The Gendered Executive

The Gendered Executive

A Comparative Analysis of Presidents,
Prime Ministers, and Chief Executives

Edited by

Janet M. Martin and MaryAnne Borrelli

TEMPLE UNIVERSITY PRESS
Philadelphia • *Rome* • *Tokyo*

Temple University Press
Philadelphia, Pennsylvania 19122
*www.temple.edu/tempres*s

Copyright © 2016 by Temple University—Of The Commonwealth System
of Higher Education

Published 2016

Library of Congress Cataloging-in-Publication Data

Names: Martin, Janet M., 1955– editor. | Borrelli, MaryAnne, editor.
Title: The gendered executive : a comparative analysis of presidents, prime
    ministers, and chief executives / edited by Janet M. Martin and MaryAnne
    Borrelli.
Description: Philadelphia : Temple University Press, 2016. | Includes
    bibliographical references and index.
Identifiers: LCCN 2016015506| ISBN 9781439913635 (cloth : alk. paper) |
    ISBN 9781439913642 (paper : alk. paper) | ISBN 9781439913659 (e-book)
Subjects: LCSH: Women heads of state. | Women government executives.
Classification: LCC HQ1236 .G46247 2016 | DDC 352.23082—dc23 LC record
    available at https://lccn.loc.gov/2016015506

♾ The paper used in this publication meets the requirements of the American
National Standard for Information Sciences—Permanence of Paper for Printed
Library Materials, ANSI Z39.48-1992

Printed in the United States of America

9 8 7 6 5 4 3 2 1

Contents

III POLITICS AND POWER

Tables and Figures

TABLES

FIGURES

Acknowledgments

As editors, we are indebted to the collaborative forces of talented authors and a supportive press. These forces united at every stage of this book's development, yielding new and dynamic ways of understanding presidents, prime ministers, and executive politics.

Our authors are an extraordinarily intelligent and collegial group of scholars. We had the privilege of learning through their chapters and through the countless e-mail exchanges that drew the chapters into harmony with one another. Our authors have benefited from numerous travel and research grants, which are acknowledged in the respective chapters.

At Temple University Press, we benefited from the highest levels of expertise and professionalism. Senior editor Aaron Javsicas had a vision for this project from its outset, and his support at every stage of its development was invaluable and deeply appreciated. We also appreciated the opportunity to work with senior production editor Dave Wilson, editor Sara Jo Cohen, rights and contracts coordinator Nikki Miller, and senior production editor Joan Vidal. Two anonymous reviewers asked questions that challenged our presumptions and expanded our imaginations. At Newgen, project manager Rebecca Logan held everyone to a tight and efficient production schedule. Temple's art manager, Kate Nichols; marketing director, Ann-Marie Anderson; advertising and promotion manager, Irene Imperio Kull; and publicity manager, Gary Kramer, made the text as beautiful as it was insightful and brought it to the attention of our readers.

Finally, we thank our readers for being open to the rigorous and original analyses that follow. We hope this book will inspire teachers, scholars, commentators, and students to ask new questions, strengthening everyone's knowledge about political executives throughout the world.

As editors, we are responsible for decisions relating to the book as a whole, including its organization, coherence, and disciplinary focus. While the contributions and insights of this book have many sources, we must take responsibility for any limitations or flaws. Without wishing to sound immodest, however, we are excited to share this book with scholars from a range of disciplines and subdisciplines; we look forward to participating in new and renewed debates about representation, identity, and power in the executive.

Janet thanks John Winship for his love and support and especially for his nuanced suggestions to make each chapter accessible to readers who are not immersed in political science. She dedicates this book to the future: to her niece Andrea; to her nephews, Luke and Matthew Sassu; and to a new generation of students of the presidency, who will build on the scholarship presented here. MaryAnne thanks her family for their understanding and patience, especially when deadlines loomed. She dedicates this book to her brother and sister-in-law, Damon and Marianna, whose questions and ideas have always pushed her to see new possibilities.

1

Learning What We Know

The Complexity of Gender in U.S.
and Comparative Executive Studies

JANET M. MARTIN AND MARYANNE BORRELLI

Change is coming. It may even be arriving.

Excluded from the ranks of elite executive decision makers for generations, women are now exercising power as chiefs of government and chiefs of state. As of April 1, 2016, 112 women have served as presidents or prime ministers, just 26 of whom have been interim or acting leaders.[1] These women have led seventy-three countries, but our knowledge of their politics is still limited and preliminary.

The United States is not one of the nations that has had a woman chief executive, but it is among those for whom gender and, much more generally, identity are assuming a no-longer-deniable importance in the executive branch. In 2008, a white woman (Hillary Clinton) and a biracial man (Barack Obama) contended for the Democratic presidential nomination for six months, precipitating national conversations about race, gender, and race-gender. When the biracial man, who self-identified as black, had the nomination in hand, he reverted to tradition and named an established white male (Joseph Biden) as his running mate. In the same election, the Republican Party nominated a Vietnam war veteran (John McCain), who was a white man, for the presidency and a white woman (Sarah Palin) for the vice presidency. These candidates challenged enduring preconceptions of who could—and even who should—be president. In 2012, identity continued to be a critical element of the campaign, with the religious affiliation of the Republican presidential nominee (Mitt Romney), the Church of Jesus Christ of

Latter-day Saints, a source of concern for many in the party's base. His vice presidential running mate (Paul Ryan) was a conservative Roman Catholic, a religious affiliation that no longer excited comment. This white and male Republican ticket signaled change in the deeply rooted conceptions of who could and should be president. Yet the 2012 reelection of the Democratic, biracial president seemed to energize the backlash that had emerged four years earlier.

As this book goes to press, new identity conversations are beginning, and old conversations are continuing as the United States undertakes its presidential primaries and caucuses. Speaker of the House Paul Ryan has sought to counter the "angry insurgent refrain" of the Republican Party by noting, "If we try to play our own version of identity politics and try to fuel ourselves based on darker emotions, that's not productive" (Steinhauer 2015, 20). As the field of presidential candidates narrows in spring 2016, the final five contenders include a white woman (Hillary Clinton), a Jewish man (Bernie Sanders), and a man of Cuban heritage (Ted Cruz). In other words, just two of the five candidates remaining in the race—John Kasich and Donald Trump—have the male, white, Protestant profile that has predominated among U.S. presidents. Once again, U.S. presidential candidates are, in varying ways and to varying degrees, part of a continuing assessment and reassessment, conducted by candidates and voters, of identity and the presidency.

For some, this inventorying by gender, race, sexuality, and religion—by any aspect of identity—edges toward objectification. Presidents, above all else, are expected to be extraordinary individuals; they are expected to withstand the pressures of society, making history rather than merely enduring or even withstanding its legacies. While acknowledging the popular appeal of this conception of a heroic chief executive, the authors and the editors of this book observe that the status and honor of being a hero have historically been reserved to men—moreover, to men whose identity conforms to a historically rooted, socially reinforced, politically endorsed set of requirements in each nation (see Duerst-Lahti 1997). However, as the numbers of women chiefs of state and chiefs of government indicate, and as this brief overview of recent U.S. presidential elections suggests, the identity of leaders is seemingly, slowly, becoming more diverse. Change is coming. It may even be arriving.

Recognizing the power and relevance of this development, the contributors to this book write from a conviction that how we study executive politics in the twenty-first century must undergo a decisive change. As scholars, we need to address new questions, use new methodologies, and seek out new intellectual resources if we are to understand just who are the top political leaders in the twenty-first century, their decision- and policy-making strategies and their impact on policy, actions, behavior, and attitudes. Accordingly, this book integrates research in U.S. politics, comparative politics, and gender-race studies; it draws on the insights of political scientists, historians, and gender scholars; and it presents diverse frameworks and research designs. In this chapter, we welcome the reader to an analytic conversation that is precise and creative, challenging and inclusive, examining institutions and individuals.

Studying Presidents, Prime Ministers, and Chief Executives

Over time, scholars have introduced new ways of looking at presidents, prime ministers, and executive leadership. Surveying scholarly works reveals the extent to which the study of these offices has undergone a series of innovations and advances since the mid-twentieth century. In the next two sections, scholarship on the U.S. presidency, and prime ministers and chief executives more broadly, provides a context for study of the gendered executive.

The U.S. presidency has received a good deal of attention. The rise of the United States as a superpower in the twentieth century encouraged such a focus, which was facilitated by campaign strategists (especially since the 1970s), citizens, the media, and, often, scholars. In fact, in the United States, political time is often described by reference to a particular presidential administration. In referring to the period surrounding the events of September 11, 2001, and the attacks on the World Trade Center and Pentagon, the "Bush presidency" is a familiar marker in political time. The administration becomes a reference to U.S. wars in Afghanistan and Iraq and to discussions of unilateral powers of the president, the global role of the United States, and enhanced measures for national security. Similarly, a reference to the "Roosevelt years" brings the Great Depression and the Second World War to mind. In both instances, a president and a presidential administration are perceived as marking an era—an indication of the extent to which a president is popularly accepted as a powerful, even defining, historical actor.

Yet while political time is still marked by presidential administrations, in the latter half of the twentieth century the presidency itself became a more familiar way to understand an institution and branch of government that extended beyond the person taking the presidential oath of office. And the subfield of presidency research has evolved and adapted new lines of inquiry, paralleling the growth and establishment of the presidency and the executive branch, especially throughout the latter half of the twentieth century.

Studies of the U.S. presidency have been identified and categorized in many different ways. For example, George C. Edwards III and Stephen

J. Wayne (1983) gathered a collection of essays by well-known students of the presidency, including John Kessel, Norman C. Thomas, Martha Joynt Kumar, Cal Mackenzie, Louis Fisher, Joseph Pika, Larry Berman, and journalist Dom Bonafede, who each addressed a different aspect of methodology in studying the presidency, from approaches and concepts to availability of data, both qualitative and quantitative. Essays featured the materials available in presidential libraries, relevant government documents, use of interviews, role of case studies, and need for concepts to guide data definition and analysis and suggested quantitative approaches to bring study of the presidency in line with behavioral approaches in vogue across the discipline. All of the points raised became a routine part of the accepted and varied methodologies drawn on by scholars studying the presidency for decades to follow.

In the brief review that follows, our goal is to sample the literature that provides a strong foundation for the chapters in this book and to demonstrate how studying the complexity of the executive's identity is a critical next step in the evolution of presidency research.

The U.S. Presidency

Two books that dramatically affected scholarship on the presidency were Richard E. Neustadt's *Presidential Power* ([1960] 1990) and Thomas E. Cronin's *The State of the Presidency* (1975). These books stimulated interest in scholarship on presidents and the presidency, becoming familiar classics.

Presidential Power reflected Neustadt's own experiences in government. Neustadt's focus was on the individual in the office—he contextualized the president as acquiring and exercising power in an institutional setting and weighed the constitutional and statutory constraints that limited a president's authority. Neustadt made clear that his sole focus was the U.S. president—not the presidency (i.e., the institutions that had grown around the president) or heads of government in other countries. Subsequent editions benefited further from his own "observation, as a consultant to the Kennedy and Johnson White House and occasionally to Carter's Reorganization Project" (Neustadt 1990, xxvii). Stressing both the academic and the practical value of his White House service, Neustadt noted, "I have always tried to turn participant-observership to the account of scholarship that might assist participants" (xxvii).

Cronin's *State of the Presidency* introduced a generation of students to the presidency. Neustadt had presented an expansive view of presidential power. Cronin, whose book was published a year after President Richard M. Nixon's resignation from office, was more tempered in his assessments. Cronin had also been a participant-observer, having worked as a White House

Fellow on domestic policy in the Johnson administration; in addition to his access to power and decision making at the highest levels, he conducted interviews that buttressed his analysis. He recommended more moderation in presidential actions and in popular expectations of what actions a president can (or should) take.

In the 1970s and 1980s, scholars addressed new questions and topics. Presidential rhetoric and communication (see Ceaser et al. 1981; Tulis 1987), in particular, fostered interdisciplinary studies (see Campbell and Jamieson 1990; Denton and Hahn 1986). This scholarship reflected and examined ongoing changes in how presidents were communicating with the public and creating a staff structure in the White House to support these new roles. As was seen earlier, in Neustadt's and Cronin's writings, political scientists were using and developing new methodologies, defining and responding to new questions about the workings of presidential power. Speeches, travel, and staged events were acknowledged and examined as leadership strategies (Kernell 1986; Stuckey 1991). Michael B. Grossman and Martha Joynt Kumar (1981) focused on the growth of the White House press operations. Jeffrey Cohen's *Going Local* (2010) followed in the path of this scholarship, noting how presidents began to use local media when traveling in order to cultivate favorable coverage.

Scholars were also attentive to changes in the White House Office staff. John Hart, in *The Presidential Branch* (1987), argued for including study of the formal advising structure surrounding presidents, in contrast to Neustadt's focus on a singular executive. Hart's study came out fifty years after the presidency as we know it today began to be established in incremental ways. Charles E. Walcott and Karen M. Hult's *Governing the White House: From Hoover through LBJ* (1995) and Karen M. Hult and Charles E. Walcott's *Empowering the White House: Governance under Nixon, Ford, and Carter* (2004) provided the nuanced analysis that gave us insight into the impact of legislative reforms that focused on providing the president with "help" in the White House. Walcott and Hult's studies demonstrated the theoretical and sophisticated analysis that can come from a rigorous use of qualitative materials, especially the documents and oral histories available in archives. Others writing in this area include Bradley Patterson (1988) and John Burke (2000). Sex-differences analyses, including that by Kathryn Dunn Tenpas (1997), began with a look at the White House Office and were complemented by gender analyses of the office of the first lady (see Borrelli 2011; Burrell 1997).

Also receiving close attention were presidential appointments throughout the wider executive branch. The confirmation process itself was examined as revelatory of legislative-executive relations, especially when partisan polarization came to dominate the U.S. political system. Richard

Fenno (1959) and Cronin (1975), focusing on the president's cabinet, studied an institution whose influence has been subjected to increasing debate across the modern presidency (see Cohen 1988; Warshaw 1996). As executives within their departments, however, cabinet secretaries continued to be recognized as elite decision makers. The appointment of women to these posts generated important research questions, initially through sex-differences studies (Martin 1989, 1991) and then through gender analysis (Borrelli 1997, 2002).

The Gendered Executive and Studies of Comparative Executives

It is no longer sufficient to say, "But a woman has never been elected president of the United States" in excusing the absence of women and gender from scholarship on the U.S. presidency. Women have become increasingly viable presidential candidates, and a corresponding literature has emerged to assess women running for president and the consequences of electing a woman as president (see, for example, Han and Heldman 2007; Lawrence and Rose 2010; Sheeler and Anderson 2013). Even absent a woman in the Oval Office, however, there is a need to study gender in the U.S. presidency. To state the obvious, men also are gendered, and the study of masculinity reveals a great deal about the U.S. presidency. Likewise, it is not appropriate to discuss race only through the study of Barack H. Obama's presidency. Deconstructing whiteness is a critically important task for scholars seeking to understand how power, privilege, and marginalization are expressed, reinforced, and changed through the presidency. The representation provided by the president as chief of state and chief of government demands close and careful study if we are to understand the U.S. polity.

In the past, methodological innovations have consistently resulted in a richer literature and a deeper understanding of the U.S. presidency and executive politics. We see every reason to expect a similar, even greater, outcome as the workings of identity in the U.S. presidency are subjected to thoughtful, close, continuing analysis.

As shown in the chapters in this book, as women have been elected president or elevated to the office of prime minister around the world, particularly in the past twenty years, women-and-politics scholars have assessed their politics in detail. This book demonstrates how the study of presidents, prime ministers, and executives is being transformed by the intellectual cross-fertilization occurring across studies of the U.S. presidency, gender and politics, and comparative politics. Quite simply, a new benchmark is being set for the research questions we ask, the concepts we develop and define, and the arguments we advance.

Identity in the Executive

In studying political change, political scientists typically focus less on individuals than on institutional forces. For U.S. presidency scholars, a more empirical and encompassing analysis has also been embraced as a corrective to the challenges of studying a singular (though not unique) decision maker. In part, in U.S. studies this reflects the shift away from leadership studies focusing on specific presidents and the move toward the study of institutions and political processes. Yet with a return of interest in studying leaders and leadership, identity can no longer escape analysis. Perhaps because the many facets of identity—including gender, race, ethnicity, religion, socioeconomic status, and sexuality—are so constitutive of individuals, some presidency scholars have been hesitant to incorporate identity in their analyses or have not been consciously aware of their exclusion of identity. Still, scholars of identity politics have firmly demonstrated that identity is both a national and a transnational construct, its performance shaped within societies, reinforced through law, and regulated and policed by governments and its changes and continuities mediated through political systems (see, for example, Kerber 1998). Recognizing and nuancing these circumstances, contributors to this collection present identity as interwoven and closely fused with national executive leadership. Identity, they argue, is as constitutive of a political system and government as it is of individual persons.

To explore the workings of identity in an executive office, however, is daunting. It must be studied comparatively if we are to understand how different political systems interweave executive and identity politics (see Andeweg 2013). It requires an extraordinary and critical awareness to examine deeply ingrained norms. It demands the acceptance of complexity. And it calls for an encompassing expertise. Each facet of identity has a rich and contentious literature, stretching across multiple disciplines, to be consulted and considered for its political implications. This is a topic that welcomes, and even commands, the attention of engaged scholars in a multiplicity of disciplines and subfields.

Shared Questions

This book had its origins in a series of decisions made by scholars in two subfields within political science, those specializing in women and politics and those focusing on the U.S. presidency.

Women-and-politics scholars have developed a strong literature centered on women legislators, which has contributed to work in U.S. politics, comparative politics, and international relations (see, for example, Krook 2010;

Krook and Zetterberg 2015; Thomas and Wilcox 2014). More gradually, women-and-politics scholars have begun to investigate the ways in which women were recognized as decision makers in and constituents of the executive branch. The descriptive, symbolic, and substantive representation of women by those with the primary responsibility for implementing public policy—and sometimes, depending on the political system, for presenting policy proposals to the legislature or even for acting unilaterally—has received increasing attention. As information, analysis, and theory building have been acquired, developed, and formulated, there has been a corresponding expansion of knowledge about women as political executives and, more generally, about gender and executive politics. That, in turn, has led many women-and-politics scholars to recognize that gender is one among many facets of identity. Intersectionality, initially formulated to examine the legal marginalization of African American women in the United States, has gradually been applied to many more persons and political contexts (Hancock 2016).

Meanwhile, scholars of the U.S. presidency have become more aware of the value and need to engage in comparative study of national executives. Organizationally, the Presidency Research Group, a formal section of the American Political Science Association (APSA), voted to rename itself the Presidents and Executive Politics Section. Subsequently, the section has sought out and welcomed contributions from comparativists, including a number of women-and-politics scholars. In 2014, a cosponsored panel at the annual APSA meeting, titled "The Gendered Dimensions of Executive Power," offered a comparative analysis of women as national political executives. The intellectual engagement of the presenters and the audience sparked a continuing, creative, collaborative process, which has culminated in this book. As Janet M. Martin wrote in one e-mail after another, to one author after another, the time has come to recognize and assess the work being done across our fields and disciplines. Our authors' strong endorsement of her worldview is evident in their intellectual investment, with chapters that offer new and often controversial conclusions about identity and executive politics.

To give structure and coherence to this analysis, we formulated a series of questions to guide the research and writing. Some of these inquiries had previously been tested and refined by the authors in earlier studies and publications. Others were new to this book. All of them stimulated our imagination and intellect. The most enduring and difficult of them were the following:

- What new research questions, designs, or methodologies can we suggest to executive-politics scholars? Why is it important to recognize and integrate the study of identity into the study of executive politics?

- What theories and frameworks are important to the research and analysis of identity and executive politics? How and why should those theories and frameworks be applied in other subfields and disciplines?
- What are the priorities in studying national executives? As we share knowledge across subfields, what are we seeking to analyze about identity, executives, and power? Why is this important?

As these questions indicate, we were at once respectful of the learning fostered within our subfields and disciplines and eager to reach across those intellectual boundaries.

Exploratory studies are meant to engage others with their questions and arguments so that the initial investigations are expanded and tested. That is exactly the hope of the editors and authors of this collection. In presenting our findings about executive decision making, leadership, representation, and power, we look forward to continuing conversations and debates about the relationships among identity, political executives, and executive politics.

Common Challenges

Just as there were shared questions, so also were there common challenges. In addition to writing for readers from widely ranging fields, the authors had to give careful consideration to the integration of diverse theories and frameworks. Of all the intellectual challenges encountered in compiling this collection, perhaps the most compelling related to the relationship between sex-differences and gender analyses. We also were concerned with incorporating the complexity of gender and, more broadly, of identity, into our studies of chief executives.

Sex-Differences and Gender Analysis

The distinction between and the respective contributions of sex-differences and gender analyses are familiar to many scholars. Sex-differences analyses routinely accept the male-female binary; subjects self-identify as male or as female, and their responses to surveys or their actions as public officials are then compared and contrasted. Sex-differences analyses might reveal the attitudes or behavior of men and women to be similar or different. In studies of the U.S. presidency, a "gender gap" has been used in describing the differing support that Republican and Democratic candidates receive from men and women in the November general election. This is a well-established area of research, and although support among women for Democratic and

Republican presidential candidates has fluctuated since 1960, Democratic presidential candidates have benefited from the votes of women since 1980 (see Carroll 2014; Martin 2003; Whitaker 2008).

Gender analyses instead examine the ideas and roles that are assigned to persons, considering the ways in which biological sexes (not limited to binaries, also including intersexual persons, for example) are defined personally, socially, and politically. Gender, then, is both idea and action—a person both *is* gendered and *does* gender. Sex-differences and gender analyses each have benefited from the other's insights, but they contrast in fundamental ways. Many gender analysts, for example, reject the strict gender binaries in sex-differences studies. The fluidity of gender definitions in gender analyses, conversely, are problematic for many sex-differences scholars. In this book, however, the argument is made that the comparisons delineated by sex-differences scholars set a foundation for the analyses offered by gender scholars, and the findings of gender scholars raise important questions for sex-differences scholars. This interchange, we maintain, facilitates a thoughtful engagement of sex and of gender as distinct yet potentially related identities.

For scholars of politics, whatever their discipline or subfield, the connection between sex and gender is among the most fascinating subjects for study. Especially in an era that has given such primacy to visuals, an elected official's person has become an extremely influential element of her or his career.

Whether campaigning or holding office, officials are intensely aware of the power of visual depiction and craft their image with corresponding care (e.g., see Kernell 1986; Lawrence and Rose 2010; Wayne 2016). Elected officials, in important ways, *embody* their politics. As Sheetal Chhabria notes in Chapter 4, Indian prime minister Narendra Modi has repeatedly relied on carefully constructed visuals to advance his political career and policy agenda. Modi's presentation—like those of many other political actors—delivers an immediate sex-and-gender message. In a world that still expects to see men as national leaders and that routinely holds masculinity as a prerequisite for leadership, sex and gender are readily conflated. As a result, the complexity of the relationship between sex and gender is ignored, overlooked, and dismissed. Working together, scholars of sex differences and of gender can highlight, investigate, and reveal the ways in which each of these facets of identity shapes a political system and its decision making.

This shared contribution is so much a part of this book that it informs the sequencing of its chapters. In each of its three parts, the first chapter is an overarching sex-differences investigation, identifying similarities and differences among women and men. Sex differences studies relating to international, comparative, and U.S. politics are presented in chapters by Amy C. Alexander and Farida Jalalzai, Catherine Reyes-Housholder and

Leslie A. Schwindt-Bayer, and Janet M. Martin, respectively. Drawing on surveys and documents, using quantitative and qualitative methodologies, these authors present findings that set an imposing agenda for future research. Using survey data from fifty-six countries, Alexander and Jalalzai, in Chapter 2, test a series of hypotheses and determine that female heads of state and government serve as symbolic representatives, sending "positive signals that improve political engagement" by women. Reyes-Housholder and Schwindt-Bayer, in Chapter 6, compare the social and political consequences of *presidentas* and *presidentes* in seventeen Latin American countries. They find that "women living under *presidentas* tend to profess higher levels of political activity, controlling for a series of potential confounders." The authors suggest that in a part of the world that has elected five women *presidentas* in just the past sixteen years yet has been "characterized as a region with low civic activity and political marginalization of women," women leaders may be important forces for mobilization.

Martin, in Chapter 10, drawing on the archival resources of presidential libraries and women's organizations, examines why women's rights were not a priority for U.S. presidents until the latter part of the twentieth century, and then only sporadically. She notes that while human rights have moved firmly onto the presidential foreign-policy agenda, women's rights in the United States have been set apart from and often set aside from these broader discussions. In these three sex-differences studies, the authors delineate political developments that have the potential to directly affect women's political engagement, mobilization, status, and power as leaders.

The consequences of these findings are explored in each of three thematic parts through gender analyses. For example, MaryAnne Borrelli and Lilly J. Goren, in Chapter 5, provide a rhetorical analysis that reveals and compares the gender ideologies of recent Republican vice presidential candidates, demonstrating that gender as an idea and as a performance is a crucial element of recent U.S. presidential campaigns. Daniela F. Melo, in Chapter 9, delineates the transnational and domestic pressures on the Portuguese government to change its women-centered policies and sets out the consequences of these policy confrontations for Portugal's political system and women. Georgia Duerst-Lahti, in Chapter 11, assesses the women-centered policies advanced by the U.S. State Department during Hillary Clinton's tenure as secretary of state, many of which were continued by her male successor, John Kerry, and finds that policy implementation is highly contingent on the department secretary's willingness to invest significant political capital in effecting change. Who is included in political processes and decision making, and how they are included, has direct consequences; decisions made by a secretary of state can affect who is, for example, an aid recipient in programs administered throughout the African continent. In these chapters, and others, authors show that gender and power are tightly interwoven. The authors also connect gender to changes in political systems, with immediate consequences for wider populations.

These connections between sex-differences and gender analyses eliminate conceptions of gender as purely personal or social. The place of gender in political calculations, as in the crafting of a party nomination speech or the implementation of a foreign-aid policy, and the consequences of gender for the public sphere are incontestable. And the ways in which gender is incorporated in decision and policy making, and the immediate and measurable consequences for individuals worldwide, are revealed. This is what is accomplished when sex-differences and gender analyses are recognized as complementary rather than competing frameworks.

The Complexity of Identity

To state the obvious, examining the contributions of sex-differences and gender analyses focuses attention on two facets of identity, sex and gender. Identity, however, has many facets. The relationships among these facets—race, ethnicity, sexuality, class, and religion, among others—must be considered if we are to understand a decision maker in her or his full complexity. Furthermore, because these facets, singly and in relationship with one another, will affect the power and positionality of an individual, we must consider how each facet is expressed by that decision maker.

This insistence that identity is complex and that its complexity will have profound consequences for a person's power and politics, owes a great deal to the scholarship of intersectionality. The origins of intersectionality can be traced to a law review article by Kimberlé W. Crenshaw (1989), which argued against the dissection of identity in U.S. law. Crenshaw rejected conceptions of persons as having race *or* gender, which had resulted in legal rulings that required African American women to choose either their race or their gender in filing antidiscrimination lawsuits; African American women could claim to have been discriminated against as African Americans or as women but not to have been discriminated against as African American women. African American women, Crenshaw argued, did not have the luxury of being African Americans or being women—they were always both. And because they were always both, always performing their gender and their race, they were affected by a constellation of forces. The ideologies and policies that marginalized women and African Americans were mutually reinforcing. Both bore down on African American women. Identity, Crenshaw wrote, was not merely intersecting—as if one facet were sufficiently distinct that it could simply interact with another—it was intersection*al*; that is, identity was a complex and deeply interwoven set of social and political roles. And the forces that created, informed, and defined those roles were mutually reinforcing. African American women were marginalized as African American women. They were not excluded as African Americans *or* as women (a legal dissection), not even as African Americans *and* as women (a conception that gender and race were distinct, if intersecting); they were marginalized as African American women (their race and gender inextricably interwoven). By ignoring the inseparability of race and gender, Crenshaw argued, the judicial system refused to remedy discrimination, so the law supported and reinforced the continuing inequality and marginalization of African American women.

Almost immediately, women-and-politics scholars began to apply intersectional frameworks to additional identities and incorporated their arguments into comparative-politics analyses. In doing so, these scholars continued and expanded understandings of identity as intersectional, as multifaceted, with a complexity that was experienced altogether and in the same moment, not separated and sequential. What was sometimes lost in these studies, however, was the importance of understanding the marginalization experienced by the persons who were living their complex identities and refusing to conform to prevailing standards. Notwithstanding the commitments to diversity and enfranchisement voiced in many countries, governments and political systems have often excluded and disempowered their people. As Janet M. Martin reminds us in Chapter 10, a powerful and too-often-overlooked example is the Fifteenth Amendment to the U.S. Constitution, which promises that "the right of all citizens of the United States to vote shall not be abridged or denied by the United States or by any State on account of race, color, or previous condition of servitude." A close reading of the Fourteenth Amendment finds that citizens are defined as "male."

It is important to emphasize, therefore, that scholars must connect the complexity of identity to practices of marginalization, assessing the complicity of the political system in furthering inequality. This understanding has informed every chapter in this book, as each author has carefully assessed the inextricability of identity and power in executive politics. Though many of the authors have presented their own interpretations of identity, their consistency in analyzing its complexity, and (more narrowly) the complexity of gender, yields three important insights.

First, authors embraced the conception of identity as multifaceted, with those facets experienced all at once rather than sequentially. In so doing, we were intellectually indebted to intersectionality. Studying decision making and decision makers in the Obama administration, for example, required a careful consideration of gender-race. Karen M. Hult's analysis, in Chapter 8, of Valerie Jarrett's office within the White House Office assesses the ways in which Jarrett's identity as an African American woman and her long-standing relationship with the president and the first lady were integral to her selection as a senior adviser and to her decisions as a presidential adviser. If Jarrett's contribution to the substantive representation of women and girls was sometimes ambiguous, so also was her status within the White House Office sometimes uncertain. The force and nuances of marginalization are a central feature of Hult's chapter, as they are in many others.

Second, and relatedly, there was a strong and continuing effort to avoid essentialist conceptions of gender. To insist that gender is one aspect of identity among many is a powerful corrective to the presumption that the "essence" of femininity or masculinity can be distilled into a finite listing of traits and actions. In this book, the awareness that women and men are diverse, though there are patterns in their inclusion or exclusion from positions of power, is showcased in Chapter 13, the comparative analysis of cabinet officers conducted by Maria C. Escobar-Lemmon and Michelle M. Taylor-Robinson. Investigating the credentials and qualifications of self-identified women and men cabinet ministers in four Latin American countries and the United States, Escobar-Lemmon and Taylor-Robinson provide inter- and intragender comparisons, controlling for ministerial post. Carefully coding the many elements of the ministers' careers, these authors mitigate the binaries of a sex-differences analysis. Then the authors weigh the response of prime ministers and presidents to the ministers' qualifications and credentials, assessing the extent to which women are at the center or the margins of the cabinets in which they serve.

Third, the authors and editors have revealed the ways in which identity is integral to decision making by national executives. Cory Charles Gooding's analysis of President Barack Obama's rhetoric, in Chapter 3, exemplifies this commitment. Examining Obama's 2013 commencement address at Morehouse College, Gooding argues that "Obama addresses the tension between the color-blind and individualistic ideals of liberalism *and* the more collective racial orientations existing in the black community through language that speaks to his racial and national communities simultaneously: the language of respectability." Analyzing the rhetoric and policies being articulated at the center, we see that the association of identity with power is intensely dynamic, rarely static, and correspondingly resistant to change.

Overturning Expectations

Scholars take pride in their questioning, even skeptical, mind-set. Political scientists, especially, seek to reveal, and challenge, the status quo. Research that tests our presumptions and expectations, that shifts perceptions and institutes new paradigms, is valued. It may also be disconcerting and uncomfortable, as learning often is.

Several chapters disrupt the status quo of executive politics and gender studies through their methodological innovations. Catherine Reyes-Housholder, in Chapter 12, for example, offers a new standard for coding policies that advance "pro-women change," which promises to advance comparative-policy research. Her coding is informed by a nation's obligations under international law, by the policy priorities of the governmental agency charged with advancing women's interests, and by women's organizations affiliated or in partnership with the government. Reyes-Housholder demonstrates the strength of this schema by comparing the policy agendas of, and the exercise of presidential power by, Chilean presidents Ricardo Lagos and Michelle Bachelet.

Other chapters introduce questions and topics that have been neglected by executive-politics scholars. More than filling a gap in the existent literature, these chapters open new possibilities for research. Ariella R. Rotramel, in Chapter 7, analyzes the outreach and lack of outreach by U.S. presidents to the lesbian, gay, bisexual, and transgender (LGBT) community. From the Carter through the Obama administrations, LGBT policies have privileged some members of the community at the expense of others—lesbian and gay persons the focus of more policies, bisexual and transgender persons the focus of far fewer. She also delineates the partisan elements of presidential outreach, assessing which administrations have advanced LGBT civil rights and which have empowered a backlash. Rotramel's analysis is highly integrative, spanning more than one subfield in U.S. politics and gender studies.

Finally, some chapters require readers to confront their preconceptions about identity and executive politics. Sheetal Chhabria's study of Indian prime minister Narendra Modi's gender performance, in Chapter 4, details how the prime minister's performance of traditional masculine *and* feminine gender roles has advanced his career and policy priorities. Her investigation of gender and power in Indian leadership suggests new avenues for research in governments, political systems, and nations.

In their theories and frameworks, research designs and methodologies, questions and findings, the contributors to this collection have acknowledged and then modified, reworked, and even rejected past conceptions of executive politics. The result is a collection that encourages readers to think, research, and write in new ways—an invitation that we hope is widely accepted.

Overview of the Book

The chapters in this book are ordered in ways that allow readers to appreciate the complementarity of their frameworks, as already noted. Also important, the chapters are brought together in ways that showcase their findings on issues and controversies of critical importance to the study of national executives. We include an editorial preface (in italics) at the beginning of each chapter to introduce its general concepts and context. Here, we set out the pivotal questions and declarations for the chapters.

Notably, each part has two chapters focusing on the U.S. presidency and two chapters focusing on comparative study of political executives. Alexander and Jalalzai (Chapter 2) and Escobar-Lemmon and Taylor-Robinson (Chapter 13) include the United States in their comparative data sets.

Identity and Ambition

In the first part of the book, the authors look at political executives and the effects of their identities and identity performances. In each instance, the authors draw a connection between the executive and the people, arguing that the identity of the executive profoundly influences the people's political engagement, political ambitions, and political attitudes.

In Chapter 2, Amy C. Alexander and Farida Jalalzai ask whether a woman head of state or government serves as a symbolic and therefore empowering representative for women, stimulating greater interest in and support for women leaders throughout the nation. Alexander and Jalalzai examine public-opinion polls in a cross-national analysis of fifty-six countries that assesses the influence of women chiefs of government and chiefs of state on political activity in the country that each leads.

In Chapter 3, Cory Charles Gooding confronts the intersections and the intersectionality of race and gender in a detailed rhetorical analysis of Obama's 2013 commencement address at Morehouse College. "Those who subscribe to respectability politics view the individual performance of standards and values imposed by white people as the most effective collective strategy for the racial group to gain equitable inclusion into the polity," he writes. "This relationship between individual and group identity is important for discussions of presidential power, whereby the president is a singular actor, using rhetoric and performance to move government."[2] This negotiation, performed by a biracial president self-identified as black, working to sustain support from a majority white electorate, has contributed to shaping the chief executive's political ambitions, policy agenda, and actions.

In Chapter 4, Sheetal Chhabria's study of India's prime minister Narendra Modi illustrates how a political leader's gender performance can win the support of the international business community while at the same time sustaining support from the Hindu Right, which seeks to protect traditional values. She also argues that the prime minister's gender performance has empowered the Hindu Right, with serious domestic and international policy consequences for India.

In Chapter 5, MaryAnne Borrelli and Lilly J. Goren provide a comparative rhetorical analysis of Sarah Palin's 2008 and Paul Ryan's 2012 acceptance speeches. In the stories that Palin and Ryan told about their lives and the partisan attacks that they directed against their Democratic opponents in their respective speeches, these two Republican vice presidential nominees revealed a great deal about workings of gender specifically, and identity more generally, in the vice presidency and the presidency.

Policy and Representation

Perhaps because scholarship on the identity of national executives has been so limited, there has been little recognition that these leaders are representatives, as are their cabinet ministers and department secretaries. This book, accordingly, investigates the contributions of the presidents and the presidents' administrations to fulfilling the obligation to represent the people in symbolic, descriptive, and substantive ways. Each of the chapters in the second part of the book offers a longitudinal analysis that delineates the complexity of change across the decades. The richness of symbolic representation in empowering citizens is an aspect of leadership not often addressed by scholars of the presidency and prime ministers.

In Chapter 6, Catherine Reyes-Housholder and Leslie A. Schwindt-Bayer's study of seventeen Latin American countries traces the impact of *presidentas* and *presidentes* on the wider population's political activity, as measured by participation in campaigning, attendance at local political meetings, and intention to vote. These authors demonstrate that a national executive's sex does influence political activity throughout the nation that she or he leads. Descriptive and symbolic representation are intertwined.

Ariella R. Rotramel's longitudinal study, in Chapter 7, reveals and evaluates the shifting engagement of the U.S. presidency with the LGBT community. Her study unites rhetorical and policy analysis, exploring the frames that presidents have used in advancing civil rights policy or in empowering the conservative backlash against this diverse community.

In Chapter 8, Karen M. Hult sets out the origins and history of President Obama's White House Office of Public Engagement, which can trace its beginnings to the Franklin D. Roosevelt administration. This office, headed by the president's senior adviser and longtime friend, Valerie Jarrett, is pivotal to the administration's initiatives for women and girls, straddling the line between representation and policy.

In Chapter 9, Daniela F. Melo looks at how Portuguese prime ministers have managed pressures to reform their country's women-centered policies. In this chapter, policy outcomes move to the forefront in discussing representation, asking whether policy outcomes generate representation. In a formidable combination of top-down and bottom-up forces, both the European Union and domestic women's organizations have sought change. Yet she finds that these prime ministers have, more often than not, retained control of the policy process and their power as national leaders.

Politics and Power

Authors in the third part of the book focus on central features of the national executive most familiar to scholars and perhaps most in need of new methods and new questions. Outcomes matter. Outcomes depend on access to power, the exercise of power, and political processes. Accordingly, the authors in this part of the book investigate executive decision making and leadership worldwide. The processes, timing, and implementation of those decisions; the impact of changes in leadership and in staff; and the consequences of executive politics for constituents are among the critical issues addressed.

In Chapter 10, Janet M. Martin focuses on executive power. She asks why U.S. presidents have not addressed women's rights as human rights. In response, she uses a model of "nondecision-making" to reveal why the absence of a decision is important. Looking at decisions and actions that could have been made, Martin demonstrates that absence of action can indicate either the use of power or the lack of access to power.

In Chapter 11, Georgia Duerst-Lahti, drawing on data from interviews, fieldwork, and focus groups, assesses the effectiveness of Secretary of State Hillary Clinton in moving U.S. foreign-policy and development bureaucracies to make gender and women's policy central in diplomatic and development strategies.

In Chapter 12, Catherine Reyes-Housholder compares two successive socialist presidents of Chile, Ricardo Lagos and Michelle Bachelet. She assesses how these leaders advanced contrasting legislative agendas, using the powers of their presidency in very different ways to promote their contrasting conceptions of a pro-women policy agenda.

There is more to understanding power and leadership than listing who is in office, as Maria C. Escobar-Lemmon and Michelle M. Taylor-Robinson note in their comparative study of cabinet members in five presidential democracies in Chapter 13. The presence of women in a room of policy makers may lead to a change in policy or consideration of viewpoints not previously taken, but a seat at the table is not sufficient for bringing about change. Even after women are included in cabinets, issues of influence, power, and resources remain. Escobar-Lemmon and Taylor-Robinson draw on social-control theory to compare and contrast the appointment of women and men cabinet officers in sixteen different presidential administrations in five countries. They investigate posts where a first woman was appointed and posts where appointing women has become the norm.

This collection is as optimistic as it is critical. Political systems are always changing, and as scholars of politics, we are committed to understanding that change. It is both historical fact and present reality that the identity of national executives influences policy, politics, and power domestically, nationally, and transnationally. We are long overdue in more comprehensively investigating the who and when, the what and where, and above all the how and why of this influence. Earlier studies in our separate disciplines and subfields have suggested answers. Now, in this book, we take the next step of pooling our accumulated wisdom, inviting the reader to join in a collaborative effort to learn what we know about the power of identity in executive politics.

NOTES

1. Officially, the leader of Taiwan is president-elect until May 2016. We thank Farida Jalalzai for the data on women presidents and prime ministers.

2. Respectability politics has, more recently, also been studied in association with other marginalized groups in U.S. society and the U.S. political system, including the LGBT community.

REFERENCES

Andeweg, Rudy B. 2013. "Cabinet Ministers: Leaders, Team Players, Followers." In *The Oxford Handbook of Political Leadership*, edited by R.A.W. Rhodes and Paul 't Hart, 532–546. New York: Oxford University Press.

Borrelli, MaryAnne. 1997. "Campaign Promises, Transition Dilemmas: Cabinet Building and Executive Representation." In *The Other Elites: Women, Politics, and Power in the Executive Branch*, edited by MaryAnne Borrelli and Janet M. Martin, 73–89. Boulder, CO: Lynne Rienner.

———. 2002. *The President's Cabinet: Gender, Power, and Representation.* Boulder, CO: Lynne Rienner.

———. 2011. *The Politics of the President's Wife.* College Station: Texas A&M University Press.

Burke, John P. 2000. *The Institutional Presidency: Organizing and Managing the White House from FDR to Clinton.* Baltimore: Johns Hopkins University Press.

Burrell, Barbara C. 1997. "The Office of the First Lady and Public Policymaking." In *The Other Elites: Women, Power and Politics in the Executive Branch*, edited by MaryAnne Borrelli and Janet M. Martin, 169–187. Boulder, CO: Lynne Rienner.

Campbell, Karlyn Kohrs, and Kathleen Hall Jamieson. 1990. *Deeds Done in Words: Presidential Rhetoric and the Genres of Governance.* Chicago: University of Chicago Press.

Carroll, Susan J. 2014. "Voting Choices: How and Why the Gender Gap Matters." In *Gender Elections: Shaping the Future of American Politics*, 3rd ed., edited by Susan J. Carroll and Richard L. Fox, 119–145. New York: Cambridge University Press.

Ceaser, James W., Glen E. Thurow, Jeffrey Tulis, and Joseph M. Bessette. 1981. "The Rise of the Rhetorical Presidency." *Presidential Studies Quarterly* 11 (2): 158–171.

Cohen, Jeffrey E. 1988. *The Politics of the U.S. Cabinet: Representation in the Executive Branch, 1789–1984*. Pittsburgh: University of Pittsburgh Press.

———. 2010. *Going Local: Presidential Leadership in the Post-broadcast Age*. New York: Cambridge University Press.

Crenshaw, Kimberlé. 1989. "Demarginalizing the Intersection of Race and Sex: A Black Feminist Critique of Antidiscrimination Doctrine, Feminist Theory, and Antiracist Politics." *University of Chicago Legal Forum* 140:139–167.

Cronin, Thomas E. 1975. *The State of the Presidency*. Boston: Little, Brown.

Denton, Robert E., and Dan F. Hahn. 1986. *Presidential Communication: Description and Analysis*. New York: Praeger.

Duerst-Lahti, Georgia. 1997. "Reconceiving Theories of Power: Consequences of Masculinism in the Executive Branch." In *The Other Elites: Women, Power and Politics in the Executive Branch*, edited by MaryAnne Borrelli and Janet M. Martin, 11–32. Boulder, CO: Lynne Rienner.

Edwards, George C, III. 1981. "The Quantitative Study of the Presidency." *Presidential Studies Quarterly* 11 (2): 146–150.

Edwards, George C., III, and Stephen J. Wayne, eds. 1983. *Studying the Presidency*. Knoxville: University of Tennessee Press.

Fenno, Richard F. 1959. *The President's Cabinet: An Analysis in the Period from Wilson to Eisenhower*. Cambridge, MA: Harvard University Press.

Grossman, Michael B., and Martha Joynt Kumar. 1981. *Portraying the President: The White House and the News Media*. Baltimore: Johns Hopkins University Press.

Han, Lori Cox, and Caroline Heldman. 2007. *Rethinking Madam President: Are We Ready for a Woman in the White House?* Boulder, CO: Lynne Rienner.

Hancock, Ange-Marie. 2016. *Intersectionality: An Intellectual History*. New York: Oxford University Press.

Hart, John. 1987. *The Presidential Branch*. New York: Pergamon Press.

Hult, Karen M., and Charles E. Walcott. 2004. *Empowering the White House: Governance under Nixon, Ford, and Carter*. Lawrence: University Press of Kansas.

Kerber, Linda K. 1998. *No Constitutional Right to Be Ladies: Women and the Obligations of Citizenship*. New York: Hill and Wang.

Kernell, Samuel. 1986. *Going Public: New Strategies of Presidential Leadership*. Washington, DC: CQ Press.

Krook, Mona Lena. 2010. *Quotas for Women in Politics: Gender and Candidate Selection Reform Worldwide*. New York: Oxford University Press.

Krook, Mona Lena, and Pär Zetterberg, eds. 2015. *Gender Quotas and Women's Representation: New Directions in Research*. New York: Routledge.

Lawrence, Regina G., and Melody Rose. 2010. *Hillary Clinton's Race for the White House: Gender Politics and the Media on the Campaign Trail*. Boulder, CO: Lynne Rienner.

Martin, Janet M. 1989. "The Recruitment of Women to Cabinet and Subcabinet Posts." *Western Political Quarterly* 42 (1): 161–172.

———. 1991. "An Examination of Executive Branch Appointments in the Reagan Administration by Background and Gender." *Western Political Quarterly* 44 (1): 173–184.

———. 2003. *The Presidency and Women: Promise, Performance and Illusion*. College Station: Texas A&M University Press.

Neustadt, Richard. E. (1960) 1990. *Presidential Power and the Modern Presidents: The Politics of Leadership from Roosevelt to Reagan*. Reprint, New York: Free Press.

Patterson, Bradley H. 1988. *The Ring of Power: The White House Staff and Its Expanding Role in Government*. New York: Basic Books.

Sheeler, Kristina Horn, and Karrin Vasby Anderson. 2013. *Woman President: Confronting Postfeminist Political Culture.* College Station: Texas A&M University Press.

Steinhauer, Jennifer, 2015. "Ryan Says 'Inclusive' House Agenda Must Counter Polarizing Campaign." *New York Times*, December 15, p. 20.

Stuckey, Mary E. 1991. *The President as Interpreter-in-Chief.* Chatham, NJ: Chatham House.

Tenpas, Kathryn Dunn. 1997. "Women on the White House Staff: A Longitudinal Analysis, 1939–1994." In *The Other Elites: Women, Power and Politics in the Executive Branch*, edited by MaryAnne Borrelli and Janet M. Martin, 91–106. Boulder, CO: Lynne Rienner.

Thomas, Sue, and Clyde Wilcox. 2014. *Women and Elective Office: Past, Present, and Future.* 3rd ed. New York: Oxford University Press.

Tulis, Jeffrey. 1987. *The Rhetorical Presidency.* Princeton, NJ: Princeton University Press.

Walcott, Charles E., and Karen M. Hult. 1995. *Governing the White House: From Hoover through LBJ.* Lawrence: University Press of Kansas.

Warshaw, Shirley Anne. 1996. *Powersharing: White House–Cabinet Relations in the Modern Presidency.* Albany: State University of New York Press.

Wayne, Stephen J. 2016. *Road to the White House, 2016.* Boston: Cengage.

Whitaker, Lois Duke. 2008. *Voting the Gender Gap.* Urbana: University of Illinois Press.

I

Identity and Ambition

2

The Symbolic Effects of Female Heads of State and Government

AMY C. ALEXANDER AND FARIDA JALALZAI

Arguably, the identity and political ambition of a female head of state or government is transformative of the views of politics held by women throughout the polity. In fact, if one considers the visibility and status of national executive office, the symbolic effects of a female head of state or head of government could trump that of an increase in the number of women in legislative bodies. This chapter therefore examines whether a recent or current female head of state or government improves support for female leaders and political engagement. Working with the most recent public-opinion data, covering years 2011 to 2014, the authors look cross-sectionally at fifty-six countries to evaluate the influence of the presence of a female head of state or head of government on acceptance of female leaders, as well as citizen interest in politics, and on the level of voting in national and local elections.

Women's representation creates "symbolic effects" when the very presence of women leaders shapes citizens' perceptions of politics and women's role in politics. Cross-national explorations of the symbolic effects of women's representation focus on women's presence in national legislatures; they largely ignore women presidents and prime ministers. This oversight stems in part from better data availability for testing the theory on female presence in legislatures. However, with the number of female heads of state and governments accelerating since the 1990s, the opportunity to investigate their symbolic effects is rapidly improving. And there are key theoretical reasons for evaluating this level of officeholding.

There is every reason to believe that the presence of a woman president or prime minister is as potentially transformative as are increased numbers of women legislators, and possibly even more so. Yet while a growing, albeit recent, literature tackles the question of the symbolic effects of female parliamentarians comparatively and over time, not a single study applies the theory of symbolic representation to the presence of women presidents and prime ministers. The research presented here attempts to fill this gap.

Women's inclusion at the highest levels of political power is a strong example of improvement in women's descriptive representation. Descriptive representation is the extent to which representatives possess the same physical or social characteristics of their constituencies (Pitkin 1967) and have shared experiences (Mansbridge 1999). For groups with a history of marginalization from political leadership, increases in their descriptive representation can be symbolically empowering. The potential for symbolic benefit is particularly applicable to women, which make up the largest politically marginalized group in most countries in the world. When women make these gains, widespread, deeply rooted perceptions of the long-held connection of political officeholding and participation with men are challenged. Seeing women hold political office sends the message that women belong in politics. This may also send broader positive cues, signaling that politics is more democratic and enhancing levels of political engagement.

Along these lines, while these symbolic effects are severely understudied, there are good reasons to expect that they will be most profound when women fill the position of president or prime minister. For example, more people likely know their president and prime minister than are aware of their percentages of women legislators and cabinet ministers. This, in part, is a function of the relatively high levels of media attention presidents and prime ministers receive (Heffernan 2006). In fact, if one considers the visibility and status of national executive office, the symbolic effects of a country electing or appointing a female executive could trump those of an increase in the number of female parliamentarians.

This chapter examines whether the presence of a woman head of state or government is associated with enhanced support for female leaders and increased political engagement among citizens. Working with the most recent public-opinion data, covering the years from 2011 through 2014, we hypothesize that female executives positively shape people's views about women in politics and increase their levels of political engagement.

Review of the Literature

Theory on the symbolic effects of descriptive representation assumes which groups hold power will strongly influence who pursues positions of power by symbolizing what is possible for some groups relative to others. The symbolism evokes rational, normative, and emotional responses from citizens.

The Symbolic Effects of Female Leaders

As rational actors, individuals develop expectations that affect their perceptions of their abilities to hold certain positions based on whether they see people like themselves—what the literature refers to as "role models" (Bussey and Bandura 1999, 685)—in those positions. An experience of fewer role models sends the signal that one or both of the following scenarios is likely: (1) one is less capable and will fail to attain the position, or (2) one will be systematically disadvantaged and, all else equal, fail to attain the position. In both cases, the absence of role models is deincentivizing.

Given that women experience some form of marginalization in political leadership in every country in the world, the symbolic implications of improvements in their inclusion are potentially profound (Mansbridge 1999; Phillips 1995; Sapiro 1981; Williams 1998; Young 2002). Increases in women's presence in positions of political power may be key to incentivizing women's political engagement as citizens and future leaders. For this reason, political scientists assess the incentivizing benefits of increases in women's inclusion in political leadership (Atkeson 2003; Burns, Schlozman, and Verba 2001; Carroll 1985; Hansen 1997; High-Pippert and Comer 1998; Koch 1997; Norris and Krook 2009; Norris, Lovenduski, and Campbell 2004; Reingold and Harrell 2010; Sapiro and Conover 1997). While there are some exceptions (Dolan 2006; Kittilson and Schwindt-Bayer 2012; Lawless 2004; Morgan and Buice 2013), the evidence largely shows that gains in women's presence in legislatures create these incentivizing symbolic effects for women. Under these gains, women become more politically engaged and see themselves as more capable of political leadership. For instance, Christina Wolbrecht and David E. Campbell (2007) find that higher percentages of female legislators lead to higher levels of political discussion and activity among women and girls in a study of twenty-three European democracies. Susan J. Carroll (1985), in a U.S. study, finds that there is a greater likelihood for women to enter the political arena when there are more women in state legislatures. And Pippa Norris, Joni Lovenduski, and Rosie Campbell (2004), through a study of constituencies across the United Kingdom, find a higher likelihood for women to volunteer in campaigns and vote when represented by a female member of parliament (MP).

In addition to the incentivizing effect, symbolic representation may improve women's engagement and inclusion through a socialization mechanism. Gains in female political leadership create a serious symbolic challenge to traditional norms that reject a role for women in politics.

Through this challenge, the norms are potentially transformed. This may affect both women and men's acceptance of female political participation and leadership. For instance, Amy C. Alexander (2012) finds that positive change in women's presence in national legislatures leads to positive change in women's beliefs in women's ability to govern across a global sample of twenty-five countries.

The Link between Symbolic and Descriptive Representation

Finally, symbolic representation also potentially evokes emotional responses toward political participation and the political system. Either through the exclusion or inclusion of certain groups, representational bodies signal how open their political systems are to a more equal competition of political interests. In the narrowest sense, gains for a marginalized group will improve how members of that group feel about political participation and their systems by symbolizing greater inclusion. In a broader sense, all citizens may feel more positive about participation and the political system when they experience increases in the descriptive representation of certain groups. These improvements may send a general signal of fairer political competition not only to women but to all members of society. This can improve trust and political engagement generally. For instance, Leslie A. Schwindt-Bayer and William Mishler (2005), in a study of thirty-one democracies, find that higher levels of women's descriptive representation increase both women's and men's trust in the legislature.

While we see growing confirmation of the symbolic effects of women's descriptive representation, the literature's evidence base contains a serious omission: not a single study applies the theory of symbolic representation to the presence of women presidents and prime ministers. We think that up until recently this was largely a data-driven issue. In the past, too few women attained these positions for comparative, systematic evaluation of their effects. But fortunately, the more recent political landscape is changing. The numbers of women presidents and prime ministers grew substantially over the last five decades. As of January 2015, ninety-eight women in sixty-seven countries have served in these positions. Fifty-seven have held the prime ministership (58 percent), and forty-one have become president (42 percent). However, eighteen of these women were "acting" or "provisional" leaders (eleven presidents and seven prime ministers). If we set these cases aside, seventy-nine noninterim women (women who were neither acting nor provisional) have held these positions of power: forty-nine prime ministers (62 percent) and thirty presidents (38 percent). While women made sluggish progress in earlier decades, dramatic changes occurred from the 1990s onward. The number of new female leaders nearly quadrupled in the 1990s, and this pattern repeated again in the 2000s. In fact, over three-quarters of all female presidents and prime ministers entered office in the last twenty years, when women's presence in these positions dramatically increased.

Research on women executives finds that women tend to enter office through appointment and often lack the ability to exercise independent authority as prime ministers or more symbolic presidents. They also benefit from political transition and instability as well as family ties to power (Jalalzai 2013). This may temper the optimism we have regarding women's ability to shape policies on behalf of women's interests. However, there is every reason to believe that women leaders would offer women enhanced symbolic representation, given their sheer visibility. Because of the recent and substantial increases in their numbers, this is the perfect time to begin analyzing the symbolic effects of women presidents and prime ministers. Before turning to our data and analysis, however, we briefly review factors in addition to the presence of a female head of state or government that potentially affect global trends in support for female leaders and women's political engagement.

Competing Country-Level Effects: Development, Secularization, and Democratic Institutionalization

The most commonly analyzed country-level factors include development (Alexander and Welzel 2011a; Inglehart and Norris 2003; Paxton and Hughes 2013), secularization (Alexander and Welzel 2011b; Inglehart and Norris 2003; Paxton and Hughes 2013; Paxton and Kunovich 2003), and democratic institutionalization (Karp and Banducci 2008; Norris and Krook 2009).

Increases in countries' levels of development are strongly linked to increases in gender-equality values, which include the acceptance of women as political leaders. These values are powerful predictors of gender equality in resources and political participation (Alexander and Welzel 2011a; Inglehart and Norris 2003).

Religion is a primary agent of gender-role socialization in every society in the world (Franzmann 1999; Inglehart and Norris 2003). Evidence shows that religious organizations from all religious faiths support traditional and subordinate roles for women (Alexander and Welzel 2011b; Inglehart and Norris 2003). Cross-national studies link religious beliefs to fewer women in national legislatures (Kenworthy and Malami 1999; Paxton and Hughes 2013; Paxton and Kunovich 2003).

With a core emphasis on human autonomy and equality of political participation, democratic principles contribute to a political climate that is conducive to gender-egalitarian attitudes and women's formal representation. Thus, many of the cross-national studies in the literature include a measure of countries' level of democracy in the analysis of the importance of symbolic representation for women (see, for instance, Karp and Banducci 2008; Norris and Krook 2009).

In the following sections, we turn to our test of the hypotheses we derive from the literature. Based on the literature, we expect the presence of a female executive to have a positive effect on support for women leaders, voter engagement in national and local elections, and political interest. We also expect the effect to be stronger for women across these categories of symbolic effects.

Sample and Methods

We draw on a cross-sectional sample of countries surveyed in the sixth and most recent wave of the World Values Survey (WVS),[1] spanning 2011–2014. At the time of the current writing, data are available for fifty-six countries. These cases span every cultural zone in the world, including countries with the largest populations, such as Germany among Western European countries, China among East Asian countries, India among countries in South Asia, and Brazil among countries in Latin America (Inglehart and Welzel 2005).

In addition to the value of having the most recent data, the sixth wave includes eleven cases: the highest number of any wave with a recent or current female head of state or government. The female heads of state and government and the countries they come from are outlined in Table 2.1. The

TABLE 2.1: LEADERS AND SURVEY YEARS

Country	Position	Leader	Years in office	Survey year
Argentina	President	Cristina Fernández de Kirchner	2007–2015	2011
Australia	Prime minister	Julia Gillard	2010–2013	2012
Chile	President	Michelle Bachelet	2006–2010	2011
Germany	Chancellor	Angela Merkel	2005–present	2013
India	President	Pratibha Patil	2007–2012	2014
Kyrgyzstan	President	Roza Otunbayeva	2010–2011	2011
New Zealand	Prime minister	Helen Elizabeth Clark	1999–2008	2011
Philippines	President	Gloria Macapagal Arroyo	2001–2010	2012
Thailand	Prime minister	Yingluck Shinawatra	2011–2014	2013
Trinidad and Tobago	Prime minister	Kamla Persad-Bissessar	2010–present	2011
Ukraine	Prime minister	Yulia Tymoshenko	2005; 2007–2010	2011

diversity of countries we cover in this sample is noteworthy. However, with just eleven cases, the female-executive effect could be especially sensitive to leverage cases. Therefore, we ran all our analyses with one of the female-executive cases excluded from the models to see if this dramatically changed the results. The results do not change statistically significantly when we conduct this exploratory procedure.

The sixth wave also has an important set of new indicators for evaluating the symbolic effects of female heads of state and government. Two of the four questions we evaluate, whether a respondent "votes in national elections" and whether a respondent "votes in local elections," were asked for the first time.

Dependent variables. To evaluate the symbolic effects of a female head of state or government, we look at the variation in average response of all female and male respondents per country to four questions that cover acceptance of female leaders, voting behavior in national elections, voting behavior in local elections, and interest in politics. On acceptance of female leaders, respondents are asked, "How strongly do you agree or disagree with the following statement: men make better political leaders than women?" Response categories range from 1 (strongly agree) to 4 (strongly disagree). On voting in national elections, respondents are asked, "When national elections take place, do you vote always, usually, or never?" Respondents have the selection of response categories 1 (always) through 3 (never). We reverse the scale so that more voter engagement has higher value. Nearly identical question and response categories are used to measure voting in local elections. The only difference is that respondents are asked, "When local elections take place, do you vote always, usually, or never?" This is rescaled so that more voter engagement has higher value to match the scores on voting in national elections. On interest in politics, respondents are asked, "How interested are you in politics?" Responses range from 1 (very interested) to 4 (not at all interested). We reverse the scale so that more interest has higher value. For all of these variables, we score countries according to the average female and male responses to the survey per country.

Independent variables. Our key variable is the recent or current presence of a female head of state or government.[2] Countries are scored a 1 if they recently or currently have a female head of state or government and a 0 if not. We control for the countries' levels of development, religiosity, democratic institutionalization, and percentage of women in parliament. To measure the countries' level of development, we use the United Nations Development Program Human Development Index for 2010. To measure level of religiosity, we take the mean response per country to the WVS question "How important is God in your life? 1 (not at all important)–10 (very important)."

To measure countries' levels of democratic institutionalization, we use Polity IV's 2010 measure of the general openness of political institutions.[3] The measure of the percentage of women in parliament is taken from the Inter-Parliamentary Union's data on women in the lower house. For this variable, we take data for the same year that our dependent variables are measured. In addition to these controls, in the models that predict voting engagement, we control for countries' level of turnout in the most recent national elections that took place prior to or in the same year as our dependent variables. These data are taken from the Inter-Parliamentary Union's PARLINE Database.[4]

Finally, we incorporate sex differences into our models by looking separately at the variation in the country averages for female and male respondents across our dependent variables. (For variable descriptives, see Table 2A.1 in the chapter appendix.)

Analysis. We test whether the presence of a female executive affects acceptance of female political leaders and women's political engagement with multivariate models. These models are estimated with Ordinary Least Squares Regression (OLS) analysis (Miles and Shevlin 2001; Tabachnick and Fidell 2000). We hypothesize that the presence of a female leader has a positive, significant effect on all the indicators of symbolic effects and that this more strongly affects women.

Results

As a first step we look at the correlations between the female-executive variable and the four indicators of symbolic effects: support for women leaders, voting in national elections, voting in local elections, and interest in politics. Table 2.2 presents these results for the female and male respondents

TABLE 2.2: CORRELATIONS BETWEEN HAVING A FEMALE EXECUTIVE AND THE MEASURE OF AVERAGE POLITICAL ENGAGEMENT

	Women respondents	Men respondents
Average support for women leaders	0.25*	0.25[†]
	(56)	(56)
Voted in national election	0.42***	0.40***
	(56)	(56)
Voted in local election	0.42**	0.41**
	(54)	(54)
Average interest in politics	0.24[†]	0.16
	(56)	(56)

Note: Entries are Pearson's *r* correlation coefficients with number of cases in parentheses.
†$p \leq 0.10$; *$p \leq 0.05$; **$p \leq 0.01$; ***$p \leq 0.001$.

separately. The data allow us to look for bivariate relationships between the presence of a female executive and the symbolic effects for women and men across fifty-six countries. As reported in Table 2.2, all but one correlation are positive and significant. Respondents in countries with a female executive have higher average levels of support for women leaders, voter engagement in national elections, voter engagement in local elections, and, for women only, political interest. In terms of sex differences, the correlation coefficients and the significance levels indicate that the presence of a female executive is a slightly stronger correlate with all indicators that measure the effect on women compared to that on men. This is especially the case with political interest. The correlation between having a female executive and average male political interest is not statistically significant. These analyses lack control variables, but this is nevertheless a first positive indication of the symbolic effects of female heads of state and government. At this stage, the data suggest that having a female executive has positive behavioral and attitudinal effects for both women and men: women are more likely than men to show interest in politics, but both women and men are likely to support women leaders and vote.

We now turn to the multivariate models. The first indicator we examine is support for female political leadership. Table 2.3 presents the results for both women and men. When we control for countries' level of development, religiosity, democratic institutionalization, and percentage of women in national legislatures, the female-executive variable is no longer a significant, positive predictor of women's or men's beliefs in women's ability to govern. Interestingly, the symbolic effect of descriptive

TABLE 2.3: MULTIVARIATE ANALYSIS OF SUPPORT FOR FEMALE LEADERS

	Women's acceptance of women's ability to govern			Men's acceptance of women's ability to govern		
	B	Beta	Standard error	B	Beta	Standard error
Female executive	0.11	0.09	0.10	0.09	0.07	0.11
Percentage of women in national legislature	0.01***	0.33	0.00	0.01**	0.29	0.00
Development	0.95*	0.27	0.37	0.81*	0.21	0.40
Level of democracy	0.05***	0.45	0.01	0.06***	0.45	0.01
Religiosity	−0.03	−0.13	0.03	−0.05†	−0.19	0.03
Adjusted R^2	0.64***			0.64***		
N	53			53		

Note: Entries are based on OLS regression analysis. †$p \leq 0.10$; *$p \leq 0.05$; **$p \leq 0.01$; ***$p \leq 0.001$. Multicollinearity diagnostics showed that this is not a problem.

representation still shows up, since the countries' percentage of women in national legislatures is a positive and significant predictor. This is a surprising result that challenges some of our core theoretical assumptions on the symbolic effects of female heads of state and government. We not only anticipated an effect, but we thought the presence of a female head of state or government might even be stronger than the presence of women in national legislatures.

Therefore, we decided to probe further with this indicator to see if the effect of the presence of a female executive on support for female leaders is conditional. From the perspective of conditionality, it may be that the effect of the presence of a female executive on support for female leaders is conditional on whether countries have crossed a certain contextual threshold. For instance, perhaps at one point, cultural or institutional support for female leaders becomes such an ingrained norm that the symbolic impact of the presence or absence of a female leader is no longer needed. In such an environment, support for female leaders could be so widespread and high that a woman's presence or absence in a position of power can no longer have an effect.

To investigate conditionality, we turned first to determining which control variable was ultimately responsible for the change in the significance of the female-executive variable. We then decided to investigate the possibility of a conditional effect by looking at whether the female-executive variable interacted with this variable.

Further analysis shows that the variable that washes away the significance of the female-executive variable when included in the same model is *level of democracy.* Theories of democratic learning have considered a longer democratic tradition to be a socialization mechanism through which respect for the equality of opportunity in political participation and inclusion is enhanced. Perhaps countries with a higher level of effective democratic institutionalization have approached a threshold of widespread respect for formal political equality that is less affected or unaffected by whether the head of state or government is female. If a strong democratic tradition has such socializing potential, acceptance of female leaders will be high regardless of whether a head of state or government is female. So we might not see a symbolic effect among the higher achievers in democratic institutionalization. However, where institutions are weaker and their learning effects lower, the symbolic power of a female executive may still matter for support for female leaders.

Table 2.4 tests this possibility by including a new variable based on an interaction term that interacts countries' level of democracy with the presence of a female executive. In both the models predicting women's and men's

TABLE 2.4: MULTIVARIATE ANALYSIS OF SUPPORT FOR FEMALE LEADERS WITH FEMALE EXECUTIVE AND DEMOCRACY INTERACTION

	Women's acceptance of women's ability to govern			Men's acceptance of women's ability to govern		
	B	Beta	Standard error	B	Beta	Standard error
Female executive	0.36*	0.30	0.17	0.40*	0.31	0.18
Percentage of women in national legislature	0.01***	0.33	0.00	0.01***	0.30	0.00
Development	0.95*	0.27	0.36	0.81*	0.21	0.38
Level of democracy	0.06***	0.56	0.01	0.07***	0.57	0.01
Religiosity	−0.02	−0.07	0.03	−0.04	−0.17	0.03
Female executive × democracy	−0.04†	−0.29	0.02	−0.05*	−0.33	0.02
Adjusted R^2	0.65***			0.66***		
N	53			53		

Note: Entries are based on OLS regression analysis. †$p \leq 0.10$; *$p \leq 0.05$; **$p \leq 0.01$; ***$p \leq 0.001$. Multi-collinearity diagnostics showed that this is not a problem.

support, the interaction is significant. Figures 2.1 and 2.2 plot the interaction with a simple analysis of variance through mean comparisons.

In Figures 2.1 and 2.2, the sample of countries is grouped as having low or high democracy based on a median split of their democracy scores. The lower half of the distribution falls into "low democracy," and the higher half of the distribution falls into "high democracy." We then plot women and men's average support for women leaders by countries with and without the presence of a female executive. The upper line in each figure depicts the average female and male support among countries with a female executive, while the lower line depicts the average support among countries without a female executive. If the effect of a female executive on support for women leaders is conditional on a weaker level of democracy, we would expect to see a difference in average support in the "low democracy" category and no or very little difference in average support in the "high democracy" category. This is exactly what the trends depict in both figures. The simple analysis of data shows us why democracy interacted with the presence of a female executive is negative and significant in Table 2.4. Thus, the evidence supports a conditional positive influence of a female executive on support for female leaders for both women and men. It is in contexts with less effective democratic institutionalization where the symbolism of a female executive significantly improves support for female leaders.

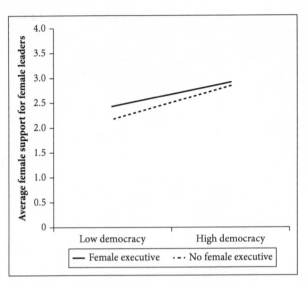

Figure 2.1   The effect of a female executive on women's support of female leaders by strength of democracy

Note: Low-democracy countries include Algeria, Armenia, Azerbaijan, Bahrain, Belarus, China, Ecuador, Egypt, Iraq, Jordan, Kazakhstan, Kuwait, Kyrgyzstan, Libya, Malaysia, Morocco, Nigeria, Pakistan, Qatar, Russia, Rwanda, Singapore, Thailand, Tunisia, Ukraine, Uzbekistan, Yemen, and Zimbabwe. High-democracy countries include Argentina, Australia, Chile, Colombia, Cyprus, Estonia, Germany, Ghana, India, Japan, Lebanon, Mexico, the Netherlands, New Zealand, Peru, the Philippines, Poland, Romania, South Africa, Slovenia, South Korea, Spain, Sweden, Taiwan, Trinidad and Tobago, Turkey, Uruguay, and the United States.

We should also note that a comparison of the figures show sex differences. Figure 2.1 graphs female support, while Figure 2.2 graphs male support. If one compares the two figures, it becomes apparent that the presence of a female executive maintains a small, independent, positive effect on female support for female leaders even among those cases grouped in the "high democracy" category, whereas this is not the case for male support of female leaders. This also shows up in the strength of the interaction's coefficients in Table 2.4. The interaction is less significant in predicting female support than male support because women's average support remains slightly higher among the countries with a female executive when compared to those countries without a female executive, even in the "high democracy" group. This is less the case for male support in the "high democracy" group. Thus, with the significant interactions, we partially confirm the expectation that the presence of a female head of state or government will positively influence support for female leaders through a symbolic effect.

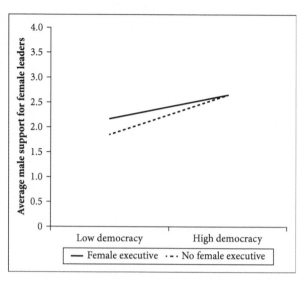

Figure 2.2   The effect of a female executive on men's support of female leaders by strength of democracy

Note: Low-democracy countries include Algeria, Armenia, Azerbaijan, Bahrain, Belarus, China, Ecuador, Egypt, Iraq, Jordan, Kazakhstan, Kuwait, Kyrgyzstan, Libya, Malaysia, Morocco, Nigeria, Pakistan, Qatar, Russia, Rwanda, Singapore, Thailand, Tunisia, Ukraine, Uzbekistan, Yemen, and Zimbabwe. High-democracy countries include Argentina, Australia, Chile, Colombia, Cyprus, Estonia, Germany, Ghana, India, Japan, Lebanon, Mexico, the Netherlands, New Zealand, Peru, the Philippines, Poland, Romania, South Africa, Slovenia, South Korea, Spain, Sweden, Taiwan, Trinidad and Tobago, Turkey, Uruguay, and the United States.

Tables 2.5 and 2.6 present the results that estimate determinants of female and male voter engagement at the national and local levels. The female-executive coefficients are positive and significant in both the female and male models in Table 2.5 and Table 2.6. This tells us that the presence of a female executive increases the average level of voting in national and local elections for both women and men. Thus, when compared to the results on support for female leaders, here the evidence runs more in favor of our original expectations. There is evidence of unconditional symbolic effects. Moreover, there is a slight indication that the effect is stronger for women when one compares the local voting models in Table 2.6. While the presence of a female executive is significant and positive for both female and male engagement, this is a more powerful predictor of female voter engagement given the larger, more significant coefficients in the female model. We should also note that in all of these voting models, symbolic effects run solely through the presence of a female executive. The percentage of women in parliament has no effect. In

TABLE 2.5: MULTIVARIATE ANALYSIS OF VOTER ENGAGEMENT, NATIONAL LEVEL

	Women who voted in national election			Men who voted in national election		
	B	Beta	Standard error	B	Beta	Standard error
Female executive	0.27**	0.35	0.08	0.23**	0.36	0.07
Percentage of women in national legislature	0.00	−0.02	0.00	0.00	−0.02	0.00
Development	0.32	0.14	0.30	0.24	0.12	0.27
Level of democracy	0.02*	0.32	0.01	0.02	0.44	0.01
Religiosity	−0.01	−0.03	0.02	0.00	−0.04	0.02
Turnout	0.01**	0.41	0.00	0.01***	0.44	0.00
Adjusted R^2	0.50***			0.45***		
N	50			50		

Note: Entries are based on OLS regression analysis. *$p \leq 0.05$; **$p \leq 0.01$; ***$p \leq 0.001$. Multicollinearity diagnostics showed that this is not a problem.

TABLE 2.6: MULTIVARIATE ANALYSIS OF VOTER ENGAGEMENT, LOCAL LEVEL

	Women who voted in local election			Men who voted in local election		
	B	Beta	Standard error	B	Beta	Standard error
Female executive	0.25**	0.32	0.09	0.20*	0.30	0.09
Percentage of women in national legislature	0.00	−0.10	0.00	0.00	−0.12	0.00
Development	0.14	0.06	0.35	−0.06	−0.03	0.33
Level of democracy	0.02*	0.30	0.01	0.02*	0.34	0.01
Religiosity	−0.02	−0.10	0.03	−0.01	−0.06	0.03
Turnout	0.01**	0.38	0.00	0.01**	0.37	0.00
Adjusted R^2	0.41***			0.32***		
N	49			49		

Note: Entries are based on OLS regression analysis. * $p \leq .05$; ** $p \leq .01$; *** $p \leq 0.001$. Multicollinearity diagnostics showed that this is not a problem.

fact, only the female-executive variable and the turnout variable are significant predictors of average voter engagement at the national and local levels.

Table 2.7 tests whether the presence of a female executive maintains a significant, positive effect on average female political interest when controlled under the multivariate analysis. We do not model men's political interest since this failed to reach significance in the test of bivariate relationships.

TABLE 2.7: MULTIVARIATE ANALYSIS OF FEMALE INTEREST IN POLITICS

	B	Beta	Standard error
Female executive	0.18[†]	0.25	0.10
Percentage of women in national legislature	0.00	−0.08	0.00
Development	−0.25	−0.12	0.35
Level of democracy	−0.02	−0.23	0.00
Religiosity	−0.06*	−0.38	0.02
Adjusted R^2	0.12*		
N	53		

Note: Entries are based on OLS regression analysis. †$p \leq 0.10$; *$p \leq 0.05$; **$p \leq 0.01$; ***$p \leq 0.001$. Multicollinearity diagnostics showed that this is not a problem.

This told us that the presence of a female executive was not a correlate of the variation in male political interest. Without the simple bivariate relationship, there is no reason to move on to the multivariate test.

In the female political-interest model, the direction of the effect is positive and significant. Thus, in countries with a female head of state or government, women have higher levels of political interest on average. Therefore, in addition to the voter-engagement models, this is yet another trend that speaks in favor of our original theoretical expectations. Also, similar to the voter-engagement models, the symbolic effect runs solely through the presence of a female executive. The percentage of women in national legislatures has no effect. While this is encouraging for our theoretical expectations, we should also note that this model performs rather low in terms of explained variance in women's average political interest across countries. The adjusted R^2 is low at 0.12.

To summarize all results, the evidence supports the hypothesis that female heads of state and government will be positive symbols for improving political engagement, particularly for women. This is especially clear in the models that explain voter engagement at the local level and political interest. Voter engagement at the national level is nearly equally higher for women and men. Support for female leaders fails to reach significance when controls are instituted, but further analysis reveals a conditional effect such that support for female leaders for both women and men is significantly higher when there is a female executive in countries with lower levels of democracy. Finally, for all but one of our measures of symbolic effects, these effects appear to run solely through the presence of a female head of state or government. This is confirmation that female heads of state and government are powerful symbols, perhaps even more powerful than women's presence in legislatures.

Conclusion

The comparative literature on the symbolic effects of women's representation must expand beyond a focus on women in national legislatures to include the effects of female heads of state and government. Arguably, the presence of a female head of state or government is as transformative of women's views of their roles in politics. In fact, if one considers the visibility and status of national executive office, the symbolic effects of a female executive could trump that of an increase in the percentage of female parliamentarians.

Toward that end we examined whether a recent or current female head of state or government improved support of female leaders and political engagement, particularly for women. We looked cross-sectionally at over fifty countries to evaluate the influence of the presence of a female executive on average support of female leaders, interest in politics, and level of voter engagement in national and local elections. The results largely supported the expectations that female heads of state and government would send positive signals that improve political engagement. This was also the case for acceptance of women leaders, but the effect was conditional on contexts where democracy was low. Importantly, we also found that when compared to the presence of women in national legislatures, the symbolic effects appear to have run solely through the presence of a female head of state or government for three out of our four indicators. This strengthened our call for the literature to expand analysis of symbolic effects beyond women's presence in national legislatures.

While our findings are promising, the data are limited to only eleven observations of countries with recent or current female executives, and the analysis is limited to a cross section of countries in the late 2000s. The universe of countries that have had a female head of state or government is, however, ninety-eight. Unfortunately, survey availability and vast differences in countries' timing in these achievements create difficulties for a wider test. As a result, there is much more comparative work to be done. Also, future research must conduct longitudinal analyses to reveal the causal direction of the relationship. In addition, our analysis in this chapter applies an aggregate-level approach to what are ultimately individual-level trends in attitudes and behavior. This raises the issue of aggregation bias. Future research must include a cross-level design that incorporates both the country level and the individual level in the same multivariate analysis to provide a microfoundation for the macrolevel evidence presented here.

Appendix

TABLE 2A.1: VARIABLE DESCRIPTIVES

Variables	Maximum value	Minimum value	Mean
Average female support of female leaders (1 low–4 high)	3.50	1.72	2.57
Average male support of female leaders (1 low–4 high)	3.38	1.39	2.29
Average females who voted in national elections (1 high–3 low)	2.56	1.11	1.57
Average males who voted in national elections (1 high–3 low)	2.38	1.09	1.55
Average females who voted in local elections (1 high–3 low)	2.68	1.13	1.62
Average males who voted in local elections (1 high–3 low)	2.60	1.12	1.60
Average female political interest (1 high–4 low)	3.47	2.15	2.77
Average male political interest (1 high–4 low)	3.26	1.98	2.54
Female executive	1.0	0	0.22
Percentage of women in national legislatures	56.3	0	20.40
Development	0.94	0.37	0.74
Level of democracy	10.0	−9.0	4.47
Religiosity	9.87	3.65	7.78
Turnout	99,000	42,000	64,760
Sample N = 56 countries			

NOTES

1. The WVS is by far the largest comparative public-opinion project in terms of both spatial and temporal coverage of countries worldwide. The WVS surveys random probability samples of residential national populations above seventeen years of age, with an average sample size of twelve hundred respondents per country. Details on the questionnaire, fieldwork, data, and sampling are available on the home page of the WVS at http://www.worldvaluessurvey.org. In six consecutive rounds between 1981 and 2014, the WVS has surveyed over one hundred countries worldwide.

2. For our recent cases, the longest gap between the time of the survey and the end of the executive's term is three years.

3. See the Polity IV Project site at http://www.systemicpeace.org/polity/polity4.htm.

4. The database is available at http://www.ipu.org/parline-e/parlinesearch.asp. See especially Inter-Parliamentary Union 2015.

REFERENCES

Alexander, Amy C. 2012. "Change in Women's Descriptive Representation and the Belief in Women's Ability to Govern: A Virtuous Cycle." *Politics & Gender* 8 (4): 437–464.

Alexander, Amy C., and Christian Welzel. 2011a. "Empowering Women." *European Sociological Review* 27 (3): 364–384.

———. 2011b. "Islam and Patriarchy." *International Review of Sociology* 21 (2): 249–276.

———. 2011c. "Measuring Effective Democracy: The Human Empowerment Approach." *Comparative Politics* 43 (3): 271–289.

Atkeson, Lonna R. 2003. "Not All Cues Are Created Equal: The Conditional Impact of Female Candidates on Political Engagement." *Journal of Politics* 65 (4): 1040–1061.

Burns, Nancy, Kay Lehman Schlozman, and Sidney Verba. 2001. *The Private Roots of Public Action: Gender, Equality, and Political Participation.* Cambridge, MA: Harvard University Press.

Bussey, Kay, and Albert Bandura. 1999. "Social Cognitive Theory of Gender Development and Differentiation." *Psychological Review* 106 (4): 676–713.

Carroll, Susan J. 1985. *Women as Candidates in American Politics.* Bloomington: Indiana University Press.

Dolan, Kathleen. 2006. "Symbolic Mobilization? The Impact of Candidate Sex in American Elections." *American Politics Research* 34 (6): 687–704.

Franzmann, Majella. 1999. *Women and Religion.* New York: Oxford University Press.

Hansen, Susan B. 1997. "Talking about Politics: Gender and Contextual Effects on Political Proselytizing." *Journal of Politics* 59 (1): 73–103.

Heffernan, Richard. 2006. "The Prime Minister and the News Media: Political Communication as a Leadership Resource." *Parliamentary Affairs* 59 (4): 582–598.

High-Pippert, Angela, and John Comer. 1998. "Female Empowerment: The Influence of Women Representing Women." *Women & Politics* 19 (4): 53–66.

Inglehart, Ronald, and Pippa Norris. 2003. *Rising Tide: Gender Equality and Cultural Change around the World.* New York: Cambridge University Press.

Inglehart, Ronald, and Christian Welzel. 2005. *Modernization, Cultural Change and Democracy: The Human Development Sequence.* New York: Cambridge University Press.

Inter-Parliamentary Union. 2015. "Women in National Parliaments." December 1. Available at http://www.ipu.org/wmn-e/world.htm.

Jalalzai, Farida. 2013. *Shattered, Cracked, or Firmly Intact: Women and the Executive Glass Ceiling Worldwide.* New York: Oxford University Press.

Karp, Jeffery A., and Susan A. Banducci. 2008. "When Politics Is Not Just a Man's Game: Women's Representation and Political Engagement." *Electoral Studies* 27 (1): 105–115.

Kenworthy, Lane, and Melissa Malami. 1999. "Gender Inequality in Political Representation: A Worldwide Comparative Analysis." *Social Forces* 78 (1): 235–269.

Kittilson, Miki Caul, and Leslie A. Schwindt-Bayer. 2012. *The Gendered Effects of Electoral Institutions.* New York: Oxford University Press.

Koch, Jeffrey. 1997. "Candidate Gender and Women's Psychological Engagement in Politics." *American Politics Quarterly* 25 (1): 118–133.

Lawless, Jennifer. 2004. "Politics of Presence? Congresswomen and Symbolic Representation." *Political Research Quarterly* 57 (1): 81–99.

Mansbridge, Jane. 1999. "Should Blacks Represent Blacks and Women Represent Women? A Contingent 'Yes.'" *Journal of Politics* 61 (3): 628–657.

Miles, Jeremy, and Mark Shevlin. 2001. *Applying Regression and Correlation.* London: Sage.

Morgan, Jana, and Melissa Buice. 2013. "Latin American Attitudes toward Women in Politics: The Influence of Elite Cues, Female Advancement and Individual Characteristics." *American Political Science Review* 107 (4): 644–662.

Norris, Pippa, and Mona Lena Krook. 2009. "One of Us." Paper presented at the annual meeting of the American Political Science Association, Toronto, September.

Norris, Pippa, Joni Lovenduski, and Rosie Campbell. 2004. *Research Report: Gender and Political Participation.* London: Electoral Commission (U.K.).

Paxton, Pamela, and Melanie M. Hughes. 2013. *Women, Politics and Power: A Global Perspective.* 2nd ed. London: Sage.

Paxton, Pamela, and Sheri Kunovich. 2003. "Women's Political Presence: The Importance of Ideology." *Social Forces* 82 (1): 87–113.

Phillips, Anne. 1995. *The Politics of Presence.* New York: Oxford University Press.

Pitkin, Hanna Fenichel. 1967. *The Concept of Representation.* Berkeley: University of California Press.

Reingold, Beth, and Jessica Harrell. 2010. "The Impact of Descriptive Representation on Women's Political Engagement: Does Party Matter?" *Political Research Quarterly* 63 (2): 280–294.

Sapiro, Virginia. 1981. "Research Frontier Essay: When Are Interests Interesting? The Problem of Political Representation of Women." *American Political Science Review* 75 (3): 701–716.

Sapiro, Virginia, and Pamela Johnston Conover. 1997. "The Variable Gender Bias of Electoral Politics: Gender and Context in the 1992 US Election." *British Journal of Political Science* 27 (4): 497–523.

Schwindt-Bayer, Leslie A., and William Mishler. 2005. "An Integrated Model of Women's Representation." *Journal of Politics* 67 (2): 407–428.

Tabachnick, Barbara, and Linda Fidell. 2000. *Using Multivariate Statistics.* 4th ed. Needham Heights, MA: Allyn and Bacon.

Williams, Melissa S. 1998. *Voice, Trust and Memory.* Princeton, NJ: Princeton University Press.

Wolbrecht, Christina, and David E. Campbell. 2007. "Leading by Example: Female Members of Parliament as Political Role Models." *American Journal of Political Science* 51 (4): 921–939.

Young, Iris Marion. 2002. *Inclusion and Democracy.* New York: Oxford University Press.

3

President Barack H. Obama and the Rhetoric of Race

Between Responsibility and Respectability

CORY CHARLES GOODING

This chapter on identity politics argues that President Obama's own gender-race performance, as a biracial man who identifies as black, is intrinsic to his presidential politics. As candidate and as president, through innumerable actions and statements, Barack Obama consistently defines black masculinity in terms of personal responsibility, as performed in the family, profession, community, and society. This principle, which has profound consequences for politics and policy, is perhaps most fully expressed in the president's 2013 Morehouse College commencement address. Setting Obama's gender-race ideology in context—examining it as a statement of African American political thought and politics made by a president whose realization of his political ambitions depended on a majority white electorate—reveals some of the challenges confronting the men and women whose identities will redefine the U.S. presidency so that it is no longer exclusively white or exclusively male.

Historically, white masculinity stood as representative of what it meant to be "American" in the United States. The early history of the country reserved citizenship rights for white men. (See Chapter 10 for a discussion of citizenship rights for white women in this early period.) Willingness to vote for a female president or a black president surpassed 50 percent only beginning in 1955 and 1965, respectively (Jones 2007; Jones and Moore 2003). Despite this history, public opinion in the twenty-first century now renders the top executive office accessible to candidates who identify outside the white male tradition, raising new questions for presidential candidates and officeholders. For example, is someone who is not white acceptable to white citizens as representing traditional American values and culture? Is this person beholden to the interests of a specific identity-based community? Does this person hold extra responsibilities to empower traditionally disenfranchised communities?

Because Barack Obama is the first black president in this nation's history, his answers to these questions have implications for his own presidency and for the relative openness of the office for future nonwhite and nonmale candidates. All presidential candidates must be able to affirmatively answer the question "Is this person capable of advancing the interests of the entire American population?" But for Obama, the emphasis on his representation of both black and white America becomes an explicit concern. Suddenly, the issue of racial inclusiveness takes center stage.

The history of racial divisions and the social, economic, and political disenfranchisement of black people in the United States raises expectations for Obama to represent the public writ large and black people in particular. However, the history of national interests subsuming those of the black community highlights an inherent tension in communicating effectively with these audiences. Obama is perpetually caught between emphasizing color-blind individualism, a proven strategy in white presidential politics, and addressing the legacy of racism in the United States, a high priority for black citizens. Throughout the first six years of his presidency, Obama's consistent strategy for balancing these priorities was to emphasize respectability.[1] He most fully expounded this strategy in his Morehouse College commencement speech delivered in 2013. In the speech, Obama presents a model of black masculinity that seeks to empower black men by balancing themes of individual and collective responsibility. At the same time, the president frames the black experience in the United States as consistent with a national history of overcoming.[2] These points of emphasis offer respectability politics as the most expedient strategy for black empowerment because it is representative of national values and consistent with African American history.

Race, Gender, and the New Presidential Body: Performing Identity at the Intersection

The election of a self-identified black man to the presidential office marked a significant historical moment in the struggle for African Americans and women for full and equitable participation in the political system of the United States. Before Obama issued a single executive order or uttered a word as president, he had already challenged the history of racial antipathy that defined U.S. society. Thus, understanding Obama's rhetorical strategies must begin not with his speeches or slogans but with the man and how he situated himself with regard to broader identity-based communities.

The rhetoric of President Obama, the son of Ann Dunham, a white woman from Wichita, Kansas, and Barack Obama Sr., a black man from Nyang'oma Kogelo, Kenya, is framed by his racial identity. The presidency and corporeal existence of Obama, as a biracial man who identifies as black, lie at the intersection of the black and white communities, so he faced representing the interests of both racial groups from a unique social location. Obama's efforts to communicate with these audiences were evident in both his racial and gender performance.

Obama's identity performance was set among diverse assessments of his background, each with implications for the United States. Political commentator Debra Dickerson argued against labeling Obama as black, stating, "In the American political context, black means . . . the descendant of West African slaves brought here to labor in the United States" ("Debra Dickerson" 2007). Because Obama did not descend from enslaved West Africans but from a white woman and a voluntary migrant from Kenya, Dickerson argued that Obama was not black. However, others did see him as black and, furthermore, saw his blackness as an obstacle to his being an effective president, depicting and rejecting him as a Muslim, Kenyan, socialist, or anti-American (Parlett 2014).[3] Recognition of these competing criticisms prompted legal scholars Devon Carbado and Mitu Gulati to argue that Obama found himself in a racial double bind between being "black enough" and "too black" (2015, 4). Each assessment of Obama's racial identity communicated an assumed tension between being black and being American.

Unfortunately, the emphasis on Obama's racial background often ignores the gendered complexities of his identity and the presidency. Discussions of gender with respect to the U.S. presidency frequently focus on the 2008 campaign, including Sarah Palin's vice presidential candidacy, Hillary Clinton's presidential candidacy, and Obama's support among women voters (Lawrence and Rose 2009). Significantly less attention is paid to Obama's own gender performance.[4] This approach is an example of the criticism levied by intersectional scholars that black people are typically studied as exclusively male, while women are studied as exclusively white (Collins 2000; Crenshaw 1991).

Analysis of Obama's gender performance reveals the nuanced relationship between race and gender in the double bind that Obama must navigate. If Obama engages the hypermasculinity used by white male candidates, he could be read as an angry or threatening black man. On the other extreme, if Obama does not assert some masculine qualities, he could be read as too weak to lead the country. Legal scholar Frank Rudy Cooper argues that Obama solves these apparent contradictions by becoming the country's first unisex president, "masculine enough to pass the Commander-in-Chief test yet feminine enough to make people comfortable with his blackness" (2009, 637). Obama maintained masculine toughness sufficient for the presidency yet emphasized qualities frequently associated with women, such as collaboration, consensus building, fairness, and inclusion. Cooper describes Obama's feminine qualities as contrasting sharply with more hawkish and assertive qualities of other candidates, including Hillary Clinton in 2008.[5]

Obama's bending of gender norms (Linsky 2008) informs broader definitions of black masculinity. African American studies scholar Ronda C. H. Anthony (2013) argues that Obama's gender performance serves to redefine black middle-class masculinity, presenting it as a cooperative process with women. Obama "employs a black male feminist consciousness to construct a progressive black masculinity that is consistently sensitive to and nurturing of women and communities around him." Obama can thus be understood as engaging "black feminist agendas and insights through intra-racial, platonic relationships with women" (154). Obama emphasizes spousal responsibilities and fatherhood as deeply connected to conceptions of masculinity. This collaborative definition of black masculinity emphasizes Obama's identity performance, particularly in the private sphere with his wife and daughters.[6] Of course, identity performance is only one component of Obama's navigation of the double bind. Rhetoric plays an important role in the navigation of such competing demands because public speech is imbued with a range of gendered norms and expectations (see Jamieson 1995). Public speech communicates the intersection of both gendered and racialized norms and expectations imposed on the president.

Navigating the Rhetoric of Responsibility: One President, Multiple Audiences

In his analysis of black public intellectuals, political scientist Adolph Reed Jr. (1995) draws a significant distinction between two types of black leaders. One speaks on behalf of the black community, articulating a black perspective to a primarily nonblack audience. Another speaks to and engages the black community to identify the best means for community empowerment.

Reed focuses on academics and civil rights leaders at the end of the twentieth century, but President Obama similarly must make decisions in the twenty-first century about what type of leader he wants to be while locating himself within the black community. The challenge for Obama is that the two types of leadership require distinct rhetorical strategies. Speaking outward translates into demonstrating black people's common humanity by articulating a common set of values that transcend race, specifically by employing color-blind individualism. Speaking inward, however, requires acknowledging the legacy of slavery and identifying collective strategies to address it, in other words, by expressing collective racial consciousness. Color-blind individualism and collective racial consciousness represent contrasting constituencies and strategies for improving race relations.

Color blindness serves as a useful approach for political leaders articulating national values while engaging a majority white U.S. population. The color-blindness philosophy emphasizes the individual over the collective and deemphasizes the persistence of racism within the structures and institutions of society (Bonilla-Silva 2009; Wise 2010). Sociologist Eduardo Bonilla-Silva identifies the roots of color-blind philosophy in an abstract liberalism that emphasizes individual freedom and choice.

Ronald Reagan demonstrated the color-blind philosophy in his appropriation of Martin Luther King Jr.'s speeches to claim that equal opportunity was achieved in the United States and that individuals needed to take responsibility for their own success (Bostdorff and Goldzwig 2005). While Obama could not throw off the ascribed racialized expectations that his racial identity produced, his capacity to downplay racial divisions and speak to liberal ideals was effective from his arrival on the national stage and throughout his presidential campaigns.

What brought Obama to national prominence was his 2004 speech at the Democratic National Convention, in which he articulated a vision for a united nation that was undivided by race, committed to the ideal that "all men are created equal." In this speech, Obama stated, "Go into any inner city neighborhood, and folks will tell you that government alone can't teach our kids to learn—they know that parents have to teach, that children can't achieve unless we raise their expectations and turn off the television sets and eradicate the slander that says a black youth with a book is acting white" (Obama 2004). By emphasizing the existence of parental and personal responsibility in the inner city, Obama attempted to counteract common stereotypes that frame black Americans as sponging off the government and lacking personal responsibility. Similarly, Obama's 2008 campaign for president was characterized by persistent neutrality on racial politics and an inclination toward emphasizing liberal ideals and American progress (Marable 2009; Wise 2010).

This rhetorical position, which Tim Wise (2010) calls color-blind individualism, contributed to the belief that the United States had entered a postracial era (Tierney 2008). Central to the postracial claim was the conviction that race no longer mattered in determining the life chances of individual Americans. After the 2008 presidential election, 22 percent of the white and 44 percent of the black population identified racism as a big problem in society. Although this represented a sharp drop from 1996, when pollsters found 52 percent of white and 70 percent of black people had identified racism as a big problem in society, white people remained less concerned than black people about racism (Craighill and Langer 2009).

Despite such individualistic trends in American political thought, black leaders and activists have largely engaged the struggle for equal rights as a collective effort. The collective framing of political claims is a signature component of black political thought and rhetoric (Dawson 2001). Whether expressed through the rhetoric of abolitionist Frederick Douglass, civil rights leader Martin Luther King Jr., or Black Nationalist Malcolm X, claims for equal rights are largely expressed in terms of a collective racial community. Studies find that many black Americans understand themselves as a part of a racial community that extends beyond their geographic location or socioeconomic class, a self-conception that is frequently described as racial group consciousness. This sense of community is sometimes measured in terms of the belief that an individual's fate is linked to the fate of the larger racial group (Dawson 1995; McClain et al. 2009).

While Obama's performative and rhetorical blackness produces a need for him to engage this rich history of black politics as a collective endeavor, as president, Obama must also engage the concepts of individualistic liberalism that traditionally inform national politics. Obama must perpetually answer the question of how to publicly, simultaneously speak both inwardly to the black community and outwardly to a majority white national audience in a way that does not betray the interests of the group in which he claims membership.

An exclusive emphasis on the performative and rhetorical components of this double bind renders this author in danger of painting a president whose public face is schizophrenic and unable to empower anyone, much less a racial community. That would be an inaccurate portrait and one that misses the unifying ethos that holds Obama's racial politics together. Obama addresses the tension between the color-blind and individualistic ideals of liberalism *and* the more collective racial orientations existing in the black community through language that speaks to his racial and national communities simultaneously: the language of respectability.

Respectability Politics: The Answer to the Double Bind?

Given the inherent constraints on Obama, these questions remain: How did he seek to empower the black population? Has this president's outreach to the white population constrained his ability to address black concerns about the legacy of racism in the United States? I argue that understanding Obama's presidential politics requires recognition of his race-gender performance and rhetoric as rooted in respectability politics. Obama's respectability politics advances an image of black masculinity that emphasizes both individual and collective responsibilities while countering negative stereotypes of black men.[7] Moreover, Obama strives to bridge the black experience with a broader national narrative.

Evelyn Brooks Higginbotham (1994) defines respectability politics as the belief that reform of individual behavior is a goal in itself as well as a strategy for broader societal reform. This philosophy is evident in sociologist W.E.B. Du Bois's gendered conception of the Talented Tenth. Du Bois noted, "The Negro race, like all races, is going to be saved by its exceptional men. The problem of education, then, among Negroes must first of all deal with the Talented Tenth; it is the problem of developing the Best of this race that they may guide the Mass away from the contamination and death of the Worst" (1903, 33). This strategy of black uplift is anchored in the representation of the race through white representations of gender roles, drawn from the Victorian era, and current internal policing of community-member behavior. Respectability politics within black politics translates to a perpetual recognition that one is under a white gaze that bases its assessment of the race on the actions of the individual. Thus, those who subscribe to respectability politics view the individual performance of standards and values imposed by white people as the most effective collective strategy for the racial group to gain equitable inclusion into the polity.[8] This relationship between individual and group identity is important for discussions of presidential power, whereby the president is a singular actor, using rhetoric and performance to move government.

This emphasis on rhetoric and performance is not exclusive to the Obama presidency. Presidential scholars historically emphasize performance and rhetoric as persuasive tools in the pursuit and execution of executive duties (see, for example, Campbell and Jamieson 2008; Hart, Childers, and Lind 2013; Leith 2012; Medhurst 2007; Mercieca and Vaughn 2014; Nelson and Riley 2010; Stuckey 1991, 2004; Tulis 1988; Zarefsky 2004). Presidential campaigns and speeches are typically highly scripted yet performative in nature (Wayne 2000). Despite this historical emphasis, Obama's performance is unique, as his race adds an additional, unprecedented layer of identity representation.

Obama's efforts to use respectability politics to balance competing interests earned him criticism. According to Frederick C. Harris (2012), Obama's emphasis on overcoming paints racism as irrelevant to outcomes; Obama does a poor job of addressing the legacy of racism that resides in the systems and institutions of American society. Similarly, political scientist Melanye Price states that "Obama does the following: he provides a racial analysis that is disconnected from historical context, suggests that prevailing isms are primarily relegated to the past, conflates oppositional racial experiences, and relies too heavily on his own personal narrative to justify claims" (2014, 573).

Ultimately, Obama's respectability politics is consistently cognizant of the white gaze. His strategy emphasizes countering negative stereotypes among white people rather than confronting the persistence of institutionalized racism. By focusing on countering negative stereotypes, Obama attempts to diminish perceptions that the nation is divided while maintaining the broadest base of support possible.

Obama's commencement speech at the historically black all-male Morehouse College represents an important articulation of his public strategy in that it was characteristic of his emphasis on individual agency over political, economic, and social systems while countering old conceptions of black masculinity. Obama frames black history as a part of national overcoming and minimizes the critique of American systems, the rhetorical strategy that predominated throughout the first six years of his presidency.

The Morehouse Speech

With the goal of inspiring an audience of optimistic young people to achieve their full potential as they enter the American workforce, Obama's commencement speeches in the United States offer unique insight into what the president understands to be the ideal strategy for attaining success. Commencement speeches also provide exceptional opportunities for the president to address audiences on major issues while appearing to transcend the usual partisan politics (Martin 1985). Between 2009 and 2015, Obama gave twenty-two commencement speeches at a range of educational institutions.[9] Among them, his commencement speech at Morehouse College presents a particularly useful opportunity to examine his efforts to empower black Americans.

Morehouse College is an all-male historically black college in Atlanta, Georgia, with an extraordinary tradition built on educating and inspiring black men, most notably civil rights leader Dr. Martin Luther King Jr.[10] Like many other historically black colleges and universities (HBCUs),[11] Morehouse espouses a type of respectability politics consistent with Du Bois's Talented Tenth philosophy. Famous for its own conceptualizations of masculinity, Morehouse holds expectations for its students that center on being Renaissance men. Expectations encompass academics (being well read and well spoken), extracurricular activities (being well traveled), and gender performance. In his 2009 town hall address, Morehouse president Robert M. Franklin enumerated these expectations: "[A Renaissance Man] should carry something to read and make good use of [his] down time." Franklin defined what it means to be well spoken as choosing one's words carefully: "Profanity does not reflect your verbal grace and style." Also articulating what it means to be well dressed, Franklin stated, "We cannot monitor what you wear when you leave campus, but while you are on the Morehouse campus, in the presence of adult learners, do not sag your pants, do not show your undergarments. Do not wear do-rags, and do not wear baseball caps in class or in the cafeteria" (Franklin 2009).

For Morehouse, overcoming the legacy of racism is as much a matter of gender performance as it is racial performance. In particular, Franklin describes dressing well in terms of gender: "And, to those who would experiment with wearing clothing associated with a women's [sic] garb (dresses, tunics, purses and pumps) I am directing that you not exhibit these items on the Morehouse campus. Wear what you wish to off campus. But, while you are here on the ground where [Benjamin] Mays and Martin [Luther King Jr.] and Maynard [Jackson] walked, those items are off limits. A man in women's clothing on campus is provocative and will not be tolerated" (Franklin 2009).[12] Franklin places the expectations of the college within the context of a broader gendered tradition of Morehouse men as unequivocally male and masculine. Although Franklin underscores the presence and contributions of gay men at Morehouse and in the African American community, he describes his expectations that Morehouse men will be exceptional leaders who do not challenge long-standing boundaries of gender representation.

Such restrictions may seem unusual to those unfamiliar with HBCUs; however, it is important to note that in its mission statement, Morehouse describes itself as developing "men with disciplined minds who will lead lives of leadership and service" (Morehouse College, n.d.). This mission is deeply connected to a historical relationship with the broader black community. Thus, countering negative stereotypes and overcoming a history of racial subordination are not exclusively academic or civic; they are also performative. Given this setting and tradition, which is aligned with respectability politics, Obama's commencement speech at Morehouse provides a way to dissect how the president uses his identity performance and rhetoric to balance the competing interests that perpetually surround him.

The Performative "We"

In the context of Morehouse College, Obama explicitly claims membership in the black racial group and positions himself in community with the audience on account of his race, gender, and new honorary degree. Throughout his presidency, Obama has frequently avoided identifying exclusively as a black man; however, in this context he does so three times over the course of the speech. Each instance serves to reinforce his commonality with the audience by identifying shared concerns, reflecting on his experience facing common obstacles, and sharing mutual capacities for success. Moreover, Obama continues, "I am humbled to stand here with all of you as an honorary Morehouse Man" (Obama 2013a). Although this might seem a reference only to his newly received honorary Morehouse degree, Obama reinforces his commonality with the audience by claiming the title of honorary "Morehouse Man."

Obama builds on his commonality with the mostly black Morehouse audience by developing his speech, with its conceptions of respectability, around three notable figures in African American history. Through the philosophy of Du Bois, the examples of Martin Luther King Jr., and his own autobiography, Obama creates a respectable black masculinity.[13] He leans on a long tradition, affirming his own racial credentials while emphasizing traditional liberal values of hard work and family values. In using these historical figures and his own autobiography, which he often incorporates into his speeches, Obama balances individual personal responsibility and collective racial responsibility. At the same moment, he emphasizes black figures, values, and history as constitutive of national identity.

Individual Responsibility and Overcoming

Obama addresses the double bind by emphasizing themes of overcoming, irrespective of race, and by placing the most notable racial barriers in the past. Obama acknowledges the physical, emotional, and psychological violence imposed on black men in particular in the United States. However, he reminds his audience that the conditions that once hindered their progress are no longer as significant as they once were, thanks to the African American civil rights movement.

Drawing on biblical references, Obama highlights the accomplishments of the civil rights movement.

> And over the last fifty years, thanks to the moral force of Dr. King and a Moses generation that overcame their fear and their cynicism and their despair, barriers have come tumbling down, and new doors of opportunity have swung open, and laws and hearts and minds have been changed to the point where someone who looks just like you can somehow come to serve as President of these United States of America. (Obama 2013a)[14]

Obama first identifies the obstacles faced by Morehouse graduate Dr. Martin Luther King Jr. and highlights the generation of individuals who fought to improve opportunities for the members of the audience.[15] He then lays down the gauntlet for his audience by identifying himself as the very product of that work and emphasizing his racial commonality with the graduates. He states, "We have individual responsibilities. There are some things, as

black men, we can only do for ourselves." This emphasis on the need for
his audience of black men to take responsibility for their own outcomes is
reminiscent of King's 1967 speech delivered before the Southern Christian
Leadership Conference, where he stated:

> Nobody else can do this for us. No document can do this for us. Not
> even an Emancipation Proclamation can do this for us. Nor can a
> Johnsonian Civil Rights Bill do this for us. If the Negro is to be free,
> he must move down into the inner resources of his own soul and sign
> with a pen and ink of self-assertive manhood his own Emancipation
> Proclamation. (King 1967)

Consistent with Martin Luther King Jr., "The Talented Tenth," and the
"Morehouse Man," Obama places responsibility on the individual graduates. He then draws from the tradition of Black Greek Letter Organizations
(BGLOs) to push his audience past the "excuses" that may restrict their
success.

> I understand there's a common fraternity creed here at Morehouse:
> "Excuses are tools of the incompetent used to build bridges to no-
> where and monuments of nothingness." Well, we've got no time for
> excuses. . . . Not because racism and discrimination no longer exist;
> we know those are still out there. It's just that in today's hypercon-
> nected, hypercompetitive world, with millions of young people from
> China and India and Brazil—many of whom started with a whole lot
> less than all of you did—all of them entering the global workforce
> alongside you, nobody is going to give you anything that you have
> not earned.

Relying on the African American tradition of the civil rights movement—
specifically Martin Luther King Jr.—and BGLOs,[16] Obama defines hard work
as the ultimate determinant of success and channels more conservative sentiments that challenge redistributive programs (i.e., welfare, affirmative action). Obama's use of the "fraternity creed" to cast racism and discrimination
as merely an "excuse" is a significant departure from the dominant black political tradition, one that, if made by a white candidate, would receive significant criticism for historical insensitivity. Gender and race intertwine in the
speech, expressing the president's identity as a black man. Certainly a white
president could not speak from within the black community or make selec-
tive use of black history without encountering great criticism. Likewise, a
woman could not comment on masculinity in terms that were self-referential
and community based without generating opposition. The Morehouse

commencement address is a speech that presents and explains Obama's race-gender performance. Yet the president does not accentuate these domestic themes. Instead, he uses international comparisons to validate his liberal claims and to further cast racism and discrimination as excuses.

Having confronted his audience, Obama then returns to identifying with them, using his autobiography as an example of overcoming and individual success: "We know that too many young men in our community continue to make bad choices. And I have to say, growing up, I made quite a few myself. Sometimes I wrote off my own failings as just another example of the world trying to keep a black man down." Obama's ability to identify with his audience in terms of both race and gender represents a powerful tool for encouraging and inspiring them. He can speak directly to an experience that is relevant while simultaneously embodying their potential. Obama uses his own social location to place the responsibility on the graduates to overcome obstacles and be successful as black men.

This success, as embodied by Obama, is defined by both the public and private spheres. Success in assuming individual responsibility in the private sphere is represented by his capacity to overcome an absentee father. "My whole life, I've tried to be for Michelle and my girls what my father was not for my mother and me. I want to break that cycle where a father is not at home, [*applause*] where a father is not helping to raise that son or daughter. I want to be a better father, a better husband, a better man." Identifying his own father as absent allows Obama to address the broader image of black men as irresponsible.[17] He also places his father's absenteeism in the realm of an excuse and pushes his audience to consider a future that is not determined by the past. By focusing on his father and his own agency in being a father, with no mention of his siblings and extended family, Obama uses a politics of respectability that is rooted in both racial and gender performance to define individual responsibility. He *speaks from* within the black tradition and *speaks to* a broader liberal tradition that can appeal to any white audience.

Collective Responsibility and Community Uplift

In the vein of the Morehouse tradition extolled by President Franklin and Du Bois's Talented Tenth, Obama emphasizes collective responsibility by arguing that the best and brightest have a responsibility to improve the conditions of the community through respectable role modeling, mentorship, and service.

Obama calls on his audience to harness "the power of your example." For Obama, a central part of the collective racial-uplift ideology is rooted in identifying and helping other men characterize positive and well-defined conceptions of manhood. This charge for role models rests at the intersection of race and gender insofar as he states, "We've got to teach [men in their communities] just like what we have to learn, what it means to be a man." While these themes are not specifically racialized, as he does not specify mentoring young black men, Obama is asking his audience to counter widely circulated stereotypes of black men as not making wise decisions or taking care of their responsibilities. Like President Franklin and Du Bois, Obama positions his audience as responsible for uplifting members of their community to represent the image of Renaissance men.

Throughout the speech, Obama takes themes from the black political tradition and stretches them to a broader national community. Acknowledging that Du Bois called for "a class of highly educated, socially conscious leaders in the black community," Obama insisted that "it's not just the African American community that needs you. The country needs you." Obama makes the same discursive move regarding the need for black businesses: "But ask yourselves what broader purpose your business might serve, in putting people to work, or transforming a neighborhood." Obama's reference to the need for black businesses draws on Black Nationalist sentiments regarding the support and development of black-owned businesses. Obama, however, defines these businesses as a matter of national inclusion, not a racial project of community exclusion.[18] Obama seeks to resolve the racialized expectations of the double bind by taking Black Nationalism and making it synonymous with American nationalism.

Obama's emphasis on collective responsibility, particularly through service, is not a theme exclusive to the Obama presidency. Among others, John F. Kennedy's 1961 entreaty to the nation to "ask not what your country can do for you—ask what you can do for your country" represents a long-standing emphasis on themes of collective responsibility through service. However, Obama's emphasis on collective responsibility is rooted in a distinct black tradition that is frequently set apart from the "American" tradition. Obama's racial identity allows him to define the national collective from the inside out. His capacity to locate himself within the black community and communicate the charge of service in terms germane to the black community expands American ideals to make them more inclusive.

Conclusion

Over the course of Obama's presidential campaigns and terms in office, political observers have identified a range of additional expectations that were placed on President Obama as a result of his racial background. Many, including Obama himself, noted that he must show that he is both black enough and not too black. Obama's efforts to resolve such overwhelming and frequently conflicting expectations are manifest in his performative and rhetorical respectability politics.

Most notably enumerated during his commencement speech at More-house College, Obama's respectability politics earned him criticism from across the ideological spectrum. However, critics frequently overlook the political payoff of Obama's respectability politics. Through this strategy, Obama balanced themes of collective and individual responsibility. He also attempted to counter negative stereotypes about black men in particular. Obama strove to define the black experience as an integral part of the nation's history and identity, thereby bridging divides between black and white communities.

While Obama's political strategy serves to reach the broadest base of voters, respectability politics is a tool that is most useful for the individual. It does not translate into positive stereotypes for an entire subjugated collective. Obama's respectability serves as an inspirational example for some black men, but it also reinforces and strengthens arguments against the existence of systemic racism. It defines success as entirely the result of determination and individual choice and implicitly identifies less successful people as lazy and bad decision makers.

Despite the race of a black president, whose racial and gender performance appealed to the majority of voters in two presidential elections, racial tensions in the United States have persisted. Between 2009 and 2015, tensions increased as a result of several high-profile events. In 2009, Henry Louis Gates Jr., an African American and Harvard professor, was arrested by Cambridge police for trespassing in his own home. Eventually, Obama intervened and held a "beer summit" where the arresting officer and the professor met with the president and vice president for a beer to discuss the incident. Demonstrating his consistent awareness of the white gaze, Obama ensured racial parity by inviting Vice President Biden and emphasized hope for positive lessons learned in his comments about the summit.

In 2012, Obama used a similar approach regarding race relations when unarmed seventeen-year-old black male Trayvon Martin was shot and killed by neighborhood watch volunteer George Zimmerman.[19] Speaking outward, Obama served as explainer-in-chief as he described the experiences of discrimination that inform the African American perspective on the case (Obama 2013b). The Trayvon Martin shooting marked only the beginning of increased media attention to the deaths of unarmed black Americans at the hands of law enforcement. Victims included Michael Brown in Ferguson, Missouri; Eric Garner in Staten Island; Freddie Gray in Baltimore; and Walter Scott in South Carolina.

Each of these events, among others, reminds us of the limitations of respectability politics to fight racism. Moreover, Obama's aggressiveness in tackling racial disparities in U.S. systems and institutions after the 2014 midterm elections also revealed that Obama's ability to address racial disparities during his presidency was limited by the white gaze before the 2014 midterms. When the national attention to race was heightened by the 2015 murder of nine parishioners (Susie Jackson, Sharonda Coleman-Singleton, DePayne Doctor, Ethel Lance, Daniel Simmons Sr., Clementa Pinckney, Cynthia Hurd, Tywanza Sanders, and Myra Thompson) by a white supremacist at Emmanuel African Methodist Church in South Carolina,[20] Obama used a very different tone from the one used at Morehouse College, at the beer summit, or in response to the George Zimmerman verdict. Addressing race relations in the eulogy for a victim of the massacre, sitting state senator Clementa Pinckney, Obama rooted his remarks in the tradition of the African Methodist Episcopal Church and passionately addressed racial discrimination in the criminal justice system, workforce, law enforcement, and voting rights. Stressing the country's persistent blindness to the impact of past injustices on the present, Obama concluded his remarks by leading the audience in singing the hymn "Amazing Grace" (Obama 2015).

Several weeks later, Obama commuted the prison sentences of forty-six nonviolent drug offenders, became the first sitting U.S. president to visit a federal prison facility to begin a national discussion of disparate sentencing for crimes committed by African Americans and Latinos, and spoke more assertively about the need to improve race relations.

Obama's respectability politics is not simply a political ploy. Obama ardently defends both his desire and practice of speaking with young men of color about personal responsibility, fatherhood, and family as a personal calling, given Obama's own experiences with having an absent father (Mathis-Lilley 2015). However, Obama's respectability politics is also a political tool that balances competing interests while trying to empower black Americans. The failings of respectability politics remain in its subdued engagement of past and persistent injustice. As the presidency becomes more inclusive, speaking inward and outward will have to accompany systemic change. While respectability politics is an effective strategy for an individual candidate, it will take much more to ensure equitable inclusion of all Americans.

NOTES

1. Obama's racial rhetoric arguably shifts significantly in year seven of his presidency, after the 2014 midterm elections, reflecting deeper criticism of racism embedded in national institutions and systems.

2. All presidents are engaged in balancing multiple interests (Stuckey 2004). However, Obama's background serves to emphasize the black-white binary in terms of his racial performance and rhetoric because he is a biracial president.

3. Obama's race informed public opinion during his presidential campaigns on even nonracialized issues such as health care (Tesler 2012; Tesler and Sears 2010).

4. Georgia Duerst-Lahti (2008) highlights the importance of analyzing gender performance even when its embodiment is consistent with the status quo.

5. Regina Lawrence and Melody Rose (2009) describe Hillary Clinton's attempt to navigate gendered double binds during the 2008 Democratic nomination contest. Throughout her campaign, Clinton emphasized her experience and sought to engage in a nuanced gender strategy between masculine toughness and feminine caring. While Lawrence and Rose recognize the significance of Clinton's gender and Obama's race, significantly less attention is paid to Obama's gender.

6. Despite Obama's performance of collaborative masculinity, his policy agenda was criticized for its inattentiveness to black feminist priorities (McClain 2014).

7. My Brother's Keeper, an initiative developed by the Obama administration to provide mentorship and guidance to boys and men of color, reflects a policy position consistent with his respectability politics. The initiative partners with cities, communities, and tribal nations to identify strategies that produce cradle to college to career pathways for the target population. Criticism of the initiative problematizes the omission of girls and women as ignoring an already underresearched and underserved population (McClain 2014).

8. Respectability politics has, more recently, also been studied in association with other marginalized groups in the U.S. society and political system, including the lesbian, gay, bisexual, and transgender (LGBT) community. See, for example, Chapter 7.

9. The types of academic institutions that Obama addressed included a liberal arts college, community college, four high schools, four large state universities, two private universities, a technical school, one military service academy each year, and two HBCUs (Morehouse College and Hampton University). While the HBCU speeches share similar audiences and common themes, the Morehouse speech provides greater depth and breadth for understanding Obama's strategies for navigating the double bind through speech making.

10. While Obama is not the first president to address an HBCU commencement (Lyndon Johnson most notably addressed the 1965 graduating class at Howard University), this is noteworthy given his social location as the first black president.

11. As defined by the amended Higher Education Act of 1965, an HBCU is "any historically black college or university that was established prior to 1964, whose principal mission was, and is, the education of black Americans, and that is accredited by a nationally recognized accrediting agency or association determined by the Secretary [of Education] to be a reliable authority as to the quality of training offered or is, according to such an agency or association, making reasonable progress toward accreditation." There are 105 private and public HBCUs, which include single-sex and coeducational community colleges, four-year institutions, and medical and law schools. Primarily established after the Civil War, HBCUs are located in nineteen states, the District of Columbia, and the U.S. Virgin Islands.

12. Benjamin Mays is a former president of Morehouse College, noted for reviving the institution and giving the benediction at the March on Washington for Jobs and Freedom in 1963. Civil rights leader Martin Luther King Jr. is the institution's most famous alumnus. Maynard Jackson was a fellow alumnus of Morehouse and a three-term mayor of Atlanta (1974–1982, 1990–1994).

13. Obama's choice of Du Bois and King stands in contrast with more revolutionary and controversial figures such as Marcus Garvey or Malcolm X. Such figures are more likely to be deemed less acceptable to white observers.

14. All quotations by Obama in this section and the next are drawn from Obama 2013a.

15. The Moses generation represents a powerful contrast and response to the "Greatest Generation" identity construction often claimed exclusively by white people. Developed by journalist and longtime broadcast news anchor Tom Brokaw, the "Greatest Generation" is used to refer to the generation of U.S. citizens who persevered through the hardship of the Great Depression and World War II to help define the nation and win the war. Obama uses the "Moses generation" to describe the black citizens who fought through the extreme hardship of racism and discrimination to redefine the nation and achieve significant gains in the fight against white supremacy.

16. BGLOs hold a unique position in African American history. Emphasizing themes such as service and leadership, BGLOs count many notable figures as members, including major leaders in the struggle for African American civil rights (e.g., W.E.B. Du Bois, Martin Luther King Jr., Thurgood Marshall, Huey Newton, A. Philip Randolph, Rosa Parks, and Fannie Lou Hamer). For additional information, see Ross 2000.

17. Obama identifies the centrality of the nuclear family and family values and in doing so uses language that connects with both liberals and conservatives, as noted by linguist George Lakoff (2002).

18. Robert Brown and Todd Shaw describe community nationalism as the belief that "African Americans should control and support communities and institutions where they predominate." This does not necessarily translate into the desire for a separate nation-state. Rather, community nationalism "reconciles a belief in black autonomy with American ideals of ethnic and racial pluralism . . . [by focusing on] black control of public and private institutions in black communities" (2002, 26).

19. Zimmerman was later acquitted of second-degree murder in July 2013.

20. National outrage in each of these instances advanced conversations on race relations. In particular, the shooting at Emmanuel African Methodist Church prompted the removal of the Confederate flag from the State Capitol of South Carolina.

REFERENCES

Anthony, Ronda C. H. 2013. *Searching for the New Black Man: Black Masculinity and Women's Bodies.* Jackson: University Press of Mississippi.

Bonilla-Silva, Eduardo. 2009. *Racism without Racists: Color-Blind Racism and the Persistence of Racial Inequality in the United States.* 3rd ed. Lanham, MD: Rowman and Littlefield.

Bostdorff, Denise M., and Stephen R. Goldzwig. 2005. "History, Collective Memory, and the Appropriation of Martin Luther King, Jr.: Reagan's Rhetorical Legacy." *Presidential Studies Quarterly* 35 (4): 661–690.

Brown, Robert A., and Todd C. Shaw. 2002. "Separate Nations: Two Attitudinal Dimensions of Black Nationalism." *Journal of Politics* 64 (1): 22–44.

Campbell, Karlyn Kohrs, and Kathleen Hall Jamieson. 2008. *Presidents Creating the Presidency: Deeds Done in Words.* Chicago: University of Chicago Press.

Carbado, Devon W., and Mitu Gulati. 2015. *Acting White? Rethinking Race in "Post-racial" America.* New York: Oxford University Press.

Collins, Patricia Hill. 2000. *Black Feminist Thought: Knowledge, Consciousness, and the Politics of Empowerment.* 2nd ed. Rev. tenth anniversary ed. New York: Routledge.

Cooper, Frank Rudy. 2009. "Our First Unisex President? Black Masculinity and Obama's Feminine Side." In "Obama Phenomena: A Special Issue on the Election of Barack Obama," special issue, *Denver University Law Review* 86 (April): 633–661.

Craighill, Peyton, and Gary Langer. 2009. "Fewer Call Racism a Major Problem Though Discrimination Remains." Available at http://abcnews.go.com/images/PollingUnit/1085a2RaceRelations.pdf.

Crenshaw, Kimberlé. 1991. "Mapping the Margins: Intersectionality, Identity Politics, and Violence against Women of Color." *Stanford Law Review* 43 (6): 1241–1299.

Dawson, Michael C. 1995. *Behind the Mule: Race and Class in African-American Politics.* Princeton, NJ: Princeton University Press.

———. 2001. *Black Visions: The Roots of Contemporary African-American Political Ideologies.* Chicago: University of Chicago Press.

"Debra Dickerson." 2007. *Colbert Report,* aired February 8. Available at http://thecolbert report.cc.com/videos/12d71h/debra-dickerson.

Du Bois, W.E.B. 1903. "Talented Tenth." In *The Negro Problem: A Series of Articles by Representative American Negroes of Today,* edited by Booker T. Washington, 31–75. New York: J. Pott.

Duerst-Lahti, Georgia. 2008. "'Seeing What Has Always Been': Opening Study of the Presidency." *PS: Political Science & Politics* 41 (4): 733–737.

Franklin, Robert. 2009. "The Soul of Morehouse and the Future of the Mystique." Speech delivered to Morehouse students, Morehouse College, Atlanta, GA, April 21. Available at https://teachbreakthroughs.files.wordpress.com/2009/05/329_the-soul-of -morehouse-and-the-future-of-the-mystique-abridged1.pdf.

Harris, Frederick C. 2012. *The Price of the Ticket: Barack Obama and the Rise and Decline of Black Politics.* New York: Oxford University Press.

Hart, Roderick P., Jay P. Childers, and Colene J. Lind. 2013. *Political Tone: How Leaders Talk and Why.* Chicago: University of Chicago Press.

Higginbotham, Evelyn Brooks. 1994. *Righteous Discontent: The Women's Movement in the Black Baptist Church, 1880–1920.* Rev. ed. Cambridge, MA: Harvard University Press.

Jamieson, Kathleen Hall. 1995. *Beyond the Double Bind: Women and Leadership.* New York: Oxford University Press.

Jones, Jeffrey M. 2007. "Some Americans Reluctant to Vote for Mormon, 72-Year-Old Presidential Candidates." Gallup, February 20. Available at http://www.gallup .com/poll/26611/some-americans-reluctant-vote-mormon-72yearold-presidential -candidates.aspx.

Jones, Jeffrey M., and David W. Moore. 2003. "Generational Differences in Support for a Woman President." Gallup, June 17. Available at http://www.gallup.com/poll/8656/ generational-differences-support-woman-president.aspx.

Kennedy, John F. 1961. "Inaugural Address." January 20. *American Presidency Project.* Available at http://www.presidency.ucsb.edu/ws/?pid=8032.

King , Martin L., Jr. 1967. "Where Do We Go from Here?" Speech delivered at the Eleventh Annual Southern Christian Leadership Conference Convention, Atlanta, GA, August 16. Available at https://kinginstitute.stanford.edu/king-papers/documents/ where-do-we-go-here-delivered-11th-annual-sclc-convention.

Lakoff, George. 2002. *Moral Politics: How Liberals and Conservatives Think.* 2nd ed. Chicago: University of Chicago Press.

Lawrence, Regina G., and Melody Rose. 2009. *Hillary Clinton's Race for the White House: Gender Politics and the Media on the Campaign Trail.* Boulder, CO: Lynne Rienner.

Leith, Sam. 2012. *Words like Loaded Pistols: Rhetoric from Aristotle to Obama.* New York: Basic Books.

Linsky, Martin. 2008. "Obama: First Female President?" *Newsweek,* February 25. Available at http://www.newsweek.com/obama-first-female-president-94065.

Marable, Manning. 2009. "Racializing Obama: The Enigma of Post-black Politics and Leadership." *Souls: A Critical Journal of Black Politics, Culture, and Society* 11 (1): 1–15.

Martin, Howard. 1985. "Presidents in Academe: Changing Uses of Commencement." *Presidential Studies Quarterly* 15 (3): 512–531.

Mathis-Lilley, Ben. 2015. "Obama Defends 'Respectability Politics' Speeches Criticized by Black Progressives." *Slate*, May 12. Available at http://www.slate.com/blogs/the_slatest/2015/05/12/obama_responsibility_politics_my_brother_s_keeper_president_defends_approach.html.

McClain, Dani. 2014. "'Black Women, like Black Men, Scar': Conversation on My Brother's Keeper Heats Up." *The Nation*, June 18. Available at http://www.thenation.com/article/black-women-black-men-scar-conversation-my-brothers-keeper-heats/.

McClain, Paula D., Jessica D. Johnson Carew, Eugene Walton Jr., and Candis S. Watts. 2009. "Group Membership, Group Identity, and Group Consciousness: Evolving Racial Identity in American Politics." *Annual Review of Political Science* 12 (1): 471–485.

Medhurst, Martin J. 2007. "Rhetorical Leadership and the Presidency: A Situational Taxonomy." In *The Values of Presidential Leadership*, edited by Terry L. Price and J. Thomas Wren, 59–84. New York: Palgrave Macmillan.

Mercieca, Jennifer R., and Justin S. Vaughn. 2014. *The Rhetoric of Heroic Expectations: Establishing the Obama Presidency*. College Station: Texas A&M University Press.

Morehouse College. n.d. "Mission." Available at http://www.morehouse.edu/about/mission.html (accessed August 5, 2015).

Nelson, Michael, and Russell L. Riley. 2010. *The President's Words, Speeches and Speechwriting in the Modern White House*. Lawrence: University Press of Kansas.

Obama, Barack H. 2004. "Transcript: Illinois Senate Candidate Barack Obama." *Washington Post*, July 27. Available at http://www.washingtonpost.com/wp-dyn/articles/A19751-2004Jul27.html.

———. 2013a. "Remarks by the President at Morehouse College Commencement Ceremony." May 19. Available at https://www.whitehouse.gov/the-press-office/2013/05/19/remarks-president-morehouse-college-commencement-ceremony.

———. 2013b. "Remarks by the President on Trayvon Martin." July 19. Available at https://www.whitehouse.gov/the-press-office/2013/07/19/remarks-president-trayvon-martin.

———. 2015. "Remarks by the President in Eulogy for the Honorable Reverend Clementa Pinckney." June 26. Available at https://www.whitehouse.gov/the-press-office/2015/06/26/remarks-president-eulogy-honorable-reverend-clementa-pinckney.

Parlett, Martin A. 2014. *Demonizing a President: The "Foreignization" of Barack Obama*. Westport, CT: Praeger.

Price, Melanye T. 2014. "Barack Obama and the Third Wave: The Syntaxes of Whiteness and Articulating Difference in the Post-identity Era." *Politics, Groups, and Identities* 2 (1): 573–588.

Reed, Adolph, Jr. 1995. "What Are the Drums Saying, Booker? The Current Crisis of the Black Public Intellectual." *Village Voice*, April 11, pp. 31–36.

Ross, Lawrence C., Jr. 2000. *The Divine Nine: The History of African American Fraternities and Sororities*. New York: Kensington.

Stuckey, Mary E. 1991. *The President as Interpreter-in-Chief*. Chatham, NJ: Chatham House.

———. 2004. *Defining Americans: The Presidency and National Identity*. Lawrence: University Press of Kansas.

Tesler, Michael. 2012. "The Spillover of Racialization into Health Care: How President Obama Polarized Public Opinion by Racial Attitudes and Race." *American Journal of Political Science* 56 (3): 690–704.

Tesler, Michael, and David O. Sears. 2010. *Obama's Race: The 2008 Election and the Dream of a Post-racial America*. Chicago: University of Chicago Press.

Tierney, John. 2008. "Where Have All the Bigots Gone?" *New York Times*, November 7. Available at http://tierneylab.blogs.nytimes.com/2008/11/07/where-have-all-the -bigots-gone/.

Tulis, Jeffrey K. 1988. *The Rhetorical Presidency*. Rev. ed. Princeton, NJ: Princeton University Press.

Wayne, Stephen J. 2000. *The Road to the White House, 2000: The Politics of Presidential Elections*. New York: St. Martin's Press.

Wise, Tim. 2010. *Colorblind: The Rise of Post-racial Politics and the Retreat from Racial Equity*. San Francisco: City Lights.

Zarefsky, David. 2004. "Presidential Rhetoric and the Power of Definition." *Presidential Studies Quarterly* 34 (3): 607–619.

4

India's Prime Minister

Narendra Modi, Gender, and Governance

SHEETAL CHHABRIA

This study of Narendra Modi's gender performance highlights some of the ways in which statesmen and stateswomen can capitalize on the inherent instability and ambiguity of gender to advance their own ambitions and agendas. When Modi became the prime minister of India in May 2014, it was due in part to his reconciliation of an enduring division between the feminine and masculine in Indian politics. This division, which can be traced to the colonial period, was evident in the gender performances of Jawaharlal Nehru and Mohandas Gandhi, two of India's foremost anticolonial leaders in the 1940s. Modi, as prime minister, has continued to present himself as a patriarchal pro-business leader like Nehru and as a feminine caretaker of "traditional" India like Gandhi. This fluidity and responsiveness in Modi's gender performance have had important consequences for Modi's ambitions as a policy maker and a leader. His masculine performance has defined India as the heart of a new international economic order, and his feminine performance has resulted in an international legitimacy for the Hindu Right.

When Narendra Modi assumed the office of the prime minister in India in 2014, he not only created new economic policies but simultaneously reconfigured understandings, representations, and meanings of culture and domestic life. He mainstreamed conservative understandings of "Indian" and "Hindu" culture, including the role of caste in the Hindu religion, the status of labor, the meaning of childhood, and the role of women. He promised that economic growth and global dominance would protect traditional India. This gained him the popular support necessary for his pro-market economic policies, which could have been seen as a threat to India's customs and culture. While many observers have studied the cultural representations and economic policies separately, I analyze them together and show how a Hindu-Right representation of Indian culture is being mainstreamed internationally. Marxist feminists have insisted that the economy and culture can never be separated. I take their argument a step further, revealing the extent to which Prime Minister Narendra Modi has immersed traditional representations of Hindu culture in his vision of the economy to advance his policy and political agenda. My strategy exemplifies a feminist critique of the presumed separation of economy from culture in which I show that the economy is never devoid of its politics of representation.

In this chapter, I argue that Modi's appeal and success as the elected prime minister of India represent a reconciliation of a long-standing dichotomy between the feminine and masculine in Indian politics. Modi simultaneously presents himself as a valiant custodian of a feminine, traditional, and Hindu India and as a masculine, future-looking, pro-development business leader. He speaks for the customs and culture of the masses while advocating for an India that is the centerpiece of a new economic international order in which globalization is inevitable. Narendra Modi deliberately crosses gendered political boundaries to put forth a new economic and Hindu India together as one and the same thing. I discuss the gendered legacy of colonialism, the way in which gender has been historically performed in colonial and subsequent postcolonial politics by the leading figures of Mohandas Gandhi and Jawaharlal Nehru, and then the way in which Narendra Modi deploys that history in his policies and in his justifications of those policies. I show that the prime minister consistently links traditional culture and economic change, mainstreaming the Hindu Right and also prioritizing Indian domestic economic growth.

The Gendered Legacy of Colonialism

Haunted by a history of foreign domination, postcolonial governments struggle to strike the right balance between being seen as internationally credible and domestically sensitive since the specter of colonial domination haunts the structure of the government itself. At worst, postcolonial constituencies see postcolonial officials as agents of neocolonial rule, especially since native leaders occupy offices created by the former colonial state. To counter this perception, political executives have relied on metaphors of the family and family life. By reformulating gendered political messages from the colonial years, elected officials have distanced themselves from colonial rule, critiqued its politics, and reclaimed the nation.

Historically, colonizers framed themselves as aggressive and masculine and framed the colonized as passive and feminine subjects unable to protect their country from outsiders. British imperialism in particular was founded on a gendering of the state and of the Orient. Gender scholar Sikata Banerjee, for example, has written that "a feminization of the Orient encompassed a disparagement of Arab and Indian men who were conquered because they were effeminate and seen as effeminate because they were conquered" (2003, 170). Nationalists such as Mohandas Gandhi and Jawaharlal Nehru, seeking independence for India, responded to this gendering: Gandhi valorized the feminine as the prized and exclusive domain of indigenous culture; Nehru competed in the masculine sphere, skillfully managing an international economic order.

From independence in 1947 to Modi's election in 2014, the Indian prime ministership's gender performance routinely performed masculinity and femininity as an exclusive binary. During these decades, prime ministers were widely viewed as specializing in one domain or the other, separating the spheres of domesticity, culture, and the household from the spheres of economics and the international arena.

Prime Minister Narendra Modi, who took office in 2014 as a member of the Hindu nationalist Bharatiya Janata Party, ended this exclusivity. Instead, he has used masculinity and femininity in tandem. By uniting previously exclusive genders in his one person, he has garnered unprecedented support from both a religiously conservative domestic constituency and liberal advocates of globalization.

Gender in Colonial and Postcolonial Politics

In the anticolonial thought of the early nationalists of the late nineteenth and early twentieth centuries, political life became separated and gendered. Economics and development became "masculine" because nationalists conceived of the economy and modern industry as residing in the outer domain of political life. In nationalist ideology, the outer domain included trade routes, which connected colonial India via its ports to distant markets, and it was there that the colonizers used their authority to dominate India. In contrast, the domestic sphere (including culture, religion, tradition, and the role of women) resided in the inner domain. The nationalists reserved a pride of place for religious and spiritual practices of identity (Chatterjee 1986). They conceived of the "East" as the site of an exalted and historical religious and spiritual knowledge, from which the colonizers needed to learn.

Orientalists undertook translations of Indic languages to understand native culture, which included religion and customs (Chatterjee 1989, 623).

This distinction separated the policy agenda and political tasks of a statesperson into the mutually exclusive masculine-feminine binary. Yet both the masculine and the feminine were absolutely necessary. One could not function without the other because the government had to attend to both the economy and the culture. In the years immediately preceding and following independence, this masculine-feminine gender binary was enacted by two men: Nehru performed masculinity as an elite statesman skilled in internationalism, statecraft, and economics; his close friend and ally Gandhi performed femininity as a personal caretaker of culture and the household.

Together, Nehru and Gandhi pieced together the popular support necessary to delegitimize the colonial state. These men convinced the Indian people that a centralized bureaucratic structure, held over from the colonial days, was necessary—and furthermore, that it would aid India in overcoming its imperial condition. To discredit the colonial state without completely rejecting the colonial-state apparatus was a delicate task; the gendered performances of these men aided in its accomplishment. Ultimately, Nehru's and Gandhi's respective and separate gender performances, *separately yet together*, made it possible for an otherwise distant and elite figure such as Prime Minister Nehru to successfully claim representation of India's wide-ranging and diverse population.

Jawaharlal Nehru: The Male Political Leader Performing Masculinity

Born in a Kashmiri upper-caste household, Jawaharlal Nehru's father, Motilal Nehru, was a prominent Indian National Congress leader in the 1920s. As reformers, Motilal Nehru and other moderates sought to effect change while positioned within colonial institutional structures. (In contrast, violent and/or radical revolutionaries, known as "extremists" by the moderates, advocated a total dismantling and replacement of the colonial state.) The moderates sought the replacement of colonial officials with native officials and the replacement of extractive economic policies with redistributive policies. This moderate anticolonialism led Motilal Nehru's son Jawaharlal Nehru, as prime minister in the initial years of India's independence, to pursue industrialization, replace imports with domestic manufactures, and undertake extensive economic planning (Chibber 2003).

Jawaharlal Nehru's personal characteristics were certainly not assets to his prime ministership. He was an English speaker educated in English institutions, an ardent secularist, unable to communicate and connect with the masses, cerebral in demeanor, and distant from the common person's concerns. Nehru thus firmly occupied the masculine political domain, so much so that he potentially alienated the feminine cultural domain; to gain popular support, he needed Gandhi.

Nehru set feminine cultural concerns aside, sidestepping them as religious sentiment. However, his friendship and alliance with Gandhi conveyed a respect for the feminine and inner domain. This alliance with Gandhi permitted Nehru to recast his flaws as strengths, as the necessary performance of masculinity. Nehru's ability to communicate in the colonizer's language and his learning, stature, and ability to mix and mingle with the officials of the British colonial state were evidence that India's leaders were authoritative in the masculine, outer, political domain. This was precisely what India needed to establish itself as an independent nation in the global economy.

Mohandas Gandhi: The Male Spiritual Leader Performing Femininity

Mohandas Gandhi solidified a popular base for anticolonial agitations through vigilant nonviolence and noncooperation. He cast himself as the bridge between the moderates and extremists during India's transition to independence in 1947. He characterized their difference as the difference between the "slow and the impatient," slow because political negotiations took time and impatient because the extremists were advocates of the violent overthrow of the colonial state. He established an ashram, a retreat house, where he spun cloth, wrote letters, fasted, rested, prepared meals, cleaned, and cared for and tended to his many visitors—all domestic feminine activities in the inner domain. Gandhi argued that political independence necessitated the extrication of the self from all forms of colonial domination and its concomitant modernity (1997, 22). The ashram was a site in which to perfect that self-rule.

Gandhi wore a loincloth that he spun himself to avoid imported and imperial cloth products. He undertook poverty not as a way to temporarily enter the masses' way of life and understand them but as a way to actually become and embody them. He fasted and took a vow of celibacy to undergo the moral transformation of the self, which he thought indispensable for the political transformations that would signal true independence. He critiqued modern civilization, its medicine, law, and education. According to Gandhi (1957, 1997), these provided only symptomatic cures for self-created ills; he concluded that modernity enslaved not just the colonized Indians but the English as well.

By the 1930s and 1940s, Gandhi explicitly endorsed women's roles in nationalist activities. His habits and rituals of daily life, which symbolically valorized domestic and feminine work by untouchables and women, aided him in making the anticolonial project a popular one (Kishwar 1985). Whereas Nehru and other Indian National Congress leaders were seen as elite figures constructing the nation in inaccessible ways, Gandhi, through his tactics, political principles, and daily practices, opened the nation-building project to untouchables, women, and the masses. All could now see clearly their role in gaining independence (Wolpert 2001). This made him an invaluable ally for Nehru.

Nonetheless, Gandhi's understanding of gender and caste, especially the role of women, was a masculine reading of domestic femininity. This is best understood through Gandhi's politics of celibacy. His asceticism was that of a masculine householder who had gained control over bodily desires through fasting and celibacy, in spite of his wife and children. He often tested his mastery over his body by sleeping next to his wife without acting on sexual temptation. Mastery over one's sexual desires was evidence of a masculine mastery over virility—it was not just evidence of a spiritual renunciant's austerity. This was a specific kind of masculinity that at once appropriated femininity and exercised mastery over it to undo colonial power from within domestic space, from within the inner domain. In other words, Gandhi (1957) spoke as a political reformer while standing outside the government and political system.

Feminist scholars critique Gandhi, pointing to the patriarchal assumptions that underlie his performances of femininity. For example, they highlight Gandhi's failure to challenge the notion that the woman's sphere is in the home, even as he politicized the domestic space and deployed it in the service of nation building. For feminist scholars, performing femininity and including women do not, in and of themselves, constitute a genuine project of liberation for women. Installing women symbolically into political life only implicates them in a patriarchal understanding of public life. Furthermore, Gandhi's efforts effectively constructed an essentialist Indian identity, which erased existing social relations and ideologies of difference—most important, those of class-caste and patriarchy (Bannerji 2000).

Gandhi's performance of femininity, then, is highly contested. Scholars have long recognized that Gandhi's self-immersion in the domestic sphere and his embodiment of marginalized peoples contributed to elevating the inner domain (Alter 1994; Rudolph and Rudolph 2010; Wolpert 2001). His practice of self-rule built influential connections between Indian culture and nationalist politics. In each of these instances, Gandhi invested femininity with power and influence, winning the support of the masses. Many historians and political scientists have perceived Gandhi's performance of femininity as an invaluable complement to Nehru's performance of masculinity. To this way of thinking, Gandhi accepted and reinforced the gender binary; his performance of femininity contributed to Indian independence and secured the importance of the inner domain.

Feminist historians and political scientists, however, are more nuanced in their judgments of Gandhi. These scholars maintain that Gandhi's performance of femininity was strongly masculine; femininity had to be mastered (through self-rule) to make a contribution to the political system. Like Nehru, Gandhi was dedicated to India's economic and political development—Nehru through economic policy, Gandhi through spiritual practices. Thus, Gandhi eroded the boundaries between the outer and inner domains, between femininity and masculinity. By performing femininity in a masculine framework, Gandhi helped India become an independent and influential nation—political goals achieved in the outer domain. With this argument, feminist historians and political scientists challenged accounts of femininity and masculinity as mutually exclusive and separately embodied by leaders in the Indian movement for independence, in the nation's transition to independence, and in its early years as an independent nation. Gandhi—who never held political office—foreshadowed the potential and the limitations of Narendra Modi's deployment of gender.

Narendra Modi: Performing Masculinity and Femininity in the Twenty-First Century

Narendra Modi's gender performances as a custodian of religious values and a technocrat conjoin the gendered feminine inner domain of culture with the gendered masculine outer domain of the economy. As India's prime minister, Modi has advanced initiatives for both a new economic India and a traditional Hindu India. This is part and parcel of a vision in which India will claim its role as an economic world leader without compromising its long-standing Hindu culture. The following sections detail the connections among Modi's vision for India, his policies and priorities, and his gender performances.

Representing Hindu India

Modi's gender performance of intertwined masculinity and femininity had its origins in his years and reelection as chief minister of Gujarat, a state in western India. In this instance, a national leader's career before becoming prime minister is profoundly revelatory of the politics he practiced as a newly elected prime minister. The discussion of Modi's years as a chief minister reveals how Modi learned to turn the liability of being a controversial figure affiliated with the Hindu Right into an asset by framing himself as a protector of traditional India in a globalizing economy.

As chief minister of Gujarat from 2001 to 2014, Narendra Modi has often been held responsible for the infamous instance of interreligious civil conflict in 2002, known as the "Godhra riots," when he allegedly ordered the withdrawal of police during several days of anti-Muslim violence, which then extended to several months. Hundreds of Muslims, the minority religious community, were killed and more than two thousand raped and injured (Brass 2005; Jaffrelot 2011; Ludden 1996; Nussbaum 2008). Despite this incident—which later resulted in Modi being denied a visa to the United States—Modi was reelected chief minister of the province in 2007. It was in this election that Modi's gender performance became clear. A special investigations team, appointed by the Supreme Court of India, conducted investigations for years after the anti-Muslim riots of 2002 and, in 2012, cleared Modi of allegations of wrongdoing. Meanwhile, Muslims failed to secure justice or reparations from the Gujarat government for their suffering in these riots (Chandhoke et al. 2007). These conflicts, which received extensive media coverage, could have ended Modi's career. Instead, they led Modi to adopt a gender performance that won the support of the Hindu Right and made the Hindu Right less controversial and more acceptable to the country's political mainstream.

Modi was widely accused of failing to protect the Muslim minority community in 2002. He responded by embracing these charges and turned them into proof of his ability to protect the Hindu community, which was especially effective with the Hindu Right. In a carefully executed reelection effort in 2007, which drew on the expertise of U.S. political consultants, including the communications firm APCO Worldwide, Modi made it clear that his personhood and personality, not just his policies, were the subject of the campaign (Jafferlot 2008, 14). It was in the election of 2007 that Modi's gender performance became clear.

Throughout this campaign, Modi made assertions that echoed those heard from Gandhi decades earlier, emphasizing the inner domain of the family and domesticity. For example, Modi asserted that Gujarat was his "only family" since he had no wife or children, casting himself as the patriarch of a household in which the government and its citizens were his domestic sphere.[1] He fulfilled this commitment to the people by "maintain[ing] a direct relation with all the citizens of Gujarat," spending four hours a day responding directly to e-mails from citizens of Gujarat and using text messages and other forms of social media to communicate directly with residents of Gujarat. His slogan was "Jeetega Gujarat" (Gujarat will win), "as if his victory could only be the victory of Gujarat" (Jaffrelot 2008, 14). He cast himself as the sole protector of Gujarat, using television advertisements that began with bomb blasts and ended in the figure of Modi against the backdrop of smoke. He turned his personhood into the state, into the body politic, into every person. This strategy culminated in supporters attending rallies while wearing masks of Modi, substituting his face for their own as if everyone were Modi and Modi were everyone.

As a chief minister, Modi effectively appealed to the Hindu Right and its patriarchal and upper-caste visions of the majority Hindu religion and culture. Modi saw India's economic well-being as wholly compatible with tradition and customs. The outer and inner domains were integrated in Modi's vision, just as the masculine and the feminine were integrated in his gender performance. Modi was reelected as chief minister of Gujarat, serving a total of four terms. In 2013, he was named to lead the party's 2014 campaign to win the Lok Sabha, the lower house of India's parliament; the Bharatiya Janata Party won a majority (282 seats, not including the seats won by its partner the National Democratic Alliance) in the chamber and resoundingly defeated the Indian National Congress party, which secured only 44 seats. Modi was subsequently appointed prime minister by the president. The joining of economic development with Hindu religion and culture set a successful, formidable precedent for his policy initiatives as prime minister, which are discussed in the following sections.

"Make in India"

The "Make in India" campaign, announced in August 2014, was Modi's appeal to foreign multinationals to make global products in India. The name superficially alluded to Nehruvian economic development, but it was markedly different from Nehru's desire to export products "made in India." Unlike Nehru's economic policies, Modi's depended on foreign capital, which the Indian people could have perceived as strikingly similar to colonial forms of exploitation. To avoid any suggestion that foreign capital threatened the hard-won independence of India, Modi spoke of acquiring foreign investments as part of a coherent nationalist agenda. In doing so, this prime minister—in contrast to Nehru and other prime ministers—connected the domestic and the international, the culture and the economy. Modi's economic policy rhetoric included many references to individuals, families, children, and the domestic sphere. He insisted that India's participation in the international economy would aid India's families and households. Thus, Modi undertook a gendered performance that knit together families and the inner domain with economics and the outer domain.

The Make in India initiative was announced at a speech on India's sixty-eighth Independence Day, in which Modi made numerous references to India's historic independence in 1947 and called for India to challenge its subordinate role in the global economy ("Narendra Modi" 2014). The prime minister spoke directly to India's families and children. He made very little

mention of the structural changes, such as regulations around land use, necessary for Make in India to work. Instead, he spoke of the character of the
children and their parents, describing these as central to India's new place
in the world, using a familial rhetoric suited to a householder speaking inti-
mately with his loved ones. He alluded to Gandhi's moral sensibility as well.
In announcing the program, for example, Modi said:

> Brothers and sisters, I want to call upon the youth of the country,
> particularly the small people engaged in the industrial sector. I want
> to call upon the youth working in the field of technical education
> in the country. As I say to the world "Come, Make in India," I say
> to the youth of the country—it should be our dream that this mes-
> sage reaches every corner of the world, "Made in India." This should
> be our dream. Whether, to serve the country, is it necessary for the
> youth of the country to be hanged like Bhagat Singh? . . . A soldier
> sacrifices himself at the border and protects Mother India. Similarly,
> a farmer serves Mother India by filling the godowns with grains.
> (Modi 2014)

Speaking to young people as if he is a parental figure, Modi calls on them to
adopt and proclaim his policies, not merely in India but throughout "every
corner of the world." Then Modi goes further. He invokes Gandhi by rejecting violence. He invokes and denounces the famous nationalist martyr
Bhagat Singh.[2] In place of rebellion, the prime minister speaks of loyalty;
in place of violence, the prime minister endorses agricultural productivity.
Modi even identifies the nation itself as feminine: "Mother India." In this
passage, Modi merges economics and culture; he reconciles the previously
exclusive gender roles of the masculine economic protector and the feminine
moral guide in his person as the prime minister. In furtherance of his desire
to deliver this message to young people, Modi later asked each government
school to install a television so he could address the students directly (Bhandary 2014).

The Make in India campaign did require extraordinary structural
changes involving land use and government policy. For multinationals to
set up manufacturing bases in India, there needed to be large parcels of land
available on which to build factories and offices. To provide this land, the
Modi government revised the historic Land Acquisition Act of 1894.

Prior to Modi's government, the Congress Party government had made
changes to the act that were widely seen as limiting corporate influence and
aiding landowners. Though these reforms were critiqued as prioritizing a
few landowners at the cost of poorer citizens, they were still a check on un-
mitigated corporate rights.[3] The Congress Party government also created

a National Green Tribunal that was "a special court with environmental expertise to hear grievances about green violations within short deadlines" (Mohan 2015a). Modi's proposed changes to the Land Acquisition Act of 2013, which would have significantly altered the historic Land Acquisition Act of 1894, would have sped up procedures for businesses and corporations to acquire land in India, reducing government oversight. As this book goes to press, some of Modi's proposed changes are still being debated, while others have come to fruition through a variety of executive maneuvers.

The effects of this bill were particularly important because agrarian crises have loomed large in India. Since 1995, more than three hundred thousand farmers have committed suicide as a result of debt (Gutierrez et al. 2015; Rukmini S. 2015; see also Sainath 1996). The Modi government took a further toll on common farmers, tenants, and agricultural laborers who had lost their land rights. Rather than alleviate the extraordinary debt crisis that had prevailed among small farmers in India for two decades, Modi imposed further stresses and difficulties by facilitating the displacement of these landowners to provide large tracts of land for large corporations.

Environmental Deregulation

Progress on the environment was quickly reversed when Modi took office. In a controversial move, Modi demanded that Greenpeace stop its activism in India and froze the organization's bank account (Mohan 2015a). Justification for his action came in the form of a report by India's Intelligence Bureau, which was leaked to the public and accused foreign-funded nonprofits such as Greenpeace of obstructing Indian development. The report stated that Indian nongovernmental organizations (NGOs), which were often funded by foreign donors, exploited "people-centric issues" against development projects and thus negatively impacted India's gross domestic product (GDP; Ranjan 2014).[4] Although the Modi government saw Greenpeace as a possible neocolonial agent that was obstructing foreign capital, it simultaneously insisted that foreign capital was benign and essential for India's progress.[5] Medha Patkar, a prominent activist, said that prior governments were "at least open to conversation with NGOs and people's groups. That door is fast shut today. They are making policies more aggressive, no matter what the cost" (Ranjan 2015).

In other action, Prime Minister Modi acted unilaterally, appointing a committee of six members to "review and draft amendments to the five key laws that protect India's environment, forest, wildlife, air and water" (Mazoomdaar 2014). Shibani Ghosh, a critic of this committee and an environmental lawyer herself, said, "Once the recommendations were out, it was clear the committee was simply meant to remove human rights and green roadblocks for investment growth" (Mohan 2015a). These recommendations asked corporations to self-regulate by predicting the potential environmental impact of their work and their own violations. While many of the recommendations have still to be implemented, some have fast-tracked business permits in the name of economic growth to support Make in India (Barry and Bagri 2014; see also Mohan 2015b).

Coal mining and the accompanying deforestation and land grabs also indicate the willingness of the Modi government to sacrifice environmental protection to advance Make in India priorities. In 2015, the Modi government passed a Coal Mines Act and a Mines and Minerals Amendment Act, both effectively privatizing the country's natural resources. For decades, such natural resource extraction was state run and regulated. Now, private mining companies—and soon foreign mining companies—can effectively sell coal. Environmental activists, organizations, and poor farmers have leaked tales of criminal behavior by corporations and private individuals who intimidate locals into accepting the confiscation of their land for natural resources. When complaints are registered to local police, the result is more intimidation, physical violence, and legal retaliation against complainants (Mohan 2015a).

All of this has been done for the sake of the economy and the Make in India promise. Modi has managed to combine Nehruvian economic technocracy—through his championing of economic growth and the allusion in the title "Make in India"—alongside Gandhian morality. In doing so, Modi has combined the inner and the outer domains of Indian politics in his person and his policies.

"Clean India"

After his election, Prime Minister Modi launched the Swachh Bharat, or "Clean India," campaign. Modi deliberately announced this initiative on Gandhi's birthday, October 2, 2014, with the goal of achieving a clean India by Gandhi's 150th birthday in 2019. Modi aligned himself explicitly with this Gandhian message, imploring every citizen to head out into the streets and wield a broom, literally cleaning up the country. The press covered Modi sweeping, visibly performing a feminine domestic function (Government of India 2014). The campaign was reminiscent of Gandhi's cleaning toilets, an act Gandhi performed quite visibly during his anticolonial agitations. Modi challenged politicians, beautiful Bollywood celebrities, and famous cricket players to clean India of its waste and dirtiness.

The average Indian was inspired to believe that she or he was caring for the whole nation through the simple act of sweeping. The line between the person and the national body politic was blurred; each person was India, and

India was each person, which conflated the nation with a home and imagined the nation as a domestic space to be sanitized. This was, in ideology and practice, Gandhi's ashram writ large, where the boundaries between domesticity and the international stage blurred, combined, and were recast as one and the same thing. Through the gender performances of Modi, which explicitly echoed those of Gandhi, the inner and outer domains of Indian politics were overlaid such that every individual citizen now cleaned India and thus remade the nation for a better future.

Unlike Gandhi, however, Modi associated cleanliness with economic development. He justified the Clean India campaign as helping Indian tourism, an industry that Modi argued would benefit all classes of Indians. In doing so, he seemed to reconcile Gandhian and Nehruvian priorities. Yet Modi did not invest many governmental resources in this campaign—it remained a personal responsibility, a matter for the inner domain, notwithstanding its significance for the outer domain. The central government did make allotments for more toilets and sanitation workers across the country and in schools. It also sought to protect women from sexual violence, since women in poor areas were often assaulted while trying to get to a toilet some distance from their home.[6] Modi reminded the people, "I come from a poor family, I have seen poverty. The poor need respect and it begins with cleanliness" (Modi 2014). Yet critics complained that sanitation expenditures actually increased by paltry amounts, while businesses benefited significantly from relaxed environmental regulations. Environmental protection was not prioritized. Therefore, even as Modi seemed to echo Gandhi, he avoided the issues that Gandhi had addressed: poverty, caste stigmas, and the negative repercussions of industry.

Conclusion

Throughout his prime ministership, Modi has depended on traditional and patriarchal understandings of gender, and of gender's roles in private and public life, to advance his political agenda. As has been shown, Modi has performed both masculinity and femininity in ways that echo both Nehru and Gandhi. Yet Modi has also innovated. In contrast to Nehru and Gandhi, Modi connects the outer and inner domains in his policies and his rhetoric. Modi presents masculinity and femininity as integrated rather than oppositional and complementary rather than exclusive. He moves fluidly between masculinity and femininity, uniting these genders in his own person.

Narendra Modi's success as India's prime minister depends on his enacting economic reforms in postcolonial India while simultaneously mainstreaming the Hindu Right's interpretation of traditional Hindu culture. Modi's conjoining of the outer and inner domains of political life, through his gender performance as masculine (the technocratic economic policy maker) and as feminine (sweeping the streets for Clean India), upholds the arguments of feminist historians and political scientists who have contended that the economy and culture are linked and mutually dependent spheres. Furthermore, this analysis shows the consequences of that theory's implementation for policy making and governing. In concluding his speech on India's independence anniversary on August 15, 2014, Modi said:

> Brothers and sisters, today, on 15th August, we also have the birth anniversary of Maharishi Aurobindo. Maharishi Aurobindo, being a rebel, moved on to achieve the status of a Yoga Guru. With regard to the destiny of India, he remarked, "I have a faith that the divine power and spiritual heritage of India will play an important role towards the welfare of the world." . . . I strongly believe in the words of legends. I have great faith in the statements made by ascetics, sages & saints and that's why today at the ramparts of Lal Quila I am reminded of the words of Swami Viveknanda. He had said—"I can see before my eyes Mother India awakening once again. My Mother India would be seated as the World Guru. Every Indian would render service towards [the] welfare of humanity. This legacy of India would be useful for the welfare of the world." . . . Friends, the words of Viveknanda ji can never be untrue. The words of Viveknanda ji, his dream of seeing India ensconced as World Guru, his vision, it is incumbent upon us to realize that dream. This capable country, blessed with natural bounty, this country of youth can do much for the world in the coming days.

In connecting these statements of past religious reformers and spiritual leaders to his policies of economic development, Modi connects religious expression to economic and international mastery. For Modi, the right to be a devout Hindu in the public sphere is one and the same as the right to participate in market life (Gopalakrishnan 2006). The prime minister has gained popular support while creating pro-market economic reforms. He has achieved this end by championing traditional religious expression for his constituency and then conjoining religion with economic freedom.

What is new and unique about Modi is that he claims economic credentials *because* of his humble origins; he was a tea seller in his youth, unlike his predecessor Manmohan Singh, for example, who had a doctor of philosophy in economics from Oxford and was a professor of economics at Delhi University. Modi's predecessor had trouble convincing the masses to support his economic reforms, but Modi has succeeded because of the reassurances of his rhetoric of cultural guardianship. Modi speaks of individual choices in ways that intertwine religion and the labor market. In connecting Hindu traditions and a globalizing economy in this way, Modi's rhetoric has effectively mainstreamed the Hindu Right.

Study of Modi's use of femininity and masculinity to advance his political ambitions (from the chief minister of Gujarat to prime minister of the nation) and his policies (intertwining free-market economic policy priorities and traditional religious practices) reveals the power of gender to advance a chief executive's political agenda. Yet his integration of the inner and outer domains is as dangerous as it is innovative. As Modi's actions demonstrate, this uniting of religion and politics privileges some (the Hindu Right) and marginalizes others (the Muslim minority). As prime minister, Modi has facilitated foreign investment while devoting few resources to correcting the inequality endemic to India's caste system. For all of these reasons, it remains to be seen whether Modi's gender performance—however successful it may seem to be in elections and in governing—will actually advance India's economy and democracy.

NOTES

1. Modi—notwithstanding his claims to be single—was actually estranged from his wife. He had apparently left her shortly after their marriage to "wander in the Himalayas" as a devout Hindu contemplating a religious life and eventually joining the Rashtriya Swayamsevak Sangh, the Hindu nationalist group. In this as well, the similarities between Gandhi and Modi were pronounced. Both distanced themselves from their wives to test their self-mastery in the inner domain and to prove their dedication to political priorities in the outer domain (Gowen 2015).

2. Bhagat Singh was a militant Marxist revolutionary of the colonial era; hanged in 1931 as an insurrectionist, he is still revered by many.

3. The Congress Party did backtrack on some of these protections for landowners as the 2009 elections neared, creating exemptions for some corporations.

4. Greenpeace was one among several NGOs that were constrained by the Modi government.

5. I thank Shatrunjay Mall for this insight.

6. In Tamil Nadu, for example, the government allied with women's self-help groups to enact training and participation in use of the toilets ("Swachh Bharat" 2015).

REFERENCES

Alter, Joseph S. 1994. "Celibacy, Sexuality, and the Transformation of Gender into Nationalism in North India." *Journal of Asian Studies* 53 (1): 45–66.

Associated Press. 2014. "For Indian Who Confronted Mining Industry, the 'Green Nobel.'" *NDTV*, April 28. Available at http://www.ndtv.com/india-news/for-indian-who-confronted-mining-industry-the-green-nobel-559237.

Banerjee, Sikata. 2003. "Gender and Nationalism: The Masculinization of Hinduism and Female Political Participation in India." *Women's Studies International Forum* 26 (2): 167–179.

Bannerji, Himani. 2000. "Projects of Hegemony: Towards a Critique of Subaltern Studies' 'Resolution of the Women's Question.'" *Economic and Political Weekly* 35 (11): 902–920.

Barry, Ellen, and Neha Thirani Bagri. 2014. "Narendra Modi, Favoring Growth in India, Pares Back Environmental Rules." *New York Times*, December 4. Available at http:// www.nytimes.com/2014/12/05/world/indian-leader-favoring-growth-sweeps-away -environmental-rules.html.

Bhandary, Shreya. 2014. "PM Narendra Modi's Address to Cost Schools Rs 5000." *Mid-Day*, September 4. Available at http://www.mid-day.com/articles/pm-narendra-modis -address-to-cost-schools-rs-5000/15577160.

Brass, Paul R. 2005. *The Production of Hindu-Muslim Violence in Contemporary India.* Seattle: University of Washington Press.

Chandhoke, Neera, Praveen Priyadarshi, Silky Tyagi, and Neha Khanna. 2007. "The Displaced of Ahmedabad." *Economic and Political Weekly* 42 (43): 10–14.

Chatterjee, Partha. 1986. *Nationalist Thought and the Colonial World: A Derivative Discourse.* London: Zed Books.

———. 1989. "Colonialism, Nationalism, and Colonialized Women: The Contest in India." *American Ethnologist* 16 (4): 622–633.

Chibber, Vivek. 2003. *Locked in Place: State-Building and Late Industrialization in India.* Princeton, NJ: Princeton University Press.

Gandhi, Mohandas. 1957. *An Autobiography: The Story of My Experiments with Truth.* Boston: Beacon Press.

———. 1997. *Hind Swaraj and Other Writings.* Edited by Anthony Parel. New York: Cambridge University Press.

Gopalakrishnan, Shankar. 2006. "Defining, Constructing and Policing a 'New India': Relationship between Neoliberalism and Hindutva." *Economic and Political Weekly* 41 (26): 2803–2815.

Government of India. 2014. "Launch of Swachh Bharat Mission by Hon PM Shri Narendra Modi." October 2. Available at https://swachhbharat.mygov.in/challenge/launch -swachh-bharat-mission-hon-pm-shri-narendra-modi.

Gowen, Annie. 2015. "Abandoned as a Child Bride, Wife of Narendra Modi Hopes He Calls." *Washington Post*, January 25. Available at https://www.washingtonpost.com/ world/abandoned-as-a-child-bride-indias-first-lady-still-hopes-her-husband-will -call/2015/01/25/3509dac5-5ac1-49e3-8b44-7d92e027c9ec_story.html.

Gutierrez, Andrew Paul, Luigi Ponti, Hans R. Herren, Johann Baumgartner, and Peter E. Kenmore. 2015. "Deconstructing Indian Cotton: Weather, Yields, and Suicides." *Environmental Sciences Europe* 27:12–29. Available at http://enveurope.springeropen .com/articles/10.1186/s12302-015-0043-8.

Jaffrelot, Christophe. 2008. "Gujarat: The Meaning of Modi's Victory." *Economic and Political Weekly* 43 (15): 12–17.

———. 2011. *Religion, Caste and Politics in India.* New York: Oxford University Press.

Kishwar, Madhu. 1985. "Gandhi on Women." *Economic and Political Weekly* 20 (41): 1753–1758.

Ludden, David, ed. 1996. *Contesting the Nation: Religion, Community, and the Politics of Democracy in India.* Philadelphia: University of Pennsylvania Press.

Mazoomdaar, Jay. 2014. "The Six Minds That Will Look Afresh at Environment Laws." *Indian Express*, September 12. Available at http://indianexpress.com/article/india/ india-others/the-six-minds-that-will-look-afresh-at-environment-laws/.

Modi, Narendra. 2014. "Full Text: Prime Minister Narendra Modi's Speech on 68th Independence Day." *Indian Express*, August 16. Available at http://indianexpress .com/article/india/india-others/full-text-prime-minister-narendra-modis-speech -on-68th-independence-day/.

Mohan, Rohini. 2015a. "After Months of Tussle with Activists, India Suspends Greenpeace." *Al Jazeera America*, April 10. Available at http://america.aljazeera.com/
multimedia/2015/4/india-greenpeace-suspension.html.

———. 2015b. "Narendra Modi's War on the Environment." *Al Jazeera America*, April 10.
Available at http://america.aljazeera.com/multimedia/2015/4/narendra-modis-war
-on-the-indian-environment.html.

"Narendra Modi Invites Global Firms to 'Come, Make in India' in Maiden Independence
Day Speech." 2014. *Economic Times*, August 16. Available at http://articles.economic
times.indiatimes.com/2014-08-16/news/52873648_1_defence-manufacturing
-manufacturing-sector-manufacturing-and-investment.

Nussbaum, Martha C. 2008. *The Clash Within: Democracy, Religious Violence, and India's
Future*. Cambridge, MA: Belknap Press.

Ranjan, Amitav. 2014. "Foreign-Aided NGOs Are Actively Stalling Development, IB Tells
PMO in a Report." *Indian Express*, June 7. Available at http://indianexpress.com/
article/india/india-others/foreign-aided-ngos-are-actively-stalling-development-ib
-tells-pmo-in-a-report/.

Rudolph, Lloyd I., and Susanne Hoeber Rudolph. 2010. *Postmodern Gandhi and Other Essays: Gandhi in the World and at Home*. Chicago: University of Chicago Press.

Rukmini S. 2015. "India's New Farm Suicides Data: Myths and Facts." *The Hindu*, July 24.
Available at http://www.thehindu.com/data/indias-new-farm-suicides-data-myths
-and-facts/article7461095.ece.

Sainath, Palgummi. 1996. *Everybody Loves a Good Drought: Stories from India's Poorest
Districts*. New York: Penguin Books.

Sinha, Mrinalini. 1995. *Colonial Masculinity: The "Manly Englishman" and the "Effeminate Bengali" in the Late Nineteenth Century*. Manchester, UK: Manchester University
Press.

"Swachh Bharat: Tamil Nadu—Where Self Help Is the Best Help." 2015. *Times of India*,
May 17. Available at http://timesofindia.indiatimes.com/India/Swachh-Bharat-Tamil
-Nadu-Where-self-help-is-the-best-help/articleshow/47315618.cms?from=mdr.

Wolpert, Stanley A. 2001. *Gandhi's Passion: The Life and Legacy of Mahatma Gandhi*. New
York: Oxford University Press.

5

Sarah Palin's and Paul Ryan's Vice Presidential Acceptance Speeches

Gender and Partisan Appeals to the Republican Party

MARYANNE BORRELLI AND LILLY J. GOREN

In this gender analysis of the U.S. presidency, the gender identity of two vice presidential running mates contributes to an understanding of political ambition. The Republican Party nominated its first woman vice presidential candidate, Governor Sarah Palin of Alaska, in 2008. Four years later, the party reverted to the established practice of nominating a man for the vice presidency, selecting U.S. Representative Paul Ryan of Wisconsin. Both Palin and Ryan were white, claimed middle-class families of origin, presented themselves as self-made, signaled a generational shift in leadership, and had strong ideological alliances throughout the Republican Party. Yet Palin was a Washington outsider and one of the few Republican women in elected office across the country, while Ryan was a Washington insider and among the gender-race majority in his party and in government. These complex identities confronted Palin and Ryan with distinctive challenges and opportunities, as individual candidates and as running mates. This chapter provides a close study of the Palin and Ryan nomination acceptance speeches delivered at the 2008 and 2012 Republican National Conventions. These speeches reveal how these candidates and this party connected gender to leadership, throughout the campaign, in anticipation of elective office.

E very four years voters in the United States assess the strengths and capacities of presidential candidates. The first major decision made by the presumptive nominee of each political party that receives intense scrutiny is his or her choice of a vice presidential running mate. So we study modern vice presidential candidates, in part, for what they reveal about the presidential candidates who selected them and the party that nominated them. For instance, then-governors William J. Clinton and George W. Bush, both Washington outsiders, chose Al Gore and Richard Cheney, respectively, as their running mates; Gore and Cheney were both white men with their own political capital to win support throughout their party and the Washington community. In 2008, campaigning for president as a first-term U.S. senator, Barack Obama similarly selected Joseph Biden, another white male Washington insider with considerable foreign-policy expertise. In selecting their running mates, these outsider presidential candidates presented themselves as anticipating the challenges that would come in governing, even in the midst of the campaign.

In 2008, this expectation that the vice presidential nominee would complement the presidential nominee was qualified. U.S. Senator and Republican presidential nominee John McCain selected Alaska governor Sarah Palin as his running mate. True, McCain was a Washington insider and Palin was an outsider. Also true, McCain was a self-proclaimed maverick, while Palin was far more a party loyalist. But their complementarity was also more complex. McCain emphasized his masculinity throughout the campaign, stressing his military heroism. Palin also presented herself *as masculine*, showcasing her accomplishments as a sitting governor. And she presented herself *as feminine* and as resolving the gender debates of economic and social conservatives. As a sitting governor, she testified to the economic conservative conviction that women and men were equally capable of succeeding in the public sphere. As a wife and mother, dedicated to upholding pro-life policy priorities, she embodied the social-conservative commitment to women as the moral compass for the family. By insisting that she brought economic and social conservatives together, Palin encouraged both party loyalists and unaffiliated voters to rethink their conceptions of the Republican Party and the 2008 Republican ticket.[1]

In 2012, however, it seemed that Republicans returned to time-honored formulae in picking their vice presidential nominee. The presidential nominee, Mitt Romney, selected U.S. Representative Paul Ryan as his running mate. Once again, there were two white males on the Republican Party's presidential ticket; the Washington-outsider presidential candidate paired himself with an insider running mate; the vice presidential candidate was a firm party loyalist. The Ryan nomination appeared predictable, a marked contrast to the innovative Palin nomination.

Yet the seemingly innovative Palin and the seemingly predictable Ryan had important underlying similarities. Both represented a generational shift in the presidency. Both were strong partisans, with long-standing ties to social conservativism. And both delivered highly strategic gender performances, explicitly advancing their political priorities and ambitions through their self-identification. Ryan, like Palin, revealed and capitalized on established Republican campaign practices but in ways that were distinctly his own.

This chapter investigates the vice presidential candidacies of Sarah Palin and Paul Ryan through careful study of their acceptance speeches at the Republican National Conventions. Addressing thousands in the convention hall and millions throughout the nation, Palin and Ryan asserted their readiness to serve and criticized their Democratic opponents. Their speeches uncovered much about the complex interweaving of gender and partisanship in the modern vice presidency.

Republican Vice Presidential Candidates in the Modern Presidency

The modern vice president, as Jody Baumgartner and Thomas Crumblin explain, "routinely acts as presidential surrogate, helping the president extend his reach. . . . Recent vice presidents are important policy advisors to their presidents. . . . In short, modern vice presidents, unlike their counterparts in previous times, are important actors in American governance" (2015, 4). Thus, the vice presidential candidate is chosen by the presidential candidate as someone whom the aspiring chief executive trusts, someone with whom the presidential candidate expects to govern. The most recent Republican vice president, Richard Bruce "Dick" Cheney, embodied these qualities; on the campaign trail and in the White House, he set a formidable precedent against which both Sarah Palin and Paul Ryan were judged.

As a vice presidential candidate, Dick Cheney had a lengthy résumé in politics, which spanned the executive and legislative branches. Cheney was Gerald Ford's chief of staff (1975–1977), among other executive branch appointments, and thus had an insider's perspective on the presidency. Subsequently elected to the U.S. House of Representatives (1979–1989), where he served in the House leadership, he had an insider's perspective on the legislative branch. Then, as defense secretary (1989–1993), he gained substantive expertise in national security and an insider's perspective on departmental and cabinet politics. Though Cheney's running mate, George W. Bush, was the son of a president, Bush's own experience and expertise were centered in the private sector and in the governor's office in Texas.[2] Cheney's résumé augmented George W. Bush's reputation, with Cheney providing the Washington wisdom, while Bush remained the independent outsider. Selecting Cheney as his vice presidential running mate was, as is typical, Bush's first major personnel decision and sent a reassuring message that the presidential candidate would recruit deeply experienced decision makers with well-known policy stances who were well respected by the Republican base (see Baumgartner 2006, 76; 2015).[3]

Cheney was not the only Republican vice presidential candidate to have strengthened support for the ticket. Cheney's Republican predecessors in the vice presidential office all made similar contributions—Richard Nixon for Dwight Eisenhower, Spiro Agnew for Richard Nixon, George H. W. Bush for Ronald Reagan, and Dan Quayle for George H. W. Bush. Each reshaped the campaign role and responsibilities of the Republican vice presidential candidate. As presidential candidates, Dwight Eisenhower, Richard Nixon, Ronald Reagan, and George H. W. Bush could present themselves as inclusive partisans because their vice presidents served as strong partisan critics of the Democratic Party and presidential ticket. The Eisenhower, Nixon, Reagan, and George H. W. Bush campaign organizations could present their policy agendas as moderate—a significant reframing when one remembers the outreach made by all four to the conservative South and by Reagan to social and economic conservatives nationally.[4]

The vice presidential candidate, particularly in this Republican tradition, is expected to be a presidential surrogate during the campaign and in the White House: the president's running mate is evaluated primarily as an advocate for the presidential candidate as a person, partisan, and decision maker. And the vice presidential candidate must do all this without overshadowing the presidential candidate. While denying their own personal ambitions, vice presidential candidates must establish their own credentials and reputations as worthy successors to the presidency in the event of the president's death. They must enact this performance on a national stage in a high-stakes, competitive political contest, closely scrutinized by diverse media outlets and publics. To fulfill these roles and responsibilities, vice presidential candidates need to constantly, successfully negotiate popular perceptions and media frames. Speeches, press conferences, and interviews become critically important (see Bode and Hennings 2012; Fridkin, Carle, and Woodall 2013; see also Witcover 2014).

Gender is integral to the campaign, as it is to governance. There is wide agreement that the presidential office is the "most masculine" of political offices in the United States. The historic origins of the office of president, the "chief among chiefs," are both military and political. Across the generations in the United States, the social roles associated with masculinity and leadership have aligned (and conflated) with the highest offices typically held by men who could exhibit qualities such as aggressiveness, strength, and self-reliance. Georgia Duerst-Lahti (1997, 2008) concluded, simply and succinctly, that campaigns showcase manly men doing manly things; even apathetic voters are typically familiar with the presidential candidates' aggressiveness (as war heroes and athletes), their sexual virility (as husbands and patriarchs), and their political acumen (as elites in state and national government). Presidents are expected to be "alpha males." It falls to vice presidents to deliver a complementary and reinforcing gender performance. For this reason, we describe vice presidential nominees as having to establish themselves as credible "beta males." Nothing less will gain a favorable frame for the campaign and the administration.

These multiple frames become even more complex and difficult to orchestrate when the vice presidential candidate is female (see Beail and Kinney Longworth 2012; more generally, see Dolan 2008; Jamieson 1995; Tolleson-Reinhart and Josephson 2005). In such a case, a biological woman needs to deliver a gender performance as a male—as the beta male to the presidential candidate's alpha male. This requires that she undo the still-prevailing conflation of sex and gender and that she break the long-standing association of elite leadership with masculine (even hypermasculine) men. To do all this during a campaign, which is a fragmented and conflicted environment that favors communication by sound bite, is extremely difficult (see Lawrence and Rose 2013). With only one woman, Geraldine Ferraro, having previously been a vice presidential nominee for one of the two major political parties, this electoral negotiation has just one precedent, a generation ago, in the Democratic Party. For Sarah Palin, a little-known governor and the first female vice presidential nominee of the Republican Party, the challenges were great. She was a gender outsider and a political novelty; could she contribute to her running mate's campaign? She was a woman seeking an intensely masculine office; could she convince the media, the party loyalists, and the voters that she was a credible beta male?

John McCain named Sarah Palin as his running mate on August 29, 2008, less than ten weeks before the presidential election. Up to this point, Democrats had provided much of the drama in the campaign, with Barack Obama and Hillary Clinton's battle for delegates extending through the entire primary season. Though McCain confronted some competitors early in 2008, he amassed sufficient delegates to become the presumptive Republican presidential nominee by March 4. In part, as McCain himself acknowledged, he selected Palin to infuse his campaign with new energy—this was much the same reason that Walter Mondale had chosen Geraldine Ferraro more than thirty years earlier.[5] As a first and as a virtual unknown, she could expect close, continuing, and critical scrutiny. And ultimately, while Palin brought strengths to the ticket, both her and the campaign's lack of preparation for the national campaign contributed to a bumpy national campaign for the Republican ticket (see Baumgartner and Crumblin 2015, 108; Heilemann and Halperin 2010, 353–376; Traister 2010; for the nominee's own account, see Palin 2009).

Mitt Romney announced his choice of Paul Ryan, a U.S. representative from Wisconsin, as his vice presidential running mate on August 11, 2012. The Ryan nomination appeared very different from the 2008 Palin nomination: The Republican ticket again consisted of a white male Washington outsider as the presidential candidate and a white male Washington insider as vice presidential candidate. Unlike Palin, Ryan had both Washington experience and a national reputation, was a regular on the Sunday-morning talkshow circuit, and had occupied congressional leadership roles both in the House minority and majority—as a committee chair or ranking member but also as a close confidant and party adviser to the Republican congressional leadership. And Romney liked him (see Baumgartner and Crumblin 2015).

The similarities between the Bush-Cheney and Romney-Ryan running mates were obvious. Romney, like George W. Bush, was running his campaign as an outsider candidate, with his economic and executive credentials as the primary focus for his strength as a presidential candidate. Ryan, like Cheney, was a Washington insider, part of the Republican elite in Congress, and had strong ties to party conservatives.

Yet there were also similarities between Ryan and Palin, with Ryan the more prepared and polished of the two. Their sexes were different, but both Palin and Ryan claimed a white, middle-class, rural identity (see Beail and Longworth 2012). While Romney was not as old as McCain, Ryan, like Palin, represented the next generation of leaders within the Republican Party. Ryan, also like Palin, was telegenic, and he insulated Romney as Palin had insulated McCain, with strong connections to the social conservatives and evangelicals of the Republican Party (Baumgartner and Crumblin 2015, 187).

Palin and Ryan were heirs to a tradition of vice presidential nominees as forceful campaigners. Republican vice presidential nominees during the modern presidency—Nixon, Agnew, George H. W. Bush, Quayle, and Cheney—presented themselves as policy spokespersons, partisan loyalists, and presidential advocates. Yet Palin and Ryan were not merely passive inheritors of these practices and expectations. They were ambitious and assertive on their own behalf; they were determined to define themselves, articulate their own agendas, and achieve their own destinies. Each self-framed as a nominee who honored established Republican factions, valued the party's past accomplishments, and were committed to empowering new cohorts of voters. They were change makers, presenting as beta males though one was a woman and one was a man, delivering a message of self-reliance and opportunity to the party that had always celebrated the American dream of personal achievement and socioeconomic mobility. Their speeches to the Republican National Conventions in 2008 and 2012, accepting the vice presidential nomination, are distinctively revealing of these complex frames and messages.

The Republican National Conventions:
Vice Presidential Candidates Make Their Mark

We assess the Palin and Ryan acceptance speeches by focusing on two critical elements, each of which is closely tied to the campaign roles assigned to modern Republican vice presidential nominees.[6] First, we examine Palin's and Ryan's life stories, as recounted in the speeches. Palin was less well known than Ryan, which likely contributed to her lengthier autobiography. Palin was also the first woman vice presidential nominee for the Republican party. Yet both she and Ryan presented their identities—not merely their career credentials—as qualifying them for high office. Both referred to their gender, religion, and socioeconomic class as part of their fitness for the vice presidency. Second, we investigate the partisan criticisms that Palin and Ryan directed at their Democratic opponents, causing them to be judged as performing a pivotal, vice presidential campaign role: they were partisan warriors, taking action in the immediate present.

Candidate Life Stories

As a Washington outsider virtually unknown to the nation, Palin was expected to spend more podium time introducing herself. Like Ryan, she acknowledged her children, husband, and parents. She then told the audience about her political offices and accomplishments. The account, nearly half of the entire speech (44.8 percent by word count), came early in her statement and was tightly compartmentalized. This arrangement was dictated by Palin's limited reputation—if she had not introduced herself, many listeners would have been ignorant of her political credentials, which would have limited her credibility as a nominee.

Palin's autobiographical statement came after a brief acceptance of the party's nomination and endorsement of her running mate as "a true profile in courage" dedicated to the nation's security. It was in this context of electing a wartime commander-in-chief that Palin introduced herself: "And as the mother of one of those troops [in Iraq], that is exactly the kind of man I want as commander-in-chief." As Palin explained, her nineteen-year-old son would deploy to Iraq in a week; her nephew was serving on a carrier stationed in the Middle East. Palin thus presented herself as a Republican Mother, proud of the sacrifices she was making on behalf of her nation. Palin's selfless caregiving was further emphasized when she introduced her five-month-old son, "a perfectly beautiful baby boy" with "special needs." Acknowledging the commitment of "families of special needs children ... to make America a more welcoming place for your sons and daughters," Palin promised to be a vice president who would realize their hopes. With these words, Palin elevated herself from being "just one of many moms" with a child in the military to a White House decision maker standing for the parents of vulnerable children. Palin thus framed Republican Motherhood as a role that extended from the private to the public sphere, from the passive acceptance of sacrifice to the active performance of representation.[7] In doing so, she aligned herself with other socially conservative women, among them the iconic Phyllis Schlafly, whose commitment to the private sphere of the family caused them to assume leadership in the public sphere.

Palin also aligned herself with economic conservativism early in her life narrative, insisting that her sex was irrelevant: "Among the many things I owe [my mom and dad] is a simple lesson that I've learned: that this is America, and every woman can walk through every door of opportunity."[8] Palin described herself as a confrontational change maker throughout her political career. As governor, she declared, she had secured ethics reform, eliminated waste, cut the budget deficit and created a surplus, suspended taxes, broken monopolies, and built infrastructure through public-private partnerships. But Palin gentled her self-promotion by referring to "we" and "our": "*Our* state budget is under control—*we* have a surplus—and *I* have protected the taxpayers by vetoing wasteful spending, nearly half a billion dollars in vetoes" (emphasis added).[9] In this one sentence, Palin combined an enduring Republican appeal ("wasteful spending"), factual claims ("nearly half a billion dollars"), and assertions of power ("vetoing"). And she deliberately moved from a close association with the people ("our budget . . . we have a surplus") to self-reflective declarations ("I have protected"). The leader-as-protector was a historically familiar frame for presidential candidates, echoing conceptions of the president as patriarch. In this instance, however, a woman claimed that masculinist role. Though some argued that Palin reinforced masculinity in politics, the notion that women and men were equal and that both could succeed in the public sphere was congruent with fundamental principles of the gender ideology advanced by economic conservatives.

This endorsement of women and men as equals in the public sphere, however, called Palin's commitment to social conservativism into question. Economic conservatives perceived gender differences as evidence of discrimination among people who were equals. Social conservatives, however, maintained that women and men had mutually exclusive gender roles. For social conservatives, the private woman–public man dichotomy was foundational: women should dedicate themselves to the private sphere, nurturing their children and serving as their husbands' moral compass; men should channel their ambitions into the public sphere, protecting their family and their nation. If women entered the public sphere, social conservatives concluded, the family would be deeply compromised, having lost its moral guardian.

Women in the public sphere, meanwhile, would either fail (because they lacked the requisite masculine self-reliance and aggressiveness) or be corrupted (because they abandoned their moral responsibilities and adopted men's priorities).[10] Social and economic conservatives, then, had contrasting gender ideologies, with social conservatives insisting that women and men should perform mutually exclusive gender roles and economic conservatives just as firm that women and men were equals, rejecting gender differences as the product of discrimination. But Palin described herself as having fulfilled her responsibilities in the private sphere *and* as having succeeded in the public sphere. She identified herself as mother, wife, *and* elected official; she was other directed and self-sacrificing *and* self-assertive and fiercely competitive.[11] In other words, Palin claimed to uphold both social and economic conservative priorities. She insisted that she had reconciled the contradictory gender ideologies of social and economic conservativism in her person, political career, and policy priorities.

Palin most clearly bridged economic and social conservativism in declaring her standards for governing: "No one expects us all to agree on everything, but we are expected to govern with integrity and good will and clear convictions and a servant's heart." The biblical and spiritual references paid homage to Palin's evangelical faith. They also tapped into the ideals of Republican Motherhood, that women would sacrifice themselves and their families for the nation's well-being. At the same time, her commitment "to govern with integrity and good will and clear convictions" fit within enduring conceptions of a self-reliant and principled leader in the public sphere. In this passage, Palin united otherwise divided partisan factions by embracing the priorities of social and economic conservatives.[12]

Like Sarah Palin four years earlier, Paul Ryan introduced his family members early in his acceptance speech. Unlike Palin, Ryan identified his living family members only through their relationship to himself ("my best friend and wife, Janna"), speaking more extensively of his deceased father: "My dad, a small-town lawyer, was also named Paul. Until we lost him when I was sixteen, he was a gentle presence in my life. I like to think he'd be proud of me and my sister and brothers." This statement set the frame for Ryan's self-depiction as a loyal son who has triumphed over loss: self-made, resilient, and successful, Ryan is the small-town boy next door—"I'm sure proud of . . . where I come from, Janesville, Wisconsin"—who has risen to national leadership. Like so many presidential and vice presidential candidates before him, Ryan appropriated a Lincolnesque narrative of upward mobility from what the vice president presents as the margins of the middle-class Midwest to the center of power in Washington, D.C.

Like Palin, Ryan articulated his achievements and political philosophy as standards for challenging his Democratic opponents. Unlike Palin, Ryan wove his autobiography throughout his entire acceptance speech, presenting himself as both representative and exemplary.

> I hope you understand this, too: if you're feeling left out or passed by, you have not failed; your leaders have failed you.
>
> None of us have to settle for the best . . . [the Obama] administration offers—a dull, adventureless journey from one entitlement to the next, a government-planned life, a country where everything is free but us. . . .
>
> It's the exact opposite of everything I learned growing up in Wisconsin or at college in Ohio. Now, when I was waiting tables, washing dishes, or mowing lawns for money, I never thought of myself as stuck in some station in life. I was on my own path, my own journey, an American journey where I could think for myself, decide for myself, define happiness for myself. That's what we do in this country. That's the American Dream. That's freedom.

Ryan makes this declaration after delivering an extended critique of the president's first-term policies and priorities. He deliberately evokes a nostalgia that lessens agency and removes responsibility: "You have not failed; your leaders have failed you." His own life, meanwhile, he describes in almost-libertarian terms that stress self-reliance and personal initiative: "think for myself, decide for myself, define happiness for myself." The contrast is complete: failed leaders drain the people of their ambition, but successful individuals—here, Ryan speaks of himself, with strong and reiterated use of "I" and "my"—prove the continuing force and value of "the American Dream" and "freedom." Ryan gives voice to betrayal and loss, even as he embodies persistence and achievement.

Both Sarah Palin and Paul Ryan delivered strongly gendered messages throughout their acceptance speeches. In 2008 and again in 2012, the Republican vice presidential nominees used their addresses to the convention to present themselves as forceful. Palin, a white woman, ascribed both feminine and masculine gender roles to herself. Her speech spanned the gender ideologies of social and economic conservatives; it connected political leadership to Republican Motherhood, democratic accountability, and biblical calls to service. Ryan, a white man, defined himself as the loyal son and the realization of the American Dream. His masculinist speech connected political leadership to self-awareness (not self-sacrifice), to personal success (not other directedness), and a commitment to self-fulfillment (not service). Although Palin and Ryan were seeking the same office and had similar partisan alliances, their acceptance speeches endorsed very different gender ideologies. These contrasts continued and grew when they turned from recounting their autobiographies to attacking their Democratic opponents. Now, Palin and Ryan shifted from claiming to be viable vice presidential nominees to acting as vice presidential candidates; their gender ideologies became even more intensely performed and embodied.

Partisan Attacks

As more than one commentator has noted, a critically important role for the vice presidential nominee is to serve as forceful partisan. When these nominees voice partisan attacks in their acceptance speeches, therefore, they are demonstrating their fitness and vitality as warrior-advocates for the campaign and the future administration. Message and gender performance become tightly intertwined, with listeners assessing the speaker as both candidate and prospective officeholder.

Though the McCain campaign had publicly distanced itself from the George W. Bush presidency, it invited one of the administration's (former) speechwriters, Matthew Scully, to draft the vice presidential acceptance speech (Meckler, Langley, and Holmes 2008). Palin's contribution to the speech came largely through its performance, in the richest sense of that term. Her task was to create a strong and positive first impression, and she was widely viewed as achieving that goal.

Palin's attack identifies three fatal flaws in presidential candidate Barack Obama: his legislative career, campaign promises, and rhetoric. As a legislator, "this is a man who has authored two memoirs but not a single major law or even a reform—not even in the state Senate." As a candidate, the "Democratic nominee for president supports plans to raise income taxes and raise payroll taxes and raise investment income taxes and raise the death tax and raise business taxes and increase the tax burden on the American people by hundreds of billions of dollars." As a rhetorician, "this is a man who can give an entire speech about the wars America is fighting and never use the word 'victory' except when he's talking about his own campaign." Throughout, Palin assigns Obama an identity that is profoundly antithetical to the presidency. The vice presidential candidate labels her presidential opponent as self-promoting and underachieving; as thoughtlessly burdening others; as unpatriotic and threatening America's security. Palin insists that Obama is a man whose masculinity fails to meet the standards set for a president of the United States.

In this section of the speech, Palin is unequivocal in her judgments, leveraging her credentials against her Democratic opponent. She is the sitting governor who had changed policy, balanced budgets, ended corruption; she could recognize an ineffective legislator. She is a woman who had proven that opportunity was open to everyone, and she is a mother whose son was being deployed to Afghanistan; she could identify an unpatriotic man. She is a vice presidential nominee; she could name the machinations of a self-absorbed candidate. This was a battle of identities, with the vice presidential candidate claiming greater authority than her Democratic opponent.[13] And it is important to note that Palin directs her challenge at the Democratic presidential candidate, asserting her self as a confident partisan warrior. She is, strongly and clearly, demonstrating that she will be a strong vice presidential candidate and a correspondingly authoritative vice president. Presenting herself as a leader mobilizing her party in support of her running mate, Palin delivers the beta-male performance expected of a vice presidential candidate.

Paul Ryan also established himself as a partisan warrior in his acceptance speech, in ways that were similar to and different from Palin's. Both appealed to economic and social conservatives. But Ryan, the Washington insider, was more ideological and more policy focused.

In marked contrast to Palin, who was handed a speech to deliver, Ryan was reportedly deeply involved in crafting his convention speech, working with a shifting constellation of party and campaign speechwriters (Schlesinger 2012). As the chair of the House Budget Committee (2011–2015), Ryan had articulated clear and strong priorities. Writing an acceptance speech consistent with that political record, however, injected strong ideological appeals into a campaign that had resisted such messaging. Romney, throughout the primary season, had framed his campaign as a referendum on the president's economic policies. Ryan more dramatically defined the election as a momentous choice, either to accept a Democratic apocalypse or to work for a Republican renewal.

> The present administration has made its choices. And Mitt Romney and I have made ours: before the math and the momentum overwhelm us all, we are going to solve this nation's economic problems. And I'm going to level with you: we don't have that much time. But if we are serious, and smart, and we lead, we can do this.

Ryan declares that there is a crisis, which will require, and foster, a virtuous people—his use of "we" is deliberately ambiguous and could refer to either the Republican ticket or to the people. All need to be "serious" and "smart" leaders. He calls on his audience to join him and Mitt Romney in saving a nation—even, in other segments of the speech, the world order. Ryan's speech strategically relies on "we" rather than "I," blurring the boundaries between himself, the people, and the Republican ticket. All join together in the great effort to avert catastrophe. Similarly, his call for action shifts between partisan and national appeals.

Ryan's more specific criticisms of Obama, Biden, and the presidential administration reinforce the sense of loss, threat, and danger invoked by his apocalyptic imagery. Palin describes candidate Obama as overreaching and underachieving. Ryan goes further. Having served in the House while Obama was in the Oval Office, and having frequently opposed the president on a wide range of issues, Ryan is a well-known critic of Obama's policy agenda. Now, as a vice presidential candidate, he reiterates his familiar, searing critiques of the administration's stimulus package, health-care reform bill, deficit spending, and debt management. These are the reasons he gives for defining President Obama as ignorant, uncaring, and ineffectual:

> He created a bipartisan debt commission. They came back with an urgent report. He thanked them, sent them on their way, and then did exactly nothing. Republicans stepped up with good-faith reforms and solutions equal to the problems. How did the president respond? By doing nothing—nothing except to dodge and demagogue the issue.

Ryan had actually been a member of the bipartisan debt commission and had blocked its issuing a unanimous report.[14] Ignoring this complication—which he could have framed more positively as leadership on his own part—Ryan instead asserts that Obama had betrayed the hopeful expectations that he raised just four years earlier: "Now all that's left is a presidency adrift, surviving on slogans that already seem tired."

Ryan's speech presented an economic, social, and political accounting of the nation's power in the present and the future. And without equivocation or hesitation, Ryan put himself at the center of this assessment: "I accept the calling of my generation to give our children the America that was given to us, with opportunity for the young and security for the old—and I know that we are ready." This is a strongly masculine speech, in ways that are familiar to observers of modern presidential campaigns. The vice presidential nominee commits himself to protecting the vulnerable (the elderly, the unemployed), the struggling (the middle class), and the disappointed (Obama voters).

At the same time, Ryan sidesteps the hypermasculinity of the alpha male with a strategic deployment of the democratic "we." Still, Ryan delivers this inclusive message by echoing Obama's 2008 presidential campaign slogan ("Yes, we can"). Ryan declares, "We can get this country working again. We can get this economy growing again. We can make the safety net safe again. We can do this." The vice presidential candidate positions himself as the beta male, promising transformation through shared commitment rather than command. Yet there are continuing overtones that he is, in fact, an alpha male: Ryan appropriates the slogan of a presidential candidate rather than makes reference to one of his vice presidential peers. Like Palin, Ryan is a vice presidential candidate who claims the authority to issue a partisan attack against the Democratic presidential candidate—neither are vice presidential candidates who content themselves with critiquing the opposing vice presidential candidate.

Conclusion

Palin's profile as a political outsider was initially part of her charm. As an Alaskan, she was the ultimate Washington outsider, extremely attractive to a nation invested in its frontier mythology and the antigovernment traditions of its revolutionary beginnings. In other words, Palin was appealing because she conformed to long-standing political values, exemplifying aspects of the nation's identity and the people's self-conceptions. This aspect of her appeal could be sustained, however, only if she demonstrated her mastery (a gendered standard) of policy substance and political process. If she was to represent a nation's mythologies, values, and politics, then she had to prove her ability to do so. Her convention speech was a step in that direction, but the narrative became difficult to sustain during the intensity of the presidential campaign.[15]

For Palin, a significant part of being a political outsider was being a gender outsider. As a woman, she was challenging presumptions that the United States needed a man to be its chief of state, its national executive, its commander-in-chief. Whatever the respect granted to women as social reformers, Republican Mothers, and elected officials, only one woman had previously been a vice presidential candidate. No woman had previously been nominated for the vice presidency by the Republican Party, whose factions remained strongly divided over women's place in politics. Palin confronted the historic challenges of running as a woman, magnified by her situation as a candidate for the historically masculine office of the vice presidency (Kornblut 2009). At the same moment, she also confronted the Republican challenges of reassuring her partisan base that she was both a dedicated mother and a person to whom gender was irrelevant and that she was family oriented and self-reliant. Palin's convention speech drew attention to areas where she was comfortable and had experience; thus, she presented herself, at this point in the campaign, as competent. She threaded the needle between alpha and beta, attacking the Democratic ticket with substantial vehemence (alpha) while supporting John McCain as the presidential candidate (beta).

Palin was both a gender outsider and a Washington outsider. Ryan, four years later, was both a gender insider and a Washington insider. Ryan's selection as Romney's running mate hewed closely to multiple norms, in ways that were distinct from Palin's selection four years earlier. Ryan embodied midwestern wholesomeness, from his boyish good looks (confirming his gender-insider position) to his geographic conventionality (representing a midwestern swing state). Ryan's political experience, as a House member and among the House leadership, again indicated both his insider position and broad acceptability among Republicans—he had already proven himself and was quite well known. Ryan's speech at the Republican convention capitalized on these capacities, highlighting his reputation as a policy expert, a member of the Republican leadership, and a strong and consistent voice for conservative values and policies.

Ryan's gender performance as the vice presidential candidate is in keeping with the gendered standards set for the vice president as beta male, showing deference to the people and to his running mate, being fiercely oppositional toward his partisan opponents, and calling for decisive and comprehensive partisan change to protect the nation. Ryan's gender performance is both clear and nuanced. His life narrative is an account of personal achievement. He attributes his social, economic, and political advancement to his own character—to his drive, competitiveness, and aggressiveness. Ryan epitomizes the American Dream, which he associates with an unfettered individualism and unlimited freedom. Ryan is both exceptional and representative, as voters would expect of a candidate for national elected office. Moderating this masculine gender performance, however, Ryan also presents himself as the loyal son who still mourns his father's death, helped care for his elderly grandmother, and has taken his mother, a successful small-business owner, as his role model. This is the beta-male gender performance required of a vice presidential nominee. Ryan's self-identification as the loyal son positioned his running mate, Mitt Romney, in the historically enduring alpha-male role of the national patriarch.

Palin and Ryan each presented, in their convention speeches, versions of the ideal Republican vice presidential candidate. They both took on the role defined by Richard Nixon as a vice presidential candidate in the 1950s, attacking the other party's ticket and allowing the Republican presidential candidate to sidestep many partisan battles. This was an intensely gendered role, and Palin and Ryan responded by carefully presenting themselves as exemplary beta males. Even as they elevated their characters and credentials—as a Republican Mother and Alaskan governor, as a loyal son and U.S. representative, as a David confronting Goliath, and as the herald of a political apocalypse—Palin and Ryan deferred to their presidential running mates as alpha males. In thirty minutes at the convention podium, these two Republican vice presidential nominees revealed much about the complexities and contradictions that characterize the modern presidential campaign and the modern presidency.

NOTES

1. Palin was not the first to seek this reconciliation. Throughout the George W. Bush administration, both economic and social-conservative gender ideologies were referenced in support of domestic and foreign policies (Ferguson and Marso 2007; see also Schreiber 2008). For a discussion of the significance of the comparisons made between Hillary Clinton and Sarah Palin in 2008 and Palin's appeal to women generally and conservative women specifically, see Rymph 2011.

2. George W. Bush's father, George H. W. Bush, had a distinctly insider résumé, as a former president, vice president, ambassador, and CIA director, among other executive posts. But in 2000 George W. Bush was making every effort to run as his own man, not as his father's son. Aside from Cheney, few of the advisers who worked with George W. Bush—on the campaign trail and in the White House—had advised Bush's father (see Baumgartner 2006; Gellman 2008).

3. When President Bush delegated critical policy decisions to Vice President Cheney, including running the transition for the incoming Bush administration and decisions relating to energy policy and foreign policy, political commentators began to refer to the Bush-Cheney co-presidency. This assessment became even more acute following the terrorist attacks of 9/11. Cheney played a major role in decision making about the military engagements in Afghanistan and Iraq. This vice presidential involvement led to the president being stigmatized as weak and the vice president as overreaching (Cheney 2009, 256–268; Gellman 2008; Lechelt 2004; Warshaw 2009). These concerns further testify to the importance of the vice president in popular and elite assessments of the president.

4. On the outreach of these Republican presidents to the conservative South, and by Reagan to social and economic conservatives, see Baumgartner 2006, 2015. For an examination of the emergence of social and economic conservative gender ideologies and their significance for partisan and electoral politics, see Klatch 1987, 1999; Nickerson 2012.

5. Mondale had promised to nominate a female running mate if he was the Democratic nominee for president in 1984, and he also hoped to capitalize on Reagan's growing gender gap among voters (see Baumgartner and Crumblin 2015, 108; Mondale 2002).

6. We generated accurate transcripts for each vice presidential acceptance speech by consulting video coverage, from multiple sources, of Sarah Palin and Paul Ryan delivering these speeches at the Republican National Conventions.

7. Palin's introduction of her three daughters and husband continued this social-conservative messaging. Her daughters were described as "strong and kindhearted," as having the fortitude to become Republican Mothers. Her husband's masculinity was highlighted with descriptions of his working career and athletic championships. For an analysis of Palin's framing of motherhood and her messaging to "conservative women activists in the Tea Party" following the 2008 campaign, see Deckman 2012, 174.

8. Palin received a strong endorsement from the leading women's economic conservative organization, the Independent Women's Forum (Beail and Longworth 2012, 105).

9. For more on the significance of pronouns in "speaker and audience construction," see Fahnestock 2011, 277–291.

10. The woman who extended her private-sphere role into the public sphere, speaking with moral force and seeking to reform a corrupt policy, was the potential exception to this dire prediction. Phyllis Schlafly, the mother of six children and a constitutional lawyer, founder of the Eagle Forum and a leader in the Republican Party, and author of more than twenty books, as well as innumerable articles and lectures, was such a woman. Arguably, Palin, as a vice presidential candidate, was similarly extending herself from the private into the public sphere.

11. Regina Lawrence and Melody Rose (2013), in contrast, focus on the continuities between Palin's postfeminism and Hillary Clinton's liberal feminism.

12. For a discussion of Palin's appeal to conservative women in 2008 and in following years, see Schreiber 2012.

13. In subsequent speeches, Palin continued and expanded this critique, polarizing and racializing her campaign rhetoric (Logan 2011, 115–117; see also Parlett 2014, 105–106). These references were foreshadowed in her convention speech.

14. Ryan's speech was strongly critiqued by fact checkers, who noted that Ryan repeatedly ignored his own role in constraining (if not obstructing) the president's actions vis-à-vis the economic recovery and social policy reform (see Fallows 2012; Kessler 2012; Matthews 2012).

15. For public-opinion data testifying to the positive effect of Palin's convention address, see Kenski, Hardy, and Jamieson 2010, 142–146. Subsequent interviews conducted by Charles Gibson and Katie Couric, however, probed assertions that Palin issued throughout her nomination acceptance speech. Palin's poor performance on these occasions seriously undermined her support among Republican party elites and throughout much of the electorate (Borrelli and Goren 2015).

REFERENCES

Baumgartner, Jody C. 2006. *The American Vice Presidency Reconsidered.* Westport, CT: Praeger.

Baumgartner, Jody C., with Thomas F. Crumblin. 2015. *The American Vice Presidency: From the Shadow to the Spotlight.* Lanham, MD: Rowman and Littlefield.

Beail, Linda, and Rhonda Kinney Longworth. 2012. *Framing Sarah Palin: Pit Bulls, Puritans, and Politics.* New York: Routledge.

Bode, Leticia, and Valerie M. Hennings. 2012. "Mixed Signals? Gender and the Media's Coverage of the 2008 Vice Presidential Candidates." *Politics & Policy* 40 (2): 221–257.

Borrelli, MaryAnne, and Lilly J. Goren. 2015. "The Sarah Palin/Katie Couric Interviews: Gendering the Executive and Contesting Feminism." Paper presented at the annual meeting of the Midwest Political Science Association, Chicago, April.

Cheney, Dick, 2009. *In My Time: A Personal and Political Narrative.* New York: Threshold Editions.

Deckman, Melissa. 2012. "Of Mama Grizzlies and Politics: Women and the Tea Party." In *Steep: The Precipitous Rise of the Tea Party,* edited by Lawrence Rosenthal and Christine Trost, 171–191. Berkeley: University of California Press.

Dolan, Kathleen. 2008. "Women as Candidates in American Politics: The Continuing Impact of Sex and Gender." In *Political Women and American Democracy,* edited by Christina Wolbrecht, Karen Beckwith, and Lisa Baldez, 110–127. Cambridge: Cambridge University Press.

Duerst-Lahti, Georgia. 1997. "Reconceiving Theories of Power: Consequences of Masculinism in the Executive Branch." In *The Other Elites: Women, Politics, and Power in the Executive Branch,* edited by MaryAnne Borrelli and Janet M. Martin, 11–32. Boulder, CO: Lynne Rienner.

———. 2008. "'Seeing What Has Always Been': Opening Study of the Presidency." *PS: Political Science & Politics* 41 (4): 733–737.

Fahnestock, Jeanne. 2011. *Rhetorical Style: The Uses of Language in Persuasion.* New York: Oxford University Press.

Fallows, James. 2012. "Paul Ryan and the Post-truth Convention Speech." *The Atlantic,* August 30. Available at http://www.theatlantic.com/politics/archive/2012/08/paul-ryan-and-the-post-truth-convention-speech/261775/.

Ferguson, Michaele L., and Lori Jo Marso, eds. 2007. *W Stands for Women: How the George W. Bush Presidency Shaped a New Politics of Gender*. Durham, NC: Duke University Press.

Fridkin, Kim L., Jill Carle, and Gina Serignese Woodall. 2013. "The Vice Presidency as the New Glass Ceiling: Media Coverage of Sarah Palin." In *Women and Executive Office: Pathways and Performance*, edited by Melody Rose, 33–52. Boulder, CO: Lynne Rienner.

Gellman, Barton. 2008. *Angler: The Cheney Vice Presidency*. New York: Penguin Press.

Heilemann, John, and Mark Halperin. 2010. *Game Change: Obama and the Clintons, McCain and Palin, and the Race of a Lifetime*. New York: HarperCollins.

Jamieson, Kathleen Hall. 1995. *Beyond the Double Bind: Women and Leadership*. New York: Oxford University Press.

Kenski, Kate, Bruce W. Hardy, and Kathleen Hall Jamieson. 2010. *The Obama Victory: How Media, Money, and Message Shaped the 2008 Election*. New York: Oxford University Press.

Kessler, Glenn. 2012. "Fact Checking the GOP Convention's Second Night." *Washington Post*, August 30. Available at http://www.washingtonpost.com/blogs/fact-checker/post/fact-checking-the-gop-conventions-second-night/2012/08/30/128cbe9e-f260-11e1-adc6-87dfa8eff430_blog.html.

Klatch, Rebecca E. 1987. *Women of the New Right*. Philadelphia: Temple University Press.

———. 1999. *A Generation Divided: The New Left, the New Right, and the 1960s*. Berkeley: University of California Press.

Kornblut, Anne. 2009. *Notes from the Cracked Ceiling: Hillary Clinton, Sarah Palin, and What It Will Take for a Woman to Win*. New York: Penguin Random House.

Lawrence, Regina G., and Melody Rose. 2013. "The Real '08 Fight: Clinton vs. Palin." In *Women and Executive Office: Pathways and Performance*, edited by Melody Rose, 11–32. Boulder, CO: Lynne Rienner.

Lechelt, Jack. 2004. "Vice President Dick Cheney: Trendsetter or Just Your Typical Veep?" In *George W. Bush: Evaluating the President at Midterm*, edited by Bryan Hilliard, Tom Lansford, and Robert P. Watson, 207–220. Albany: State University of New York Press.

Logan, Enid. 2011. *"At This Defining Moment": Barack Obama's Presidential Candidacy and the New Politics of Race*. New York: New York University Press.

Matthews, Dylan. 2012. "The True, the False, and the Misleading: Grading Paul Ryan's Convention Speech." *Washington Post*, August 30. Available at http://www.washingtonpost.com/blogs/ezra-klein/wp/2012/08/30/the-true-the-false-and-the-misleading-grading-paul-ryans-convention-speech/.

Meckler, Laura, Monica Langley, and Elizabeth Holmes. 2008. "GOP Tightens Image Control as Palin Prepares for Debut." *Wall Street Journal*, September 3. Available at http://www.wsj.com/articles/SB122039868736392867.

Mondale, Walter. 2002. Lecture delivered at St. Catherine University, St. Paul, MN, April.

Nickerson, Michelle M. 2012. *Mothers of Conservativism: Women and the Postwar Right*. Princeton, NJ: Princeton University Press.

Palin, Sarah. 2009. *Going Rogue: An American Life*. New York: HarperCollins.

Parlett, Martin A. 2014. *Demonizing a President: The "Foreignization" of Barack Obama*. Santa Barbara, CA: Praeger.

Rymph, Catherine E. 2011. "Political Feminism and the Problem of Sarah Palin." In *Obama, Clinton, Palin: Making History in Election 2008*, edited by Liette Gidlow, 137–147. Urbana: University of Illinois Press.

Schlesinger, Robert. 2012. "Meet Paul Ryan's Speechwriters." *U.S. News and World Report*, August 29. Available at http://www.usnews.com/opinion/blogs/robert -schlesinger/2012/08/29/meet-paul-ryans-speechwriters.

Schreiber, Ronnee. 2008. *Righting Feminism: Conservative Women and American Politics.* New York: Oxford University Press.

———. 2012. "Dilemmas of Representation: Conservative and Feminist Women's Organizations React to Sarah Palin." In *Women of the Right: Comparisons and Interplay across Borders,* edited by Kathleen M. Blee and Sandra McGee Deutsch, 273–289. University Park: Pennsylvania State University Press.

Tolleson-Reinhart, Sue, and Jyl J. Josephson, eds. 2005. *Gender and American Politics: Women, Men and the Political Process.* 2nd ed. New York: Routledge.

Traister, Rebecca. 2010. *Big Girls Don't Cry: The Election That Changed Everything for American Women.* New York: Free Press.

Warshaw, Shirley Anne. 2009. *The Co-presidency of Bush and Cheney.* Stanford, CA: Stanford University Press.

Witcover, Jules. 2014. *The American Vice Presidency: From Irrelevance to Power.* Washington, DC: Smithsonian Books.

II

Policy and Representation

6

The Impact of *Presidentas* on Political Activity

CATHERINE REYES-HOUSHOLDER
AND LESLIE A. SCHWINDT-BAYER

In this comparative analysis, the impact of women presidents is shown to facilitate the representation of women by contributing to women's increased political participation. While Latin America continues to exhibit significant gender inequality in citizens' political participation, women were elected president eight times between 1999 and 2015 throughout the continent: twice in Chile, Brazil, and Argentina; and once in Costa Rica and Panama. Extant research predicts that the representation provided by women leaders will lead to increased political activity by women in the society. Using public-opinion data for seventeen countries, gathered from 2004 to 2012, analysis reveals that presidentas *do augment three measures of women's political participation: vote intention, rates of campaigning, and attendance at local meetings. Furthermore, evidence is provided that* presidentas *challenge conventional notions of the appropriateness of political activity for women.*

From 1999 to 2015, five women democratically won the presidency in Latin America, a region known for machismo. Mireya Moscoso was elected president of Panama in 1999, and between 2006 and 2010, Michelle Bachelet (2006–2010) in Chile, Cristina Fernández de Kirchner (2007–2011) in Argentina, Laura Chinchilla (2010–2014) in Costa Rica, and Dilma Rousseff (2010–2014) in Brazil were elected president. Between 2011 and 2014, three of these women mounted reelection campaigns and won office for a second time. Fernández de Kirchner and Rousseff won reelection in Argentina and Brazil, respectively, and Bachelet was reelected in 2013 in Chile (immediate reelection is prohibited in Chile).

The *presidenta* (female president) phenomenon suggests major advances in women's political representation in the region. There is little doubt that the presidency is the most visible political office in Latin America. Latin American presidents enjoy greater constitutional prerogatives than U.S. presidents (Mainwaring and Shugart 1997), and they tend to attract more media attention because of their political power.

Despite the novelty and importance of the rise of *presidentas* in Latin America, research on them has been limited. The most popular topics have been how these women have won office and what they have accomplished in office (Franceschet and Thomas 2010; Jalalzai 2013; Jensen 2008; Morales Quiroga 2008; Piscopo 2010; Ríos Tobar 2008; Staab and Waylen 2016; Thomas and Adams 2010; see also Chapter 12). Although most of these studies have been president or country specific, a few cross-national analyses do exist (see, for example, Barnes and Jones 2011; Thames and Williams 2013).

What has received no serious attention, however, are the societal consequences of women's election to the presidency in Latin America. Existing research from around the world suggests that increased visibility of historically marginalized groups in elected political offices will augment the political participation of those groups in society (Atkeson 2003; Banducci, Donovan, and Karp 2004; Barreto 2007; Bobo and Gilliam 1990; Burns, Schlozman, and Verba 2001; Campbell and Wolbrecht 2006; Wolbrecht and Campbell 2007). Building from this literature, we analyze whether the presence of *presidentas* in Latin America increases the political activity of women in society and, if so, how much and why.

The election of women to the presidency in Latin America should have positive effects on political participation of women and work to close long-standing gender gaps (Desposato and Norrander 2009).[1] We suggest three causal pathways that could theoretically link the *presidentas* to increased political activity among women. First, *presidentas* may change cultural beliefs about the appropriateness of politics for women and, in turn, encourage women to become politically involved. Second, the election of *presidentas* could make women believe that the government will be more responsive to their concerns, thereby raising the potential payoffs of political activities. Third, *presidentas* could make women more interested in politics or more likely to follow it in the news. This augmented psychological engagement in politics could then increase their political participation.

We use the AmericasBarometer public-opinion data from Vanderbilt University's Latin American Public Opinion Project (LAPOP) for seventeen

Latin American countries over an eight-year period as a tool to explore the relationship between *presidentas* and political activity.[2] We demonstrate that *presidentas* exert a positive impact on three forms of women's political activity—voting intentions, campaign participation, and attendance at local meetings—and have no statistically significant impact on men's behavior. The presence of *presidentas* almost entirely closes the gender gap in these three forms of political activity.

It is unclear which mechanism underlies the relationship between *presidentas* in office and women's political activity. Empirical analyses show that citizens living under *presidentas* do not sense greater government responsiveness; nor are they more psychologically engaged. However, the presence of *presidentas* is positively related to citizens' views of how appropriate it is to have women in politics. The fact that these effects are not statistically different for women and men suggests that this mechanism is not necessarily responsible for closing the gender gap in political activity. More research is needed to determine exactly how and why the election of *presidentas* increases women's political activity and whether the phenomenon occurs outside Latin America.

Should *Presidentas* Affect Women's Political Activity?

Members of historically marginalized groups tend to participate less often in politics. Most scholars converge on the same general prediction: enhanced descriptive representation will augment the corresponding group's political participation. It is the increased visibility of in-group members that is believed to spur political activity (Atkeson 2003; Banducci, Donovan, and Karp 2004; Barreto 2007; Bobo and Gilliam 1990; Burns, Schlozman, and Verba 2001; Campbell and Wolbrecht 2006; Wolbrecht and Campbell 2007). This research motivates our study's central hypothesis: *presidentas* will exert a positive impact on women's political activity. Three causal mechanisms may link the presence of a *presidenta* to increased female political activity—cultural appropriateness, government responsiveness, and psychological engagement.

Cultural Appropriateness

The cultural-appropriateness mechanism derives from an account of women and men behaving according to cultural norms. This is a version of what has become known as cue theory (Atkeson 2003), and it posits that citizens are socialized to believe that politics is a "man's world" because men dominate politics. According to this logic, the rising visibility of female leaders should challenge traditional conceptions of the inappropriateness of female leadership in politics (Burns, Schlozman, and Verba 2001; Hansen 1997). In Latin America, women profess stronger support for female leadership than men do, according to 2008 and 2012 LAPOP data, and it could be that both women's and men's views on the appropriateness of female political activity constrain women's actual activity. Indeed, Jana Morgan and Melissa Buice (2013) found that women are sensitive to gender-equality cues, such as increased female descriptive representation, but men are even *more* susceptible to these cues. If *presidentas* challenge those beliefs, then women may feel encouraged to participate. Therefore, we hypothesize that the presence of a *presidenta* should make citizens feel more positively inclined toward women in political leadership.

Government Responsiveness and External Efficacy

Another line of reasoning suggests that women may infer that male politicians know less and care less about their concerns than female politicians do; thus, government is less responsive to them. Because men dominate politics, women may calculate that political activity is not worth their time and effort. Still, rising visibility of female leaders sends the message to women that their in-group is gaining power. Since female leaders may share their policy concerns, increased visibility of female politicians may send women the message that the potential policy payoffs from participating are greater and that government will be more responsive to their needs and concerns. In other words, descriptive representation of women will lead to better substantive representation. We hypothesize that the presence of a *presidenta* should exert a positive impact on women's perceptions of government responsiveness.

Indeed, multiple studies show that greater descriptive representation augments historically marginalized groups' external efficacy—their perception of how much government leaders care about them and thus will respond to their concerns (Atkeson and Carrillo 2007; Banducci, Donovan, and Karp 2004; Bobo and Gilliam 1990; Burns, Schlozman, and Verba 2001; High-Pippert and Comer 1998). Examining this in the context of contemporary Latin America is important because it offers a strict test of the effect of sex in producing changes in perceptions of government responsiveness. All of the *presidentas* under study here are ideological moderates whose administrations have been characterized more by policy continuity than change. Bachelet, Chinchilla, and Rousseff were cabinet ministers who succeeded popular male presidents from their same party. Fernández de Kirchner succeeded her husband. The *presidenta* administrations largely promoted the continuation of economic policies.[3] As a result, if sex of the president has an effect on perceptions of government responsiveness, we can be confident that it is largely independent of dramatic economic policy change.

Psychological Engagement

The third line of reasoning is that *presidentas* may affect political activity through increased psychological engagement with politics. Gender gaps in political engagement exist in Latin America, just as they do in many parts of the world (Kittilson and Schwindt-Bayer 2012). *Presidentas* could increase women's psychological engagement, which in turn could lead them to become more politically active.[4] A psychological mechanism could link the *presidentas*' rise in power to increased female political activity. Studies conducted in the United States have shown that the presence of female legislators augments women's engagement, measured by interest in politics, political discussion, and political knowledge (Reingold and Harrell 2010). Christina Wolbrecht and David Campbell (2007) and Campbell and Wolbrecht (2006) argue that discussion about politics is the causal mechanism linking increased female presence in parliaments to increased political activity. The emergence of *presidentas* attracts public attention and may produce greater interest in, discussion about, and attention to political news. Along these lines, we hypothesize that the election of female presidents could increase political engagement among women in Latin America.

Sex and Political Activity in Latin America

Although Latin American women tend to report voting in elections at similar rates as men (Carreras and Castañeda-Angarita 2014; see also Desposato and Norrander 2009), they are less active in other forms of political participation. Three forms of political activity where substantial gender gaps exist are the intention to vote, campaign participation, and local-meeting attendance.[5] We use data from LAPOP's AmericasBarometer project from 2004 to 2012 to assess gender gaps in political activity and analyze the role of *presidentas* in explaining women's political activity.

The first way we operationalize political activity is with vote intention. Elections are a unique moment when citizens can directly manifest their preferences. Vote intention reflects whether citizens would go to the polls in the hypothetical case that an election were held this week.[6] In Latin America, on average, 84 percent of men say that they would vote if a presidential election were held this week, whereas only 80 percent of women say that they would do the same. Yet variation exists across countries. Guatemala features the largest gender gap: 82 percent of men say they would vote, but just 75 percent of women said the same. Nearly nonexistent gaps exist in Honduras, Costa Rica, Panama, Peru, and Uruguay.

Our second measure of political activity is participating in a campaign. Arguably, those who campaign can influence an electoral outcome more than those who only vote. If women and men display different levels of campaign participation, this can translate into men's disproportionate power over electoral outcomes. In Latin America, the regionwide gender gaps in campaign participation are substantial—12.2 percent of men and 8.7 percent of women said they had campaigned.[7] Figure 6.1 shows the variation in women's and men's campaign activity across countries. Chileans campaign the least—only 3 percent said they had helped out during the last presidential election—but the gender gap of one percentage point is statistically significant. Uruguayans are the most active campaigners—13 percent of citizens said they campaigned, but a 1.4 percent gender gap exists and is borderline significant (p-value of 0.10). Gender gaps in campaigning are statistically

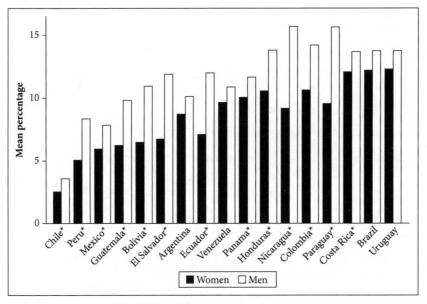

Figure 6.1 Variation in women's and men's responses about campaign participation, 2004–2012

Source: Data from Latin American Public Opinion Project (LAPOP) surveys.
Note: Asterisks indicate countries where the gender gap is statistically significant at $p < 0.05$.

significant at the $p < 0.05$ level in every country except Brazil, Uruguay, Venezuela, and Argentina. As discussed later, *presidentas* have led the government in Brazil, Argentina, Chile, Costa Rica, and Panama during the time frame studied. Paraguay had the largest gender gap. While 16 percent of Paraguayan men said they campaigned, only 9 percent of women said the same.

Attendance at political meetings at the local level assesses the extent to which citizens voice their opinion on issues that directly affect their lives. While 11.9 percent of Latin American men from 2004 to 2012 said they had attended local political meetings, only 9.9 percent of women said they had done so.[8] Gender differences in local-meeting attendance vary across Latin American countries. All countries have statistically significant gender disparities in this measure of local political involvement except Argentina, Chile, and Uruguay. This could be related to the fact that Chile had *presidentas* governing during the 2006 and 2008 LAPOP survey fieldwork, and Argentina had a *presidenta* governing during the 2008, 2010, and 2012 LAPOP fieldwork. Gender gaps favor men in all countries except Venezuela. Venezuelan women participated more in local political meetings than did men, with a gap of 2.8 percentage points. This is not surprising given that the 2004–2012 period was the heyday of former President Hugo Chávez's efforts to increase participatory democracy in Venezuela, and women were a key target of those efforts.

Gender gaps in these three forms of political activity are evident in most countries of Latin America. Fewer women than men express intentions to vote; women are less involved in political campaigns than men; and in all countries but Venezuela, fewer women than men attend local political meetings. Has the rise of the *presidentas* in some Latin American countries reduced these gaps by disproportionately increasing women's political activity relative to men's?

Presidentas *and Political Activity:* *Variables and Methods*

The three measures of political activity just described are the first part of this study's main dependent variables. They capture fundamental but diverse types of political activity, and the correlations among them are low. The strongest correlation ($r = 0.16$) is between campaigning and attending local meetings. The correlation between vote intention and campaigning and vote intention and attending local meetings is 0.07 and 0.05, respectively. Because of these low correlations, we examine the impact of *presidentas* on each indicator separately.

We use logistic regression with country and year fixed effects to estimate the effect of *presidentas* on citizens' political activity.[9] We include country weights, as provided by LAPOP, which in addition to appropriately balancing the different number of and representativeness of responses helps account for the problem of lack of independence across respondents within countries, a problem that typically requires clustered standard errors. In addition to the country and year fixed effects, we control for individual- and country-level factors that could confound or mediate the relationship between the presence of a *presidenta* and women's political activity (as described later and elaborated on in notes and Table 6A.1 in the chapter appendix).

The main independent variable is the presence of a *presidenta* in office at the time the fieldwork for the AmericasBarometer was conducted. A female president was in power during the fieldwork for the 2004 survey in Panama, the 2006–2008 surveys in Chile, 2008–2012 surveys in Argentina, and the 2012 surveys in Costa Rica and Brazil. Our statistical models, which include seventeen Latin American countries and all applicable LAPOP years, allow us to generate the expected change in the dependent variable's value while holding all other variables constant. Although the number of cases with female presidents is small, the analyses allow us to provide an initial test of the effect of women's presence on political activity. This study provides a start to theorizing about and empirically validating the relationship between female presidents in Latin America and women's political activity.

The models all include an interaction term between the sex of the respondent (the *female* variable) and the presence of a female president (the *presidenta* variable). This interaction—that is, the *presidenta* × *female* variable—tests whether *presidentas* have significantly different effects on men and women and whether the gender gap in political activity is significantly reduced under female presidents. We then can show what those different effects look like with calculations of marginal effects from the interaction models (Brambor, Clark, and Golder 2006). All of the models also control for other factors that may mediate the relationship between female presidents and political activity. These control variables include individual-level factors such as respondent sex, education, wealth, age, party preference, and presidential approval and country-level factors such as gender-equality measures. We also include a variable for whether a presidential campaign was happening at the time of the survey fieldwork and whether a viable female candidate was running. (See Table 6A.1 in the chapter appendix for a full list of controls and descriptive statistics.)

Presidentas *and Political Activity: Analysis*

Table 6.1 presents the statistical results for the three dependent variables measuring political activity. The interaction terms in all three models are statistically significant. This means that the presence of female presidents has significantly different effects on men's and women's political participation.

TABLE 6.1: LOGIT MODELS EXPLAINING POLITICAL ACTIVITY

	Would vote	*Campaign*	*Local meeting*
Female	−0.13	−0.35	−0.30
	(0.02)***	(0.02)***	(0.02)***
Presidenta	0.17	0.18	0.13
	(0.11)	(0.12)	(0.10)
Presidenta × female	0.19	0.18	0.27
	(0.06)***	(0.07)***	(0.08)***
Wealth	0.03	−0.02	−0.08
	(0.01)***	(0.01)**	(0.01)***
Age	0.12	0.10	0.15
	(0.01)***	(0.01)***	(0.01)***
Presidential party congruence	1.75	—	—
	(0.10)***		
Presidential approval	0.16	0.15	0.14
	(0.01)***	(0.02)***	(0.01)***
Presidential election proximity	0.003	−0.001	−0.001
	(0.001)***	(0.001)	(0.001)
Election season	0.32	0.07	0.11
	(0.18)*	(0.11)	(0.09)
Viable female candidate	0.09	−0.13	−0.11
	(0.15)	(0.11)	(0.09)
Average female education	0.20	0.10	−0.05
	(0.04)***	(0.04)**	(0.04)
Fertility rate	−0.87	−0.16	−0.67
	(0.21)***	(0.18)	(0.18)***
GDP per capita (log)	0.94	−0.18	−0.05
	(0.26)***	(0.16)	(0.18)
Compulsory voting	0.10	—	—
	(0.14)		
N	63,739	105,140	110,762
Years included in model	2008–2012	2004–2012	2004–2012

Note: Logit estimates with standard errors in parentheses. Year and country dummies not shown. *$p < 0.10$; **$p < 0.05$; ***$p < 0.01$.

The top rows of Table 6.2 present the marginal-effects calculations from the model to show the estimated effect of *presidentas* on men and on women. For men, the presence of female *presidentas* has no significant effect on their likelihood of acting politically. For women, however, *presidentas* have significant positive effects. Converting the logit estimates in Tables 6.1 and 6.2 into more substantively intuitive average partial derivatives, we can estimate that women living under a *presidenta* have almost a 5 percent higher probability of saying how they would vote if the presidential election were this week than women living under a male president.[10] The probability that women will participate in a campaign is 3 percent higher in a country with a *presidenta* than one with a *presidente* (male president). Women in countries with female presidents have a 3.4 percent higher probability of participating in local political meetings than women in countries run by male presidents.

Does the strong positive effect on women lead to smaller gender gaps in political activity? Yes. The bottom rows of Table 6.2 show the effect of the *female* variable (i.e., the gender gap) on political activity under male and female presidents. Under male presidents, significant gender gaps favor men over women for all three forms of political activity. Under female presidents, the gender gap is no longer significant for intention to vote or attending local meetings and is significantly reduced for campaigning.

TABLE 6.2: MARGINAL EFFECTS OF *PRESIDENTAS* ON MALE AND FEMALE RESPONDENTS

Effect of presidentas

	Male	Female
Vote intention	0.17	0.36**
	(0.11)	(0.11)
Campaign participation	0.18	0.37**
	(0.12)	(0.12)
Local meeting attendance	0.13	0.40**
	(0.10)	(0.10)

Gender gap (female effect)

	Presidente	Presidenta
Vote intention	−0.13**	0.06
	(0.02)	(0.05)
Campaign participation	−0.35**	−0.17*
	(0.02)	(0.07)
Local meeting attendance	−0.30**	−0.03
	(0.02)	(0.08)

Note: Logit estimates with standard errors in parentheses. *$p < 0.05$; **$p < 0.01$.

In sum, the results of all three models support the conclusion that women living under *presidentas* tend to profess higher levels of political activity, controlling for a series of potential confounders. Women under *presidentas* intend to vote more frequently. They also help out more on political campaigns and are more active in local politics. Their increased probability of being politically active under female presidents is substantial enough to close the gender gap in "intention to vote" and "local-meeting attendance" and reduce it significantly for "campaign participation." This provides initial evidence that the presence of *presidentas* is related to increased political activity among women.

Why Are Women in Countries with *Presidentas* More Politically Active?

We have now established that, holding constant a host of potential confounders, female presidents are correlated with women's political activity. The next question is, why? Earlier, we outlined three causal pathways that could link *presidentas* to increased female political activity. Here we empirically evaluate whether the sex of the president has different effects on men's and women's perceptions of the appropriateness of women in politics, feelings of government responsiveness, and political engagement. If having a female president is positively associated with women's positive views of women in government, government responsiveness, and/or political engagement but not men's, then we have initial evidence that those mechanisms could be the path through which sex of the president affects political activity among women and the gender gaps in political activity.

The next set of statistical models tests these posited causal mechanisms by using different dependent variables—again measured by the LAPOP AmericasBarometer. Table 6A.1 in the chapter appendix shows the years that each question was asked (and descriptive statistics for the dependent variables). Cultural appropriateness is captured by respondents' level of agreement/disagreement with the statement "Men are better political leaders than women." Responses are coded from 1 to 4 so that positive effects in the statistical models indicate greater acceptance of women in politics. Government responsiveness (or external efficacy) is captured by respondents' agreement/disagreement with the assertion "Those who govern this country are interested in what people like you think." Responses are coded 1 through 7 so that positive effects reflect a greater perception that government is responsive to citizens. Finally, two indicators capture political engagement. First, interest in politics is coded 1 through 4 with higher values indicating greater interest. The second indicator is about news consumption—coded from 1 through 5 with higher values indicating greater news consumption.

Our statistical methodology is similar to that in the previous section; however, we run ordered logit regressions for all of these models because the dependent variables are ordinal rather than dichotomous. Again, the key variables here are the dichotomous *female* and *presidenta* variables and an interaction between the two. We again include control variables to isolate the effect of *presidentas* (see Table 6A.1 in the chapter appendix).

Table 6.3 presents the results for the tests to see if the mechanisms that we hypothesized were actually at work. In only one of the models is the interaction term between female and sex of the president significant: interest in politics. Except for this relatively weak relationship, sex of the president has no statistically significant different effect on men's and women's views of the cultural appropriateness of women in politics, their expectations of government responsiveness, or their political engagement as measured by news consumption. This suggests that these three mechanisms do not explain why sex of the president closes gender gaps in political activity. We tested this further by rerunning the models from the previous section with the four possible causal mechanisms included. None of the four possible causal mechanism variables eliminated the effect of sex of the president on women's political activity. Thus, the explanation for why sex of the president is related to women's political activity must derive from something else. We are unsure about what this is.

Even though a president's sex does not have different effects on women than men, it importantly does have effects on both women and men, as shown in Table 6.4. This table simply removes the interaction term between

TABLE 6.3: TESTS OF APPROPRIATENESS, RESPONSIVENESS, AND ENGAGEMENT

	Support of female leadership	*Sense of government responsiveness*	*Interest in politics*	*News consumption*
Female	0.70	−0.03	−0.36	−0.21
	(0.02)***	(0.01)**	(0.01)***	(0.02)***
Presidenta	0.52	−0.06	−0.10	0.08
	(0.12)***	(0.07)	(0.06)	(0.18)
Presidenta × female	−0.08	−0.05	0.07	−0.01
	(0.06)	(0.04)	(0.04)*	(0.06)
N	45,638	76,582	94,715	52,904
Year included	2008, 2012	2008–2012	2006–2012	2010–2012

Note: Logit estimates with standard errors in parentheses. Control variables and year and country dummies were included in the model but are not shown here. *$p < 0.10$; **$p < 0.05$; ***$p < 0.01$.

TABLE 6.4: TESTS OF APPROPRIATENESS, RESPONSIVENESS, AND ENGAGEMENT
(NO INTERACTION)

	Support of female leadership	Sense of government responsiveness	Interest in politics	News consumption
Female	0.70	−0.03	−0.35	−0.21
	(0.02)***	(0.01)***	(0.01)***	(0.02)***
Presidenta	0.48	−0.09	−0.07	0.07
	(0.12)***	(0.07)	(0.06)	(0.18)
Education	0.23	−0.07	0.50	0.45
	(0.02)***	(0.01)***	(0.01)***	(0.02)***
Wealth	0.04	0.01	0.05	0.14
	(0.01)***	(0.01)	(0.01)***	(0.01)***
Age	−0.05	0.01	0.02	0.21
	(0.01)***	(0.01)	(0.01)***	(0.01)***
Presidential party congruence	0.01	0.36	1.09	0.21
	(0.03)	(0.02)***	(0.02)***	(0.03)***
Presidential approval	−0.08	0.59	0.11	0.05
	(0.01)***	(0.01)***	(0.01)***	(0.01)***
Presidential election proximity	−0.02	−0.002	0.001	−0.01
	(0.003)***	(0.001)**	(0.001)	(0.002)***
Election season	−0.52	−0.12	0.46	−0.08
	(0.23)**	(0.13)	(0.06)***	(0.18)
Viable female candidate	0.84	−0.003	−0.04	−0.02
	(0.21)***	(0.11)	(0.06)***	(0.11)
Average female education	0.09	0.11	0.10	0.09
	(0.05)*	(0.03)***	(0.03)***	(0.05)*
Fertility rate	0.29	−0.44	−0.24	1.21
	(0.18)	(0.14)***	(0.10)**	(0.62)*
GDP per capita (log)	−0.34	0.03	−0.08	0.38
	(0.23)	(0.15)	(0.12)	(0.42)
N	45,638	76,582	94,715	52,904
Year included	2008, 2012	2008–2012	2006–2012	2010–2012

Note: Logit estimates with standard errors in parentheses. Year and country dummies not shown. * $p < 0.10$; ** $p < 0.05$; *** $p < 0.01$.

female and *presidenta* from the statistical model and shows the estimated effect of respondent sex and having a female president on citizens (both men and women). The first notable findings are the gender gaps in all the dependent variables, revealed by the statistical significance of the *female* variable, but the direction of that gender gap varies across models. Under a *presidenta*, women have a higher likelihood of professing much stronger support for women's leadership than men do. Men demonstrate a higher likelihood of efficacy, interest in politics, and rates of following political news. The effect of *presidentas* on these dependent variables, however, is limited to the support for female leaders among women and men. Having female presidents leads to greater levels of support for female political leaders, but it has no effect on women's or men's efficacy, interest in politics, or following politics in the news.

Results from the model of beliefs about female leadership support the hypothesized appropriateness mechanism. *Presidentas* exert a positive and highly significant impact on citizens' support for female leaders, and there is no differential impact between male and female respondents. Table 6.5 shows the changes in predicted probabilities for support of female leaders when citizens are governed by a *presidenta*. The highest level of support for female leadership is measured by a "strongly disagree" response to the statement "In general, men are better political leaders than women." Most of the movement in public opinion occurs between the "disagree" and "strongly disagree" answers. Living under a *presidenta* means that citizens are 2 percent less likely to "strongly agree" with the statement, 5 percent less likely to "agree," 3 percent less likely to "disagree," and 10 percent *more* likely to "strongly disagree." The beliefs data capture only the effects of the Fernández de Kirchner, Rousseff, and Chinchilla presidencies because the question was asked only in 2008 and 2012 and did not include Chile in 2008. Nevertheless, the observation that under *presidentas* the predicted probability for disagreeing strongly with the statement "Men are better political leaders than women" changes by 10 percent is remarkable.

The findings concerning the effect of the campaign of a viable female candidate are also consistent with the general prediction that increased visibility of female political leaders can change citizens' views about the capacity of female leaders. In this model, the *viable female candidate* variable

TABLE 6.5: CHANGES IN PREDICTED PROBABILITIES FOR SUPPORT OF FEMALE LEADERS

"Men are better political leaders than women"	*Impact under a presidenta*
Disagree strongly	0.10
Disagree	−0.03
Agree	−0.05
Strongly agree	−0.02

Note: All changes are significant at the $p \leq 0.01$ level; calculated with the margins command in Stata; holding all other variables at their means. Average interest levels for women in seventeen Latin American countries from 2004 to 2012 is 1.94.

captures the highly competitive but ultimately unsuccessful presidential runs of Paraguayan Blanca Ovelar in 2008 and Mexican Josefina Vázquez Mota in 2012. Ovelar ran for the Colorado Party and did not win, since she received only 31 percent of the vote. Backed by the Partido Acción Nacional (PAN), Vázquez Mota captured 26 percent of the vote. The dummy for the election season is also significant, but it is negative. The combined impact of both variables is positive and significant at the 0.01 level. Results, therefore, show that if a viable female candidate is campaigning during the LAPOP survey fieldwork dates, then the men and women profess stronger support for female leaders. The findings of the appropriateness model are strengthened by the observation that other key variables are significant, and their coefficients accord with our expectations.

Although our empirical results do not support the conclusion that cultural appropriateness of women in politics, government responsiveness, and psychological engagement in politics are the *causal* mechanisms by which the sex of the president is linked to women's political activity, our results do show that the sex of the president is *related* to views of cultural appropriateness for both men and women. Whereas previous research has found this when focusing on women's representation in legislatures in Latin America (Morgan and Buice 2013), we show support for it through women's representation in top executive-office positions. Whether a president is a woman, however, does not affect citizen perceptions of government responsiveness or their political engagement. This is important as well for showing the limits of the effects that female presidents can have on society. While they do seem to have an impact on our indicators of women's political activity, *presidentas* are not panaceas for all political inequalities between women and men.

Conclusion

The number of women elected to presidencies in Latin America is still quite low, but the election of five women eight times in just the last sixteen years is remarkable. This chapter offers one of the first studies of the societal consequences of the presence of *presidentas*. Latin America has often been characterized as a region with low civic activity and political marginalization of women (Craske 1999; Klesner 2007), but we show that the rise of *presidentas* could have a positive impact on these democratic deficiencies. Statistical evidence is largely consistent with the proposition that the presence of *presidentas* in Latin America relates to women's political activity, as measured by intention to vote, campaign participation, and attendance at local political meetings.

Our empirical analyses do not allow us to identify which causal mechanisms could link *presidentas* to increased political activity among women. But we do show evidence that the presence of female presidents is associated with more positive cultural attitudes about politics being an appropriate arena for women's participation. Scholars have empirically demonstrated that the rise of women in legislatures contributes to greater acceptance of women in politics. We find evidence that *presidentas* also help positively change these attitudes.

Contrary to many studies of the effect of descriptive representation on historically marginalized groups in the developed world (Atkeson and Carrillo 2007; Bobo and Gilliam 1990), *presidentas* do not produce greater feelings of government responsiveness or more psychological engagement with politics for women (or men). Furthermore, there is little evidence to support the idea that *presidentas* generally augment women's interest in politics.

Because of the unavailability of data, we were unable to test another plausible mechanism: political discussion. Campbell and Wolbrecht's (2006) and Wolbrecht and Campbell's (2007) studies of adolescents in the United States and Europe revealed that girls—on observing larger numbers of women in office—begin to discuss politics more with their friends and family. This increased discussion leads to greater anticipated political involvement. LAPOP's question on political discussion was asked in 2006 and 2008, when only Chile and Argentina (2008 only) had a female president, and this provides too little variation on sex of the president to test any political-discussion hypotheses. A related factor—general interest in politics—was found to be unaffected by *presidentas*. Future research on the impact of a president's sex on political activity should try to study the political discussion-mechanism more directly.

Much scholarship has examined the impact of female legislators on women's symbolic representation (see, for example, Atkeson 2003; Kittilson and Schwindt-Bayer 2012; Lawless 2004; Schwindt-Bayer 2010). To our knowledge, however, this is the first empirical exploration of the impact of *presidentas* in Latin America. Extant research has been conducted on Latin American voting behavior and civic activities (Desposato and Norrander 2009; Klesner 2007), but no study so far has examined political activity as measured by rates of intention to vote, campaign participation, and attendance at local political meetings. This study, therefore, contributes to the literature on contextual effects and political behavior in Latin America as well as the possible impact of female presidents. We expect the rise of the *presidentas* to continue, and much research remains to be conducted on how *presidentas* affect citizens' political attitudes and behavior.

Appendix

TABLE 6A.1: DESCRIPTIVE STATISTICS FOR ALL VARIABLES

Variable	Survey years	N	Mean (standard deviation)	Range
Presidenta	All	137,550	0.11 (0.004)	0–1
Would vote	2008–2012	72,062	0.81 (0.003)	0–1
Campaign	All	129,554	0.10 (0.31)	0–1
Attend local meeting	All	134,229	0.11 (0.31)	0–1
Support for female leadership	2008, 2012	51,627	2.89 (0.01)	1–4
Sense of government responsiveness	2008–2012	87,102	3.34 (0.01)	1–7
Interest in politics	2006–2012	118,039	2.04 (0.96)	1–4
Follow political news	2010–2012	60,513	4.39 (0.01)	1–5
Female	All	137,550	0.52 (0.50)	0–1
Education	All	135,771	1.97 (0.004)	1–3
Wealth	All	124,981	3.87 (1.75)	0–7
Age cohort	All	135,123	2.57 (1.25)	1–5
Presidential party congruence	2006–2012	105,669	0.17 (0.37)	0–1
Presidential approval	All	134,124	0.21 (0.95)	–2–2
Presidential election proximity	All	137,550	14.22 (9.83)	0–40
Election season	All	137,550	0.08 (0.27)	0–1
Viable female candidate	All	137,550	0.05 (0.003)	0–1
Fertility rate	All	137,550	2.70 (0.60)	1.7–4.5
Average female education	All	137,550	7.31 (1.57)	3.2–10
GDP per capita (log)	All	137,550	8.43 (0.01)	6.8–9.6
Compulsory voting	All	137,550	0.70 (0.01)	0–1

NOTES

1. By "gender gap," we mean the difference between men's and women's rates of participation in a political activity, whether by voting, campaigning, protesting, or some other means.

2. The survey data are available at http://www.vanderbilt.edu/lapop/survey-data.php. We thank LAPOP and its major supporters (the United States Agency for International Development, the Inter-American Development Bank, and Vanderbilt University) for making the data available. Political science research on Spanish and Portuguese Latin America usually includes eighteen countries: Mexico, Guatemala, Honduras, El Salvador, Nicaragua, Costa Rica, Panama, Colombia, Venezuela, Ecuador, Bolivia, Peru, Chile,

Brazil, Argentina, Paraguay, Uruguay, and the Dominican Republic. Haiti is not included because it is French speaking, and Cuba is excluded because it is not democratic. In this study, we exclude the Dominican Republic because it has unusually high levels of political activity by women and men, making it an outlier.

3. However, some *presidentas* made important shifts in pro-women policies. See Chapter 12.

4. We found the mean for interest in politics (measured on a 1–4 scale) for women in Latin America from 2006 to 2012 is 1.9, while the mean for men is 2.1. The mean for following news (measured on a 1–5 scale) for women from 2010 to 2012 is 4.3, and for men, 4.4.

5. Questions about working on campaigns and participating in local meetings were included in every survey beginning in 2004, but questions on vote intention were asked only in 2008–2012. Only about 10 percent of all respondents claim to have participated politically by campaigning and attending meetings, whereas, on average, over 80 percent of all respondents claim they would vote in a hypothetical upcoming election.

6. The exact wording of the survey question is "If the next presidential elections were held this week, what would you do?" Respondents are given four options: not vote, vote for the incumbent candidate or party, vote for a candidate or party different from the incumbent's, and vote blank/null. We recode this variable as 0 if respondents said they would not go to vote and 1 if the respondents said they would vote for the incumbent, vote for the challenger, or vote blank. Our variable is binary and captures whether the respondents would vote at all.

7. We assess campaign participation according to the question "Did you work for any candidate or party in the last presidential election?" We coded "yes" responses as 1 and "no" responses as 0.

8. The exact wording of the question is "Have you attended a town meeting, city council meeting, or other meeting in the past twelve months?" We coded "yes" responses as 1 and "no" responses as 0.

9. Hierarchical modeling is not appropriate for these data, since only seventeen countries are included in the study. This is not enough to justify the hierarchical modeling's assumption that the countries are a random sample.

10. We generated the change in probabilities reported here by using Stata's margins option with partial derivatives after the logit models and then calculating the marginal effects of those estimated probabilities for women and men (Brambor, Clark, and Golder 2006).

REFERENCES

Atkeson, Lonna R. 2003. "Not All Cues Are Created Equal: The Conditional Impact of Female Candidates on Political Engagement." *Journal of Politics* 65 (4): 1040–1061.

Atkeson, Lonna Rae, and Nancy Carrillo. 2007. "More Is Better: The Influence of Collective Female Descriptive Representation on External Efficacy." *Politics & Gender* 3 (1): 79–101.

Banducci, Susan A., Todd Donovan, and Jeffrey A. Karp. 2004. "Minority Representation, Empowerment, and Participation." *Journal of Politics* 66 (2): 534–556.

Barnes, Tiffany D., and Mark P. Jones. 2011. "Latin America." In *Women in Executive Power: A Global Overview*, edited by Gretchen Bauer and Manon Tremblay, 105–121. New York: Routledge.

Barreto, Matt A. 2007. "¡Sí se puede! Latino Candidates and the Mobilization of Latino Voters." *American Political Science Review* 101 (3): 425–441.

Bobo, Lawrence, and Franklin D. Gilliam Jr. 1990. "Race, Sociopolitical Participation, and Black Empowerment." *American Political Science Review* 84 (2): 377–393.

Brambor, Thomas, William Roberts Clark, and Matt Golder. 2006. "Understanding Interaction Models: Improving Empirical Analyses." *Political Analysis* 14 (1): 63–82.

Burns, Nancy, Kay Lehman Schlozman, and Sidney Verba. 2001. *The Private Roots of Public Action: Gender, Equality, and Political Participation.* Cambridge, MA: Harvard University Press.

Campbell, David E., and Christina Wolbrecht. 2006. "See Jane Run: Women Politicians as Role Models for Adolescents." *Journal of Politics* 68 (2): 233–247.

Carreras, Miguel, and Néstor Castañeda-Angarita. 2014. "Who Votes in Latin America? A Test of Three Theoretical Perspectives." *Comparative Political Studies* 47 (8): 1079–1104.

Craske, Nikki. 1999. *Women and Politics in Latin America.* New Brunswick, NJ: Rutgers University Press.

Desposato, Scott, and Barbara Norrander. 2009. "The Gender Gap in Latin America: Contextual and Individual Influences on Gender and Political Participation." *British Journal of Political Science* 39 (1): 141–162.

Franceschet, Susan, and Gwynn Thomas. 2010. "Renegotiating Political Leadership: Michelle Bachelet's Rise to the Chilean Presidency." In *Cracking the Highest Glass Ceiling: A Global Comparison of Women's Campaigns for Executive Office*, edited by Rainbow Murray, 177–196. Santa Barbara, CA: Praeger.

Hansen, Susan B. 1997. "Talking about Politics: Gender and Contextual Effects on Political Proselytizing." *Journal of Politics* 59 (1): 73–103.

High-Pippert, Angela, and John Comer. 1998. "Female Empowerment: The Influence of Women Representing Women." *Women & Politics* 19 (4): 53–66.

Jalalzai, Farida. 2013. *Shattered, Cracked, or Firmly Intact: Women and the Executive Glass Ceiling Worldwide.* New York: Oxford University Press.

Jensen, Jane S. 2008. *Women Political Leaders: Breaking the Highest Glass Ceiling.* New York: Palgrave Macmillan.

Kittilson, Miki Caul, and Leslie A. Schwindt-Bayer. 2012. *The Gendered Effects of Electoral Institutions: Political Engagement and Participation.* New York: Oxford University Press.

Klesner, Joseph L. 2007. "Social Capital and Political Participation in Latin America: Evidence from Argentina, Chile, Mexico, and Peru." *Latin American Research Review* 42 (2): 1–32.

Lawless, Jennifer. 2004. "Politics of Presence? Congresswomen and Symbolic Representation." *Political Research Quarterly* 57 (1): 81–99.

Mainwaring, Scott, and Matthew Soberg Shugart, eds. 1997. *Presidentialism and Democracy in Latin America.* New York: Cambridge University Press.

Morales Quiroga, Mauricio. 2008. "La primera mujer presidenta de Chile: ¿Qué explicó el triunfo de Michelle Bachelet en las elecciones de 2005–2006?" [The first woman president of Chile: What explains the triumph of Michelle Bachelet in the elections of 2005–2006?]. *Latin American Research Review* 43 (1): 7–32.

Morgan, Jana, and Melissa Buice. 2013. "Latin American Attitudes toward Women in Politics: The Influence of Elite Cues, Female Advancement and Individual Characteristics." *American Political Science Review* 107 (4): 644–662.

Piscopo, Jennifer M. 2010. "*Primera dama, prima donna?* Media Constructions of Cristina Fernández De Kirchner in Argentina." In *Cracking the Highest Glass Ceiling: A Global Comparison of Women's Campaigns for Executive Office*, edited by Rainbow Murray, 197–220. Santa Barbara, CA: Praeger.

Reingold, Beth, and Jessica Harrell. 2010. "The Impact of Descriptive Representation on Women's Political Engagement: Does Party Matter?" *Political Research Quarterly* 63 (2): 280–294.

Ríos Tobar, Marcela. 2008. "Seizing a Window of Opportunity: The Election of President Bachelet in Chile." *Politics & Gender* 4 (3): 509–519.

Schwindt-Bayer, Leslie A. 2010. *Political Power and Women's Representation in Latin America*. New York: Oxford University Press.

Staab, Silke, and Georgina Waylen. 2016. *Gender, Institutions, and Change in Bachelet's Chile*. New York: Palgrave Macmillan.

Thames, Frank C., and Margaret S. Williams. 2013. *Contagious Representation: Women's Political Representation in Democracies around the World*. New York: New York University Press.

Thomas, Gwynn, and Melinda Adams. 2010. "Breaking the Final Glass Ceiling: The Influence of Gender in the Elections of Ellen Johnson-Sirleaf and Michelle Bachelet." *Journal of Women, Politics & Policy* 31 (2): 105–131.

Wolbrecht, Christina, and David E. Campbell. 2007. "Leading by Example: Female Members of Parliament as Political Role Models." *American Journal of Political Science* 51 (4): 921–939.

7

U.S. Presidents and LGBT Policy

Leadership, Civil Rights, and Morality Claims, 1977–2015

ARIELLA R. ROTRAMEL

This chapter focuses on the substantive representation provided by U.S. presidents. As the lesbian, gay, bisexual, and transgender (LGBT) movement has gained traction in the United States, it has called on presidents to advocate for the protections necessary for LGBT people to become fully incorporated into society. Yet multiple and layered tensions within the LGBT community have complicated this policy making. Presidents have, moreover, encountered a strong conservative backlash to LGBT rights since 1977. In response to these cross-cutting pressures, Democrats have largely embraced a civil rights/equality frame, while Republicans have either embraced or mediated a morality frame. The result has been wide swings in presidential responsiveness to the LGBT community, arguably undermining the well-being of LGBT people throughout the United States.

It was not until 2000 that a president mentioned "gay" people in a State of the Union address (Clinton 2000). And it was not until 2015 that the full phrase "lesbian, gay, bisexual or transgender" was included in a State of the Union address (Obama 2015a). The status of this speech—constitutionally mandated, delivered before both houses of Congress, televised nationally—gave these references great significance. However, both President Bill Clinton and President Barack Obama had waited until late in their second terms to make this reference, speaking only after there was no possibility of an electoral backlash. And rather than use the State of the

TERMINOLOGY

LGBT (lesbian, gay, bisexual, transgender) is an umbrella term commonly used to refer to the overarching community of people who share historical and contemporary experiences of oppression regarding their sexuality and/or gender identities. While gender and sexual practices are highly variable, LGBT refers to people who *identify* with these sexual or gender categories. Other variations of the LGBT acronym include categories that have yet to be overtly addressed in presidential politics, such as intersex, asexual, or gender nonconforming, as well as culturally specific categories such as two-spirit or aggressive. For the purposes of this chapter, "LGBT" is used when referring to the community at large, while "gay and lesbian" is used when these identities are the particular groups being acknowledged or represented. This choice is used to highlight the frequent silences about the range of community members participating in and/or affected by the issues discussed in this chapter.

Lesbian, gay, and bisexual refer to sexual orientations, women same-gender attraction, men same-gender attraction, and men and women or no gender-preference attraction, respectively.

Transgender refers to the range of people who identify as a gender that is not the gender commonly associated with the sex they were assigned at birth (e.g., infants sexed as female are assigned a girl/woman gender identity). There is a range of gender expressions among transgender people, as there is among *cisgender* people (those whose assigned birth sex aligns with their gender identity). Transgender and cisgender people identify with the range of sexual orientations, including identifying as heterosexual.

Heterosexism is the ideology that rejects, degrades, and devalues actual or perceived nonheterosexual people, activities, culture, and communities. Within a heterosexist culture and social structure, institutional supports, such as religious and legal ideologies, promote prejudice and institutional discrimination. Heterosexism is entwined with sexism, the similar devaluing of women, and *heteropatriarchy* is used to name overlapping investments in hierarchal gender and sexual categories.

Transphobia, homophobia, and *biphobia* are forms of bias against transgender or gender nonconforming, gay or lesbian, and bisexual people, respectively. These biases constrain the lives and expression of all people, including heterosexual or cisgender people. For example, sexist ideas about appropriate *gender expression* (e.g., men performing masculinity through violence or sexual aggression) combine norms around heterosexuality and gender conformity that circumscribe men's lives.

Union address to push for legislation, the presidents only issued a predict-able call for an end to discrimination. Clinton and Obama were "voic[ing] national values," without suggesting that they should have the force of law (Campbell and Jamieson 2008, 164).

LGBT activists have lobbied presidents for many years, but only recently have presidents even begun to respond to their efforts. Presidential responses reflect the complexity of partisan and electoral politics, particularly in the midst of increasing polarization and enduring culture wars. Also complicat-ing the presidential response is the diversity of the LGBT community: LGBT Americans are a heterogeneous community with profound demographic differences and correspondingly diverse interests. Presidents have only just begun to understand how to respond to this diversity with policies that are both constructive and nuanced.

In addition, there are enduring patterns of privilege among lesbian, gay, bisexual, and transgender people. Power inequities also reflect discrimina-tion in the wider society: though all LGBT people have confronted powerful opposition, bisexual and transgender people have continually encountered a higher level of stigma (Norton and Herek 2013, 750). Anti-bisexual and anti-transgender biases within the LGBT movement further this marginalization. Gay men and lesbian women have predominated among the leaders of the gay rights movement, and they have acted to further their interests. Think-ing of lesbian, gay, bisexual, and transgender people as a unified community is, therefore, highly problematic. They are more accurately understood as a richly diversified cohort of people whose status as sexual and gender minori-ties leads them to share some policy priorities.

Presidential efforts to protect LGBT people from discrimination, as ar-ticulated in the Clinton and Obama addresses, reflect a shift in social atti-tudes that has encouraged greater tolerance but not wholesale acceptance of LGBT members in U.S. society. A 2004 *Los Angeles Times* survey found that 47 percent of respondents agreed with the statement "Homosexuality should be accepted by society"; a 2013 Pew survey, posing the same statement, found that 60 percent of respondents agreed. Likewise, in 2004, 45 percent agreed with the statement "Homosexuality should be discouraged by society," while just 31 percent agreed nine years later (Pew Research Center 2013, 2). Neither survey asked about attitudes toward bisexual and transgender people. In this, the survey reflected the common practice of placing bisexual and trans-gender people in an umbrella "LGBT" category or ignoring their existence entirely (Flores 2014; Mehren 2004; Walls 2008).

Conservative and religious constituencies have mobilized in response to the LGBT community, with profound consequences for electoral and parti-san politics in the Democratic and Republican Parties. This chapter delin-eates and examines these politics, assessing their significance for presidential decision making. Democratic administrations since 1977 are examined first, followed by Republican administrations. Often presidents have abdicated leadership in favor of compromise and damage control, endorsing policies that fail to acknowledge—let alone address—the needs of bisexual and transgender people, as well as lesbians and gays.

Democratic Administrations: *In*equality and Civil Rights

As the LGBT community has become a significantly Democratic voting bloc (see Figure 7.1), it has been increasingly integrated into the Democratic Party. Yet Democratic presidents have struggled with the potential political costs of supporting the rights of LGBT Americans during times of backlash. Moreover, having few LGBT staff members, Democratic administrations have frequently demonstrated a limited understanding of issues faced by bisexual and transgender people. Democratic presidents are routinely presumed to be allies of the LGBT community, and their policies have sometimes advocated for civil rights. However, these presidential efforts have also sometimes reinforced inequities among the members within the LGBT community. To say the least, the LGBT policy legacy of Democratic presidents is far more complicated and nuanced than is often realized or acknowledged.

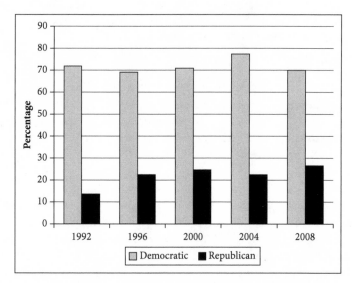

Figure 7.1   **Presidential election voting patterns of lesbian/gay/bisexual voters, 1992–2008**

Sources: Data compiled from Roper Center 1992, 1996, 2000, 2004, 2008.

Carter Administration, 1977–1981

The Democratic Party's response to the disastrous 1968 Democratic National Convention included the formation of the Commission on Party Structure and Delegate Selection, also known as the McGovern-Fraser Commission. As participation in the primary elections expanded and the party sought to include marginalized groups, Jimmy Carter's 1976 presidential campaign organization focused on the Democratic base. Although the Democratic platform made no mention of gay or lesbian people or policies, Carter actively sought the support of these voters. During the campaign, he expressed his opposition to discrimination against lesbians and gays; he publicly supported a proposal by Representative Bella Abzug to amend the 1964 Civil Rights Act to protect people from discrimination based on "sexual or affectional preference" (Turner 2000, 6).[1]

Carter's administration inaugurated outreach to LGBT people as constituents through the National Gay Task Force (NGTF).[2] A leader within the gay rights movement, this organization advocated antidiscrimination initiatives to protect gay men and lesbian women. White House staff arranged meetings for NGTF activists at the White House and with the Department of Justice, Immigration and Naturalization Service, and Federal Communications Commission. These meetings addressed concerns related to the treatment of gay and lesbian employees, as well as anti-gay and anti-lesbian practices (Turner 2000, 4–9).

This engagement prompted anti-gay activist Anita Bryant to attack the administration:

> I protest the action of the White House staff in dignifying these activists for special privileges with a serious discussion of their alleged "human rights." . . . Behind the high-sounding appeal against discrimination . . . they are really asking to be blessed in their abnormal life style by the office of the President of the United States. (Parrott 1977, B20A; see also "Anita Bryant" 1977, 56; Mattingly and Boyd 2013, 371)

Despite Bryant's inflammatory language, Carter refused to make public statements opposing her campaign to repeal antidiscrimination ordinances in Dade County, Florida.

In fact, Carter made few public statements in support of gay or lesbian rights. None of his State of the Union addresses directly or indirectly addressed discrimination against lesbians and gays. The president was also unwilling to lobby for the inclusion of "sexual orientation" as a protected category in his major overhaul of the Civil Service System in 1978 (Turner

2000, 13–15). The president, a former governor of Georgia, abdicated leadership to local and state governments and to private-sector employers, many of which led equality efforts.

Clinton Administration, 1993–2001

Bill Clinton announced his support for ending the ban on lesbians and gays in the military in the same month that he declared his candidacy for the presidency, October 1991. In response to a student's question at a Harvard University presidential forum, Clinton declared, "I think people who are gay . . . should be given the opportunity to serve the country." It was a pledge that he repeated throughout his campaign (Rimmerman 1996, 113). The 1992 Democratic Party platform promised "civil rights protection for gay men and lesbians and an end to Defense Department discrimination" ("Democratic Party Platform of 1992" 1992). When Clinton won the election, Urvashi Vaid, executive director of the National Gay and Lesbian Task Force, declared, "For the first time in our history, we're going to be full and open partners in the Government" (Schmalz 1992).

Clinton's administration did provide the LGBT community with some representation, through the appointments of Robert Hattoy (gay and HIV positive) as White House associate director of personnel, Roberta Achtenberg (lesbian) as assistant secretary for fair housing and equal opportunity in the Department of Housing and Urban Development, and Bruce A. Lehman (gay) as assistant secretary in the Department of Commerce (Haeberle 1999, 149). In addition, James Catherwood Hormel was the first openly gay ambassador, to Luxembourg; after conservative Republicans blocked his confirmation in the Senate for over eighteen months, President Clinton made a recess appointment (Smith and Haider-Markel 2002, 218–220).

Substantively, however, the Clinton administration failed to uphold the campaign promise and the platform plank that promised an end to the military's exclusion of homosexuals. Confronted with strong opposition from the military and Congress, the Clinton administration quickly backed away from its campaign commitments. Instead, the administration negotiated the "Don't ask, don't tell" (DADT) policy. This prohibited the military from asking question about service members' sexuality and prohibited gay, lesbian, and bisexual personnel from being open about their identity (U.S. Department of Defense 1993). Announced just weeks after the Clinton inauguration, this was a compromise that did not have the support of the military or the LGBT community: the military believed that any acceptance of homosexuality would endanger unit cohesion; the LGBT community objected to the demands for secrecy about such a fundamental aspect of one's identity. Ultimately, the DADT policy contributed to an even more toxic environment for LGBT servicemen and servicewomen, who continued to be discharged for their sexuality. When a gay soldier, Private First Class Barry Winchell, was beaten to death by members of his own unit, the Department of Defense added "don't harass" to DADT (Rimmerman 1996, 116–124; 2007, 117–121; see also Wilcox and Wolpert 1996, 137–142).

The Clinton administration subsequently downplayed its support for a range of issues affecting LGBT Americans throughout the first and second terms.[3] In 1996, with Republicans in majority control of the House and Senate, the president acquiesced on two major pieces of bipartisan legislation welcomed by religious conservatives, the Personal Responsibility and Work Opportunity Reconciliation Act (PRWORA) and the Defense of Marriage Act (DOMA). PRWORA funded heterosexual marriage-promotion programs, which advanced conservative fatherhood and marriage movements; these movements would come to drive the anti-gay-marriage backlash of the 2000s (Clinton 1996; Stone 2012, 31–32). DOMA allowed states to refuse to recognize same-sex marriages conducted in other states; a couple legally married in one state was not necessarily married in another, a change in status that could affect virtually every aspect of their lives, including child custody and tax status.

In sum, the Clinton administration embraced LGBT constituents but acceded to important demands from anti-LGBT conservatives. The Ronald Reagan and George H. W. Bush administrations had firmly established Republican support for social and religious conservatives, who opposed civil rights for LGBT people. Clinton's management of the DADT and the conservative PROWRA and DOMA victories all demonstrated the inability—or unwillingness—of this Democratic president to provide strong substantive representation for this constituency (Cohen 1997; Haeberle 1999, 166; see also Lewis and Edelson 2000; Rimmerman 2002, 156–161).

Obama Administration, 2009–2015

The 2008 Democratic Party platform stated:

> We support the full inclusion of all families, including same-sex couples, in the life of our nation, and support equal responsibility, benefits, and protections. We will enact a comprehensive bipartisan employment non-discrimination act. We oppose the Defense of Marriage Act and all attempts to use this issue to divide us. ("2008 Democratic Party Platform" 2008)

Four years later, the Democratic platform described antidiscrimination initiatives for the members of the LGBT community as a domestic and international priority.

At the core of the Democratic Party is the principle that no one should face discrimination on the basis of race, ethnicity, national origin, language, religion, gender, sexual orientation, gender identity, or disability status. Democrats support our civil rights statutes and we have stepped up enforcement of laws that prohibit discrimination in the workplace and other settings. . . . We support the Employment Non-Discrimination Act because people should not be fired based on their sexual orientation or gender identity. . . . Recognizing that gay rights are human rights, the President and his administration have vowed to actively combat efforts by other nations that criminalize homosexual conduct or ignore abuse. Under the Obama administration, American diplomats must raise the issue wherever harassment or abuse arises, and they are required to record it in the State Department's annual report on human rights. And the State Department is funding a program that finances gay rights organizations to combat discrimination, violence, and other abuses. ("2012 Democratic Party Platform" 2012)

The Obama administration followed through on this commitment. As had President Clinton, President Obama included lesbians and gays among his appointees; he also made a groundbreaking move to include two transgender women and two transgender men in his administration.[4] There were also policy changes for LGBT people. Among these were a 2012 antidiscrimination rule for U.S. Department of Housing and Urban Development housing programs, including financing, rental, and homeownership programs (Hudson 2014; Kinder 2012) and Executive Order 13672 (2014), which amended Lyndon B. Johnson's Executive Order 11246 (see Johnson 1965) to prohibit discrimination on the basis of sexual orientation and gender identity by federal contractors (U.S. Department of Labor 2015). With these actions, the president began to address the antidiscrimination concerns of the full LGBT community.

The president's response to Supreme Court rulings that upheld LGBT rights also provided substantive representation to members of the LGBT community. In 2011, a federal appellate court upheld an injunction on DADT, ruling it unconstitutional. Though difficult and contentious, bipartisan legislation was eventually passed to repeal the policy, ending the ban on homosexuals serving in the U.S. military in 2011. Four years later, on September 18, 2015, Obama nominated an openly gay man, Eric Fanning, to be secretary of the army (Wagner 2015). This historic nomination suggested an effort by the administration to close the chapter on one component of institutionalized sexual orientation–based discrimination.

In 2013, when the U.S. Supreme Court declared DOMA unconstitutional, Obama declared, "I applaud the Supreme Court's decision to strike down the Defense of Marriage Act. This was discrimination enshrined in law" (White House 2013). His analysis was in stark contrast to that of President Clinton, who, twenty years earlier, had claimed there was no inherent discrimination in this law. And Obama greeted the 2015 Supreme Court's ruling legalizing same-sex marriage with approval:

> Our nation was founded on a bedrock principle that we are all created equal. . . . This decision affirms what millions of Americans already believe in their hearts: When all Americans are treated as equal, we are all more free. . . . [T]oday we can say in no uncertain terms that we've made our Union a little more perfect. (Obama 2015b; see also "Transcript: Obama's Remarks" 2015)

This phrasing was a thematic echo of statements made during the president's State of the Union address earlier in the year. That speech had, in a historic first, made three references to LGBT people and rights, including a specific mention of bisexual and transgender people:

> There's one last pillar of our leadership, and that's the example of our values. . . . That's why we defend free speech and advocate for political prisoners and condemn the persecution of women or religious minorities *or people who are lesbian, gay, bisexual, or transgender.* We do these things not only because they are the right thing to do, but because ultimately, they will make us safer [by countering threats to our national security]. . . . I believe this because over and over in my six years in office, I have seen America at its best. . . . I've seen something like *gay marriage* go from a wedge issue used to drive us apart to a story of freedom across our country, a civil right now legal in States that seven in ten Americans call home. So I know the good and optimistic and big-hearted generosity of the American people who every day live the idea that we are our brother's keeper and our sister's keeper. . . . I want future generations to know that we are a people who see our differences as a great gift, that we're a people who value the dignity and worth of every citizen: man and woman, young and old, Black and White, Latino, Asian, immigrant, Native American, *gay*, *straight*, Americans with mental illness or physical disability. Everybody matters. (Obama 2015a; emphasis added)

In his remarks and in his State of the Union address, Obama's references to equality and freedom echoed the statements of other Democratic presidents—this was a familiar frame for the party. But Obama also applied the morality frame, which was used by the Republican Party to reject LGBT claims, and turned it into a reason for endorsing those same claims to make "our union a little more perfect" and to demonstrate a fulfillment of the religious call to be "our brother's keeper and our sister's keeper." Mixing equality and morality frames, Obama's rhetoric reconciled these otherwise competing conceptions of LGBT policies, using both in support of civil rights for all members of the LGBT community.[5] He added a national security argument, maintaining that the practice of equality and morality would make the United States less vulnerable in a world where human rights were often denied.

However, the Obama administration also demonstrated its limits in understanding and communicating about LGBT concerns. In 2013 and again in 2014, Secretary of State John Kerry confused sexual and gender identity, memorializing a gay man, Matthew Shepard, in a statement for the Transgender Day of Remembrance (Kerry 2013, 2014). The secretary's remarks demonstrated a failure to understand the distinct communities within LGBT and contributed to the pervasive character of transphobia, which puts transgender people at risk as targets of violence and severely limits their ability to flourish in the United States.

Substantively, although the Obama administration moved the country forward on antidiscrimination policies relating to housing and to federal contractors, the president pursued a limited agenda. Notably, anti-transgender military policies remained largely untouched, and advocacy for transgender people remained in its infancy. Bisexuals received little attention beyond the ending of DADT (Weiss 2011). There were advances, but lesbian and gay rights still received greater attention, relative to bisexual and transgender people's rights, during the Obama presidency.

Democratic Presidents: Fostering LGBT Equality or Inequality?

An April 2013 Pew study found that LGBT adults strongly held a positive view of the Obama administration (63 percent favorable, 30 percent neutral) and were in even stronger agreement that the Republican Party was "unfriendly" (Kiley 2013). This partisan divide is likely to continue as long as social and religious conservatives in the Republican Party reject pro-LGBT policies—though Democratic support for pro-LGBT policy has been uneven, it has been considerably stronger than that provided by the Republican Party, as discussed in the next section. And because the Democratic Party can be fairly confident that it will have the support of the LGBT community, its presidents can set their own pace and priorities in addressing LGBT policies. Complicating Democratic leadership will be tensions among LGBT people, to the extent that these presidents are not positioned to referee struggles within the LGBT community.

Republican Administrations: Morality and Compromise

The LGBT policy priorities articulated by the Ronald Reagan, George H. W. Bush, and George W. Bush administrations revealed the continuing conflict within the party between social and economic conservatives. Social conservatives were morally, and therefore politically, opposed to LGBT civil rights policies. Economic conservatives focused more on the market than social policy and, often in alliance with more libertarian-trending members of the party, accepted the need for some antidiscrimination legislation. In the Reagan administration, this tension was often resolved in favor of social conservatives. Yet both Bush administrations acknowledged the political need to acknowledge LGBT Americans as members of society if the party was to uphold its contemporary tenets (Pew Research Center 2015). If the Republican Party did not, for instance, accept same-sex marriage, lesbian women and gay men would be prevented from participating in a nuclear family structure. Then the Republican Party could no longer claim to be the guardian of family values. For these Republican administrations, the challenge was to find the balance between morality and civil rights in order to sustain the support of opposing factions within their party. This became especially challenging as young Republican voters began to voice their support for LGBT rights (Pew Research Center 2015).

Reagan Administration, 1981–1989

A keyword search of Republican platforms from 1972 through 2012 revealed no mention of "sexual orientation," "LGBT" people or policies, or "gay" or "lesbian" people. In these same decades, Democratic presidential candidate Jimmy Carter was reaching out to LGBT voters and constituents; the 1984 Democratic platform referenced the need to "address, document, and end . . . violence" against "gay men and lesbians"; and by the 1990s Democratic platforms were consistently promising various antidiscrimination initiatives for lesbians and gays, expanded slightly during the Obama administration to include bisexuals and transgender people. If the Republican Party was not endorsing LGBT rights, then what was it doing in this policy arena?

The 1980 Republican Party platform emphasized the Judeo-Christian foundation of the United States and the need to defend families and their values, including "support for legislation protecting and defending the traditional American family against the ongoing erosion of its base in our society" ("Republican Party Platform of 1980" 1980). The 1984 platform argued for the evaluation of sex education programs, stating, "Many health problems arise within the family and should be dealt with there" ("Republican Party Platform of 1984" 1984). Emphasizing the importance of family and faith, the Republican Party in these years ignored the increasing needs of an emerging constituency.

The AIDS epidemic, which emerged and spread throughout the Reagan years, is particularly revealing of this administration's response to the LGBT community. Sustaining a relationship with Christian conservatives that he had forged long before becoming president, Reagan made a number of statements that attributed the crisis to the "immoral behavior" of gay men. With these words, the president framed HIV/AIDS—and, by extension, LGBT-related policies—as a moral issue. Attributing HIV/AIDS to the immoral decisions of individuals excused public health institutions, throughout the nation, from responding to the disease.

The president's reluctance to identify AIDS as a public health crisis has led to strong condemnations of the Reagan administration, which is widely perceived as failing the LGBT community with its slow and inadequate response (Rimmerman 2007, 37–39). Yet there were tensions within the administration: Senior officials in the Department of Health and Human Services pushed for greater funding behind the scenes, notwithstanding their public statements that existent funding levels were sufficient. Surgeon General C. Everett Koop, prevented from publicly commenting on AIDS in Reagan's first term, responded to the president's 1986 request for a report with a "call for federal action," which "underscored the importance of a comprehensive AIDS education strategy" (Rimmerman 2002, 888). This led to the dissemination of some information by the Public Health Service and to strong conflicts with the conservative secretary of education, William Bennett. In brief, efforts to cut federal spending and promote socially conservative values remained predominant throughout Reagan's two terms (Brier 2009). Even the recommendations of the Presidential Commission on the Human Immunodeficiency Virus Epidemic (established in the summer of 1987) went largely unimplemented (Rimmerman 2002, 86–90; 2007, 37–40).

Reagan's 1987 remarks at a luncheon for members of the College of Physicians exemplify the administration's mixed messages in regard to the government's obligation to mitigate the suffering caused by AIDS:

We've declared AIDS public health enemy number one. And this fiscal year we plan to spend $416 million on AIDS research and education and $766 million overall. Next year we want to spend 28 percent more on research and education and a total of $1 billion. . . . Spending on AIDS has been one of the fastest growing areas of the budget. . . . We are also unlocking the chains of regulation and making it easier to move from the pharmaceutical laboratory to the market with AIDS drugs. . . . But all the vaccines and medications in the world won't change one basic truth: that prevention is better than cure. And that's particularly true of AIDS, for which right now there is no cure. This is where education comes in. . . . The Federal role must be to give educators accurate information about the disease. Now, how that information is used must be up to schools and parents, not government. But let's be honest with ourselves. AIDS information cannot be what some call "value neutral." After all, when it comes to preventing AIDS, don't medicine and morality teach the same lessons? (Reagan 1987)

The president alternately favors government action and government restraint, concluding with a rhetorical question that frames AIDS as a moral crisis: "After all, when it comes to preventing AIDS, don't medicine and morality teach the same lessons?" Reagan references free-market economics, responsible government, and family values, but he concludes with, and thus emphasizes, the perspective of the Christian conservatives.

While never the sole issue encountered by the LGBT community, the AIDS crisis—and the failures of the Reagan administration to respond to the epidemic—propelled recognition of LGBT people by the general public. Those diagnosed with AIDS came out, and lawmakers were lobbied to increase their support for medical research (Turner 2000, 28). LGBT organizations advocated for LGBT- and non-LGBT-identified people living with AIDS and gained new funding for crucial services (Brier 2009; Fee and Fox 1988).

Reagan's strong alliance with social and religious conservatives limited his ability to respond to LGBT concerns, even though the general public was becoming more aware and empathetic toward LGBT people. Reagan's successor and former vice president, George H. W. Bush, therefore inherited policies that were geared toward satisfying these members of the Republican base and were failing to respond to shifts in mainstream American attitudes.

George H. W. Bush Administration, 1989–1993

The 1988 Republican Party platform continued the trajectory set by the Reagan administration. Under a section titled "Equal Rights," the platform highlighted religion and "traditional family values." The planks called for a greater investment in programs such as the "Adolescent Family Life program to teach teens the traditional values of restraint and the sanctity of marriage." And the party continued its morality-based approach to AIDS, affirming that "AIDS education should emphasize that abstinence from drug abuse and sexual activity outside of marriage is the safest way to avoid infection with the AIDS virus" ("Republican Party Platform of 1988" 1988). The platform gave no recognition to LGBT people. However, the party was diverging from public opinion. The 1988 National Election Survey revealed a nation split over "laws to protect homosexuals against job discrimination," with 52 percent in favor, 44 percent against, and 3 percent responding "it depends" (Hertzke 1993, 229). By 1992, eight states and one hundred municipalities had instituted policies banning discrimination based on sexual orientation (Haeberle 1999, 146).

In this political environment, George H. W. Bush's signing—rather than vetoing—of the 1990 Hate Crime Statistics Act (HCSA) was a stunning shift in support for civil rights–related legislation. In remarks delivered at the signing ceremony, Bush declared,

> Hate breeds violence, threatening the security of our entire society. We must rid our communities of the poison we call prejudice, bias, and discrimination. . . . I will use this noble office, this bully pulpit, if you will, to speak out against hate and discrimination everywhere it exists. . . . Until we reach that day when the bigotry and hate of mail bombings, and the vandalisms of the Yeshiva school and the Catholic churches we've seen recently, and so many other sad, sad incidents are no more. (Bush 1990a)

Bush sought to diffuse conservative anxieties by foregrounding the violence targeted at Catholics and Jews—a message of religious freedom that could resonate with Christian conservatives. (This was also a potentially bipartisan appeal directed at core constituents of the Democratic Party.) But the president offered no examples of violence targeting the LGBT community, although its members were included in the law. Ultimately, Bush offered a morality-centered defense for civil rights legislation.

Like the Reagan administration, the Bush administration was criticized for weak leadership in regard to the continuing AIDS epidemic. Bush continued Reagan's moralizing language about HIV/AIDS; in 1990, his remarks to the National Leadership Coalition on AIDS concluded, "Let me state clearly: People are placed at risk not by their demographics but by their deeds, by their behavior" (Bush 1990b). In that same speech, Bush called for passage of the Americans with Disabilities Act (ADA), which included protections for HIV-positive people against employment and housing discrimination. These and other conflicting statements led people across the political spectrum—including members of the LGBT community and of conservative-issue networks—to criticize the president and his administration as inconsistent and often obstructive. In 1992, members of the National Commission on AIDS went public with their frustrations with the Bush administration's lack of responsiveness (Haeberle 1999, 147).[6] The commission had pressed for a unified national strategy, increased drug treatment and needle-swap programs, an end to the AIDS immigration ban, and comprehensive sexual education (Hilts 1992). The administration's limited efforts to increase funding in a time of budget deficits, coupled with its efforts to retain the electoral support of social and religious conservatives, left it unable to act in this critical policy area.

Thus, the George H. W. Bush presidency reveals the extent to which presidents could at once succeed and fail in responding to the LGBT community's needs. On the one hand, this administration significantly advanced lesbian, gay, and bisexual interests, signing the first federal hate crimes legislation that addressed sexual orientation. On the other hand, this same administration marginalized the LGBT community by failing to strongly address the AIDS epidemic or engage the LGBT people as constituents.

George W. Bush Administration, 2001–2009

In the 2000 presidential election, 71 percent of gay/lesbian/bisexual voters cast a ballot for Democratic candidate Al Gore and 25 percent for Republican George W. Bush (Roper Center 2000). Despite the increasing presence of Republican gay partisans, the 2000 Republican Party platform took an aggressive stance against LGBT rights ("Republican Party Platform of 2000" 2000; Lewis, Rogers, and Sherrill 2011). It included statements such as:

> We affirm that homosexuality is incompatible with military service. . . . We do not believe sexual preference should be given special legal protection or standing in law. . . . We renew our call for replacing "family planning" programs for teens with increased funding for abstinence education, which teaches abstinence until marriage as the responsible and expected standard of behavior. ("Republican Party Platform of 2000" 2000)

The 2004 Republican Party platform also opposed lesbians and gays in the military; supported abstinence education to avoid AIDS/HIV, sexually transmitted disease, and pregnancy; and supported the Defense of Marriage Act as a "common sense law" that "reaffirms the rights of states not to recognize same-sex marriages licensed in other states" ("Republican Party Platform of 2004" 2004). These Republican commitments meant that the Bush administration would not be expected to undertake—and could avoid—outreach to the LGBT community.

A notable exception was the administration's concession on civil unions, though it remained strongly opposed to gay marriage. In an October 2004 interview, in the final weeks of his reelection campaign, Bush publicly disagreed with the Republican Party platform: "I don't think we should deny people rights to a civil union, a legal arrangement, if that's what a state chooses to do" (Bumiller 2004). The same year, however, as state and local governments began to extend marriage to same-sex couples, Bush called for a constitutional amendment to "protect marriage":

> The amendment should fully protect marriage, while leaving the state legislatures free to make their own choices in defining legal arrangements other than marriage. . . . America is a free society. . . . Our government should respect every person, and protect the institution of marriage. There is no contradiction between these responsibilities. (White House 2004)

With this statement and others, Bush attempted to reconcile conflicting Republican priorities over same-sex marriage, as had previous Republican presidents confronting important LGBT policies. The concern to "protect marriage," which Bush reiterated, provided a moralistic judgment that resonated with social conservatives. The insistence that "America is a free society" and that the "government should respect every person" appealed to small-government libertarians, opposed to the regulation of personal choices. These assertions were also congruent with the Democrats' civil rights/equality frame for LGBT policy. Like George H. W. Bush, George W. Bush attempted to reconcile opposing forces.

The Bush administration also provided federal support to faith-based organizations, some of which were later found to espouse anti-LGBT views, under Executive Order No. 13198 (Bush 2001; Sacks 2011). Domestically, funding for abstinence education programs increased dramatically (Barroso and La Rosa 2007). Internationally, the President's Emergency Plan for AIDS Relief (PEPFAR) program provided massive funding to global HIV/AIDS, tuberculosis, and malaria health efforts, resulting in dramatic increases in the number of people (from 50,000 to 1.5 million) receiving medical treatment (Cahill 2008). However, with the majority of prevention education funding going to abstinence programs, the *Journal of the American Medical Association* noted that "seventeen of twenty country HIV/AIDS prevention teams reported that requiring that funds be spent on abstinence-focused prevention programs would prevent them from allocating prevention resources in accordance with local HIV/AIDS needs" (Mitka 2006, 2130; see also U.S. Government Accountability Office 2006).[7] Increased funding for

PEPFAR during the Bush administration was, therefore, of limited aid to members of the LGBT community.

The Bush White House took a lower profile and a more savvy approach to navigating the tensions within the Republican Party when it distanced itself from the *Lawrence v. Texas* (2003) ruling.[8] Libertarians were concerned about the privacy violations evident in the case, while social conservatives were opposed to legally supporting homosexuality; the Bush administration simply avoided this conflict by not filing a brief. The Supreme Court subsequently found that sodomy laws were unconstitutional, ruling that the use of these laws to target people based on their sexual identities was a violation of due process and equal protection. Through *Lawrence*, much of the moral argument against the LGBT community was set aside, and the Supreme Court recognized LGBT people as having rights protected by the Constitution.

Republican Presidents: Protecting Whose Morality?

The LGBT policy legacy of Republican presidents demonstrates the difficulties of applying the morality frame to sexual and gender issues or of claiming to reconcile the morality and civil rights frames. George H. W. Bush took steps to respond to particularly heinous forms of discrimination, signing the HCSA and the ADA. He found it difficult to defend himself as a compassionate conservative, however, when conservative Christians interpreted LGBT civil rights as threats to their religious freedom. It remains to be seen whether the LGBT community will be able to exploit the schisms within the party to their own advantage, perhaps forming alliances with libertarians concerned about protecting civil rights and liberties.

Conclusion

As the LGBT movement has gained traction in the United States, presidents have confronted multiple and layered tensions associated with ending the marginalization of these people in electoral politics and in governing. Presidents have been called on to advocate for the protections necessary for LGBT people to become fully incorporated into society. Presidents have also encountered a strong conservative backlash to LGBT rights. This ongoing battle has chiefly been framed as a confrontation between civil rights and morality, with partisan implications. Democrats have largely embraced a civil rights/equality frame, while Republicans have either embraced or mediated a morality frame. The result has been wide swings in presidential responsiveness to the LGBT community, arguably undermining the well-being of LGBT people throughout the United States. A president willing to go beyond the dichotomy of civil rights/equality and morality could find more nuanced approaches to policy making that will benefit all the people in this emerging constituency.

For scholars of the presidency, it is critical to recognize that the internal diversity of the LGBT community and the long-standing privileging of gay and lesbian concerns in mainstream LGBT organizing have restricted the issues brought to the president. Even as the Obama administration has supported key advances in military, marriage, and other rights, the detention of LGBT undocumented immigrants has exposed the limits of presidential engagement as well as tensions among LGBT advocates. In June 2015, these tensions were very much in evidence at a White House pride event: when Jennicet Gutiérrez, a transwoman activist, disrupted the event, protesting the treatment of undocumented transgender people, the president responded angrily that such actions were unacceptable in "my house"; she was booed, and the president was cheered by gay and lesbian activists present at the event (Ennis 2015; Gutiérrez 2015; Moyer 2015). Media coverage of the exchange led to criticism of the president, though there is little evidence that the status of transgender people has improved.

In the future, as it has in the past, White House outreach to LGBT Americans will require careful consideration of the presidents' electoral and policy priorities; a better understanding of the diversity within the LGBT community and of its corresponding policy priorities; and an awareness of the sometimes-contradictory character of the conservative response to LGBT rights.

NOTES

1. The terms used to name these identities reflect the language of the period, including the primacy given to gay men and the marginalization of transgender and bisexual activists. The LGBT acronym emerged and became more commonly used in the 1990s.

2. The NGTF later changed its name to the National Gay and Lesbian Task Force and is currently called the National LGBTQ Task Force.

3. For a more extended discussion of the "promises and disappointments" of lesbian and gay rights policy during the Clinton administration, see Rimmerman 2002, 156–161. For a comparative analysis of congressional politics relating to gay rights before and after the 104th Congress, which saw Republicans gain the majority in both chambers for the first time in forty years, see Campbell and Davidson 2000.

4. Amanda Simpson was first named to a Commerce Department post in 2010; she subsequently was named to Department of Defense posts, and as this book goes to press in 2016, she has been promoted to deputy assistant secretary of defense for operational energy. In 2015, Raffi Freedman-Gurspan was named the outreach and recruitment director for presidential personnel in the White House Office of Presidential Personnel. In 2009, Dylan Orr was named a special assistant in the Labor Department's Office of Disability Employment Policy. Shannon Price Minter was appointed to the Commission on White House Fellowships in 2015 (Abeni 2016; Goldman 2010; Ohlheiser 2015).

5. Obama's stance on same-sex marriage changed throughout his years as an Illinois state senator, a U.S. senator, a presidential candidate, and a president. In 1996, in response

to a questionnaire distributed and published by the *Windy City Times*, he wrote, "I favor legalizing same-sex marriages, and would fight efforts to prohibit such marriages." In 1998, however, he responded "undecided" to all questions related to support of legalizing same-sex marriage (Baim 2009, 5). On June 5, 2006, as a U.S. senator, Obama issued a statement opposing a constitutional amendment to define marriage as occurring only between a man and a woman, describing it as a "political ploy" (Obama 2006). Then, in the midst of his 2008 presidential campaign, Obama declared, "I believe that marriage is a union between a man and a woman. Now, for me as a Christian . . . it is also a sacred union. God's in the mix." He added that he considered marriage a matter for the states to legislate (Obama 2008). In 2012, he declared his support for same-sex marriage in an exclusive interview ("Transcript: Robin Roberts" 2012; see also Axelrod 2015).

6. Congress established the National Commission on AIDS on November 4, 1988, after the Reagan administration failed to respond to recommendations of the President's Commission on the HIV Epidemic.

7. Uganda, in particular, gained international attention for its anti-LGBT policies, which were influenced by U.S.-based evangelicals (Bosia 2013, 47–48; Sadgrove et al. 2012, 113).

8. *Lawrence v. Texas* involved the arrest and charging of a white man, John Lawrence, and a black man, Tyron Garner, for homosexual conduct. Police entered Lawrence's apartment in response to a false gun report and found the men involved in same-sex activities in the privacy of Lawrence's bedroom. The case raised questions about the nature of American sodomy laws and their intent. Notably, historians identify these laws as based in Puritanical theology that applied to all people, though the laws have often targeted LGBT people, especially in the twentieth century (Hurewitz 2004). *Lawrence* overturned the 1986 *Bowers v. Hardwick* decision, which had upheld a long-standing moral basis for sodomy laws. The *Bowers* decision had been embraced by social conservatives, who saw it as empowering the government to defend Christian moral values.

REFERENCES

Abeni, Cleis. 2016. "Meet the First Trans White House LGBT Liaison." *The Advocate*, March 14. Available at http://www.advocate.com/transgender/2016/3/14/latina-just -became-first-transgender-white-house-lgbt-liaison.

"Anita Bryant Scores White House Talk with Homosexuals." 1977. *New York Times*, March 28, p. 56.

Axelrod, David. 2015. *Believer: My Forty Years in Politics*. New York: Penguin Press.

Baim, Tracy. 2009. "Obama Marriage Story Goes National." *Windy City Times*, January 21, p. 5. Available at http://www.windycitymediagroup.com/images/publications/ wct/2009-01-21/current.pdf.

Barroso, Carmen, and Zhenja La Rosa. 2007. "Bush's War on Sexual Health and Defensive Strategies against It." *International Journal of Sexual Health* 19 (3): 25–34.

Bosia, Michael J. 2013. "Why States Act: Homophobia and Crisis." In *Global Homophobia: States, Movements, and the Politics of Oppression*, edited by Meredith L. Weiss and Michael J. Bosia, 30–54. Urbana: University of Illinois Press.

Brier, Jennifer. 2009. *Infectious Ideas: U.S. Political Responses to the AIDS Crisis*. Chapel Hill: University of North Carolina Press.

Bumiller, Elisabeth. 2004. "Bush Says His Party Is Wrong to Oppose Gay Civil Unions." *New York Times*, October 26. Available at http://www.nytimes.com/2004/10/26/ politics/campaign/bush-says-his-party-is-wrong-to-oppose-gay-civil-unions.html.

Bush, George. 1990a. "Remarks on Signing the Hate Crime Statistics Act." April 23. *American Presidency Project.* Available at http://www.presidency.ucsb.edu/ws/?pid=18394.
———. 1990b. "Remarks to the National Leadership Coalition on AIDS." March 29. Available at http://bush41library.tamu.edu/archives/public-papers/1706.
———. 2001. "Executive Order 13198: Agency Responsibilities with Respect to Faith-Based and Community Initiatives." January 29. *American Presidency Project.* Available at http://www.presidency.ucsb.edu/ws/index.php?pid=45708.
Cahill, Sean. 2008. "HIV: The Forgotten Election Issue." *Gay and Lesbian Review Worldwide* 15 (5): 18–20.
Campbell, Colton C., and Roger H. Davidson. 2000. "Gay and Lesbian Issues in the Congressional Arena." In *The Politics of Gay Rights*, edited by Craig A. Rimmerman, Kenneth D. Wald, and Clyde Wilcox, 347–376. Chicago: University of Chicago Press.
Campbell, Karlyn Kohrs, and Kathleen Hall Jamieson. 2008. *Presidents Creating the Presidency: Deeds Done in Words.* Chicago: University of Chicago Press.
Clinton, William J. 1996. "Statement on Signing the Personal Responsibility and Work Opportunity Reconciliation Act of 1996." August 22. *American Presidency Project.* Available at http://www.presidency.ucsb.edu/ws/?pid=53219.
———. 2000. "Address before a Joint Session of the Congress on the State of the Union." January 27. *American Presidency Project.* Available at http://www.presidency.ucsb.edu/ws/?pid=58708.
Cohen, Cathy J. 1997. "Punks, Bulldaggers, and Welfare Queens: The Radical Potential of Queer Politics?" *GLQ* 3 (4): 437–465.
"Democratic Party Platform of 1992." 1992. *American Presidency Project.* Available at http://www.presidency.ucsb.edu/ws/?pid=29610.
Ennis, Dawn. 2015. "Booing Jennicet Was Wrong, but Was What She Did Worse?" *The Advocate*, July 1. Available at http://www.advocate.com/commentary/2015/07/01/booing-jennicet-was-wrong-was-what-she-did-worse.
Executive Order No. 13672 [Further Amendments to Executive Order 11478, Equal Employment Opportunity in the Federal Government, and Executive Order 11246, Equal Employment Opportunity]. 2014. 79 Federal Register 42971, July 21.
Fee, Elizabeth, and Daniel M. Fox, eds. 1988. *AIDS: The Burdens of History.* Berkeley: University of California Press.
Flores, Andrew R. 2014. "National Trends in Public Opinion on LGBT Rights in the United States." Williams Institute, UCLA School of Law, November. Available at http://williamsinstitute.law.ucla.edu/wp-content/uploads/POP-natl-trends-nov-2014.pdf.
Goldman, Russell. 2010. "First Transgender Presidential Appointee Fears Being Labeled 'Token.'" *ABC News*, January 5. Available at http://abcnews.go.com/Politics/amanda-simpson-transgender-presidential-appointee-begins-work-commerce/story?id=9477161.
Gutiérrez, Jennicet. 2015. "Exclusive: I Interrupted Obama Because We Need to Be Heard." *Washington Blade*, June 25. Available at http://www.washingtonblade.com/2015/06/25/exclusive-i-interrupted-obama-because-we-need-to-be-heard/.
Haeberle, Steven H. 1999. "Gay and Lesbian Rights: Emerging Trends in Public Opinion and Voting Behaviors." In *Gays and Lesbians in the Democratic Process: Public Policy, Public Opinion, and Political Representation*, edited by Ellen D. B. Riggle and Barry L. Tadlock, 146–169. New York: Columbia University Press.
Hertzke, Allen D. 1993. *Echoes of Discontent: Jesse Jackson, Pat Robertson, and the Resurgence of Populism.* Washington, DC: CQ Press.

Hilts, Philip J. 1992. "Magic Johnson Quits Panel on AIDS." *New York Times*, September 26. Available at http://www.nytimes.com/1992/09/26/us/magic-johnson-quits-panel-on-aids.html.

Hudson, David. 2014. "President Obama Signs a New Executive Order to Protect LGBT Workers." *White House* (blog), July 21. Available at https://www.whitehouse.gov/blog/2014/07/21/president-obama-signs-new-executive-order-protect-lgbt-workers.

Hurewitz, Daniel. 2004. "Sexuality Scholarship as a Foundation for Change: *Lawrence v. Texas* and the Impact of the Historians' Brief." *Health and Human Rights* 7 (2): 205–216.

Johnson, Lyndon B. 1965. "Executive Order 11246: Equal Employment Opportunity." September 24. *American Presidency Project*. Available at http://www.presidency.ucsb.edu/ws/index.php?pid=59153.

Kerry, John. 2013. "Transgender Day of Remembrance." November 20. Available at http://www.state.gov/secretary/remarks/2013/11/217776.htm.

———. 2014. "Transgender Day of Remembrance." November 20. Available at http://www.state.gov/secretary/remarks/2014/11/234297.htm.

Kiley, Jocelyn. 2013. "Obama Had Strong Support from LGBT Adults Even before Stance on Sochi Olympics." Pew Research Center, December 26. Available at http://www.pewresearch.org/fact-tank/2013/12/26/obama-had-strong-support-from-lgbt-adults-before-stance-on-sochi-olympics/.

Kinder, Charmion. 2012. "HUD Secretary Donovan Announces New Regulations to Ensure Equal Access to Housing for All Americans Regardless of Sexual Orientation or Gender Identity." U.S. Department of Housing and Urban Development, January 30. Available at http://portal.hud.gov/hudportal/HUD?src=/press/press_releases_media_advisories/2012/HUDNo.12-014.

Lewis, Gregory B., and Jonathan L. Edelson. 2000. "DOMA and ENDA: Congress Votes on Gay Rights." In *The Politics of Gay Rights*, edited by Craig A. Rimmerman, Kenneth D. Wald, and Clyde Wilcox, 193–216. Chicago: University of Chicago Press.

Lewis, Gregory B., Marc A. Rogers, and Kenneth Sherrill. 2011. "Lesbian, Gay, and Bisexual Voters in the 2000 U.S. Presidential Election." *Politics & Policy* 39 (5): 655–677.

Mattingly, Doreen J., and Ashley Boyd. 2013. "Bringing Gay and Lesbian Activism to the White House: Midge Costanza and the National Gay Task Force Meeting." *Journal of Lesbian Studies* 17 (3–4): 365–379.

Mehren, Elizabeth. 2004. "Acceptance of Gays Rises among New Generation." *Los Angeles Times*, April 11. Available at http://articles.latimes.com/2004/apr/11/nation/na-gaypoll11.

Mitka, Mike. 2006. "U.S. Global AIDS Effort Criticized." *Journal of the American Medical Association* 295 (18): 2130.

Moyer, Justin William. 2015. "Transgender Obama Heckler Jennicet Gutiérrez Hailed by Some LGBT Activists." *Washington Post*, June 26. Available at https://www.washingtonpost.com/news/morning-mix/wp/2015/06/26/transgender-obama-heckler-hailed-by-some-lgbt-activists/.

Norton, Aaron T., and Gregory M. Herek. 2013. "Heterosexuals' Attitudes toward Transgender People: Findings from a National Probability Sample of US Adults." *Sex Roles* 68 (11–12): 738–753.

Obama, Barack. 2006. "Floor Statement of Senator Barack Obama on the Federal Marriage Amendment." June 5. Available at http://web.archive.org/web/20090106065533/http://Obama.senate.gov/speech/060605-floor_statement_5/index.php.

——. 2008. "Forum on Civil Leadership and Compassion." *C-SPAN*, August 16. Available at http://www.c-span.org/video/?280492-1/forum-civil-leadership -compassion&start=1320.

——. 2015a. "Address before a Joint Session of the Congress on the State of the Union." January 20. *American Presidency Project*. Available at http://www.presidency.ucsb .edu/ws/index.php?pid=108031.

——. 2015b. "Remarks on the United States Supreme Court Ruling on Same-Sex Mar- riage." June 26. *American Presidency Project*. Available at http://www.presidency.ucsb .edu/ws/index.php?pid=110386&st=remarks&st1=.

Ohlheiser, Abby. 2015. "Meet the White House's First Transgender Staffer." *Washing- ton Post*, August 18. Available at http://www.washingtonpost.com/news/the-fix/ wp/2015/08/18/the-white-house-has-appointed-its-first-transgender-staffer/.

Parrott, Jennings. 1977. "Gays' White House Visit Angers Anita." *Los Angeles Times*, March 28, p. B20A.

Pew Research Center. 2013. "In Gay Marriage Debate, Both Supporters and Opponents See Legal Recognition as 'Inevitable.'" June 6. Available at http://www.people-press.org/ files/legacy-pdf/06-06-13%20LGBT%20General%20Public%20Release.pdf.

——. 2015. "Most Young Republicans Favor Same-Sex Marriage." February 27. Available at http://www.pewresearch.org/fact-tank/2015/02/27/63-of-republican-millennials -favor-marijuana-legalization/ft_15-02-27_ageptymarriage_420px/.

Reagan, Ronald. 1987. "Remarks at a Luncheon for Members of the College of Physicians in Philadelphia, Pennsylvania." April 1. *American Presidency Project*. Available at http://www.presidency.ucsb.edu/ws/?pid=34054.

"Republican Party Platform of 1980." 1980. *American Presidency Project*. Available at http://www.presidency.ucsb.edu/ws/?pid=25844.

"Republican Party Platform of 1984." 1984. *American Presidency Project*. Available at http://www.presidency.ucsb.edu/ws/?pid=25845.

"Republican Party Platform of 1988." 1988. *American Presidency Project*. Available at http://www.presidency.ucsb.edu/ws/?pid=25846.

"Republican Party Platform of 2000." 2000. *American Presidency Project*. Available at http://www.presidency.ucsb.edu/ws/?pid=25849.

"Republican Party Platform of 2004." 2004. *American Presidency Project*. Available at http://www.presidency.ucsb.edu/ws/index.php?pid=25850.

Rimmerman, Craig A. 1996. "Promise Unfulfilled: Clinton's Failure to Overturn the Mili- tary Ban on Lesbians and Gays." In *Gay Rights, Military Wrongs: Political Perspectives on Lesbians and Gays in the Military*, edited by Craig A. Rimmerman, 111–126. New York: Garland.

——. 2002. *From Identity to Politics: The Lesbian and Gay Movements in the United States*. Philadelphia: Temple University Press.

——. 2007. *The Lesbian and Gay Movements: Assimilation or Liberation?* Boulder, CO: Westview Press.

Roper Center. 1992. "How Groups Voted in 1992." Available at http://www.ropercenter .uconn.edu/polls/us-elections/how-groups-voted/how-groups-voted-1992/.

——. 1996. "How Groups Voted in 1996." Available at http://www.ropercenter.uconn .edu/polls/us-elections/how-groups-voted/how-groups-voted-1996/.

——. 2000. "How Groups Voted in 2000." Available at http://www.ropercenter.uconn .edu/polls/us-elections/how-groups-voted/how-groups-voted-2000/.

——. 2004. "How Groups Voted in 2004." Available at http://www.ropercenter.uconn .edu/polls/us-elections/how-groups-voted/how-groups-voted-2004/.

———. 2008. "How Groups Voted in 2008." Available at http://www.ropercenter.uconn
.edu/polls/us-elections/how-groups-voted/how-groups-voted-2008/.

Sacks, Jonathan. 2011. "'Pray Away the Gay?' An Analysis of the Legality of Conversion
Therapy by Homophobic Religious Organizations." *Rutgers Journal of Law and Religion* 13 (1): 67–86.

Sadgrove, Joanna, Robert M. Vanderbeck, Johan Andersson, Gill Valentine, and Kevin
Ward. 2012. "Morality Plays and Money Matters: Towards a Situated Understanding
of the Politics of Homosexuality in Uganda." *Journal of Modern African Studies* 50
(1): 103–129.

Schmalz, Jeffrey. 1992. "The 1992 Elections: The States—the Gay Issues; Gay Areas Are
Jubilant over Clinton." *New York Times*, November 5. Available at http://www.nytimes
.com/1992/11/05/nyregion/the-1992-elections-the-states-the-gay-issues-gay-areas
-are-jubilant-over-clinton.html.

Smith, Raymond A., and Donald P. Haider-Markel. 2002. *Gay and Lesbian Americans and
Political Participation: A Reference Handbook*. Denver, CO: ABC Clio.

Stone, Amy L. 2012. *Gay Rights at the Ballot Box*. Minneapolis: University of Minnesota
Press.

"Transcript: Obama's Remarks on Supreme Court Ruling on Same-Sex Marriage." 2015.
Washington Post, June 26. Available at https://www.washingtonpost.com/news/post
-nation/wp/2015/06/26/transcript-obamas-remarks-on-supreme-court-ruling-on
-same-sex-marriage/.

"Transcript: Robin Roberts ABC News Interview with President Obama." 2012. *ABC
News*, May 9. Available at http://abcnews.go.com/Politics/transcript-robin-roberts
-abc-news-interview-president-obama/story?id=16316043.

Turner, William B. 2000. "Mirror Images: Lesbian/Gay Civil Rights in the Carter and Reagan Administrations." In *Creating Change: Sexuality, Public Policy, and Civil Rights*,
edited by John D'Emilio, William B. Turner, and Urvashi Vaid, 3–28. New York: St.
Martin's Press.

"2008 Democratic Party Platform." 2008. *American Presidency Project*. Available at http://
www.presidency.ucsb.edu/ws/?pid=78283.

"2012 Democratic Party Platform." 2012. *American Presidency Project*. Available at http://
www.presidency.ucsb.edu/ws/index.php?pid=101962.

U.S. Department of Defense. 1993. "Directive Number 1304.26." December 21. Available at
http://biotech.law.lsu.edu/blaw/dodd/corres/pdf/d130426wch1_122193/d130426p.pdf.

U.S. Department of Labor. 2015. "Amended Regulations: Executive Order 11246 Prohibiting Discrimination Based on Sexual Orientation and Gender Identity." Available at
http://www.dol.gov/ofccp/LGBT.html.

U.S. Government Accountability Office. 2006. "Global Health: Spending Requirement
Presents Challenges for Allocating Prevention Funding under the President's Emergency Plan for AIDS Relief." GAO-06-395, April 4. Available at http://www.gao.gov/
assets/250/249585.pdf.

Wagner, Laura. 2015. "Obama to Nominate First Openly Gay Military Service Secretary." NPR, September 18. Available at http://www.npr.org/sections/thetwo-way/
2015/09/18/441521134/obama-to-nominate-first-openly-gay-military-service
-secretary.

Walls, N. Eugene. June 2008. "Toward a Multidimensional Understanding of Heterosexism: The Changing Nature of Prejudice." *Journal of Homosexuality* 55 (1): 20–70.

Weiss, Jillian. 2011. "GL versus BT: The Archaeology of Biphobia and Transphobia within
the U.S. Gay and Lesbian Community." *Journal of Bisexuality* 11 (4): 498–502.

White House. 2004. "President Calls for Constitutional Amendment Protecting Marriage." February 24. Available at http://georgewbush-whitehouse.archives.gov/news/releases/2004/02/20040224-2.html.

———. 2013. "Statement by the President on the Supreme Court Ruling on the Defense of Marriage Act." June 26. Available at https://www.whitehouse.gov/doma-statement.

Wilcox, Clyde, and Robin M. Wolpert. 1996. "President Clinton, Public Opinion, and Gays in the Military." In *Gay Rights, Military Wrongs: Political Perspectives on Lesbians and Gays in the Military*, edited by Craig A. Rimmerman, 127–145. New York: Garland.

8

Representation in and by the White House

KAREN M. HULT

This chapter examines the Office of Public Engagement and Intergovernmental Affairs, an office directly associated with representation in the White House, in the Obama administration. Although there have been White House offices focused on outreach to the public at least since the Truman presidency, the Obama office appears distinctive in several ways. The office includes staffers with explicit ties to several "communities" (e.g., Arab Americans, LGBT individuals, seniors); houses the White House Council on Women and Girls; participates in outreach through social media; and, unlike in prior administrations, is overseen by a senior adviser to the president, Valerie Jarrett.[1] Descriptive and symbolic representation is seemingly quite high; the encompassing scope of the office, its connections with subnational officials, and its ties to more senior White House officials evidently provide access to policy makers and possible input into policy decisions. Whether such outreach systematically influences actions throughout the executive branch, however, is less clear.

Representation in and by the White House has received considerably less attention than legislative representation (e.g., in Congress, state legislatures, county boards; see Jalalzai 2008, 207). Scholarship on representative bureaucracy has devoted more emphasis to how well officials in government agencies reflect the characteristics of those in the broader public (e.g., Dolan 2002; Riccucci 2009; Riccucci, Van Ryzin, and Li 2015).

Another, more-concentrated focus has centered on the numbers of women and racial/ethnic minorities among political appointees (Clark, Ochs, and Frazier 2013).

In this chapter, I examine political appointees in the White House Office (WHO) under Barack Obama, particularly those staff members charged with establishing, maintaining, and nurturing relationships with women. I explore the positions in which women have served in the WHO. I also look closely at units designed to reach out to women; to provide information about administration initiatives for women and report on policy impacts on women; and to bring female voices, suggestions, and demands to policy and political discussion. Although the Office of Public Engagement and Intergovernmental Affairs and at least one of the entities it oversees—the Council on Women and Girls (CWG)—have performed well at outreach and information dissemination, they have been less prominent as channels of two-way communication and influence.

After a brief discussion of the chapter's analytic grounding, I trace the background of a White House focus on women and on women's gender concerns more broadly. Then attention turns to women and gender dynamics in the Obama White House, highlighting the evolution and activities of the Office of Public Engagement and the CWG. Finally, I profile Valerie Jarrett and her distinctive role in the White House. Weaving throughout the discussion are questions of whether women have had meaningful influence over actual policy and political decisions in the administration or whether they have been only what Carole Pateman terms "pseudo" or "partial" participants (1970, 67–84).

Analytic Framework

Representation can be probed in numerous ways and along multiple dimensions. Here, following Hanna Pitkin (1967) and others, emphasis pivots around substantive, descriptive, and symbolic representation of and by women in the Obama White House. Substantive representation involves acting in ways consistent with the values, expectations, and interests of those being represented, in this case, women and girls. Descriptive representation taps the extent to which staffers "possess the same physical and social characteristics [and] have shared experiences" with those being represented (Alexander and Jalalzai 2014). It "allocates power by determining who will be considered in deliberations, negotiations, and decisions" (Borrelli 2011, 11); it arguably "enhances the substance of representation of interests by improving the quality of deliberation" (Mansbridge 1999, 628). Finally, symbolic representation expresses a complex, often abstract, idea and emotional commitment; in this context, it is presidential support for and acknowledgment of the significance of female involvement in politics and governance (e.g., Borrelli 2011, 198; Pitkin 1967, chap. 5).

It must be reiterated that such representational dimensions likely are related to and reinforce one another (Schwindt-Bayer 2010). Meanwhile, concerns with intersectionality remind us that sex and gender interact in complex ways with factors like race, class, and sexuality (Bearfield, 2009; Crenshaw 1991).

Women and the White House Office

Over the last several decades, scholars have devoted more serious, systematic attention to the involvement (and exclusion) as well as the influence (and marginalization) of women in and around the presidency. Janet M. Martin (2003), for example, traced women's growing presence in the U.S. executive branch, among presidential supporters and advisers and as advocates and targets of presidential action. She underscores as well the barriers and limits to their full inclusion. Kathryn Dunn Tenpas (1997), also in collaboration with Stephen Hess (Tenpas and Hess 2002), has provided informative data on the descriptive representativeness of the White House staff, spotlighting growth in the proportions of professional women and people of color in recent White Houses. Several other examinations of the staff discuss but do not concentrate on the inclusion of women or on gender representativeness (e.g., Hult and Walcott 2004; Pika 2009).

Individual Women

Like those of its immediate predecessors, Bill Clinton and George W. Bush, the Obama White House has included numerous female profession-als. These have been long-awaited changes in a largely masculine institu-tion like the U.S. presidency (on the executive branch more generally, see Duerst-Lahti 1997, 18). As detailed later, the first senior female presidential staffer, Anne Armstrong, a counselor to the president with cabinet rank, did not appear on the WHO staff listings until 1973, in the Richard Nixon administration. In the Obama White House, numerous women have held senior positions, including assistant to the president (a coveted and rela-tively rare title), national security assistant, chair of the Council of Eco-nomic Advisers, White House counsel, director of the Domestic Policy Council, deputy chief of staff, and chief technology officer. Indeed, in 2015, thirteen of twenty-four senior staffers—all assistants to the president— were female (Jackson 2015).

Although advocates did not succeed in persuading the new adminis-tration to create a separate cabinet-level slot focusing on women, Lynn

Rosenthal, an aide to Vice President Joe Biden dating back to his days in the Senate, was named to a new position, the White House adviser on violence against women, in July 2009, a post she occupied until January 2015. Rosenthal's position was both a powerful symbol and substantive indicator of the attention the president devoted to domestic violence and sexual assault more generally. Many advocates credited her with sustaining a high-level focus on sexual assault, including the first presidential recognition of Sexual Assault Awareness Month, and with pushing for assault provisions in the 2013 reauthorization of the Violence against Women Act (Bendery 2015). Departing for a leadership post with the National Domestic Violence Hotline, Rosenthal was promptly replaced by Caroline Bettinger-Lopez, director of the Human Rights Clinic at the University of Miami Law School and a former social services professional (White House 2015b). This suggests that the significance of the emphasis has persisted beyond its initial advocate. Its longer-term institutionalization in the White House, of course, awaits the next administration.

Despite the challenges of determining the influence of such individuals and the nature of their impact on key policy and political decisions, women's presence throughout the WHO in both Obama's first and second terms indicates considerable gender integration, with women appearing as "full members" of the organization (Borrelli 2010, 737). The policy staffs and counsel's office, for example, are mostly integrated, with women and men in a range of positions in the units with few differences in rank or nature of their jobs (such as policy analyst or associate counsel). However, women are more likely to occupy redistributive policy positions (such as in the areas of health care or education policy) or hold staff positions specializing in female-focused policy like sexual-assault prevention. Administrative/coordinative slots such as staff secretary and deputy chief of staff have also been held by both women and men throughout Obama's tenure. That this has happened under four male chiefs of staff (Rahm Emanuel, William Daley, Jack Lew, and Denis McDonough) indicates the persistence of a "glass ceiling": a woman has never been chief of staff, the post that most consider to be the pinnacle of White House staff, with both political and policy influence. As Georgia Duerst-Lahti has noted, "The term [chief] is seldom associated with traditional women's work" (1997, 21).

As in past administrations, women have been somewhat more visible in outreach and boundary-spanning positions in communications, media affairs, and public liaison (see Tenpas 1997). Such jobs in and of themselves, of course, can be important for symbolic and substantive as well as descriptive representation, as illustrated in the next section. Waiting further verification, however, is concrete policy impact of such representation.

Beyond Individuals

Many examinations of representation appropriately focus on individuals' identification, activities, and formal titles. For example, that a female staffer has explicit responsibilities for "Hispanic media" acknowledges the distinctiveness and significance of such outlets (intertwining symbolic and descriptive representation), while highlighting (potential) responsiveness to the concerns and objectives of Latinas/Latinos (intertwining symbolic and substantive representation). In addition, organizational structures and processes also have representational features and implications. As MaryAnne Borrelli reminds us, for example, the president's spouse "performs public liaison tasks," and associated expectations have contributed to the emergence, institutionalization, and specialization of the Office of the First Lady (Borrelli 2011, 5, 18; see also Burrell 1997).

Along similar lines, administrations since at least Franklin Roosevelt's have placed individual aides and units charged with outreach to specific interests and constituencies in the "West Wing." Formal White House structuring for outreach to organized constituencies emerged in the 1940s; such initiatives went beyond individuals serving as informal liaisons to, for example, business executives or religious denominations. Scholars trace these arrangements to the David Niles (and later Philleo Nash) operation in the FDR and Truman presidencies, continuing to the establishment of public liaison units under Nixon and his successors, and culminating in the new Office of Public Engagement under Obama (see, e.g., Hult and Walcott 2004; Pika 2009; Walcott and Hult 1995). As the diversity and number of interests exploded in the 1960s and 1970s, administrations engaged in numerous strategies for gathering input, protecting presidential time and political autonomy, mobilizing support, and quelling opposition.

Individual positions and units devoted to explicit representation of women did not appear in the WHO until the late 1960s under President Nixon. Earlier, President John F. Kennedy appointed Esther Peterson, a longtime representative of labor, to be assistant secretary of labor and direct the department's Women's Bureau. Peterson worked to help pass the Equal Pay Act of 1963 and was among those who urged Kennedy to create the President's Commission on the Status of Women. Following Kennedy's assassination, Lyndon Johnson named her to an additional post on the White House staff as special assistant for consumer affairs. Indeed, continuing an initiative from the Kennedy administration, some of the Johnson administration's efforts to boost representation of women revolved around highlighting consumer issues (Martin 2003; Walcott and Hult 1995).

Nevertheless, throughout the 1960s, riding the crest of the second wave of feminism, clamor mounted for the appointment of women to more senior and more visible posts in the federal executive branch and for greater substantive policy responses to women's problems and perspectives. Nixon did not heed the recommendation of the President's Task Force on Women's Rights and Responsibilities to name an assistant for women's rights, but he did appoint Anne Armstrong to the most senior WHO position held by a woman until Karen Hughes under George W. Bush. Armstrong, the outgoing cochair of the Republican National Committee, had the title and position of counselor to the president with cabinet rank; she served as "liaison with grassroots party members" and, in effect, was an assistant for women's affairs (Hult and Walcott 2004, 84). She and her small staff of two professionals, however, quickly became overloaded with myriad outreach tasks, most of which did not explicitly involve representing women. Even so, Janet M. Martin finds that Armstrong contributed to all three dimensions of representation: more than a "symbol of the representation of women in the administration," Armstrong "brought a new perspective to White House deliberations which was important both in terms of ensuring that names of women were included on lists of candidates for vacant positions . . . and that issues of concern to women were brought to the table" (2003, 159–160). Moreover, she was among the earliest professional women staffers with direct access to the president. Meanwhile, personnel chief Fred Malek initially assigned his assistant, Barbara Franklin, to identify possible female appointees to executive branch positions. As the 1972 election approached, Franklin pivoted to overseeing "outreach efforts directed at women" (Hult and Walcott 2004, 84).

Such efforts at establishing and maintaining ties with women—as voters, as consumers, and in other roles—continued into the Ford administration. As Ford assumed the presidency following Nixon's resignation in 1974, he sought to reengage with Congress and the numerous constituencies in the American public. The Office of Public Liaison (OPL) was established formally in September 1974 to house a wide variety of White House staff liaisons, including those to consumers, women, and African Americans. Like those of its predecessors, most of OPL's activities focused on outreach, with few promises of substantive policy input or influence.

Since the Nixon presidency, women on occasion have received focused attention in the White House but often in terms of traditional gender roles that mark them as consumers, mothers, or housewives. Although both national party organizations continue to have women's sections (in 2015, "RNC Women" and the Democratic "Women's Leadership Forum"), the Clinton White House sought to build support among women more generally, especially following the early 1990s health-care debacle and the disastrous (for

Democrats) 1994 midterm elections. In June 1995, the administration created the White House Office for Women's Initiatives and Outreach (OWIO) "to better serve and listen to [President Clinton's] constituents." According to its website, the unit sought to link "the White House and women's organizations, listening to women's concerns and proposals and bringing these ideas to the President and others in the Administration" (Office for Women's Initiatives and Outreach 1995). The OWIO sponsored numerous events and roundtables and established relationships with a range of external organizations. These efforts mostly involved symbolic representation, providing a dedicated channel to the president and underscoring the importance of women. At the outset, the unit promised potential substantive representation as well: it "was initially successful at connecting with women's groups and in translating . . . findings to the president" (Norton and Morris 2003, 478). Yet following the 1996 election and organizational and staff changes, the OWIO's activities declined, and it ultimately "became invisible to the women's community and to the president himself" (478).

When Republican George W. Bush entered the White House, the OWIO was among the three units that he decided to abolish. The addition of offices of Strategic Initiatives and Faith-Based and Community Initiatives evidently highlighted the seeming distance of staffing arrangements from the new president's "W is for Women" campaign slogan. Even so, Bush "appointed more women to more influential positions" than any of his predecessors (Tenpas and Hess 2002, 39).

The challenges of—and the varying organizational arrangements for—representing women in and by the presidency clearly had not disappeared. Even as Democratic and Republican presidents responded to differing electoral coalitions and pressures, administrations of both parties sought to position themselves as accessible to and symbolically representative of varying values and interests of (at least some) women.

OPL to OPE: Old Wine in New Bottles?

These dynamics continued in the Obama administration. The creation of the Office of Public Engagement (OPE) on May 11, 2009, can be seen both as an effort to rebrand a unit with a somewhat sullied reputation for manipulation by and of external interests and as an initial vehicle to mobilize support for what would become the Affordable Care Act (see White House 2009). More generally, the OPE appears distinctive in several ways. First, it includes staffers with explicit ties to organizations that had links to previous White House staffs (e.g., organized labor), to advocacy organizations (e.g., American Farm Bureau, Ploughshares Fund), and to communities and groups throughout society (e.g., Arab Americans, LGBT individuals, seniors). Second, it houses the White House Council on Women and Girls, only the third such unit with a specific focus on women, placed in the Executive Office of the President. In addition, OPE staffers participate in varied efforts at outreach through social media; for example, the "social hub" includes links to Twitter, Facebook, YouTube, and others. Unlike in most prior administrations, a senior adviser and assistant to the president, Valerie Jarrett, directs the unit. The OPE is part of a larger entity that includes responsibilities for intergovernmental affairs, an office that had appeared in White Houses dating back to the Eisenhower administration (Walcott and Hult 1995, 134). Placing intergovernmental affairs within a prominent unit headed by Jarrett (a senior aide who had been a deputy chief of staff to Chicago mayor Richard M. Daley) signaled the new administration's systematic attention to issues of federalism; these were key concerns in the wake of the difficulties exposed by Hurricane Katrina and the crucial role for states that the administration envisioned in health-care reform.[2]

Throughout the Obama years, between eighteen and twenty-five professional staffers worked in the public liaison/public engagement and intergovernmental affairs offices at any one time, with somewhat more than half handling public engagement. The offices appeared to be gender integrated. Between 2009 and July 1, 2015, for example, fifty-nine individuals were listed in the White House's annual reports to Congress on staffing, thirty-seven of whom were women. Senior Advisor and Assistant to the President Jarrett directed the unit. Directors of the offices included both women and men; as of August 2015 two women and one man have directed the OPE, and the intergovernmental affairs office has had one man and one woman director (White House 2010, 2011, 2012, 2013, 2014, 2015a).

Calling itself "the open front door to the White House," the "friendlier" OPE sought to "allow ordinary Americans to offer their stories and ideas regarding issues that concern them and share their views on important topics" (Olopade 2009, 27). As discussed later, the OPE claimed "responsibility for 'crowdsourcing of ideas,'" requesting, first, submissions to a "suggestion box" and, later, the creation and signing of "petitions" on various policy ideas (Katz, Barris, and Jain 2013, 86; We the People, n.d.). OPE staffers' representation tasks have also included serving on interagency task forces such as the White House Rural Council (Executive Order 13575, 2011) and the Council on Native American Affairs (Executive Order No. 13647, 2013); they have collaborated on the White House Initiative on Asian Americans and Pacific Islanders (Hune and Kagawa-Singer 2011). Senior OPE staffers represented the president at the funeral of Michael Brown in Ferguson, Missouri. Much of the unit's work included using digital and social media to promote key administration policies like signing up for health insurance coverage, addressing domestic violence, moving toward immigration reform, and increasing the federal minimum wage (e.g., Eilperin 2015).

Such efforts were highlighted by the launching of the We the People website in September 2011, along with shifting the OPE website to the domain whitehouse.gov/engage (Campbell 2015). This new web presence sought to support administration objectives of transparency and open government. In an effort to solicit citizen input, for example, "'We the People' served as an online tool that allowed individuals to sign or initiate petitions. If a petition garnered sufficient support, the White House staff agreed to review it, send it to the appropriate policy experts and provide an official response" (Katz, Barris, and Jain 2013, 90). Despite the strong initial response and ongoing media coverage, few of the petitions have garnered more than several hundred signatures, and even fewer seem to explicitly address serious matters of particular concern to or focus on women. This in turn suggests that whether or not petitioners are asking for actions that directly affect women or gender concerns more broadly, the web links have contributed little to substantive representation.

Council on Women and Girls

Similar to the Clinton administration's placement of the Office for Women's Initiatives and Outreach in the Office of Public Liaison (Norton and Morris 2003), the Obama Council on Women and Girls is lodged in the OPE. Established by Executive Order 13506 on March 11, 2009, the council is chaired by Valerie Jarrett. It includes representatives of departments and agencies in the executive branch as well as in the Executive Office of the President; the number of members listed increased slightly between 2009 and 2015, but presidential assistants for domestic and for economic policy notably were *not* included in the later listings. The council's stated purpose is to "provide a coordinated Federal response to issues that have a distinct impact on the lives of women and girls" and to make policy recommendations and suggestions. It also has been directed to "conduct outreach with representatives of nonprofit organizations," elected officials, and state and local government agencies (Executive Order No. 13506, 2009). Considerably less clear are the extent and seriousness of the involvement of its formal members and whether their efforts have produced careful consideration of the concerns of many females, in the United States and elsewhere. (For further discussion of how various foreign-policy and development-policy actions result in change because of top-down and bottom-up leadership, see Chapter 11.)

Even so, council members have been involved in numerous activities, including engaging in outreach to women's organizations, serving on relevant interagency committees, and preparing reports on matters of contemporary importance. Members "fought for passage of the Affordable Care Act" and continued to stress "equal pay for women" (Jarrett and Tchen 2011, iv). The council addressed sexual assault on college campuses (A. Davis 2015; Geoff 2014) and in the U.S. military (Shane 2013). The council fielded a representative to the interagency working group created to address "gender-based violence" around the world (Executive Order No. 13623, 2012), an effort coordinated by deputy assistant to the president and later ambassador-at-large for women's issues Catherine M. Russell. In addition, the CWG has hosted women's entrepreneurship and other conferences focused on women. Among its most visible products has been "Women in America: Indicators of Social and Economic Well-Being," produced with the Office of Management and Budget (OMB), the Budget and Economics and Statistics Administration (in the Commerce Department), and other executive branch agencies. The "first comprehensive federal report on women since 1963," the document presented quantitative indicators and summaries of the status of U.S. women in areas such as education, employment, health, violence and crime, and demographic and household changes ("White House Releases" 2011; see also U.S. Department of Commerce and Executive Office of the President 2011).

For the most part, the council's efforts encompass both symbolic representation, highlighting the critical nature of the issues affecting females, and ways of addressing a host of those concerns in substantive policy terms. Even so, placement of the CWG in the outreach/liaison orbit of the WHO (which Noelle Norton and Barbara Morris call "a public relations branch" [2003, 482]) rather than, for example, in the Office of Policy Development or as a freestanding unit also reveals its lower ranking among policy priorities. The disappearance of policy staffers from the list of council participants is consistent with weaker substantive representation.

Perhaps a related signal is CWG executive director Tina Tchen's eventual naming as chief of staff to First Lady Michelle Robinson Obama. Indeed, the close links between the OPE and the Office of the First Lady suggest both proximity to power and the possible gender segregation of women's and girls' concerns. The OPE website, for example, spotlights Michelle Obama's initiatives, "Let's Move!" and (with Dr. Jill Biden) "Joining Forces." Generally less controversial, these programs focus on children and on more traditional families, identifying women primarily as mothers and wives.

In sum, the Council on Women and Girls is an explicit presidential acknowledgment of the political and policy significance of females. Its accomplishments, however, are more ambiguous. Its participants and activities have enhanced descriptive representation; perhaps especially in the global context and in heightening attention to gender-based violence, it has been an important vehicle for symbolic representation. Less immediately evident are more substantive policy impacts. Of concern as well is the possibility that some of the council's activities and emphases may reinforce gender-role stereotypes.

Valerie Jarrett

Valerie Jarrett deserves particular attention, given her status among the highest-ranking women and staffers in the Obama White House. At the outset of the administration, she was one of three senior advisers to the president, along with David Axelrod and Peter Rouse. She alone, however, continued to serve well into the second term. By August 2015, she shared the senior adviser spotlight with Brian Deese (who "oversee[s] climate, conservation and energy policy and advis[es] the President on a range of domestic and international policy issues" [White House, n.d., "Senior Advisor Brian Deese"]). Contemporary White Houses, including Obama's, frequently are cast as being driven by public relations and outreach emphases and strategies. These, of course, are among Jarrett's strengths and primary responsibilities. At the same time, the public distinctions drawn between Jarrett's and Deese's tasks also mirror Tenpas's observation that men tend to be placed in the highest policy positions (1997, 100).

Yet Jarrett's activities are more varied and complicated than a simple politics/policy dichotomy may suggest. Her "large portfolio" has included overseeing the Office of Public Engagement and Intergovernmental Affairs and serving as liaison to the business community (Axelrod 2015, 329; see also Draper 2009; O'Sullivan 2013; White House, n.d., "Senior Advisor Valerie Jarrett"). According to David Axelrod, the president "made it clear he wanted [her] at his side in the White House. She was fiercely loyal, and he felt she brought an invaluable perspective as an African American woman to an operation dominated by white men. She would also serve as a conduit to the First Lady" (2105, 328). Obama has told journalists that "he consults Jarrett on every major decision, something current and former aides corroborate" (Scheiber 2014). Similarly, *New York Times* reporter Jo Becker observes that "her unmatched access to the Obamas has made her a driving force in some of the most important domestic policy decisions" of the first term (2012, A1). As "the president's liaison to gay voters," Jarrett reportedly was among those who "encouraged" Obama to openly support same-sex marriage (Becker 2014), and she is credited with persuading other professional women to join the staff (J. Davis 2015). Journalists' profiles also note her efforts to interject ideologically liberal ideas and values into White House debate and to help assure that the president is exposed to a range of perspectives (Becker 2012; Draper 2009; Scheiber 2014). More generally, Jarrett has performed all four roles that scholars have associated with White House chiefs of staff, serving as presidential adviser, guardian, administrator, and proxy (e.g., Cohen, Hult, and Walcott 2012).

Much like the presence of Karen Hughes and Condoleezza Rice in the first-term George W. Bush White House, Jarrett's proximity to the Oval Office and to the president highlights important opportunities for symbolic, descriptive, and (at least potentially) substantive representation. Perhaps tellingly as well, Jarrett has been a frequent target, with many inside and outside the White House criticizing her actions and expressing concern about her closeness to and influence over the Obamas. Former colleague David Axelrod made a point of not including her in weekly gatherings at his apartment to discuss electoral strategies (Axelrod 2015; Draper 2009). The 2014 congressional midterm losses triggered a new outflowing of criticism. Generally unfavorable labels of Jarrett abound: "the spy, the chief sycophant, the night stalker, the Obama whisperer, the consigliere, and the human decoder ring." Of course, such "complaints about presidential advisers have a long tradition" (Henderson 2014), as negative commentary about aides like Harry Hopkins (Franklin Roosevelt), Sherman Adams (Dwight Eisenhower), H. R. Haldeman (Richard Nixon), Hamilton Jordan (Jimmy Carter), Michael Deaver (Ronald Reagan), Karl Rove (George W. Bush), and others underscore. Yet former Obama counselor John Podesta has called a good deal of the vitriol aimed at Jarrett a "sexist attack" (Henderson 2014; see also Brzezinski 2015; Capehart 2014). Rita Mae Kelly and Georgia Duerst-Lahti might find evidence as well of the persistent "symbolic gender biases of political institutions" like the presidency (1995, 270).

Still others would underscore the racial dimension of such criticism. Similar gender and racial biases have enmeshed First Lady Michelle Robinson Obama. Despite her significant educational and professional accomplishments, she has moved carefully from being cast as an "angry black woman" to being the "Mom-in-chief." Only after her husband's reelection has the first lady spoken more forthrightly about the "myths" and constraints of race and sex (e.g., Baker 2015).

Reactions to Valerie Jarrett may capture a discomfort and distrust that at least some white people and some males harbor toward both high-achieving African Americans (including Barack Obama) and high-ranking, influential professional women. In turn, hers may be a cautionary tale for those who believe that descriptive representation readily translates into productive symbolic and substantive representativeness.

Conclusion

Like its immediate predecessors, the two-term Obama White House has seen considerable continuity and change. A unit for involving and mobilizing external interests, organizations, and individuals continues, albeit with a different name. Women again have a dedicated office, once more lodged in a "public relations" setting, with other key constituencies. A longtime, senior presidential adviser with broad responsibilities is a woman, as are other top officials such as National Security Adviser Susan Rice. Under Obama and the OPE, efforts at outreach, collaboration, and engagement with women have diversified and multiplied.

Somewhat less clear are the implications of these political, policy, and administrative arrangements for women's representation. It appears that descriptive and symbolic representativeness is quite high. Descriptive representation of women—of differing races, ethnicities, ages, and sexualities, in professional positions, at varying hierarchical levels, and in diverse areas—has continued in the Obama White House, including in the OPE. Clearly, this carries powerful symbolic messages as well. Some of these signals are complicated by the tone and volume of the attention to Valerie Jarrett as an individual and by the overlap and seeming blurring between the OPE and the Office of the First Lady. At the very least "the political and gender boundaries within the White House Office" (Borrelli 2011, 60) appear subject to continual shifting and some contention. Also rising to the surface may be reinscribed gender binaries, such as those defining women as mothers and wives (Duerst-Lahti 1997, 13).

The impacts on substantive representation are even more difficult to pinpoint. The encompassing scope of the OPE, its connections with subnational officials, and its ties to more senior White House aides and executive agencies evidently provide access to policy makers and possible input into policy decisions. Whether such outreach channels systematically influence actions (an indicator of more substantive representation) is less apparent, particularly for those who must judge decision making from the outside. Unclear as well is whether specific individuals or units who seek to shape policy or advance particular values and objectives reflect the aspirations and concerns of classes, ages, abilities, races, and ethnicities of women who are not directly present.

In the Obama White House, staffers of both sexes have complained about being closed out of presidential meetings where decisions are made. Some have expressed concern that women and girls have been excluded from significant presidential initiatives. The signature "My Brother's Keeper" program (with President Obama's direct involvement), for instance, was placed under cabinet secretary Broderick Johnson, who worked with Marlon Marshall, deputy director of the OPE. It focuses on at-risk men and boys of color, seeking to improve their opportunities. The program's initial public-private partnership raised over three hundred million dollars in its first year, and it has been supplemented by a nonprofit organization, My Brother's Keeper

Alliance (A. Davis 2015). (See Chapter 3 for further discussion of the My Brother's Keeper initiative.) Despite suggestions by several African American men's groups and numerous feminists that these efforts be expanded to include girls and women, the White House responded—via Valerie Jarrett—that the Council on Women and Girls was an appropriate place for attention to females (Crenshaw 2015; Henderson 2014). To some, this suggests that the concerns of females are of lower priority or that their needs, aspirations, and demands are defined to be "different" and hence compartmentalized. Once more, this may be evidence of gender binaries and of regendering, as enduring gender roles and even stereotypes are reinforced.

Perhaps more persuasive are contentions that the Obama administration's attention to women's representation has focused more on outreach, information gathering and dissemination, and mobilization than on incorporating what it learns into policy deliberation and decision making. On the one hand, it has dramatically "increased access to participatory venues" (Bryer 2011, 6). Through social media and other tools, the administration has collected public opinion and other information from users and also assembled and reported the results. On the other hand, little evidence suggests that such materials and involvement have meaningfully influenced policy (Katz, Barris, and Jain 2013; Olopade 2009). In its pursuit of public participation and transparency, the administration evidently has achieved something close to "partial participation" but not full engagement in or substantial influence over decisions (Pateman 1970). Indeed, observers like Thomas Bryer (2011) worry about the emergence and subsequent deflation of a "democracy bubble" when heightened participatory access raises expectations that then are not fulfilled. Others are concerned that "many participants may find fulfillment in 'just being involved' and 'being heard' by someone in authority" (Katz, Barris, and Jain 2013, 95), so that "symbolic interactivity [becomes] a substitute for substantive engagement" (159).

Influence on political and policy decisions is notoriously difficult to unravel and isolate. Many may never be fully evident. Even as women inch ever closer to the presidential "inner circle" (Martin 2003, 58), evidence of their policy influence and substantive representation remains elusive.

NOTES
1. Valerie Jarrett's title, senior advisor and assistant to the president for intergovernmental affairs and public engagement, has sometimes created the misunderstanding that the Office of Public Engagement and the Office of Intergovernmental Affairs are a single office—the so-called Office of Public Engagement and Intergovernmental Affairs—but these are two, distinct offices. Adding to the misunderstanding, for instance, the *2015–2016 Official Congressional Directory, 114th Congress* (2016, 596) lists an "Office of Public Engagement and Intergovernmental Affairs" in its directory of White House offices. References such as this notwithstanding, the Office of Public Engagement and the

Office of Intergovernmental Affairs are distinct subunits. The combined name is used in this chapter for ease of reference to both offices.

2. Valerie Jarrett was named senior advisor and assistant to the president for intergovernmental affairs and public liaison in January 2009. In previous administrations, there had been separate offices for intergovernmental affairs and public liaison, and at the time of Jarrett's appointment, an Office of Public Engagement had yet to be created. As noted, the prioritization in the title given Jarrett, with "intergovernmental affairs" listed first, was of symbolic as well as substantive importance, especially given the significant role states were to play in regard to health-care reform.

The White House established the OPE acronym in May 2009 for the Office of Public Engagement; it refers only to this office. An acronym for the Office of Intergovernmental Affairs has not been designated. Instead, the Obama administration has referred to the Office of Intergovernmental Affairs in various ways, such as OPE-IGA or OPE/IGA (see, e.g., White House, n.d., "Presidential Department Descriptions").

REFERENCES

Alexander, Amy, and Farida Jalalzai. 2014. "The Symbolic Effects of Female Heads of State and Government." Paper presented at the annual meeting of the American Political Science Association, Washington, DC, August.

Axelrod, David. 2015. *Believer: My Forty Years in Politics*. New York: Penguin Books.

Baker, Peter. 2015. "Michelle Obama Talks about Race and Success, and Makes It Personal." *New York Times*, June 10. Available at http://www.nytimes.com/2015/06/11/us/michelle-obama-king-college-prep-and-tuskegee-graduation-speeches.html?partner=Bloomberg.

Bearfield, Dominic A. 2009. "Equity at the Intersection: Public Administration and the Study of Gender." *Public Administration Review* 69 (3): 383–386.

Becker, Jo. 2012. "The Other Power in the West Wing." *New York Times*, September 2, p. A1.

———. 2014. "How the President Got to 'I Do' on Same-Sex Marriage." *New York Times Magazine*, April 16. Available at http://www.nytimes.com/2014/04/20/magazine/how-the-president-got-to-i-do-on-same-sex-marriage.html.

Bendery, Jennifer. 2015. "White House Loses Top Adviser on Violence against Women." *Huffington Post*, January 16. Available at http://www.huffingtonpost.com/2015/01/16/white-house-violence-against-women_n_6488456.html.

Borrelli, MaryAnne. 2010. "Gender Desegregation and Gender Integration in the President's Cabinet, 1933–2010." *Presidential Studies Quarterly* 40 (4): 734–749.

———. 2011. *The Politics of the President's Wife*. College Station: Texas A&M University Press.

Bryer, Thomas A. 2011. "Online Public Engagement in the Obama Administration: Building a Democracy Bubble?" *Policy & Internet* 3 (4): 1–22.

Brzezinski, Mika. 2015. "Valerie Jarrett Deserves Credit, Not Sexist Attacks." *MSNBC Morning Joe*, January 23. Available at http://www.msnbc.com/morning-joe/valerie-jarrett-deserves-credit-not-sexist-attacks.

Burrell, Barbara C. 1997. "The Office of the First Lady and Public Policymaking." In *The Other Elites: Women, Politics, and Power in the Executive Branch*, edited by MaryAnne Borrelli and Janet M. Martin, 169–187. Boulder, CO: Lynne Rienner.

Campbell, Leah C. 2015. "Why Taking the White House Online Does Not Make It More Accessible to the Public." *Student Pulse* 7 (2). Available at http://www.studentpulse.com/a?id=989.

Capehart, Jonathan. 2014. "The Problem with Valerie Jarrett." *Washington Post*, November 10. Available at https://www.washingtonpost.com/blogs/post-partisan/wp/2014/11/10/the-problem-with-valerie-jarrett/.

Clark, Ronald C., Jr., Holona LeAnne Ochs, and Michael Frazier. 2013. "Representative Bureaucracy: The Politics of Access to Policy-Making Positions in the Federal Executive Service." *Public Personnel Management* 42 (1): 75–89.

Cohen, David, Karen M. Hult, and Charles E. Walcott. 2012. "The Chicago Clan: The First Chiefs of Staff in the Obama White House." *Social Science Quarterly* 93 (5): 1101–1126.

Crenshaw, Kimberlé. 1991. "Mapping the Margins: Intersectionality, Identity Politics, and Violence against Women of Color." *Stanford Law Review* 43 (July): 1241–1299.

———. 2015. "Black Girls Matter." *Ms.* 25 (2): 26–29.

Davis, Aaron C. 2015. "Obama Launches My Brother's Keeper Alliance to Help Young Men of Color." *Washington Post*, May 4. Available at https://www.washingtonpost.com/politics/obama-launches-my-brothers-keeper-alliance-to-help-young-men-of-color/2015/05/04/405fd47c-f286-11e4-bcc4-e8141e5eb0c9_story.html.

Davis, Julie Hirschfeld. 2015. "Adviser Guides Obamas into the Google Age." *New York Times*, January 3. Available at http://www.nytimes.com/2015/01/04/us/politics/her-task-weaning-the-white-house-off-floppy-disks.html.

Dolan, Julie. 2002. "Representative Bureaucracy in the Federal Executive: Gender and Spending Priorities." *Journal of Public Administration and Theory* 12 (3): 353–375.

Draper, Robert. 2009. "The Ultimate Obama Insider." *New York Times Magazine*, July 21. Available at http://www.nytimes.com/2009/07/26/magazine/26jarrett-t.html.

Duerst-Lahti, Georgia. 1997. "Reconceiving Theories of Power: Consequences of Masculinism in the Executive Branch." In *The Other Elites: Women, Politics, and Power in the Executive Branch*, edited by MaryAnne Borrelli and Janet M. Martin, 11–32. Boulder, CO: Lynne Rienner.

Eilperin, Juliet. 2015. "Here's How the First President of the Social Media Age Has Chosen to Connect with Americans." *Washington Post*, May 26. Available at https://www.washingtonpost.com/news/politics/wp/2015/05/26/heres-how-the-first-president-of-the-social-media-age-has-chosen-to-connect-with-americans/.

Executive Order No. 13506 [Establishing a White House Council on Women and Girls]. 2009. 74 Federal Register 11271, March 11.

Executive Order No. 13575 [Establishment of the White House Rural Council]. 2011. 76 Federal Register 34839, June 9.

Executive Order No. 13623 [Preventing and Responding to Violence against Women and Girls Globally]. 2012. 77 Federal Register 49345, August 10.

Executive Order No. 13647 [Establishing the White House Council on Native American Affairs]. 2013. 78 Federal Register 39539, June 26.

Geoff, Earle. 2014. "Bam Targets College Rape." *New York Post*, January 23, p. 20.

Henderson, Nia-Malika. 2014. "Jarrett: Five Myths about Longtime White House Adviser Valerie Jarrett." *Newsday*, November 14. Available at http://www.newsday.com/opinion/oped/jarrett-five-myths-about-longtime-white-house-adviser-valerie-jarrett-1.9618143.

Hult, Karen M., and Charles E. Walcott. 2004. *Empowering the White House: Governance under Nixon, Ford, and Carter.* Lawrence: University Press of Kansas.

Hune, Shirley, and Marjorie Kagawa-Singer. 2011. "Closing the Research and Data Gap in Order to Serve Asian Americans and Pacific Islanders Better." *AAPI Nexus: Policy, Practice and Community* 9 (1–2): vii–xii.

Jackson, David. 2015. "Obama's Staff: 13 Women, 11 Men." *USA Today*, April 16. Available at http://www.usatoday.com/story/theoval/2015/04/16/obama-white-house-staff-jen -psaki/25865279/.

Jalalzai, Farida. 2008. "Women Rule: Shattering the Executive Glass Ceiling." *Politics & Gender* 4 (2): 205–231.

Jarrett, Valerie, and Tina Tchen. 2011. "Helping Women Reach Their Economic Potential." *Washington Post*, September 25. Available at https://www.washingtonpost .com/opinions/helping-women-reach-their-economic-potential/2011/09/25/gIQA1d ODxK_story.html.

Katz, James E., Michael Barris, and Anshul Jain. 2013. *The Social Media President: Barack Obama and the Politics of Digital Engagement*. New York: Palgrave Macmillan.

Kelly, Rita Mae, and Georgia Duerst-Lahti. 1995. "Toward Awareness and Gender Balance in Leadership and Governance." In *Gender Power, Leadership and Governance*, edited by Georgia Duerst-Lahti and Rita Mae Kelly, 259–271. Ann Arbor: University of Michigan Press.

Mansbridge, Jane. 1999. "Should Blacks Represent Blacks and Women Represent Women? A Contingent 'Yes.'" *Journal of Politics* 61 (3): 628–657.

Martin, Janet M. 2003. *The Presidency and Women: Promise, Performance, and Illusion*. College Station: Texas A&M University Press.

Norton, Noelle, and Barbara Morris. 2003. "Feminist Organizational Structure in the White House: The Office of Women's Initiatives and Outreach." *Political Research Quarterly* 56 (4): 477–487.

Office for Women's Initiatives and Outreach. 1995. "White House Office for Women's Initiatives and Outreach." Available at http://clinton2.nara.gov/WH/EOP/Women/ OWIO/.

Olopade, Dayo. 2009. "Charm Offensive: How the White House Manages the Expectations of Its Base." *American Prospect* 20 (6): 27–30.

O'Sullivan, Jim. 2013. "The Valerie Jarrett Moment." *National Journal*, February 16, p. 12.

Pateman, Carole. 1970. *Participation and Democratic Theory*. New York: Cambridge University Press.

Pika, Joseph A. 2009. "The White House Office of Public Liaison." *Presidential Studies Quarterly* 39 (3): 549–573.

Pitkin, Hanna Fenichel. 1967. *The Concept of Representation*. Berkeley: University of California Press.

Riccucci, Norma M. 2009. "The Pursuit of Social Equity in the Federal Government: A Road Less Traveled?" *Public Administration Review* 69 (3): 373–382.

Riccucci, Norma M., Gregg G. Van Ryzin, and Huafang Li. 2015. "Representative Bureaucracy and the Willingness to Coproduce: An Experimental Study." *Public Administration Review* 76 (1): 121–130.

Scheiber, Noam. 2014. "The Obama Whisperer: No One Has Understood Valerie Jarrett's Role, until Now." *New Republic*, November 9. Available at https://newrepublic.com/ article/120170/valerie-jarrett-obama-whisperer.

Schwindt-Bayer, Leslie A. 2010. *Political Power and Women's Representation in Latin America*. New York: Oxford University Press.

Shane, Leo, III. 2013. "Sexual Assault in the Military Gets Attention at the White House." *Stars and Stripes*, May 9.

Tenpas, Kathryn Dunn. 1997. "Women on the White House Staff: A Longitudinal Analysis, 1939–1994." In *The Other Elites: Women, Politics, and Power in the Executive*

Branch, edited by MaryAnne Borrelli and Janet M. Martin, 91–106. Boulder, CO: Lynne Rienner.

Tenpas, Kathryn Dunn, and Stephen Hess. 2002. "'The Contemporary Presidency': The Bush White House; First Appraisals." *Presidential Studies Quarterly* 32 (3): 577–585.

2015–2016 Official Congressional Directory, 114th Congress. 2016. Washington, DC: U.S. Government Publishing Office.

U.S. Department of Commerce and Executive Office of the President. 2011. "Women in America: Indicators of Social and Economic Well-Being." March. Available at https://www.whitehouse.gov/sites/default/files/rss_viewer/Women_in_America.pdf.

Walcott, Charles E., and Karen M. Hult. 1995. *Governing the White House: From Hoover through LBJ.* Lawrence: University Press of Kansas.

We the People. n.d. "Introduction." Available at https://petitions.whitehouse.gov/how-why/introduction (accessed May 14, 2016).

White House. n.d. "Presidential Department Descriptions." Available at https://www.whitehouse.gov/participate/internships/departments (accessed May 12, 2016).

———. n.d. "Senior Advisor Brian Deese." Available at https://www.whitehouse.gov/administration/senior-leadership/brian-deese.

———. n.d. "Senior Advisor Valerie Jarrett." Available at https://www.whitehouse.gov/administration/senior-leadership/valerie-jarrett (accessed May 10, 2016).

———. 2009. "President Obama Launches Office of Public Engagement." May 11. Available at https://www.whitehouse.gov/the-press-office/president-obama-launches-office-public-engagement.

———. 2010. "2010 Annual Report to Congress on White House Staff." Available at https://www.whitehouse.gov/briefing-room/disclosures/annual-records/2010.

———. 2011. "2011 Annual Report to Congress on White House Staff." Available at https://www.whitehouse.gov/briefing-room/disclosures/annual-records/2011.

———. 2012. "2012 Annual Report to Congress on White House Staff." Available at https://www.whitehouse.gov/briefing-room/disclosures/annual-records/2012.

———. 2013. "2013 Annual Report to Congress on White House Staff." Available at https://www.whitehouse.gov/briefing-room/disclosures/annual-records/2013.

———. 2014. " 2014 Annual Report to Congress on White House Staff." Available at https://www.whitehouse.gov/briefing-room/disclosures/annual-records/2014.

———. 2015a. "2015 Annual Report to Congress on White House Staff." Available at https://www.whitehouse.gov/briefing-room/disclosures/annual-records/2015.

———. 2015b. "Vice President Biden Announces New White House Advisor on Violence against Women." March 4. Available at https://www.whitehouse.gov/the-press-office/2015/03/04/vice-president-biden-announces-new-white-house-advisor-violence-against-.

"White House Releases First Comprehensive Federal Report on the Status of American Women in Almost 50 Years." 2011. *Policy & Practice* 69 (3): 25.

9

The European Union, Executive Politics, and the Women's Movement in Portugal

The Consequences of Europeanization, 1986 to the Present

DANIELA F. MELO

This chapter investigates the representation of Portuguese women through a study of executive politics, the women's movement, and gender policy making in Portugal since 1986, when the country became a member of the European Union (EU). Over the past three decades, the EU has gradually become a dynamic gender-policy actor, obliging member countries to align their policies and legislation with the European acquis communautaire, *the "body of common rights and obligations that is binding on all the EU member states," on gender. In Portugal, this "Europeanization" has led to the creation and institutionalization of governmental gender actors. This development, however, has been uneven. Conservative prime ministers have often adopted gender legislation in response to EU pressures, but policy implementation has sometimes not occurred until power shifted to the left. This chapter examines the interactions among the prime minister and cabinet (the center of executive power), the women's movement, and the parties to better understand why (and how) executive officials ostensibly provide women with representation, adopting policy congruent with the* acquis communautaire, *even as they resist implementing that same policy.*

The prime minister of Portugal faces two challenges in setting gender policy: external pressure from the European Union (EU) and internal pressure from women's organizations. This power struggle adds a layer of complexity to policy making for a prime minister who, though in a centralized state with a strong executive system, also confronts external pressures for decentralization of powers in the government.

In this chapter, I investigate how Europeanization affects Portuguese prime ministers and women's organizations in the process of defining and implementing gender policy.[1] I argue that Portuguese prime ministers have adapted to EU expectations while resisting pressures to decentralize policy-making powers over gender policy. The executive's establishment of a state feminism agency in Portugal provides compelling evidence in support of this contention.[2]

The EU provides a particularly interesting context for national executives, who often become wedged between internal and external pressures to change gender regimes. A significant number of studies have focused primarily on how political executives adapt to EU pressures, transforming their gender-equality policies and legislation to align with the European *acquis communautaire*, the "body of common rights and obligations that is binding on all the EU member states" (European Commission 2012). Some scholars have proposed that this "Europeanization" is often synonymous with a diminishing and dispersing of executive power. However, fewer have examined how executives can simultaneously adapt while also resisting pressures for power sharing on gender policy making and remaining distant from the women's movement. Portugal provides an excellent case study to analyze the extent to which this process occurs and to consider the implications for executive power in relation to nonstate actors, like the women's movement.[3] To illustrate this point, I discuss the interaction between prime ministers and women's organizations that culminated with the legalization of abortion in 2007.

Portugal has a strong, centralized executive, led by prime ministers who have historically maintained weak or no ties with women's organizations.[4] Yet in the 1970s and early 1980s, as the country prepared for EU membership, and in the years that followed, Portugal often demonstrated high degrees of party-elite responsiveness to EU recommendations and directives (Ruivo et al. 2012). In sum, Portuguese political executives have become legal entrepreneurs on gender policy and enthusiastic Europeanists, but their relations with the women's movement have not become more cooperative. Ultimately, the Portuguese executive has centralized and strengthened its power, positioning prime ministers and their selected ministers as the principal arbiters of domestic gender-regime transformation and subordinating the state feminism agency to executive agendas. At the same time, paradoxically, these executive strategies have created opportunities for women's organizations to become relatively stronger domestic actors.

In this chapter, I first discuss some expectations in the literature regarding the relationship between Europeanization, the executive, and women's organizations, including an explanation of the structure of the Portuguese executive and a brief overview of the Portuguese women's movement and its relationship with the executive. In a case study of abortion policy, I analyze how Portuguese prime ministers have responded to internal and external pressures to share power in gender policy making since the revolution of 1974–1976. Finally, I discuss how Portuguese executives have adapted to, but also resisted, internal and external pressures to share power over gender policy.

Europeanization, National Executives, and Women's Groups

Europeanization is an ongoing process through which EU member states are compelled to change domestic institutions, legislation, regulation, procedures, and norms in response to EU-level pressures (Börzel and Risse 2000). The aim of this analysis is not to explore all the possible levels at which Europeanization affects the Portuguese executive. Instead, the focus is on two aspects: (1) Portuguese prime ministers' responses to internal (women's movement) and external (EU directives and norms) pressures to meet the *acquis* on gender equality and (2) the extent to which Europeanization has affected the leverage of the women's movement in relation to the executive.

Some theoretical approaches to Europeanization suggest that the impact of Europeanization on national executives is mediated by the degree to which power is centralized in the executive. The argument follows that in centralized states with strong executives, such as Portugal, the executive is often rendered weaker by integrating into European structures. This happens because Europeanization creates pressures to share power both upward (with the EU) and downward (with nonstate actors, such as the women's movement, or regional governments) (Banaszak, Beckwith, and Rucht 2003; Jessop 1994; Schmidt 2002). However, in countries such as Portugal, where the women's movement has not secured strong representation or an alliance with the parties in the executive, executives have few incentives to be responsive to women's interests. In this situation, we would expect women's organizations to seek alternative (or indirect) routes to pressure the executive, both transnationally and domestically.

Transnationally, to gain support in pressuring the executive, Portuguese women's organizations should have become more dynamic in their pursuit of alliances within EU institutions (e.g., the European Women's Lobby) and with similar organizations in other European countries (e.g., Spanish feminist organizations) (Imig and Tarrow 2001; Keck and Sikkink 1998; Sikkink 2005). Domestically, Portuguese women's organizations should have crafted "velvet triangles," informal channels consisting of strategic partnerships between three types of actors: (1) women's organizations and/or other nongovernmental organizations, (2) femocrats (feminist bureaucrats) and/or feminist politicians, and (3) experts and academics (Holli 2008; Woodward 2004). Cumulatively, these alliances could be expected to enhance gender policy in national or international contexts (EU) in which opportunities would otherwise be closed by the Portuguese executive.

The Portuguese Executive

Portugal is a semipresidential system, with a president, a prime minister (PM), and a multiparty, unicameral National Assembly. The president and the PM (the premier or PM) are selected in different elections and serve terms of five and four years, respectively. The president is weaker than counterparts in other semipresidential systems.[5] Executive power rests in the hands of the PM, the ministers, and the ministers' deputies (secretários de estado). In Portugal, the executive (the PM and entire cabinet, both ministers and junior ministers) is often referred to as "the government."

Once elected, PMs enjoy great independence to select (and fire) their cabinets (Conselho de Ministros [CM; Council of Ministers]), assign portfolios, and determine the direction of executive policy. The PM presides over the CM, which is tasked with drafting, adopting, and implementing the government's policy. Overall, the PM and selected council ministers have the dual responsibility of conducting the country's "general policy" and functioning as the "highest organ of public administration" (Art. 182 of the Constitution, cited in Cardoso 2000, 78).

Following a constitutional revision in 1982, the president's powers over the policy-making process were decreased (Neto and Lobo 2009; Pinto and Almeida 2009).[6] In turn, PMs have progressively gained power and independence in regard to the presidency and their own parties.[7] PMs have increased their power by centralizing decision-making instruments within the executive branch, to the point that "political decision-making takes place in an inner cabinet, formed around the premier and including most senior party members" (Lobo 2005; Neto and Lobo 2009, 245–246). Since EU accession in 1986, all Portuguese PMs have belonged to one of two parties: the center-left Partido Socialista (PS; Socialist Party) or the center-right Partido Social Democrata (PSD; Social Democratic Party; see Table 9.1). Neither party has had a strong relationship with the women's movement, though over the years the PS has become more responsive than the PSD to women's issues.

**TABLE 9.1: PRIME MINISTERS AND PRESIDENTS
SINCE PORTUGAL JOINED THE EUROPEAN UNION**

Name	Term(s)	Party
Prime ministers		
A. Cavaco Silva	1985–1995	PSD
A. Guterres	1995–2002	PS
J. M. Barroso	2002–2004	PSD
P. Santana Lopes	2004–2005	PSD
J. Sócrates	2005–2011	PS
P. Passos Coelho	2011–2015	PSD
A. Costa	2015–present	PS
Presidents		
M. Soares	1986–1996	PS
J. Sampaio	1996–2006	PS
A. Cavaco Silva	2006–2016	PSD
M. Rebelo de Sousa	2016–present	PSD

Note: Full prime ministerial terms are four years; full presidential terms are five years. Consecutive terms under the same prime minister or president are merged. PSD = Social Democratic Party; PS = Socialist Party.

The Women's Movement and Domestic Gender Dynamics prior to Portugal's Membership in the European Union

For a great part of the twentieth century, Portuguese women lived under a constitution and civil code that enshrined their second-class citizenship. The Constitution of 1933, under the Estado Novo (New State) regime (1926–1974), declared that all citizens except women enjoyed equal access to opportunities, "due to her nature and for the well-being of the family" ("Constituição" 1933, art. 5). The Civil Process Code of 1939 established that the male was the "chief of the family" (*chefe de família*), with the wife as his subordinate (Wall 1995, 437). The right to vote (in the Estado Novo's rigged elections) was extended only to a minority of women who had completed at least high school, while the threshold for men was a basic knowledge of reading and writing. Under this code, professional women—in any "liberal profession" (e.g., lawyers)—could not continue to work after marriage without their husbands' formal consent.[8] Likewise, women were not allowed to acquire a passport, travel, or enter into financial agreements without male parental or spousal agreement (Guimarães 1986; Pimentel 2002). In 1940, the government also signed a concordat with the Roman Catholic Church that rendered religious marriages (which were the vast majority) indissoluble (Cova and Pinto 1997). Women's rights in Portugal changed substantially only after 1976. The Constitution of 1976 established a democratic regime that enshrined male and female equality throughout private and public life, including familial duties, professional achievements, and political participation.

The wave of women's mobilization that began in the late 1960s and continued throughout the 1970s encompassed what were first-wave and second-wave feminist demands in the United States. Similar to U.S. first-wave feminists in the late nineteenth and early twentieth centuries, Portuguese women's groups demanded suffrage, legal emancipation, and equal citizenship, which were granted with the Constitution of 1976. And similar to second-wave feminists in the 1960s and 1970s, they sought sexual and reproductive rights. Their efforts contributed to many of the changes introduced in the Constitution of 1976. Other issues, such as reproductive rights, have been in contention since the revolution.

Starting in the late 1960s, some social-movement organizations, small cooperatives, and professional women's organizations took up these banners in Portugal (Tavares 2000, 2011).[9] One of the earliest women's groups to emerge was the Movimento Democrático de Mulheres (MDM, Women's Democratic Movement). This organization, which peaked in the early 1980s with nearly eleven thousand members, was formed in 1968 within the ranks of the then-illegal Portuguese Communist Party (PCP). During the revolution, they were joined by the small but evocative Movimento de Libertação da Mulher (MLM; Women's Liberation Movement). In 1976, another group came onto the scene, a women's group within the far-left party União Democrática Popular (UDP; Popular Democratic Union): the União de Mulheres Anti-Fascistas e Revolucionárias (UMAR; Union of Anti-fascist and Revolutionary Women).

Thus, from 1974 to 1976, a highly polarized period in Portuguese history, women's groups were either small, local associations without ties to political parties or organizations that owed their origins to radical-left political parties.[10] As a result, women's organizations were disconnected from the center-left and center-right political parties, the PS and the PSD, which would dominate governments and elect PMs in the postrevolutionary democratic period. In turn, the two strongest Portuguese parties did not cultivate a relationship with the women's movement. In fact, the PS and the PSD remained detached and generally resistant to pressures from women's groups to legalize abortion, the main issue driving the movement during that period (Prata 2010; Tavares 2003). Consequently, Portuguese PMs have generally failed to recognize women's organizations as a relevant constituency.

Executive Responses to Top-Down and Bottom-Up Pressures

The postrevolutionary democratic governments in Portugal were markedly pro-European and invested in preparing the country for full membership in the EU. To meet the criteria for accession, Portugal needed to catch up in several economic and social areas, including gender-equality measures. In fact, membership in the EU provided a powerful incentive to align Portuguese legislation with international expectations set by the EU, the United Nations, and the Council of Europe (Rêgo 2012). Facing a strong executive with centralizing tendencies regarding state feminism and gender policy, women's organizations took advantage of existing spaces for networking to build successful interorganizational coalitions. In doing so, they did not necessarily weaken executive power, but they did increase their own power resources.

Institutionalizing State Feminism

One key effort taken to achieve the goal of addressing gaps between the European gender *acquis* and Portuguese practice, and the goal of responding to internal pressures from women's organizations wanting a say in gender policy, was the institutionalization of a state agency for the study, promotion, and implementation of gender-equality policies. That state agency is currently known as Comissão para a Cidadania e Igualdade de Género (CIG; Commission for Citizenship and Gender Equality). In past years, the commission has had different designations: from 1975 to 1991, it was known as Comissão para a Condição Feminina (CCF; Commission on the Feminine Condition), and between 1991 and 2007, it was named Comissão para a Igualdade e para os Direitos das Mulheres (CIDM; Commission for Equality and Women's Rights). To avoid confusion, henceforth I use only the term "commission" when referring to this body.

The commission was intended as an organization that would help the government achieve international standards for gender equality. The law institutionalizing the commission ("Council of Ministers' Law Decree 485/77") stipulated that the PM selected the commission's president, who in turn was charged with setting the commission's agenda. The commission's mandate limited its legislative influence to consultation and prescription on legislation dealing with gender issues (Monteiro 2010, 2013). Thus, the commission's leadership and resources depended directly on the executive, especially on the PM.

Throughout its existence, the commission has been tasked with contributing to the government's formulation of gender policy by serving as a bridge between women's groups and the government. The commission's power was always limited—its recommendations remained nonbinding. And from 2002 to 2005, with the center-right PSD in power, the government sought to regulate the nongovernmental status of women's groups, adding technocratic and bureaucratic hurdles to participation in the commission's section for nongovernmental organizations (NGOs). Yet there were periods when the commission became more influential. Since the late 1990s, for example, the commission has helped develop, implement, and analyze the government's Planos Nacionais (National Plans), which delineate national-level strategies to combat gender discrimination, domestic violence, human trafficking, and other types of discrimination that affect women.

In 2007, under the center-left PS, the commission's structure changed in substantive ways. Its membership was extended to incorporate other types of organizations, including lesbian, gay, bisexual, and transgender (LGBT), migrant, and even religious organizations, such as Cáritas. At the same time, women's party sections were excluded from the commission's NGO section.[11] Thus, the commission ceased to be an organization for state feminism in the strict sense.

For women's organizations, this rebranding and restructuring presented a combination of costs and new opportunities. On the one hand, women's organizations were now competing for funds with more organizations and had to share their agenda with others. Some groups, such as the Women's Democratic Movement, viewed the commission's new focus on citizenship and the welcoming of other types of organizations as marginalizing women's groups and their interests. On the other hand, the commission's aggregation of various new members provided new opportunities for interorganizational cooperation in addressing cross-cutting grievances and demands.

The government justified this restructuring as part of a broader strategy for streamlining and modernizing the public-administration sector to render it more efficient. At the same time, this reimagining of the commission can be understood as a response to EU pressures for the executive to become more proactive in other areas of discrimination. In doing so, Portugal was aligning with an EU move away from focusing on gender inequality toward policies addressing many types of inequalities and their intersectionality.[12]

In brief, from the years immediately following the 1974–1976 revolution onward, the executive's rapprochement with women's organizations followed a centralizing logic, in which social-movement organizations and other types of NGOs were invited to work with the government through the commission. They were encouraged to promote gender equality and align their activities with the government's gender-policy goals. The relationship remained extremely asymmetric—the government received recommendations but had no legal obligation to follow them. Yet by tasking the commission with gathering information, promoting gender equality, and issuing reports on women's conditions, the executive created a "school for organizations." Through their participation in these projects, women's organizations gained new expertise in European gender laws and good understanding of where the Portuguese government fell short.

However, as mentioned previously, the executive monopolized the commission's agenda, and projects developed by women's organizations had to fall within the parameters set by the commission's presidency. As Rosa Monteiro and Virgínia Ferreira (2012) point out, the commission has played an active and persistent role in the production and dissemination of knowledge about gender rights, but it has been less efficacious concerning the executive, which often ignores or engages in foot-dragging in the implementation of the commission's recommendations. The origins of this executive resistance were both organizational and partisan. The law did not require the executive to act on commission recommendations, and movement relationships with the parties in power were weak, as discussed earlier, thus giving the executive few electoral incentives to act.

Finally, the executive's decision to expand the commission's membership and scope after 2007 avoided the creation of new state agencies (or other institutional mechanisms) to deal with various types of discrimination and inequalities. This move allowed the executive to bring these new organizations into the same type of asymmetric, centralizing relationship that characterized its interactions with women's organizations. The executive was responsive to EU pressures and sustained its power while keeping these organizations in participative, but subordinate, positions in the policy-making process.

The Executive and Women's Networks: Abortion Rights

The Portuguese executive's responses to EU pressures have, over the years, altered the relationship between the executive branch and women's organizations, bringing the two into closer contact through the commission. As discussed in the previous section, these changes have nonetheless followed a centralizing logic. The executive has maintained a monopoly over decisions regarding gender policies while keeping the commission and its women's organizations limited in power, though women's organizations continued to seek strategies to enhance their voice.

The commission has shied away from taking positions on contentious topics, such as abortion rights. This absenteeism has also been tied, in part, to the commission's subordination to conservative executive agendas (Monteiro 2011). Portuguese PMs—who have been generally opposed to or silent on abortion—appoint the commission's president and thus influence its agenda.

In this section, I discuss how pro-choice women's organizations have sought to circumvent their subordinate position regarding the executive by forming networks that operate beyond the commission. As a short case study, the campaigns for abortion rights in the 1990s and 2000s reveal how women's organizations have used velvet triangles as leverage against the executive. A comparison of the two campaigns also suggests that the PMs' positioning on the issue influenced the different outcomes.

In mobilizing to pressure the executive for change, the women's movement has relied primarily on domestic networks rather than European transnational networks. Portuguese women's groups have seldom resorted to the help of women's organizations in other EU states to pressure the Portuguese executive directly. Several factors may contribute to this, including resource scarcity and language barriers, but the research needed to address this issue is beyond the scope of this chapter.

Since the 1974–1976 revolution, the struggle for abortion rights has drawn many women's organizations toward common ground. Groups like the MLM, MDM, and UMAR, which historically mistrusted each other and seldom cooperated in protest activities, have been on the same side of this cause.[13]

In 1983, pursuant to a successful bill introduced by the center-left PS, abortion was decriminalized under restricted circumstances.[14] Dissatisfied with this law, pro-choice women's organizations continued to mobilize for a woman's right to choose. There were two more campaigns: one in the 1990s that culminated in an unsuccessful referendum in 1998 and one in 2007 that resulted in the legalization of abortion at the woman's request up to the tenth week ("National Assembly's Law 16/2007"). The latter was a major victory for the pro-choice activists, who were opposed by a strong pro-life movement, directly and indirectly influenced by the Roman Catholic Church and its teachings.

The 1990s campaign unfolded under a PS government. A devout Catholic, PM António Guterres expressed publicly that he opposed abortion on demand and used his executive position to prevent a vote in the National Assembly (Alves et al. 2009; Tavares 2003). In response, women's organizations pursued a coalitional strategy that included the three types of actors in velvet triangles: women's organizations and other NGOs, femocrats and feminist politicians, and experts and academics. In 1994, several women's and family-planning organizations formally created the Movimento de Opinião pela Despenalização do Aborto (MODAP; Opinion Movement for the Decriminalization of Abortion).[15] MODAP's coalition consisted of women's organizations, women's party sections, professional associations, and unions.[16] Most of these organizations were already working together within the commission's NGO section, which served as an incubator for the emergence of the newly renamed "Platform Right to Choose." Later, the campaign would also receive the support of the PCP and the PS's youth wing (Juventude Socialista, Socialist Youth).

PM Guterres countered the movement's strategy with a proposal for a referendum to be held in 1998. This solution would clear the ruling PS party of responsibility if voters opted for legalization. However, the referendum would be binding *only* if over half of the electorate participated. This created an opportunity for the Catholic countermovement, with the right-wing parties, to call for an abstention strategy; they succeeded, with only 32 percent of the voters showing at the polls (Comissão Nacional de Eleições 2015a). The pro-choice campaign thus failed to win the referendum because of a number of factors, summarized by Monteiro:

> The concentration of the pro-legalization militancy in one movement (Tavares 2008), the greater level of unity of the right than on the left (Freire and Baum 2001, Freire 2008a), especially the Socialist Party's lack of support and involvement in the campaign (Freire 2008a), the strength of the Church's movement, emerge as the main factors leading to the "No" victory in the referendum. (Monteiro 2012, 597)

Though failing to achieve the campaign's main goal, the 1990s strategy demonstrated to women's organizations that velvet coalitions produced enough momentum to provoke the recalcitrant executive to respond with a referendum. Thus, between 2000 and 2007, they used a similar strategy. In this campaign, women's organizations expanded their domestic velvet triangles to more organizations (including LGBT groups), as well as experts, academics, public figures, and artists. The famous painter Paula Rego and sculptor João Cutileiro, for instance, donated work to raise funds for the movement ("Aborto" 2006).

On a much smaller scale, the campaign also expanded these networks to include one external women's organization—the Dutch organization Women on Waves (WoW)—and the moral support of international personalities. The PCP, with the MDM, brought in the support of international scholars and intellectuals, such as Noam Chomsky and Pierre Bourdieu, who expressed solidarity with Portuguese women then on trial for undergoing abortions (Tavares 2011, 422).[17] In 2004, UMAR, along with other human-rights and sexual-rights organizations,[18] invited WoW to bring its ship to Portugal (424). WoW provides legal abortions by performing the procedure aboard the ship while in international waters. The ship's arrival unleashed a media frenzy that internationalized and shamed the Portuguese government, especially after the minister of defense sent two warships to impede the ship from entering Portuguese waters.[19]

This new campaign for abortion rights had started under less-than-ideal political conditions, since in 2002 the PSD retook the premiership. During the campaign, then-PSD candidate José Manuel Barroso promised not to legislate on the abortion issue if elected. In a preelection interview Barroso had stated, "I oppose a new referendum on abortion in the next legislature. . . . Personally, I am opposed to the legalization of the voluntary interruption of pregnancy" ("Durão Barroso" 2002). Barroso's statements indicated that his government would close opportunities for a discussion on the issue at the executive level. When Prime Minister P. Santana Lopes stepped into office, little changed in the PSD's approach to abortion policy.[20] This closed context likely increased incentives for the pro-choice coalitions to expand their velvet triangles.

The national and international amplification of the discussion on abortion, and the PSD PM's refusal to address the issue, created a campaign opportunity for the PS. In 2005, the new PS leader, José Sócrates, ran on a platform that openly called for a new abortion referendum and portrayed the PS as an ally of the pro-choice movement (Monteiro 2012, 598). Once Sócrates won the election, a new referendum was scheduled for 2007. At 59.3 percent, the vote overwhelmingly supported the legalization of abortion on demand. However, under Portuguese law, when there is voter turnout of less than 50 percent, a referendum is nonbinding; turnout for the 2007 abortion referendum was only 43.57 percent (Comissão Nacional de Eleições 2015b). In spite of this low turnout, PM Sócrates used his party's majority in the National Assembly, with the support of other left-wing parties, to approve Law 16/2007. This law allowed women to seek abortions up until the tenth week of pregnancy. It also allowed for late-term abortions in special cases, such as fetal malformation, the mother's health, and sexual crimes.

Thus, the velvet alliances of several politically marginal groups had produced enough leverage to shame PM Barroso's PS government internationally and to spur a national conversation on abortion under a right-wing government. The mounting domestic pressures and EU soft pressures bore fruit once the PS returned to power under PM Sócrates in 2005.[21] Under the leadership of PM Sócrates—who did not share the previous PS premier's religious opposition to legalizing abortion—the left-wing socialists took advantage of the opportunity to cast the party as "in with the times." In this manner, the PS was able to attract young voters and align with European expectations at the same time, follow through on the promised referendum, and when it failed, pass a new law.

In summary, women's organizations campaigning for the right to have an abortion in the 1990s and early 2000s confronted PMs supporting the status quo—that is, a governmental antiabortion policy and an absentee commission. Consequently, women's organizations seeking legalization had two options in terms of pressuring the executive: (1) form networks that would operate outside the commission or (2) take advantage of new opportunities for network formation at the EU level to seek the help of external allies. As this discussion shows, women's organizations pursued primarily the first option.

The resulting velvet triangles, their campaigns, and the media attention they generated pressured PMs to take positions on the abortion debate. In 1998, PM Guterres agreed to a referendum in spite of his opposition to abortion. It failed. In 2005, opportunities changed at the executive level, as PM Sócrates ran on a platform that indicated a clear positioning in favor of the legalization campaign.[22] This case study suggested that the PM's position on a policy issue remained a determining factor in gender-policy outcomes and that the executive remained very strong in relation to women's organizations, in spite of the latter's relative increase in power resources through velvet triangles and transnational outreach. Power remained centralized in the executive, despite external pressures from the EU and internal pressures from women's organizations.

Conclusion

Europeanization has been a powerful engine for political and social transformation in Portugal, leading the executive to implement significant gender-related policy changes. Portuguese PMs' agendas for gender policy since EU membership have consistently paralleled the direction of gender policy at the EU level. In that sense, Portuguese PMs have been "good students" in adapting to Europeanization. But overall, the Portuguese case does not conform to expectations that Europeanization weakens strong, centralized executives.

The executive has resisted pressures to decentralize power. The commission's continuing subordination testifies to this fact. Commission recommendations remained nonbinding, and goals were often co-opted by the executive. At no time, however, did the executive share policy-making power with the commission. Instead, Portuguese PMs have successfully resisted pressures to decentralize control over gender policy or to share it with women's organizations. Contrarily, PMs consolidated their power and set the commission's agenda. The commission has consistently been the executive's principal instrument to gather and disseminate information about gender equality in Portugal, as well as a partner in implementing gender policy.

Europeanization has had more indirect than direct effects on the Portuguese women's movement and its position in relation to the executive. The commission has been the main instrument for executive responses to external EU pressures on gender policy. Its existence did help strengthen and expand a severely fragmented, resource-poor women's movement. Importantly, the commission gave women's organizations access to an exclusionary executive office, albeit under constrained participation rules. As an agency for state feminism, it improved the access of women's groups to the executive, but its organizational structure has maintained women's organizations in subordinate positions regarding the executive and gender policy making.

EU membership has opened new political opportunity structures for women's mobilization to pressure the executive. However, it is not enough that opportunities are available—they must be activated by domestic groups using the transnational arena to effect change in their executives. Portuguese women's movements still rely primarily on domestic coalitions in lobbying the executive, though the abortion campaign in the 2000s shows signs of greater awareness of these transnational opportunities. Yet the relative improvement in the position of women's organizations over the years is not a result of executive weakening and has not significantly enfeebled executive power over gender policy.

An old Portuguese proverb teaches that water flowing against a hard rock will eventually break the rock (*àgua mole em pedra dura tanto bate que até fura*). This piece of popular wisdom provides a fitting metaphor for the persistent struggle that the women's movement has waged to chip away at the PM's centralization of power, especially regarding gender policies and the women's movement. Some gains are clearly visible, but there is still a long road ahead.

NOTES

1. In this analysis, I focus on the prime minister because he or she plays a pivotal role in the policy-making process. Unless otherwise noted, I use "prime minister" and "executive" interchangeably. Note, however, that frequently authors refer to the executive as including the prime minister and the ministers (cabinet) and junior ministers (Lobo 2005; Pinto and Almeida 2009).

2. State feminism agencies are organizations established to further women's rights and advancement in society (Stetson 2002; Stetson and Mazur 1995).

3. For studies on Portuguese Europeanization, see Jalali 2012; Magone 1999, 2004; and Teixeira and Pinto 2012. For a discussion of the Europeanization of gender policy in Portugal, see Ribeiro et al. 2014. For more on Portuguese internal dynamics between executives/parties/state and domestic gender actors, see Ferreira 2000, 2011; Ferreira, Coelho, and Lopes 2006; Freire 2008b; Monteiro 2012; Monteiro and Ferreira 2012; and Tavares 2011. This chapter builds on these studies by analyzing the Portuguese executive both in relation to Europe and to the women's movement in Portugal.

4. The sole exception was Prime Minister Maria de Lourdes Pintasilgo (1979). During the Portuguese revolution (1974–1976), she presided over the Commission on the Feminine Condition, an organization that in 1977 was converted into the main agency for state feminism in Portugal (Monteiro 2010). To date, Pintasilgo has been the only woman to hold the prime minister's seat, albeit for a short period.

5. According to Alan Siaroff (2003), when compared with other semipresidential systems, the Portuguese president holds less power than is common (see also Freire and Pinto 2005; Pinto and Almeida 2009). The president retains only limited authority to interfere in the PM's affairs. For instance, the president cannot sit in cabinet meetings unless invited by the PM. Yet the president retains a constitutional right to veto the executive's bills on political grounds (Presidência da República Portuguesa 2015).

6. One of the main goals of the 1982 constitutional revision was to distance the military—which had played a leading role during the 1974–1976 revolution—from political power. Between 1976 and 1982, the military was represented in the Revolutionary Council (RC), a political institution that had broad powers over domestic and international matters involving the military. The RC was the official overseer of the Constitution of 1976 and had to be consulted by the president before he appointed the PM. In 1982, the RC was dissolved and the military was subordinated to political power (see Pinto and Almeida 2009).

7. For example, until 1982, the president could withdraw confidence in the government, forcing the PM to resign even if the National Assembly supported the government (Freire and Pinto 2005; Pinto and Almeida 2009). After 1982, these presidential powers were circumscribed, tipping the balance in favor of the PM.

8. This specific provision was changed in the revised Civil Code of 1966, after which women no longer needed spousal consent to undertake liberal professions (e.g., lawyers, notaries, doctors, and other specialized professions). For other professions, the husband retained the right to revoke his wife's work contract at will (Guimarães 1986).

9. Note that the Estado Novo sanctioned some women's organizations, mostly charitable and religious groups. For overviews of those organizations, see Cova and Pinto 1997 and Pimentel 2002.

10. MDM and UMAR were close to political parties that played visible roles during the revolution (especially the PCP) but that have been perennially in the opposition in the democratic regime. Other organizations were mostly alienated from national political parties.

11. The PCP, for instance, protested vociferously against this decision, claiming that it represented "the 'governmentalization' of this new [commission's] Consultative Council and an attempt to instrumentalize it to serve the government's agenda" (Partido Comunista Português 2008).

12. See Verloo 2006 for a detailed analysis of this process at the EU level. For more on intersectionality in Portugal, see Alonso 2010.

13. The first organization to publicly demand abortion rights was the MLM during the revolution, but no party was willing to take up the cause at that time.

14. The exceptions were granted (1) when the mother's life or her psychiatric health were at risk, (2) in cases of fetal *malformação* (malformation), and (3) if the pregnancy resulted from rape (Tavares 2003).

15. The organizations in MODAP had previously formed a working group on the issue of abortion in 1990. In 1998, MODAP changed its name to Plataforma Direito de Optar (Platform Right to Choose) (Tavares 2011).

16. The coalition brought together UMAR, the MDM, the Organização das Mulheres Comunistas (Organization of Communist Women), and Associação Portuguesa de Mulheres Juristas (APJM; Portuguese Association of Women Jurists) with women's departments from UDP, the PS, two union confederacies (CGTP and UGT), Associação para o Planeamento Familiar (APF; Family-Planning Association), and a doctors' union (Sindicato de Médicos do Sul, Southern Doctors' Union) (Tavares 2011).

17. Between 2000 and 2006, the number of women tried for undergoing abortions increased. In a case that unfolded between 2001 and 2003, which galvanized the country, seventeen women were tried in the town of Maia (Tavares 2011, 419). Fifteen were exonerated and two were convicted; the nurse accused of performing the abortions received 8.5 years in jail. The nurse was eventually pardoned by President Jorge Sampaio (PS) on Christmas in 2003. (Per Portuguese law, the president has the right to grant pardons and reduce sentences, in consultation with the government. This practice traditionally takes place on Christmas.)

18. These included Acção Jovem para a Paz (AJP; Youth Action for Peace), a human-rights organization; Clube Safo, a lesbian-rights group; and Não te Prives (Don't Deprive Yourself), an organization fighting sexual discrimination.

19. WoW estimated that the stalemate generated more than seven hundred newspaper articles in Portugal, thus propelling the pro-choice campaign into the headlines and promoting a national conversation on abortion (Women on Waves, n.d.).

20. P. Santana Lopes became PM following Durão Barroso's resignation to become president of the European Commission. He took office in July 2004, resigning later that year in December. The WoW incident took place one month into his premiership and was one of several controversial issues that led President Sampaio to dissolve the Assembly and call for early elections to be held in February 2005.

21. In the 2000s, the European Parliament became an ally of pro-choice movements across Europe, framed the matter in terms of inalienable rights, and pressured governments to adopt appropriate legislation and stop prosecuting abortion cases. In 2002, the European Parliament adopted the Van Lancker Report, which urged member states to make abortion legal, accessible, and safe for women and to stop prosecutions of illegal abortions. This recommendation had been opposed by pro-life and pro-family EU groups. See, for instance, the criticisms on the report by the Irish LifeZone organization (LifeZone 2002).

22. The following excerpt from the 2005 government's program shows this alignment: "The Government's position on the Voluntary Interruption of Pregnancy [VIP] is very clear. Six years have passed since the referendum on this matter. In these six years, the Country watched a succession of women being tried for the crime of abortion. [These trials] confronted our society with an obsolete and unjust law that coexists with the drama of clandestine abortion. . . . The legalization of VIP is an undelayable exigency for justice and dignity towards women" (Presidência do Conselho de Ministros 2005, 88).

REFERENCES

"Aborto: Movimento 'Jovens Pelo Sim' arranca em Janeiro" [Abortion: Movement "Youth for Yes" takes off in January]. 2006. *Diário Digital* [Digital Daily], December 28. Available at http://diariodigital.sapo.pt/news.asp?id_news=255915.

Alonso, Alba. 2010. "A introdução da interseccionalidade em Portugal: Repensar as políticas de igualdade(s)" [The introduction of intersectionality in Portugal: Rethinking equality policies]. *Revista de Ciências Sociais* [Social Science Journal] 90:25–43.

Alves, Magda, Ana C. Santos, Carlos Barradas, and Madalena Duarte. 2009. *A despenalização do aborto em Portugal: Discursos, dinâmicas e acção colectiva; Os referendos de 1998 e 2007* [The decriminalization of abortion in Portugal: Discourses, dynamics and collective action; the 1998 and 2007 referenda]. Coimbra, Portugal: Oficina do Centro de Estudos Sociais.

Banaszak, Lee Ann, Karen Beckwith, and Dieter Rucht, ed. 2003. *Women's Movements Facing the Reconfigured State.* Cambridge: Cambridge University Press.

Börzel, Tanja A., and Thomas Risse. 2000. "When Europe Hits Home: Europeanization and Domestic Change." *European Integration Online Papers* 4 (15). Available at http://eiop.or.at/eiop/pdf/2000-015.pdf.

Cardoso, João C. 2000. "Making Women Count in Portugal." In *Making Women Count: Integrating Gender into Law and Policy-Making,* edited by Fionam Beveridge, Sue Nott, and Kylie Stephen, 77–106. Burlington, VT: Ashgate.

Comissão Nacional de Eleições. 2015a. "Resultados eleitorais: Referendo 28-06-1998" [Election results: Referendum 28-06-1998]. Available at http://eleicoes.cne.pt/raster/index.cfm?dia=28&mes=06&ano=1998&eleicao=rel.

———. 2015b. "Resultados eleitorais: Referendo 11-02-2007" [Election results: Referendum 11-02-2007]. Available at http://eleicoes.cne.pt/raster/index.cfm?dia=11&mes=02&ano=2007&eleicao=rel.

"Constituição de 1933" [Constitution of 1933]. 1933. Available at http://www.parlamento.pt/Parlamento/Documents/CRP-1933.pdf.

"Council of Ministers' Law Decree 485/77 of 17 November 1977." 1977. *Diário da República* [Official Gazette of the Republic] 1 (266): 2752–2755.

Cova, Anne, and António C. Pinto. 1997. "O salazarismo e as mulheres: Uma abordagem comparativa" [Salazarism and women: A comparative approach]. *Penélope* 17:71–94.

"Durão Barroso contra novo referendo ao aborto" [Durão Barroso against new referendum on abortion]. 2002. *TSF Rádio Notícias* [TSF Radio News], January 29. Available at http://www.tsf.pt/PaginaInicial/Interior.aspx?content_id=759803&page=1.

European Commission. 2012. "Acquis." Available at http://ec.europa.eu/enlargement/policy/glossary/terms/acquis_en.htm.

Ferreira, Virgínia. 2000. "A globalização das políticas de igualdade entre os sexos: Do reformismo social ao reformismo estatal" [The globalization of equality policies between the sexes: From social reformism to state reformism]. *Ex Aequo* [Equally] 2:13–42.

———. 2011. "Engendering Portugal, Social Change, State Politics, and Women's Social Mobilization." In *Contemporary Portugal: Politics, Society, and Culture,* 2nd ed., edited by António Costa Pinto, 153–192. New York: East European Monographs.

Ferreira, Virgínia, Lina Coelho, and Mónica Lopes. 2006. *Estudo diagnóstico e prospectivo sobre o papel das ONG na promoção da igualdade de oportunidades entre homens e mulheres* [A diagnostic and prospective study about the role of NGOs in the promotion of equal opportunities between men and women]. Coimbra, Portugal: Centro de Estudos Sociais.

Freire, André. 2008a. "Os referendos sobre a interrupção voluntária da gravidez: A participação diferencial como chave dos resultados" [The referendum on the voluntary interruption of pregnancy: Differential participation as key to the results]. In *Sociedade civil, democracia participativa e poder político: O caso do referendo do aborto, 2007* [Civil society, participatory democracy, and political power: The case of the abortion referendum, 2007], edited by André Freire, 41–68. Lisbon, Portugal: Fundação Friedrich Ebert. Available at http://library.fes.de/pdf-files/bueros/lissabon/06862.pdf.

———. ed. 2008b. *Sociedade civil, democracia participativa e poder político: O caso do referendo do aborto, 2007* [Civil society, participatory democracy, and political power: The case of the abortion referendum, 2007]. Lisbon, Portugal: Fundação Friedrich Ebert. Available at http://library.fes.de/pdf-files/bueros/lissabon/06862.pdf.

Freire, André, and Michael Baum. 2001. "Partidos políticos, movimentos de cidadãos e referendos em Portugal: Os casos do aborto e regionalização" [Political parties, citizen's movements and referenda in Portugal: The abortion and regionalization cases]. *Análise Social* [Social Analysis] 36 (158–159): 9–41.

Freire, André, and António C. Pinto. 2005. *O poder dos presidentes: A República Portuguesa em debate* [The power of presidents: Debating the Portuguese Republic]. Lisbon, Portugal: Campo da Comunicação.

Guimarães, Elina. 1986. "A mulher Portuguesa na legislação civil" [Portuguese women in civil legislation]. *Análise Social* [Social Analysis] 22 (3–4): 557–577.

Holli, Anne M. 2008. "Feminist Triangles: A Conceptual Analysis." *Representation* 44 (2): 169–185.

Imig, Douglas, and Sidney Tarrow, eds. 2001. *Contentious Europeans: Protest and Politics in an Integrating Europe*. Lanham, MD: Rowman and Littlefield.

Jalali, Carlos. 2012. "Governing from Lisbon or Governing from Brussels? Models and Tendencies of Europeanization of the Portuguese Government." In *The Europeanization of Portuguese Democracy*, edited by Nuno Severiano Teixeira and António Costa Pinto, 61–84. Boulder, CO: East European Monographs.

Jessop, Robert. 1994. "The Transition to Post-Fordism and the Schumpeterian Workfare State." In *Towards a Post-Fordist Welfare State?* edited by Roger Burrows and Brian D. Loader, 13–37. London: Routledge.

Keck, Margaret E., and Kathryn Sikkink. 1998. *Activists beyond Borders: Advocacy Networks in International Politics*. Ithaca, NY: Cornell University Press.

LifeZone. 2002. "Van Lancker Report." July 3. Available at http://www.prolifeinfo.ie/resources/eu-documents/van-lancker-report/.

Lobo, Marina C. 2005. *Governar em democracia* [Governing in democracy]. Lisbon, Portugal: Instituto de Ciências Sociais Universidade de Lisboa.

Magone, José. 1999. "Portugal: Party System Installation and Consolidation." In *Changing Party Systems in Western Europe*, edited by David Broughton and Mark Donovan, 232–254. London: Bloomsbury Academic.

———. 2004. *The Developing Place of Portugal in the European Union*. New Brunswick, NJ: Transaction.

Monteiro, Rosa. 2010. *A emergência do feminismo de estado em Portugal: Uma história da criação da Comissão da Condição Feminina* [The emergence of state feminism in Portugal: A history of the creation of the Commission on the Feminine Condition]. Lisbon, Portugal: Comissão para a Cidadania e Igualdade de Género.

———. 2011. "Feminismo de estado em Portugal: Mecanismos, estratégias, políticas e metamorfoses" [State feminism in Portugal: Mechanisms, strategies, politics and metamorphoses]. Ph.D. diss., Universidade de Coimbra.

———. 2012. "A descriminalização do aborto em Portugal: Estado, movimentos de mulheres e partidos políticos" [The decriminalization of abortion in Portugal: State, women's movements and political parties]. *Análise Social* [Social Analysis] 47 (3): 506–605.

———. 2013. "Feminismo de estado na transição democrática em Portugal na década de 1970" [State feminism in Portugal's democratic transition in the 1970s]. *DADOS— Revista de Ciências Sociais* [DADOS—Social Science Journal] 56 (4): 841–866.

Monteiro, Rosa, and Virgínia Ferreira. 2012. "Metamorfoses das relações entre o estado e os movimentos de mulheres em Portugal: Entre a institucionalização e a autonomia"

[Metamorphoses in the relations between the state and the women's movements in Portugal: Between institutionalization and autonomy]. *Ex Aequo* [Equally] 25:13–27.

"National Assembly's Law 16/2007 of 17 April 2007." 2007. *Diário da República* [Official Gazette of the Republic] 1 (75): 2417–2418.

Neto, Octavio A., and Marina C. Lobo. 2009. "Portugal's Semi-presidentialism (Re)Considered: An Assessment of the President's Role in the Policy Process, 1976–2006." *European Journal of Political Research* 48 (2): 234–255.

Partido Comunista Português. 2008. "Mulheres comunistas fora da CIG" [Communist women out of CIG]. Available at http://www.pcp.pt/index.php?option=com_content&task=view&id=31701&Itemid=195.

Pimentel, Irene F. 2002. "Women's Organizations and Imperial Ideology under the Estado Novo." *Portuguese Studies* 18:121–131.

Pinto, António C., and Pedro T. de Almeida. 2009. "Portugal: The Primacy of Independents." In *The Selection of Ministers in Europe: Hiring and Firing*, edited by Keith Dowding and Patrick Dumont, 147–158. New York: Routledge.

Prata, Ana. 2010. "Finding a Voice: Abortion Claims-Making during Portuguese Democratization." *Women's Studies International Forum* 33 (6): 579–588.

Presidência da República Portuguesa. 2015. "Funções do presidente" [Duties of the president]. Available at http://www.presidencia.pt/?idc=1.

Presidência do Conselho de Ministros. 2005. "Programa do XVII governo constitucional" [The XVII constitutional government program]. Available at http://www.umic.pt/images/stories/publicacoes/ProgramaGovernoXVII.pdf.

Rêgo, Maria do Céu da Cunha. 2012. "Políticas de igualdade de género na União Europeia e em Portugal: Influências e incoerências" [Gender equality policies in the European Union and in Portugal: Influences and incoherences]. *Ex Aequo* [Equally] 25:29–44.

Ribeiro, Norberto, Pedro D. Ferreira, Carla Malafaia, and Isabel Menezes. 2014. "The 'Europeanisation' of Gender Policies in Europe." In *Political and Civic Engagement: Multidisciplinary Perspectives*, edited by Martyn Barrett and Bruna Zani, 403–419. New York: Routledge.

Ruivo, João P., Diogo Moreira, António C. Pinto, and Pedro T. Almeida. 2012. "The Portuguese Political Elites and the European Union." In *The Europeanization of Portuguese Democracy*, edited by Nuno Severiano Teixeira and António Costa Pinto, 27–60. Boulder, CO: East European Monographs.

Schmidt, Vivien. 2002. "Federalism and State Governance in the European Union and the United States: An Institutional Perspective." In *The Federal Vision: Legitimacy and Levels of Governance in the United States and the European Union*, edited by Kalypso Nicolaidis and Robert Howse, 335–354. New York: Oxford University Press.

Siaroff, Alan. 2003. "Comparative Presidencies: The Inadequacy of the Presidential, Semi-presidential and Parliamentary Distinction." *European Journal of Political Research* 42 (3): 297–312.

Sikkink, Kathryn. 2005. "Patterns of Dynamic Multilevel and Inside-Outside Coalition." In *Transnational Protest and Global Activism: People, Passions, and Power*, edited by Donatella della Porta and Sidney Tarrow, 151–174. Lanham, MD: Rowman and Littlefield.

Stetson, Dorothy McBride, ed. 2002. *Abortion Politics, Women's Movements, and the Democratic State: A Comparative Study of State Feminism*. New York: Oxford University Press.

Stetson, Dorothy McBride, and Amy G. Mazur, eds. 1995. *Comparative State Feminism*. Thousand Oaks, CA: Sage.

Tavares, Manuela. 2000. *Movimentos de mulheres em Portugal nas décadas de 70 e 80* [Women's movements in Portugal in the 1970s and 1980s]. Lisbon, Portugal: Livros Horizonte.

———. 2003. *Aborto e contracepção em Portugal* [Abortion and contraception in Portugal]. Lisbon, Portugal: Livros Horizonte.

———. 2008. "Feminismos em Portugal" [Feminisms in Portugal]. Ph.D. diss., Universidade Aberta.

———. 2011. *Feminismos: Percursos e desafios (1947–1990)* [Feminisms: Paths and challenges (1947–1990)]. Lisbon, Portugal: Texto Editora.

Teixeira, Nuno Severiano, and António Costa Pinto, eds. 2012. *The Europeanization of Portuguese Democracy.* Boulder, CO: East European Monographs.

Verloo, Mieke. 2006. "Multiple Inequalities, Intersectionality, and the European Union." *European Journal of Women's Studies* 13 (3): 211–228.

Wall, Karin. 1995. "Apontamentos sobre a família na política social Portuguesa" [Notes about the family in Portuguese social policy]. *Análise Social* [Social Analysis] 30 (2–3): 431–458.

Woodward, Alison E. 2004. "Building Velvet Triangles: Gender and Informal Governance." In *Informal Governance in the European Union,* edited by Thomas Christiansen and Simona Piattoni, 76–93. Northampton, MA: Edward Elgar.

Women on Waves. n.d. "What Happened in Portugal . . . ." Available at http://www.women onwaves.org/pt/page/3131/in-collection/560/what-happened-in-portugal (accessed August 1, 2015).

III

Politics and Power

10

The U.S. Presidency and the Aftermath of Revolution

Are Women's Rights Human Rights?

JANET M. MARTIN

Human rights were fundamental to the American Revolution and have remained a focus in U.S. foreign policy, but a dichotomy has continued between women's rights and human rights in the presidents' agendas for domestic policy. This has endured even though several presidents have acknowledged that "women's rights are human rights" in their speeches and actions internationally. Furthermore, the policy efforts of first ladies, including Eleanor Roosevelt, an architect of the Universal Declaration of Human Rights, and Hillary Rodham Clinton, who delivered an internationally renowned speech in Beijing at the 1995 Fourth World Conference on Women, have repeatedly stressed this same theme. However, women's rights in foreign and domestic policy are framed and interpreted differently. This chapter draws on a theoretical framework of Peter Bachrach and Morton S. Baratz to better understand why these distinctions have endured and to delineate their consequences for women and politics in the United States.

Human rights were fundamental to the American Revolution. While the words "human rights" are not in the Declaration of Independence itself, the intent and meaning of the declaration are clear in invoking the idea of a government to preserve "unalienable rights." President George Washington equated those rights with human rights in a message to Congress near the end of his presidency: in his sixth Annual Message to Congress, on November 19, 1794, Washington ended with a call for Congress "to verify the anticipations of this Government being a safeguard of human rights."

Historically, however, in looking at civil and political rights for women, U.S. presidents failed to work toward systemic change to political institutions and in society until the latter half of the twentieth century, and only then on rare occasions. For example, in a patriotic Fourth of July oration, delivered at Independence Hall in Philadelphia in 1914, President Woodrow Wilson eloquently stated:

> As the years go on and the world knows more and more of America it will also . . . turn to America for those moral inspirations which lie at the basis of all freedom; that the world will never fear America unless it feels that it is engaged in some enterprise which is inconsistent with the rights of humanity; and that America will come into the full light of the day when all shall know that she puts human rights above all other rights and that her flag is the flag not only of America but of humanity. (Wilson 1914)

Essential to the human rights of which Wilson spoke was the right to vote. He noted that "85% of the Mexican people have never been allowed to have any genuine participation in their own government or to exercise any substantial rights with regard to the very land they live upon" (Wilson 1914). Yet he failed to note that those same rights were denied many women in the United States. The movement toward a suffrage amendment for women in the United States did not gain Wilson's support for several years after that Independence Day oration and then only after suffragists had protested in front of the White House, chained themselves to the White House gates, and endured prison.

There are parallels between the American Revolution, the subsequent formation of a representative democracy, and the role of women in that government and in civil society that foreshadow similar developments in other countries. (For discussion of a modern revolution and the impact on the rights of women, see Chapter 9.) However, the concept of women's rights as human rights has only recently become a part of a U.S. president's domestic agenda.

In the twenty-first century, human rights are a focus of democratic revolutions around the world, and human rights have become a part of modern American presidents' foreign policy, especially following the presidency of Jimmy Carter. So how did a dichotomy develop in which U.S. presidents speak of human rights only in other countries? How is it that customarily and traditionally, presidential rhetoric on human rights has only rarely included rights for women in the United States? A brief survey of American political history can shed light on the role of presidents in defining a human-rights policy that excludes women.

In this chapter I provide a brief introduction to the role of women in the American Revolution and the framing of human rights in the early years of the American republic. In particular, we see that the institution of slavery, written into the Constitution, had a long-lasting impact in framing a domestic agenda. Mention of human rights virtually disappears from presidential rhetoric after the first generation of presidents, only to reappear in the twentieth century following World War II. The formation of the United Nations in the 1940s and the crafting of a Universal Declaration of Human Rights, which served as a foundation for the procurement of rights for women worldwide, helped return the discussion of human rights to front and center for American presidents. However, presidential rhetoric and action regarding human rights became intertwined with strategic foreign policy—not domestic policy. Women's rights within the United States were not viewed as a part of a dialogue or action agenda on human rights.

Beginning with President Harry S. Truman in 1945 during the final months of World War II, examples of the rhetoric and actions of several presidents, including John F. Kennedy and Jimmy Carter, are used to illustrate when a link has been made between women's rights and human rights in the United States and when they have remained in different and distinct policy arenas, a dichotomy with implications in the foreign-policy arena. This chapter draws on Peter Bachrach and Morton S. Baratz's (1963, 632) theoretical framework of "nondecision-making" to better understand how and why these distinctions have endured; to delineate their consequences in terms of domestic policy and of U.S. presidents taking a global leadership role on issues of human rights; and to demonstrate how scholars can change the nature of research questions asked and approaches taken in their research.

Methodology

This research is primarily qualitative in nature, drawing on the speeches of presidents, archival documents, and executive actions. In addition, several databases are used to systematically look at presidential speeches and news coverage. In this chapter, the research is driven by the work of comparativists in the area of human rights and is inspired by the classic study "Two Faces of Power," by Peter Bachrach and Morton S. Baratz (1962), published over fifty years ago. Bachrach and Baratz provide a context in which to understand "what might be called 'nondecision-making,' i.e., the practice of limiting the scope of actual decision-making to 'safe issues' by manipulating the dominant community values, myths, and political institutions and procedures" (1963, 632).

Bachrach and Baratz's seminal studies of political power became a well-known part of the "power elite" literature of urban politics scholars in the 1960s and 1970s but were rarely integrated into the presidency literature. Bachrach and Baratz's study appeared two years after the publication of Richard Neustadt's *Presidential Power* (1960), which focused on the power of one individual—the president—in looking at case studies of presidential actions.

Yet Bachrach and Baratz's work provides a framework for presidency scholars to better understand why the subject of human rights is rarely a focus of their studies. Presidency scholars seldom focus on issues of human rights, except those presidents who advance a human rights foreign policy, such as Jimmy Carter. Following Bachrach and Baratz's determination to investigate what is missing from politics, this chapter focuses on why women's rights are absent from a president's agenda for human rights and the context and consequences of that absence.

The Declaration of Independence, Revolution, and Representative Democracy

The American Revolution, 240 years ago, can offer insight into what happens as the fervor for human rights during revolution is tempered over time by governments and political and societal institutions. As is true in most revolutions, the American Revolution was not inclusive of all individuals. Its aftermath witnessed the exclusion of women, enslaved people, Native Americans, and others not included in the shaping of the revolution and the government that emerged.

The Continental Congress was a loose governing structure for the colonies during the Revolutionary War. While the Congress was meeting in Philadelphia, the correspondence between Abigail Adams in Boston and John Adams gives insight into issues of concern from two perspectives—the framers of a revolution and citizens about to be subjected to that revolution. It is important to note that the Declaration of Independence did not result in the immediate formation of a government or a guarantee of fundamental rights. It would take thirteen years until the Constitution was in place and a government formed, with a Bill of Rights to follow.

Slavery and a Revolution for Human Rights

In March 1776, in an exchange of letters just before independence from Great Britain was declared, Abigail Adams queried her husband and future president, John Adams, about how a revolution could succeed without addressing the question of slavery (Adams 1776). The Continental Congress struck down Thomas Jefferson's effort to abolish slavery in the Declaration of Independence, proclaimed a few months later (Allen 2014). Over a decade later, the Constitution would protect slavery in several ways. The Constitution included a reference to the apportionment of representatives for the House of Representatives based on the populations of states, determined by adding the "number of free persons, including those bound to service for a term of years, and excluding Indians not taxed, three fifths of all other persons" (Article I, Section 2). In addition, the Constitution allowed the "Migration or Importation" of enslaved people to continue until 1808 (Article I, Section 9).

As President Thomas Jefferson observed in his annual message to Congress in December 1806, three decades after the Declaration of Independence:

> I congratulate you, fellow citizens, on the approach of the period at which you may interpose your authority constitutionally to withdraw the citizens of the United States from all further participation in those violations of human rights which have been so long continued on the unoffending inhabitants of Africa, and which the morality, the reputation, and the best of our country have long been eager to proscribe. Although no law you may pass can take prohibitory effect till the first day of the year 1808, yet the intervening period is not too long to prevent by timely notice expeditions which can not be completed before that day. (Jefferson 1806)

The son of John and Abigail Adams and sixth president of the United States, John Quincy Adams, noted the passing of the first generation of leaders and referred back to the theory of human rights on which the nation was founded. In his inaugural address, Adams (1825) noted that "it is a source of gratification and of encouragement to me to observe that the great result of this experiment upon the theory of human rights has at the close of that generation by which it was formed been crowned with success equal to the most sanguine expectation of its founders." In this speech, Adams ignored the country's failure to address slavery, which led to a devastating civil war a generation later, and ignored the marginalization of innumerable peoples through political disenfranchisement and economic exploitation.

The compromise that allowed the formation of the United States, with both centralized, national powers of the Union and reserved powers for the states, kept slavery largely off the agenda until the Civil War. Rights for women, at times a subject linked to the work of abolitionists, was essentially kept off the table, especially at the national level.[1] A discussion of human rights was removed from the rhetoric of presidents for nearly one hundred years. Instead, with the next generation of presidents, rhetoric on human rights would undergo a systemic change.

Inalienable Rights

Whereas George Washington and Thomas Jefferson spoke of human rights, the term "inalienable rights" soon replaced human rights in presidential rhetoric. "Inalienable" no longer had a singular application to *inherent* rights, as was evident in the Declaration of Independence. Instead, inalienable rights became something more malleable and situational. This new definition actually allowed for an obfuscation of human rights, and the concept of basic human rights all but disappeared.

As Bachrach and Baratz note, to fully understand the nature of power, one needs to have studied "the dominant values, the myths and the established political procedures and rules of the game . . . which persons or groups, if any, gain from the existing bias and which, if any, are handicapped by it" (1962, 952). Throughout the mid-1800s to the early twentieth century, these "values," "myths," and "rules of the game" can be discerned from the party platforms, which laid out the issue positions of presidents (and presidential candidates). The Republican Party platforms of 1856 and 1860 both drew on the words of the Declaration of Independence and the Constitution to reject slavery, with similar planks (see "Republican Party Platform of 1856" 1856; "Republican Party Platform of 1860" 1860). The Republican Party platform of 1860, in conjunction with the campaign and election of Abraham Lincoln, stated:

> As our Republican fathers, when they had abolished slavery in all our national territory, ordained that "no persons should be deprived of life, liberty or property without due process of law," it becomes our duty, by legislation, whenever such legislation is necessary, to maintain this provision of the Constitution against all attempts to violate it; and we deny the authority of Congress, of a territorial legislature, or of any individuals, to give legal existence to slavery in any territory of the United States. ("Republican Party Platform of 1860" 1860)

The Democratic Party platforms of this period had a different interpretation of the Declaration of Independence and Constitution. In the Democratic Party Platform of 1848, the party stated

> that Congress has no power under the Constitution to interfere with or control the domestic institutions of the several States, and that such States are the sole and proper judges of everything appertaining

to their own affairs, not prohibited by the Constitution; that all efforts of the Abolitionists or others made to induce Congress to interfere with questions of slavery, or to take incipient steps in relation thereto, are calculated to lead to the most alarming and dangerous consequences; and that all such efforts have an inevitable tendency to diminish the happiness of the people, and endanger the stability and permanence of the Union, and ought not to be countenanced by any friend to our political institutions. ("Democratic Party Platform of 1848" 1848)

As Abraham Lincoln observantly noted in 1857, the "Nebraska policy . . . seeks to bring the people of the nation to not care anything about slavery" (Lincoln 2001). Slavery as an issue of human rights was no longer the subject of national political debate, in effect the subject of "nondecision-making." Yet, by 1861, with Lincoln as president, a civil war had begun.[2]

After the Civil War, it would take a number of decades before "human rights" would return to the lexicon of presidents. Some presidents, however, referred to "inalienable rights." President Rutherford B. Hayes, for example, used the term "inalienable" in referring to the inherent rights of "free migration and emigration" (Hayes 1879). Hayes also used the term in reference to agreements with Native Americans for annuities in exchange for settlement of "certain lands designated for that purpose, as farmers, holding individual title to their land in fee simple, inalienable for a certain period" (Hayes 1880).

Suffrage

Participation in governing is a basic human right written into the United Nations Declaration of Human Rights (1948), modeled after the U.S. Declaration of Independence. However, suffrage for women was not an agenda item for presidents until the Nineteenth Amendment was nearing approval. Even Abraham Lincoln (2016), who spoke of suffrage for women as a lawyer in 1836 and included women in discussing equal rights, did not talk of suffrage for women once he became president.

In his public speeches as president, there is no reference to the 1848 Seneca Falls Woman's Rights Convention. In spite of the convention's Declaration of Sentiments (see "Declaration of Sentiments" 1848), with lines paralleling those in the Declaration of Independence, there is no public mention of the convention by any president, including Lincoln, until the one hundredth anniversary of that convention.

Presidency scholars can study a strong president, such as Lincoln, dissect actions taken, examine speeches and documents, and then look at the risks that could have been taken to be more inclusive in decisions. One outcome of the Civil War and the ending of slavery, and thus the removal of the immediate issue of rights for African Americans from the table, is that human rights were also taken off the table. Not until the post–World War II period and the founding of the United Nations did human rights make a consistent return to presidential rhetoric in the United States. While the Republican Party took the lead on support for issues of concern to women in the late 1800s, there is an absence of discussion on the part of presidents on this topic (see Martin 2003).

U.S. Presidents, Human Rights, and Women

Within the U.S. government, the president was designed to be co-equal with the Congress and the Supreme Court. However, in the eyes of observers and students of the U.S. government, as well as presidents themselves, U.S. presidents have a special role that comes from the office's singularity and the fact that a president is able in many situations to act quickly and unilaterally (Howell 2003). This singularity results in an intense media focus on the office, and political socialization studies reveal that the public often views government in terms of the president.

In the rhetoric of presidents in the twentieth century, discussion of human rights reemerges out of a context of war and the actions of other nations. Presidents begin to talk about human rights in terms of foreign policy, not domestic policy.[3] The words of presidents were important, and in addition, travel and staged events were identified as leadership strategies (see, e.g., Campbell and Jamieson 2008; Cohen 2010; Kernell 1986; Stuckey 1991). Throughout this period, intense study of presidential speeches and remarks gave insight into presidential leadership, and these speeches and remarks are drawn on in the case studies that follow.

President Harry S. Truman

The Universal Declaration of Human Rights, crafted at the United Nations in 1948, with its articles espousing equal pay, equal marriage rights, and universal suffrage as basic human rights, was a foundational document in the struggle for global women's rights. In 1949, President Truman declared December 10 as "United Nations Human Rights Day" in recognition of the anniversary of the passage of the Universal Declaration of Human Rights by the General Assembly. At that time, Truman noted that the declaration was "a common standard of achievement for all peoples and all nations" (Truman 1949).

Truman had used the one hundredth anniversary of the Seneca Falls Convention the previous year to address the opening session of the Women's

Bureau Conference. At that time, he pointed out "successes" for women, including suffrage and women serving in various capacities at the United Nations. But he also noted that there were

> many unfinished tasks. . . . [T]hings cannot be accomplished all at once, or all by the same means. Some of them are now before the Congress, like equal pay for equal work, and the ending of specific discriminations against women, such as limitations on the right to serve on Federal juries. It is within your strength to accomplish these things in which you believe, but only if you make your goals known and persist in demanding action. There isn't a single man in Government can resist you, if you really want him to do so. (Truman 1948)

Taking these two events together, we see the first stirrings of a U.S. president linking domestic women's issues to universal human rights. Truman's remarks highlight the role of men as setting the agenda and making the decisions in government. At the same time, he describes issues such as "equal pay" as requiring the activism of women to be on the national agenda, in order to be addressed by decision-making processes. However, no more than ten women then served in Congress. And no woman served in Truman's cabinet, Truman himself having removed the one woman in Roosevelt's cabinet, Frances Perkins, within three months of his entry into the Oval Office (Perkins 1955). As Bachrach and Baratz would assess the power situation over a decade later, "when the dominant values, the accepted rules of the game, the existing power relations among groups, and the instruments of force, singly or in combination, effectively prevent certain grievances from developing into full-fledged issues which call for decisions, it can be said that a nondecision-making situation exists" (1963, 641). It would be over a decade before action would be taken to address the issue of equal pay, Truman's rhetoric of responsiveness notwithstanding.

President John F. Kennedy

The next president to address human rights, with a link to rights for women, was President John F. Kennedy. In the 1960 election, the Republican Party candidate, Richard Nixon, won 51 percent of the women's vote (Gallup, n.d.). While this may have been a motivating factor in his addressing issues of equal rights for women, John F. Kennedy, having been present as a reporter at the birth of the UN Charter, reintroduced the nation to the fundamental issue of human rights. President Kennedy used historical remembrance to link ratification of the Nineteenth Amendment, extending the political right of voting to women, with the subject of human rights. In his first year in the

White House, he announced the creation of a President's Commission on the Status of Women, forty-one years after the Nineteenth Amendment was added to the Constitution.

The bipartisan membership of the President's Commission on the Status of Women was high powered. The commission chair was Eleanor Roosevelt, former first lady and an architect of the United Nations Universal Declaration of Human Rights. Also serving on the commission were key members of House and Senate committees, cabinet members, heads of nonprofit organizations, business leaders, leaders of labor unions, and educators. Thus, the participants in and the nature of decision making would change as a more inclusive process was designed. Kennedy (1961) noted:

> Women should not be considered a marginal group to be employed periodically only to be denied opportunity to satisfy their needs and aspirations when unemployment rises or a war ends. Women have basic rights which should be respected and fostered as part of our Nation's commitment to human dignity, freedom, and democracy. It is appropriate at this time, when we are observing Human Rights Week, to set forth before this world the story of women's progress in a free, democratic society, to review recent accomplishments, and to acknowledge frankly the further steps that must be taken. This is a task for the entire Nation.

Kennedy overtly made the link: women's rights are human rights. He also explicitly stated that rights for women were currently limited and reflected on the actions of past administrations that recognized the service of women during war, including the words of Abraham Lincoln in observing the work of women during the Civil War. In addition, Kennedy recounted the steps taken by both Republican and Democratic administrations during the Great Depression to limit the numbers of women in the workforce. Kennedy saw the economic contributions to be made by women, a common theme as other countries embraced provisions of the UN's Universal Declaration of Human Rights in subsequent decades (see Martin 2003 for further discussion, especially regarding unilateral actions taken by Kennedy; also see Burri and Prechal 2014 regarding women's rights and economic strength under the European Union's gender equality *acquis*).

Just a few months before his death, the president signed the Equal Pay Act into law. Kennedy (1963b) remarked:

> I am delighted today to approve the Equal Pay Act of 1963, which prohibits arbitrary discrimination against women in the payment of wages. This act represents many years of effort by labor, management,

and several private organizations unassociated with labor or management, to call attention to the unconscionable practice of paying female employees less wages than male employees for the same job. This measure adds to our laws another structure basic to Democracy. It will add protection at the working place to the women, the same rights at the working place in a sense that they have enjoyed at the polling place....

We also need the provisions in the tax bill that will permit working mothers to increase the deduction from income tax liability for costs incurred in providing care for their children while the mothers are working.

This problem should have a high priority.

The work of the Commission on the Status of Women was a constant reminder to the president of the issue of equal rights for women. Kennedy realized that the work of such an eminent commission could bring some change in how issues moved onto the national agenda and in making the decision-making process more inclusive. Yet he was keenly aware of endemic obstacles to women's full participation in society and the workforce. Before the commission turned in its final report, President Kennedy met with a gathering of women pilots at the White House to honor the memory of Amelia Earhart with a commemorative stamp. President Kennedy (1963a) used this act of symbolic representation as an occasion to empower women:

I sometimes wonder whether we make as much use of all of our talent that we have in this country as we should. I think particularly of the hundreds of thousands and millions of women teachers, doctors, flyers, a whole variety of skills which they possess which I think we should use to the maximum. And I am concerned that we sometimes do not for one reason or another . . . but it seems to me in a far more dramatic way perhaps, than even a commission can show is this ceremony here which brings all of you to the White House, which shows to the people of our country the skills which you have, particularly very special skills.

I think that is very useful. It is useful for remembering Miss Earhart. It is useful also for our country, taking pride in what you do, and reminds our women that they ought to get out of the house into the air. So we are glad you are here.

However, just as the Nineteenth Amendment did not result in full civil and political rights or equality for women, the Equal Pay Act would be resurrected again in the late twentieth and early twenty-first centuries, as women's pay continued to lag behind that of men. Moreover, the link Kennedy made between women's rights and human rights was not sustained by his immediate successors in the Oval Office.

In the 1960s and 1970s, women's rights became part of the president's human rights strategy in foreign policy but were no longer seen as a domestic human rights issue. The emphasis on women's rights as human rights, a part of President Kennedy's rhetoric in addressing issues such as equal pay, child care, and pensions, disappeared.

It is beyond the scope of this chapter to detail how and why this split occurred, but two factors seem especially salient. First, the focus on adding an equal rights amendment to the Constitution replaced the emphasis on securing the individual and specific rights for women laid out in the United Nations Universal Declaration of Human Rights. Second, the United Nations International Women's Year Conference, and follow-up conferences over the next two decades, provided a way for administrations to address women's rights within an international institutional framework. The absence of women's rights in U.S. presidential rhetoric about human rights worldwide, and the simultaneous rhetorical failure to mention women's rights in the United States, contributed to international challenges to the leadership of the United States on issues of human rights.

President Gerald R. Ford

In a gathering at the White House to mark the signing of an executive order to establish the National Commission on the Observance of International Women's Year (IWY) in 1975, President Gerald Ford's remarks placed ratification of the Equal Rights Amendment, as well as specific rights for women such as equal pay and access to education, in a global context:

> Let 1975, International Women's Year, be the year that ERA is ratified. . . . [W]e must . . . break new ground. . . . It means equal pay for equal work for the one woman of every three workers in the world labor market. It means educational and social opportunities for women of all nationalities. Equality for women is one objective of International Women's Year; another is integration of women into the social and economic development of all nations; and third, recognition of women's increasing contributions to world peace. . . . Opening up new doors to approximately half the world's population is vital to solving many of our international problems. (Ford 1975)

While Ford, unlike Kennedy, did not explicitly link women's rights and human rights, Ford stated that he hoped the IWY Commission would "infuse the Declaration of Independence with new meaning and promise for women here as well as around the world" (Ford 1975). Still, Ford's reference to the Declaration of Independence seems less an invocation of fundamental values than a recognition that its bicentennial celebration was less than a year in the future. Ford did, however, include in his speech some provisions of the Universal Declaration of Human Rights, such as "equal pay for equal work."

Once again, equal rights for women were dependent on actions taken by women. Ford, echoing Truman, told women present at the signing, "We on the other side of the spectrum—us men—applaud your efforts, and we urge you to continue in this very important effort" (Ford 1975). With his reference to "us men" as being "on the other side of the spectrum," Ford presented women and men as having contrasting, even opposing, priorities. Women now seemed to confront a more hostile political environment than had been suggested by Truman (1948), who had stated, "There isn't a single man in Government can resist" women dedicated to the cause of women's rights.

Given the limited role of women in the government at this time, with women holding less than 5 percent of the seats in Congress, getting an item on the agenda and having it enter the decision-making process, would be a challenge. Bachrach and Baratz were correct in their estimation of the difficulties that would stand in the way of dislodging the status quo and bringing about change.

President Jimmy Carter

Early in his presidency, President Jimmy Carter made it clear that the issue of human rights was to be a cornerstone of his foreign policy. The Soviet Union was a definite target of his policy on human rights, especially regarding emigration of Jews from the Soviet Union to Israel and the treatment of prisoners in Soviet prisons. In fact, in Jimmy Carter's (1977) remarks to members of the National Women's Political Caucus at a White House reception two months into his presidency, after a discussion of major matters of foreign policy, he clearly noted that the Equal Rights Amendment (ERA) was an issue of *domestic* policy: "On the domestic scene, there are just two or three other items I'd like to mention to you. One, of course, is the passage of the equal rights amendment."[4]

Meanwhile, the Soviet ambassador to the United States, Anatoly Dobrynin, connected human rights and the not-yet-ratified ERA to the disadvantage of the United States. Carter responded by rhetorically distancing himself from the amendment. This became the president's means of deflecting international consideration of the ERA as an issue of human rights:

> You might be interested in knowing that the first time I met Ambassador Dobrynin from the Soviet Union he brought up the subject of human rights. And I said, "Well, my position is strong. It's not going

to change." He said, "Well, let me point out that the United States is not without fault itself." I said, "I know that, but what do you mean?" He said, "Well, you still haven't ratified the equal rights amendment." And I said, "I tell you what. I'll try to help you with human rights in the Soviet Union; you help me get the equal rights amendment passed in the United States." [Laughter]

But to be serious about it, our failure to pass the equal rights amendment hurts us as we try to set a standard of commitment to human rights throughout the world. I hope we can correct that defect by next year at the latest. (Carter 1977)

In this instance, Bachrach and Baratz's (1963) emphasis on the importance of values in a nondecision-making framework is distinctly relevant—the ERA was so marginalized as a value in U.S. and international policy that it triggered laughter rather than political commitment.[5]

In his farewell address to the nation, defeated in his bid for reelection, Carter (1981) finally linked women's rights in the United States to global human rights:

If we are to serve as a beacon for human rights, we must continue to perfect here at home the rights and the values which we espouse around the world: a decent education for our children, adequate medical care for all Americans, an end to discrimination against minorities and women, a job for all those able to work, and freedom from injustice and religious intolerance.

This is the first substantive connection that the president drew between human rights and equal rights for women. But the focus is on the United States being a model for the rest of the world. And Carter, the president dedicated to advancing human rights, waited to do this in his farewell address.

Hillary Rodham Clinton

In 1995, First Lady Hillary Clinton led a U.S. delegation to attend the United Nations Fourth World Conference on Women in Beijing. Clinton forcefully stated that "human rights are women's rights . . . and women's rights are human rights (H. Clinton 2004, 305; 1995b).[6] In the years since, the words that Clinton included in her address to the delegates have resonated around the world.

More important for this analysis, no attention seemed to be given to a speech that Clinton delivered in Guam on her way to Beijing. In that short address, she noted:

The main goal of our delegation of 45 men and women will be to promote policies around the world—including in our own country—that improve the status of women, children, and families and enable all women to fulfill their God-given potential. The conference will focus on issues that matter most to women, children, and families: education, health care, economic opportunity, freedom from violence, and the protection of human rights. It is important that America play a leadership role at the conference. Issues of concern to women are crucial not only to the economic and social progress of our nation, but of every other nation. (H. Clinton 1995a)

Clinton had explicitly turned attention to issues in the United States, but media coverage in the United States continued to focus on issues of human rights in China and the status of the American delegation.[7]

Hillary Clinton's initiatives in the area of human rights for women continued when she became secretary of state in the Obama administration. Clinton linked human rights to issues in the United States, carrying through on the issues she first raised as first lady over a decade earlier. As secretary of state, Clinton addressed the appointment and hiring of women to the Senior Executive Service, Foreign Service, and other posts in foreign policy, as well as issues such as family leave (H. Clinton 2009). (For a more extended discussion of Secretary Clinton's actions, see Chapter 11.)

Notwithstanding these efforts by his secretary of state, President Obama faced the same criticisms of his foreign policy as had President Carter in regard to human rights, especially for not doing more to further the economic rights of women in the United States. Specifically, officials in China and Cuba homed in on an issue that Barack Obama himself had drawn attention to: equal pay for women in the United States.

President Barack H. Obama and Equal Pay

President Obama selected an issue raised by President Kennedy, equal pay for women, for his first bill-signing ceremony. Such ceremonies are rich in symbolic meaning, and a president's first such ceremony draws added attention. For this administration, it seemed, equal pay for women would be a priority.

However, the legislation signed by President Obama, the Lilly Ledbetter Fair Pay Act, was limited in scope and did not immediately narrow the pay gap between men and women. Instead, the act extended the period in which one could bring suit against an employer for a potentially discriminatory discrepancy in pay, which also had the effect of increasing the damages that could be awarded a successful plaintiff. Even so, the value of drawing attention to an issue of women's rights was evident in Obama's subsequent mention of the act, which often came in remarks delivered at fund-raising events around the country. For over 40 percent of the speeches in which the president mentioned the keywords "equal pay" and "women," the event was a campaign fund-raiser, often for the Democratic National Committee or for Democratic candidates running for the House or the Senate.[8]

Having reminded Americans that "more needs to be done" throughout his terms (see Obama 2010, 2014, 2016), the president returned to a concerted focus on equal pay in the final years of his presidency. Admitting that the pay gap between women and men had hardly budged during his administration, with women of color especially disadvantaged, Obama gave specific guidance and action plans to his departments and agencies through such unilateral actions as executive orders and administrative actions (Obama 2014, 2016; White House 2014). In 2014, he issued an executive order to "create more pay transparency" among federal contract employees (Obama 2014); in 2016, he included all workers in the private sector in this initiative, and he proposed collecting data on occupation and salary "by race, ethnicity, and gender" (Obama 2016).[9]

Obama's remarks framed equal pay as an issue of "social change" and "a fair shot at success." He stated that with equal pay each woman would have "the rights and the opportunities and the freedom to go as far as her dreams will take her" (Obama 2016). However, this president did not connect equal pay for women to human rights. What is missing from his statements, which is found in the rhetoric of other world leaders, is that this is an economic right that will empower women *and* strengthen the nation's economy.

Reestablishing diplomatic relations with Cuba also increased scrutiny of the administration's record on human rights. Just as Ambassador Dobrynin questioned President Carter's commitment to human rights while the Equal Rights Amendment languished, Cuban officials released statements expressing "'serious concerns' over human rights in the United States, citing everything from detentions at Guantanamo Bay . . . [to] gender inequalities." *CNN* reported that "Cuban diplomats . . . [were] concerned about racial disparities in the application of the death penalty in the U.S. as well as the state of unequal pay for men and women in the United States" (Diamond 2015). In a joint press conference with Secretary of State John Kerry, Cuban foreign minister Bruno Rodriguez commented that "we consider equal pay for equal work for women and men as a key principle ("Bruno Rodríguez" 2015; see also "U.S. Restores Embassy" 2015).[10]

When President Obama traveled to Cuba in March 2016, the first sitting president to do so since Calvin Coolidge in 1928, the issue of equal pay again came up, this time during his press conference with President Raúl Castro. Comparing his and President Castro's differing perspectives on human rights, Obama explained:

> The United States will continue to speak up on behalf of democracy, including the right of the Cuban people to decide their own future. We'll speak out on behalf of universal human rights, including freedom of speech, and assembly, and religion. . . . But as you heard, President Castro has also addressed what he views as shortcomings in the United States around basic needs for people, and poverty and inequality and race relations. (White House 2016)

When pressed by reporters on the subject of human rights, President Castro responded:

> How many countries in the world comply with all the human rights and civil rights that have been included in these 61 [international] instruments? . . . None. None, whatsoever. . . . Cuba has complied with 47 of these human rights instruments. . . . Do you think there's any more sacred right than the right to health . . . the right to a free education . . . ? Do you think that for equal work, men get better paid than women just for the fact of being women? Well, in Cuba, women get the same pay for the same work. (White House 2016)

President Obama is continuing a dialogue that is a legacy of the Cold War, defending the human rights record of the United States against the nations whose policies it has challenged. Whether this will shift the political agenda within the United States, raising the salience of women's rights as human rights and leading to decision making that advances these rights, remains in question.

Conclusion

President George Washington called on the new government to be "a safeguard of human rights," in keeping with the values of the Declaration of Independence and the American Revolution (Washington 1794). However, basic human rights of full participation for women in society and the political process did not apply. References to "human rights" soon disappeared from presidential rhetoric. And even as suffrage was universally attained, references to "human rights" remained rare in presidential rhetoric throughout the nineteenth and most of the twentieth century.

The United Nations' 1948 Universal Declaration of Human Rights provided a framework through which U.S. presidents finally, sporadically, could begin linking women's issues with human rights. Though several modern presidents have included women's rights in their agendas for domestic policy (equal pay and the Equal Rights Amendment are illustrative examples), presidential rhetoric continues to confine women's rights as human rights largely to an international context. This impedes progress for women within the United States. As we have seen in interactions with China and Cuba, it also undercuts the effectiveness of U.S. presidents in confronting human rights issues in the world.

A lack of presidential leadership has also resulted in the failure of the United States to ratify several international conventions that would implement the Universal Declaration of Human Rights. It is an issue requiring Senate action, but Bachrach and Baratz's analytic framework is helpful in understanding the nature of power to see if, how, and when presidential leadership can move policy forward in securing women's rights as human rights.

NOTES

1. It is important to note that for African American women, the experience of gaining suffrage, as African Americans and as women, is far more complicated an analysis than can be provided in this chapter. For more elaboration and discussion of political rights, especially suffrage, see Brown 1997 and Locke 1997.

2. There is a temporal dimension to what actions presidents can take. Presidents have a four-year term of office, and as John Kessel (1974) has noted, there is a clear cycle to what a president can accomplish, for example, in the first year of a presidency or in the fourth year when seeking reelection. By the seventh year, one begins to think of a president as a lame duck. It took Lincoln nearly a term of office to free enslaved people. Lincoln realized the Emancipation Proclamation was not enough, and neither was the Thirteenth Amendment. Further legislation was required, as noted in the excerpt from the Republican Party platform of 1860, as well as two additional amendments added after Lincoln's assassination: the Fourteenth Amendment (on equal protection, due process, and male suffrage) and the Fifteenth Amendment (on black suffrage). The legislation he knew was needed for enforcement was not passed until one hundred years after the Civil War, with the Voting Rights Act of 1965.

3. This marks a period when intense study of the president's communication with the public began. In addition, political socialization studies reveal how children and adults in the United States have familiarity with government through the president (Carter and Teten 2002; Greenberg 1970; Hess 1995; Prewitt 2005; Sears 1975).

4. The Equal Rights Amendment had been an agenda item in the party platforms of Democrats and Republicans for decades (Martin 2003). But movement for ratification by the states became more of an issue during the Carter administration. Congress had passed the amendment in 1972 and sent it to the states for ratification. By 1977, thirty-five states had ratified the amendment, with ratification needed by three more states for the amendment to be added to the Constitution. With no additional movement toward ratification, Congress granted a three-year extension. No more states ratified the amendment by the time the extension expired. (For a full discussion of the history and politics surrounding the ERA, see Mansbridge 1986.)

5. This was not the only time that Carter invoked laughter in commenting on the Soviet ambassador's statement and the status of the Equal Rights Amendment in the United States. Meeting with ERA supporters two years later, Carter noted that ratification of the ERA was a "human rights issue" and then evoked laughter from his assembled guests through his retelling of Dobrynin's reminder about the lack of "'equal rights for women in the United States'" (Carter 1979).

6. At the time of the speech, there was concern over the message that would be sent if the first lady attended a conference in China (see, e.g., Albright 2003, 246–252; Clinton 2004, 295–308; Crossette 1995; Faison 1995; Purdum 1995). After the conference, media attention focused less on Clinton's words than on the treatment of some delegation members, who were closed out of the meeting, and issues of human rights in China (Cullum 1995).

7. When Clinton's husband, President Bill Clinton, visited China three years later, there was little evidence in his briefing materials of advance preparation in the area of human rights for women (Blinken 1998a, 1998b). Once again, as it had been before the first lady's visit to China, the focus of American media attention was on issues of human rights in China. Clinton was the first president to visit China since the Tiananmen Square demonstrations in 1989 and the violent government response to the demonstrators. While Clinton was in China, the U.S. Supreme Court handed down rulings in the area of sexual harassment for the first time (Greenhouse 1998). The cases were *Gebser et al. v. Lago Vista Independent School District* (524 U.S. 274 [1998]), *Burlington Industries, Inc. v. Ellerth* (524 U.S. 742 [1998]), and *Faragher v. City of Boca Raton* (524 U.S. 775 [1998]). There was an abundance of media coverage of these landmark rulings in the United States, but this coverage did not assess the decisions in terms of human rights in the United States. However, President Clinton was asked a question at Beijing University regarding whether there were any "problems in the area of democracy, freedom, and human rights" in the United States (W. Clinton 1998b). The student appeared to be making the link between human rights and women's rights in the United States. President Clinton responded with an answer related to racial discrimination. It seemed that Hillary Clinton's effort, three years earlier, to resurrect a dialogue in which women's rights would be viewed as human rights had apparently not taken root. (To be fair to President Clinton, a major initiative on race was under way in his administration, so his focus was more on issues of race and civil rights than on rights for women per se. In addition, the day before Clinton departed for China, he sent a letter to congressional leaders urging fast passage of a hate crimes bill. It was evident that the brutal and senseless, racially motivated murder of James Byrd Jr., which had occurred two weeks earlier in Jasper, Texas, was very much on his mind [W. Clinton 1998a].)

8. A keyword search for "equal pay" and "women" was conducted of all President Obama's remarks and speeches from January 20, 2009, through February 29, 2016. For examples of fund-raising speeches in which these keywords appear, see Obama 2009, 2011, 2012.

9. President Kennedy had taken stronger executive action, resulting in a more immediate response. For example, the requirement that departments and agencies posting civil service jobs justify a sex preference stated in a posted job resulted in a dramatic change. Prior to this action, "67 percent of the job announcements listed a preferred sex; immediately after . . . only 14 percent of the listings indicated a sex preference" (Martin 2003, 67).

10. China has also placed the record of the United States regarding women and human rights under scrutiny, as is evident in China's white paper "Human Rights in China" (Information Office of the State Council of the People's Republic of China 1991) and in China's taking a leadership role in the UN's Global Leaders' Meeting on Gender Equality and Women's Empowerment (Beijing+20) in 2015 (Sengupta 2015).

REFERENCES

Adams, Abigail. 1776. "Letter from Abigail Adams to John Adams, 31 March–5 April 1776." *Adams Family Papers: An Electronic Archive.* Available at http://www.masshist .org/digitaladams/archive/doc?id=L17760331aa&bc=%2Fdigitaladams%2Farchive%2 Fbrowse%2Fletters_1774_1777.php.

Adams, John Quincy. 1825. "First Annual Message." December 6. *American Presidency Project.* Available at http://www.presidency.ucsb.edu/ws/?pid=29467.

Albright, Madeleine. 2003. *Madam Secretary: A Memoir.* New York: Hyperion.

Allen, Danielle. 2014. *Our Declaration: A Reading of the Declaration of Independence in Defense of Equality.* New York: W. W. Norton.

Bachrach, Peter, and Morton S. Baratz. 1962. "Two Faces of Power." *American Political Science Review* 56 (4): 947–952.

———. 1963. "Decisions and Nondecisions: An Analytical Framework." *American Political Science Review* 57 (3): 632–642.

Blinken, Anthony. 1998a. Briefing materials. "China Trip—Beijing University Speech 6/29/98 [OA/ID 3380]" folder. Box 36. National Security Council—Speechwriting collection. White House Staff and Office Files series. National Archives and Records Administration. William Clinton Presidential Library. Little Rock, Arkansas.

———. 1998b. Briefing materials. "China Trip—POTUS Pre-trip Speeches 6/98 [OA/ID 3380]" folder. Box 36. National Security Council—Speechwriting collection. White House Staff and Office Files series. National Archives and Records Administration. William Clinton Presidential Library. Little Rock, Arkansas.

Brown, Elsa Barkley. 1997. "Negotiating and Transforming the Public Sphere: African American Political Life in the Transition from Slavery to Freedom." In *Women Transforming Politics*, edited by Cathy J. Cohen, Kathleen B. Jones, and Joan C. Tronto, 343–376. New York: New York University Press.

"Bruno Rodríguez and John Kerry Hold Joint Press Conference." 2015. *Granma*, August 14. Available at http://en.granma.cu/cuba/2015-08-18/bruno-rodriguez-and -john-kerry-hold-joint-press-conference.

Burri, Susanne, and Sacha Prechal. 2014. "EU Gender Equality Law: Update 2013." European Network of Legal Experts in the Field of Gender Equality. Available at http:// www.ec.europa.eu/justice/gender-equality/files/your_rights/eu_gender_equality _law_update2013_en.pdf.

Campbell, Karlyn Kohrs, and Kathleen Hall Jamieson. 2008. *Presidents Creating the Presidency: Deeds Done in Words.* Chicago: University of Chicago Press.

Carter, Amy, and Ryan L. Teten. 2002. "Assessing Changing Views of the President: Revisiting Greenstein's 'Children and Politics.'" *Presidential Studies Quarterly* 32 (3): 453–462.

Carter, Jimmy. 1977. "National Women's Political Caucus Remarks at a Reception for Members of the Organization." March 30. *American Presidency Project.* Available at http://www.presidency.ucsb.edu/ws/?pid=7265.

———. 1979. "Equal Rights Amendment Remarks at a White House Reception for Supporters of the Amendment." October 23. *American Presidency Project.* Available at http://www.presidency.ucsb.edu/ws/?pid=31578.

———. 1981. "Farewell Address to the Nation." January 14. *American Presidency Project.* Available at http://www.presidency.ucsb.edu/ws/?pid=44516.

Clinton, Hillary Rodham. 1995a. "Remarks for Arrival Ceremony in Guam." September 4. Available at https://clintonlibrary.gov/assets/storage/Research-Digital-Library/ flotus/20060198F4/Box-003/42-t-20060198f4-003-011.pdf.

———. 1995b. "Remarks to the United Nations Fourth World Conference on Women, Beijing, China." September 5. Available at http://clinton3.nara.gov/WH/EOP/First _Lady/html/generalspeeches/1995/plenary.html.

———. 2004. *Living History*. New York: Scribner.

———. 2009. "Town Hall Marking Women's History Month at the Department of State." March 12. Available at http://www.state.gov/secretary/20092013clinton/ rm/2009a/03/120309.htm.

Clinton, William J. 1998a. "Letter to Congressional Leaders on Proposed Hate Crimes Prevention Legislation." June 24. *American Presidency Project*. Available at http:// www.presidency.ucsb.edu/ws/index.php?pid=56204&st=&st1=.

———. 1998b. "Remarks and a Question-and-Answer Session with Students at Beijing University in Beijing, China." June 29. *American Presidency Project*. Available at http://www.presidency.ucsb.edu/ws/index.php?pid=56236&st=&st1=.

Cohen, Jeffrey E. 2010. *Going Local: Presidential Leadership in the Post-broadcast Age*. New York: Cambridge University Press.

Crossette, Barbara. 1995. "U.S. Upholds Role at Talks on Women: Critics Are Repulsed by Administration." *New York Times*, August 6, p. 6.

Cullum, Lee. 1995. "Women's Conference a Success despite China's Efforts." *All Things Considered*, September 15.

"Declaration of Sentiments and Resolutions: Woman's Rights Convention, Held at Seneca Falls, 19–20 July 1848." 1848. *Elizabeth Cady Stanton and Susan B. Anthony Papers Project*. Available at http://ecssba.rutgers.edu/docs/seneca.html.

"Democratic Party Platform of 1848." 1848. *American Presidency Project*. Available at http://www.presidency.ucsb.edu/ws/?pid=29574.

"Democratic Party Platform of 1904." 1904. *American Presidency Project*. Available at http://www.presidency.ucsb.edu/ws/?pid=29588.

Diamond, Jeremy. 2015. "Cuban Diplomats Slam U.S. on Human Rights." *CNN*, January 23. Available at http://www.cnn.com/2015/01/23/politics/cuba-us-human -rights/.

Faison, Seth. 1995. "Chinese Convict Harry Wu as Spy and Order Him Out: Swift Expulsion Is Seen." *New York Times*, August 24, p. A1.

Ford, Gerald R. 1975. "Remarks upon Establishing the National Commission on the Observance of International Women's Year, 1975." January 9. *American Presidency Project*. Available at http://www.presidency.ucsb.edu/ws/?pid=4894.

Gallup. n.d. "Election Polls: Vote by Groups, 1960–1964." Available at http://www.gallup .com/poll/9454/election-polls-vote-groups-19601964.aspx.

Greenberg, Edward S. 1970. "Black Children and the Political System." *Public Opinion Quarterly* 34 (3): 333–345.

Greenhouse, Steven. 1998. "Companies Set to Get Tougher on Harassment." *New York Times*, June 28, Late edition, p. 1.

Hayes, Rutherford B. 1879. "Third Annual Message." December 1. *American Presidency Project*. Available at http://www.presidency.ucsb.edu/ws/?pid=29520.

———. 1880. "Fourth Annual Message." December 6. *American Presidency Project*. Available at http://www.presidency.ucsb.edu/ws/?pid=29521.

Hess, Stephen. 1995. "My Presidency." *Presidential Studies Quarterly* 25 (4): 663–668.

Howell, William. 2003. *Power without Persuasion: The Politics of Direct Presidential Action*. Princeton, NJ: Princeton University Press.

Information Office of the State Council of the People's Republic of China. 1991. "Human Rights in China." Available at http://china.org.cn/e-white/7/index.htm.

Jefferson, Thomas. 1806. "Sixth Annual Message." December 2. *American Presidency Project*. Available at http://www.presidency.ucsb.edu/ws/?pid=29448.

Kennedy, John F. 1961. "Statement by the President on the Establishment of the President's Commission on the Status of Women." December 14. *American Presidency Project*. Available at http://www.presidency.ucsb.edu/ws/?pid=8483.

———. 1963a. "Remarks to Members of the '99 Club' of Women Pilots Following Issuance of an Amelia Earhart Commemorative Stamp." July 26. *American Presidency Project*. Available at http://www.presidency.ucsb.edu/ws/?pid=9359.

———. 1963b. "Remarks upon Signing the Equal Pay Act." June 10. *American Presidency Project*. Available at http://www.presidency.ucsb.edu/ws/?pid=9267.

Kernell, Samuel. 1986. *Going Public: New Strategies of Presidential Leadership*. Washington, DC: CQ Press.

Kessel, John H. 1974. "The Parameters of Presidential Politics." *Social Science Quarterly* 55 (1): 8–24.

Lincoln, Abraham. 2001. "Fragment of a Speech (c. December 28, 1857)." In *Collected Works of Abraham Lincoln, 1809–1865*, vol. 2. Ann Arbor: University of Michigan Digital Library Production Services. Available at http://quod.lib.umich.edu/l/lincoln/lincoln2/1:496?rgn=div1;singlegenre=All;sort=occur;subview=detail;type=simple;view=fulltext;q1=women.

———. 2016. "Letter to the Editor of the *Sangamo Journal*." In *The Annotated Lincoln*, edited by Harold Holzer and Thomas A. Horrocks, 30. Cambridge, MA: Belknap Press.

Locke, Mamie E. 1997. "From Three-Fifths to Zero: Implications of the Constitution for African American Women, 1787–1870." In *Women Transforming Politics*, edited by Cathy J. Cohen, Kathleen B. Jones, and Joan C. Tronto, 377–386. New York: New York University Press.

Mansbridge, Jane J. 1986. *Why We Lost the ERA*. Chicago: University of Chicago Press.

Martin, Janet M. 2003. *The Presidency and Women: Promise, Performance, and Illusion*. College Station: Texas A&M University Press.

Neustadt, Richard E. (1960) 1991. *Presidential Power and the Modern Presidents: The Politics of Leadership from Roosevelt to Reagan*. Reprint, New York: Free Press.

Obama, Barack H. 2009. "Remarks at a Democratic National Committee Fundraiser in Beverly Hills, California." May 27. *American Presidency Project*. Available at http://www.presidency.ucsb.edu/ws/index.php?pid=86231.

———. 2010. "Statement on the Anniversary of the Equal Pay Act." June 10. *American Presidency Project*. Available at http://www.presidency.ucsb.edu/ws/?pid=87994.

———. 2011. "Remarks at a Democratic National Committee Fundraiser in Chicago, Illinois." April 14. *American Presidency Project*. Available at http://www.presidency.ucsb.edu/ws/index.php?pid=90264.

———. 2012. "Remarks at an Obama Victory Fund 2012 Fundraiser in New York City." May 14. *American Presidency Project*. Available at http://www.presidency.ucsb.edu/ws/index.php?pid=100850.

———. 2014. "Remarks on Signing an Executive Order on Non-retaliation for Disclosure of Compensation Information and a Memorandum on Advancing Pay Equality through Compensation Data Collection." April 8. *American Presidency Project*. Available at http://www.presidency.ucsb.edu/ws/?pid=105100.

———. 2016. "Remarks Commemorating the Seventh Anniversary of the Lilly Ledbetter Fair Pay Act." January 29. *American Presidency Project*. Available at http://www.presidency.ucsb.edu/ws/?pid=111491.

Perkins, Frances. 1955. "Reminiscences of Frances Perkins: Oral History." Columbia University Oral History Collection, Columbia Center for Oral History, New York.

Prewitt, Kenneth. 2005. "The Two Projects of the American Social Sciences." *Social Research* 72 (1): 219–236.

Purdum, Todd S. 1995. "Hard Choice for White House on Hillary Clinton and China." *New York Times*, August 17, p. A1.

"Republican Party Platform of 1856." 1856. *American Presidency Project*. Available at http://www.presidency.ucsb.edu/ws/?pid=29619.

"Republican Party Platform of 1860." 1860. *American Presidency Project*. Available at http://www.presidency.ucsb.edu/ws/?pid=29620.

Sears, David O. 1975. "Political Socialization." In *Handbook of Political Science*, vol. 2, edited by Fred I. Greenstein and Nelson W. Polsby, 93–153. Reading, MA: Addison-Wesley.

Sengupta, Somini. 2015. "U.N. Meeting on Women's Rights Brings More Discord for U.S. and China." *New York Times*, September 27, Late edition, p. A12.

Stuckey, Mary E. 1991. *The President as Interpreter-in-Chief*. Chatham, NJ: Chatham House.

Truman, Harry S. 1948. "Remarks at the Opening Session of the Women's Bureau Conference." February 17. *American Presidency Project*. Available at http://www.presidency.ucsb.edu/ws/?pid=13106.

———. 1949. "Proclamation 2866—United Nations Human Rights Day." December 6. *American Presidency Project*. Available at http://www.presidency.ucsb.edu/ws/?pid=87226.

United Nations Universal Declaration of Human Rights. 1948. Available at http://www.ohchr.org/EN/UDHR/Documents/UDHR_Translations/eng.pdf.

"U.S. Restores Embassy while Pushing for Changes in Cuba." *PBS NewsHour*, August 14. Available at http://www.pbs.org/newshour/bb/u-s-restores-embassy-pushing-changes-cuba/.

Washington, George. 1794. "Sixth Annual Message." November 19. *American Presidency Project*. Available at http://www.presidency.ucsb.edu/ws/?pid=29436.

White House. 2014. "Fact Sheet: Expanding Opportunity for All: Ensuring Equal Pay for Women and Promoting the Women's Economic Agenda." April 8. Available at https://www.whitehouse.gov/the-press-office/2014/04/08/fact-sheet-expanding-opportunity-all-ensuring-equal-pay-women-and-promot.

———. 2016. "Remarks by President Obama and President Raul Castro of Cuba in a Joint Press Conference." March 21. Available at https://www.whitehouse.gov/the-press-office/2016/03/21/remarks-president-obama-and-president-raul-castro-cuba-joint-press.

Wilson, Woodrow. 1914. "Address at Independence Hall: 'The Meaning of Liberty.'" July 4. *American Presidency Project*. Available at http://www.presidency.ucsb.edu/ws/?pid=65381.

11

U.S. Development Policy
and Women's Empowerment

Challenging the Foreign-Policy Bureaucracy
to Implement Fully Integrated Gender Policy

GEORGIA DUERST-LAHTI

This study of the U.S. presidency and bureaucratic politics delineates the power dynamics that have affected the implementation of policy in the State Department during the Obama administration. During President Barack Obama's first term, Hillary Clinton exercised her power as secretary of state to reframe understandings of gender and women's policy. Clinton's efforts established gender equality and women's empowerment as central components of U.S. diplomatic and development strategy. Full integration—gender mainstreaming—had not previously been attempted on this grand scale within the U.S. foreign- and development-policy bureaucracies. Drawing on government documents, participant observation, and a diverse range of interviews throughout Africa and in Washington, D.C., this chapter reviews the political obstacles to implementation and assesses the effectiveness of Clinton's strategies for achieving enduring, widespread policy reform.

Achieving our objectives for global development will demand accelerated efforts to achieve gender equality and women's empowerment. Otherwise, peace and prosperity will have their own glass ceiling.

—**Hillary Clinton**, quoted in U.S. Agency for International Development, "Gender Equality and Female Empowerment Policy" (2012)

During President Barack Obama's first term, Secretary of State Hillary Clinton reframed understandings of gender and women's policy to be central components of U.S. diplomatic and development strategy. Clinton's drive to fully incorporate gender equity and women's empowerment represented a marked shift in U.S. commitment and approach. This policy focused on women and men, boys and girls, and the forces that enforced cultural constructions of masculinity and femininity, norms, and so forth.[1] The work begun by Secretary Clinton continued under Secretary of State John Kerry in President Obama's second term.

Attempts at implementing gender policy had shown moderate success elsewhere in the federal government. Yet fully integrated gender policy inside the U.S. foreign- and development-policy bureaucracies had not been attempted in the fifty-year period since presidents began slowly to increase the number of women receiving political appointments and end barriers to women being hired into professional federal career positions (Martin 2003). Clinton's policies were comprehensive; she concentrated exclusively on women, later including girls, *and* developed more inclusive gender-mainstreaming initiatives (Roggeband 2013). Further, she created the Office of Global Women's Issues, headed by an ambassador, and insisted on widespread training led by expert gender specialists, achievements that allayed fears that gender mainstreaming would be poorly implemented.

This chapter undertakes a preliminary analysis of the implementation of gender-equity and women's-empowerment policies by the U.S. Department of State, U.S. Agency for International Development (USAID), the Peace Corps, and the Millennium Challenge Corporation (MCC). Drawing on implementation theory, especially from bureaucratic politics and policy-feedback perspectives, I assess the deliberate efforts taken to change the norms and cultures of the organizations, as well as the policy targets of U.S. international development (Schneider and Ingram 1993). For evidence of success or failure, I draw on evidence gathered through interviews, participant observation, and focus-group studies, as well as documentary and archival research.[2]

This research explores how and how well foreign-policy bureaucracies have adapted to full integration of gender-equity and women's-empowerment policy. "Gender equality" and "women's empowerment" are the terms used most often, a nomenclature that mirrors the primary language used by Clinton's Department of State. However, as policy efforts matured and the policy process progressed, the focus shifted to girls also; toward the end of her tenure, Department of State (DOS) language sometimes shifted to "female empowerment," which signified efforts on behalf of girls. Similarly, as gender-equality policy initiatives developed and innovations to bring men and boys into programs expanded, "equity" sometimes replaced "equality," likely in recognition that statuses and power need not be the same to achieve equitable results.

In this chapter, I detail the obstacles to implementing a fully integrated gender policy and identify astute and effective strategies for gender mainstreaming. Evidence suggests that in the areas of diplomatic and development strategies, gender policy achieved extensive integration by 2014. However, because implementation can take decades, its long-term success depends on an ongoing commitment to these policies by future presidents and secretaries of state.

I begin with an extended discussion of implementation theory and bureaucracies, which also introduces the gender-policy initiatives of Secretary of State Hillary Clinton, continued by Secretary John Kerry, and the foreign-policy bureaucracies in which the integrated gender policy is designed. Following this analysis, I turn to my fieldwork, interviews, and participant observation throughout Africa and in Washington, D.C., to look at efforts to integrate gender policy from the perspective of careerists, contractors, and clients in the field.

Implementation Is Never Easy

No single implementation theory can explain all cases (Ryan 1995), but Joe Soss and Donald Moynihan detail two major approaches in which "policy implementation matters for the polity" (2014, 322). The first "locates administration at the receiving end of politics," with political forces acting on the bureaucracy through a hierarchy of relationships and "enacting coalitions" striving to gain advantages (322). This schema perceives political principles as imposing agendas unpredictably and without understanding bureaucratic capacities, cultures, and operations. Administrators then strive to manage "multisided networks of administrative organizations." Soss and Moynihan's second approach, in contrast, "identifies politics as a terrain that administrators navigate in their efforts to achieve goals" (322). Public managers approach the polity with creativity and actively engage stakeholders to acquire political support and legitimacy (Meier and O'Toole 2006). In this process, politics shapes bureaucracy while bureaucracy implements policy. Soss and Moynihan contend that "policies are forces that reconfigure terms of power, reposition actors in political relations, and reshape political actors' identities, understandings, interests, and preferences . . . and can reshape the assumptions, positions, interests, identities, and capacities of elite actors in the state, surrounding issue networks, and interest group systems" (2014, 322). Applied to this study of Clinton's gender initiatives, this approach hypothesizes that successful gender-equity and women's-empowerment policy would change the bureaucracies themselves and the way incumbent officials understand the place of women in development programs, their own orientation toward gender equity and women's empowerment, and the power afforded to gender- and women's-issue networks.

Such extensive transformation generates further challenges. To be implemented, policies must have political support. The directives must be clear enough for implementers to understand, and they must fit within the routines of the organizations to which they are assigned. The requisite technology must exist, and personnel must possess the necessary expertise (Halperin and Clapp 2006). Successful implementation usually requires coordinating multiple programs, which in turn requires setting and incorporating new priorities. Powerful resistance can come from actions as simple as refusing to alter bureaucratic momentum, for example, when specialists in other policy areas resist new priorities.

The approach to achieving gender equity and women's empowerment initiated by Secretary Clinton and continued by Secretary Kerry clearly attempted to make these changes. To implement gender and women's policy successfully, foreign-affairs bureaucracies *themselves* needed to be transformed. This was accomplished partly through deliberate internal policies to change priorities, build gender knowledge and capacity, and redirect strategic resources to "lead by example" (U.S. Department of State 2009). It also occurred through the implementation of programs for external targets such as multilateral coalitions, governments of countries, and nongovernmental organizations (NGOs), foundations, corporations and their networks, and groups and individuals.

Gender and women's policy adds a particular flavor to implementation challenges. Mary Hawkesworth identified "sanctioned ignorance," which "suggests that every culture has blind spots that render aspects of power relations invisible and that those blind spots are integral to the legitimating myths that sustain the system" (2012, 7). (See Chapter 10 for discussion of "nondecision-making," which has had a similar impact.) Implementing policy that is mindful of gender equity and women's empowerment means first making the nonconscious conscious, creating awareness that the "natural" gender power differences between women and men are not natural (Duerst-Lahti and Kelly 1995). It means tackling deeply held beliefs, rooted in gender ideology, about what is right, just, proper, and good, questioning the norms of normal (Johnson, Duerst-Lahti, and Norton 2006). And it means disrupting and replacing the assumptions and values that hold cultural, social, and political practices in place.

In response to gender and women's policy, the resistance to implementation can become actively hostile; overt sexism may couple with national, race, class, caste, ethnic, and urban-rural dilemmas. The fact that women and their status concerns are part of *every* policy and program initiative is likely to pose enormous challenges to bureaucratic systems. If women are everywhere and gender (cultural constructions for both males and females) carries its own policy status and expertise, then the changes in policy and budget metrics are all encompassing.

Prioritizing gender-equality and female-empowerment policy as a core component of twenty-first-century U.S. diplomacy is in essence the approach of gender mainstreaming, "the (re)organization, improvement, development and evaluation of policy processes, so that a gender equality perspective is incorporated in all policies at all levels and at all stages, by the actors normally involved in policy-making" (Council of Europe 1998, 15; Verloo 2001, 2–3). It targets policy *processes* as the main object of change by reorganizing procedures and routines, capacities and responsibilities, to achieve gender equality. While women and girls remain a target of gender mainstreaming, its scope is broader: It seeks to transform the gendering of organizations by disrupting and replacing gender-biased rules, processes, assumptions, distribution of resources, and so on. It seeks to change the organizations themselves.

Under the leadership of Secretaries Clinton and Kerry, elements of strategic implementation were targeted internally to the Department of State and related agencies and externally to, for example, multilateral coalitions, other governments, NGOs, corporations, and foundations. Since 2009, the policy outputs and outcomes in the areas of U.S. diplomatic and development policy show strategic, determined, smart implementation that bolstered internal capacity.

Establishing New Foreign-Policy Priorities: Clinton, Gender Equality, and Women's Empowerment

> Our foreign policy must reflect our deep commitment to help millions of oppressed people around the world, and of particular concern to me is the plight of women and girls, who comprise the majority of the world's unhealthy, unschooled, unfed, and unpaid. If half of the world's population remains vulnerable to economic, political, legal, and social marginalization, our hope of advancing democracy and prosperity is in serious jeopardy. The United States must be an unequivocal and unwavering voice in support of women's rights in every country on every continent.
> —**Hillary Clinton**, *Nomination of Hillary R. Clinton to Be Secretary of State* (2009)

The ability to understand and predict implementation obstacles has come a great distance since 1973 when Jeffrey L. Pressman and Aaron Wildavsky published *Implementation: How Great Expectations in Washington Are Dashed in Oakland*. While Soss and Moynihan (2014) may need to persuade researchers that policy implementation affects both the bureaucracy and its clients, one suspects that savvy Washington insiders are aware of the dynamic. Hillary Rodham Clinton qualifies as a savvy insider. Her career began with service as a House committee staffer during the 1973 Watergate hearings and included time as first lady (1993–2001), eight years as a U.S. senator from New York (2001–2009), and as a presidential candidate (2008 and subsequently in 2016). As its new department secretary starting in 2009, it certainly appears that Secretary Clinton understood that the State Department would need to transform itself to achieve the goal of empowering women.

Helen Derbyshire, who studied gender organizations in the United Kingdom, concluded that all organizations pursuing gender change engage in five sets of activities: internal influence; reviews, policies, and strategies; awareness raising and skill development; systems and incentives for planning and monitoring; and promoting equality at work (2012, 409). Each set of activities is examined here for what it reveals about the extent and effectiveness of the initiatives advanced by Secretary Clinton and continued by Secretary Kerry to empower women.

Internal influence. Hillary Clinton made clear, in both her Senate confirmation hearing and her opening address to State Department employees, that women and girls and gender equality would be a top priority. Her message remained clear and unambiguous throughout her tenure: support of women was demonstrably a key to development and an aid to diplomacy. First, Clinton strategically reframed women and gender concerns away from a rights or morality frame. Instead, she made the case and put resources behind the research-driven claim that gender equality and women's empowerment was a key to development and an aid to diplomacy, essential to the success of the United States and at the core of the DOS mission (U.S. Department of State 2012a, 2012b, 2013, 2014).

Second, Clinton spent her first five months as secretary trying to build up the stature of the department and solve the concerns of its employees. One critical aspect was to build loyalty through genuine attempts to improve work-life conditions (Allen and Parnes 2014, 166). Clinton became known for her trips outside foreign embassies to interact with staff in the field offices as well as with local people.

Third, the president supported her initiative and established the Office of Global Women's Issues, which reported directly to the secretary (Obama 2013). The office thus could include "S/" before its acronym of GWI, indicating that it was part of the secretary's office, with the weight of the secretary. Symbolically, this carried great weight, as did the creation of a new post, ambassador for global women's issues. The new ambassador, nominated by the president and confirmed by the Senate, was a Washington insider and trusted Clinton ally: Melanne Verveer, Clinton's deputy chief of staff during her first term and chief of staff during her second term as first lady. Beyond symbols, the ambassador and the GWI office staff could support embassies and programs around the world and function as the "fixers" needed when implementation bogged down (Mazmanian and Sabatier 1989).

Fourth, Secretary Clinton went everywhere, often traveling with Ambassador Verveer, and routinely included a high-visibility event that elevated gender-equity and women's-empowerment policy initiatives. For example, among her first stops was Rwanda, where she visited war-rape victims in refugee camps.

Finally, Secretary Clinton consistently mobilized activists, professionals in the bureaucracy and NGOs, and political leaders. Bureaucracies have reason to strengthen interest groups and their issue networks because outside interests provide critical political support for the aims of the agencies. These issue networks become critical for agency and program success (Duerst-Lahti 1989; Meier and O'Toole 2006).

Reviews, policies, and strategies. An innovation initiated by Secretary Clinton, "Leading through Civilian Power: The First Quadrennial Development and Diplomacy Report," was issued in 2010 (U.S. Department of State and U.S. Agency for International Development 2010); it mandated that each division and region of the development bureaucracy and in the State Department, USAID, and Peace Corps create its own gender policy and strategy and then issue "guidance." A guidance document generally provides a short, clear statement about the vision and direction the agency is pursuing in a broad policy area. Often guidance is issued for prototype projects or other new initiatives within a broad policy, such as gender equity and women's empowerment. Among other aspects, the guidance required that gender-policy documents be kept clear and simple. In response, one agency replaced a forty-three-page document on gender with a three-page document. Review processes, along with explicit strategies for dissemination of learning, were built into all related program funding, facilitating and encouraging implementation of the policies.

Awareness raising and skill development. By 2011, gender specialists were incorporated into each department, agency, or major program. These individuals included seasoned gender specialists as well as longtime members of the department who received additional gender-focused training. Importantly, the gender specialists and their offices received budget support, which in the past had been borrowed from other units.

Generally, the gender specialists' first task was to provide awareness training. The goal was to make *every* employee aware of gender concepts and research findings about the impact of women's empowerment for a country's development, peace, and prosperity. Field-level employees received training on how to conduct proper gender analysis as the first step in program design and skills development. This training became ubiquitous and mandatory. It was offered through the Foreign Service Institute, as an online course for USAID agents (U.S. Agency for International Development, n.d.) and for all Peace Corps volunteers. Gender specialists brought additional education and expertise to settings to support and enhance widespread training.

Systems and incentives for planning and monitoring. As a first-round initiative, gender specialists "led by doing" in reviewing every program proposal. According to one specialist I interviewed in 2014, "Our goal was to make it simple, to show how a very small set of changes could make a big difference by incorporating women through processes already part of various field programs."

Each proposal was required to plan for gender and women at every stage and had to create metrics for impact. Requiring reports during and at the close of projects gave gender specialists an opportunity to work with implementing staff to improve skills and debrief them on related efforts. Rather than ignore problems, assessments openly discussed successes and failures and continually updated best practices. These improvements were fed into all new program designs. That is, the department and agencies did much more than monitor programs; they also explicitly and consistently disseminated findings to improve program delivery, rewarding experimentation and treating failures as lessons learned to be incorporated into plans for the next round of program funding.

Incentives came in many forms, most consistently in funding for proposals that fully incorporated gender equality and women's empowerment. Ambassadors were given discretionary funds and urged to support such programs. By 2014, Secretary Kerry had developed a fund for every mission to update its internal systems and external programming to strengthen gender policy. These internal practices offered further support for the policy-feedback model.

Promoting equality at work. A fundamental element of the Obama gender strategy as executed by Secretary Clinton was to lead by doing. All of the above reforms constitute one aspect of promoting equality at work. Another was the selection and assignment of personnel to posts of high status.

Historian and former foreign service officer Beatrice McKenzie (2011, 2015) has studied sexism in the State Department through the methodology "new biography," which studies individuals to shed light on a larger culture. She has documented both sexism and reform. In 2014, McKenzie reported that women composed less than 30 percent of the senior Foreign Service. Geographically, women were disproportionately located in Africa, especially at the higher levels. However, half of the U.S. deputy chiefs of mission in G8 countries were now women, as were half of the department's undersecretaries.[3] Thus, at the highest levels of the career civil service and the departmental appointees, it seemed that "someone is tracking equality and has fifty percent female representation in mind as a goal" (McKenzie, pers. comm. 2014).

Implementation and Integration

In many regards, implementation is evolution (Majone and Wildavsky 1978). Although gender equity and women's empowerment incorporate a range of goals, the key measure for implementation success is the degree of integration across all aspects of the foreign-policy bureaucracies, both internally and externally. Too often, success for gender and development policies has been declared with short-term, albeit unsustainable gains. Meanwhile, other gender and development policies have been declared failures because incremental step-by-step reform was undervalued when measured against the vision rather than all the stages required to achieve the envisioned policy ends (Derbyshire 2012, 416). Nonetheless, short-term visible success usually accompanies long-term impact if top-level commitment is visible, if there is support to avoid policy "evaporation," and if a clear vision of gender equity and women's empowerment exists.

Symbolism. As Murray Edelman (1964) and other constructivists suggest, the names and symbolic location of bureaucratic units matter. Thus, one measure of success in advancing gender equity and female empowerment includes the creation and prominent location of units dedicated to this purpose. While symbolic gestures risk being ineffectual without sustained and visible commitment, the symbols speak volumes and contribute substantially to concrete capacity when coupled with resources and enduring high-level support. During Clinton's tenure as secretary of state, several units were created at the top levels within the Executive Office of the President and the State Department with this focus. Clinton's activities fit readily into the Obama administration's executive actions that reestablished a White House attentiveness to issues of gender equity and women's empowerment (White House, n.d., 2013). (See Chapter 8 for a discussion of how the Obama White House has responded to and represented women and girls.)

Requirements, incentives, and compliance. By 2014, several gender-related requirements were in place. These included the President's Emergency Plan for AIDS Relief (PEPFAR) at the State Department, which had informed its teams that every country receiving funds must "undertake a gender analysis related to HIV at the country-level by March 2016" (President's Emergency Plan for AIDS Relief 2013, 4). USAID required gender analysis to be incorporated into every step of a program's design and provided assistance of many types to make doing so simple yet effective.

The well-funded MCC, created in 2004 to facilitate achieving the UN's Millennium Challenge Goals, stated in 2011 that without a gender commitment, there would be no money for any of the other seven MCC goals: eradicating poverty, improving education, reducing child mortality, improving maternal health, combating disease, ensuring environmental sustainability, and joining global partnerships. Women and girls feature prominently in each of these goals, so treating gender and female empowerment as central made policy sense. Additionally, the Peace Corps required training in gender equity and women's empowerment for all its volunteers.

Incentives, the "carrot" to the requirements' "stick," also figured as an indicator of visible success. MCC provided assistance at every step of the policy process, reaching into high levels of government.

Most prominent among State's recent incentives were highly flexible funds spent at the ambassador's discretion to improve gender equality and female empowerment in country or for specific projects.

Additionally, the Peace Corps now rewarded explicit attention to gender through extensive training in gender analysis generally and in project design specifically, with gender assistance at each post. In short, since 2010, each of these entities, as well as the State Department's subunits, produced a myriad of tools for guidance, assistance, internal improvements, and best practices. In spite of Hillary Clinton's interests and intentions, it took at least a year after she entered the secretarial office to initiate change.

Integration of gender equity and female empowerment. How well did these policies and processes lead to integration of gender equity and female empowerment? Following an initiative from the top levels of the administration, actions to integrate gender equity and empowerment for women and girls—female empowerment—began to take root in the foreign-policy bureaucracies. Halfway through Secretary Clinton's tenure as secretary of state, the MCC issued its gender policy, which included country consultation, imposed a score card that prioritized receptiveness to gender equality in funding decisions, and, perhaps most important, required gender to be incorporated into the design of all supported programs at every stage, including monitoring and closing compacts (Millennium Challenge Corporation 2011).

USAID issued its policy to integrate gender equity and female empowerment in March 2012 (see U.S. Agency for International Development 2012). This policy combined and strengthened previous efforts, brought in more staff, and commenced consultation and awareness efforts, making USAID a leader among the foreign-policy agencies. Prominent among its accomplishments has been the creation of training modules, which all field staff must complete. The Peace Corps also brought on two staff people dedicated to gender; all Peace Corps volunteers now receive training in this policy area.

While training sometimes focused only on women and girls, often it addressed how volunteers could engage men to work with women or to establish gender-complementarity efforts. These offered men and boys roles that
supported and advanced efforts for women and girls. Interestingly, because
the Peace Corps already considered women and girls to be fully integrated
into their approach and mission, they embraced the explicit gender training
with less visible enthusiasm than USAID (Peace Corps gender specialists,
telephone interviews by the author, June 2014).

An important measure of policy success is interest and integration that
extend beyond the government itself. As an illustrative case study, the Society of International Development (SID) is a nongovernmental group and the
leading association for development professionals. The Washington, D.C.,
chapter (SID-W) supports eighteen working groups that sponsor programming to build professional capacity. The Gender in Development Workgroup
is strong enough to have published annual reports since 2012. Suggesting
dispersal of gender-integration policy, it held a session on "Getting the Most
out of USAID's Gender 101 Training Tool" on September 11, 2014 (Society
of International Development, Gender in Development Workgroup 2014).
SID-W also held a session on new strategies for civil-society development
based on greater collaboration among private, public, and nonprofit sectors,
an approach central to Clinton's early efforts for gender and women, a hall-
mark of her twenty-first-century diplomacy (Allen and Parnes 2014), and a
reflection of Secretary Kerry's continuation of Clinton's policy.

Whether these visible signifiers of gender commitment actually succeed in
producing gender-policy integration remains for further study. Recent analysis
of the UN Millennium Development Goals (MDGs) suggests shortcomings
(UN Women, n.d.). Only some elements have achieved the status of standard
operating procedures (SOPs), which Daniel Mazmanian and Paul Sabatier
(1989) declared to be the litmus test of implementation. However, across all
agencies, the most important SOP seems to be an endorsement of gender analysis and a commitment to improving the status of women because these efforts
are good policy. Further, gender specialists in each agency and Office of the
White House have developed many tools to help in achieving integration: creating awareness and providing training, insisting on gender analysis in project
design, consulting during implementation, monitoring and gathering data,
disseminating best practices, and adjusting and updating gender guidelines.

In the Field: An Evolving Story Told through Interviews and Participant Observation

I conducted interviews and focus groups throughout Africa annually and
with former and current officials in Washington, D.C., from 2010 through

2014 that revealed important steps for implementation, which are detailed later. In general, initial Washington, D.C., interviews were secured through gender-specialist networks. Then I focused on those who had participated in policy implementation. All of these interviews were on background only. For interviews in Africa, I recruited interviewees through women's producer groups, the U.S. government embassies, and my own participation in the 2013 African Women's Entrepreneurship Program (AWEP) conference. Ultimately, I conducted three focus groups. I also conducted structured follow-up interviews with a number of focus-group participants and with development personnel in projects sponsored by U.S. government projects, NGOs, or their contractors.

Overall, the study spanned six years, the full four years during which Hillary Clinton served as secretary of state and the first two years of John Kerry's tenure in that same cabinet post. Such a lengthy duration allowed me to examine implementation as a process, from the earliest months of Clinton's outreach to the status of gender programming at the time of her exit, and then to assess the impact of a change in departmental leadership. The longitudinal approach also led to refinements in research design, as interview and focus-group questions became more focused, my own participant observation analyses became more informed, and my networks extended further throughout the government bureaucracies and NGOs and among program participants. Ultimately, the study encompassed Nigeria in west-central Africa and six countries in southern Africa: Botswana, Mozambique, Namibia, South Africa, Swaziland, and Zimbabwe. Each country offered a representative case of State Department gender-equity and women's-empowerment policy, with numerous agency personnel advancing diverse programs; a wide engagement of activists and NGO leaders in Washington, D.C., and abroad; and the continuing participation of officials and local people in the specific countries.

To further enhance the study, I focused on local production programs and rural women's cooperatives. These initiatives have the potential to greatly affect women's economic standing, so they are especially revealing of the extent to which the U.S. foreign-policy and development agencies are achieving their articulated goals of equity and empowerment.

What follows is a narrative of my experiences, with a preliminary analysis of the stages of implementation. The account gives careful consideration to the impact of the programs on the personnel implementing the programs, the activists and leaders mobilizing and facilitating around these programs, and the individuals who have been the clients of these programs. Conclusions will be developed further in future publications, but this early statement offers invaluable insights on research methods unfamiliar to many presidency scholars. It also suggests an important research agenda for comparative-policy scholars.

Initial focus groups were conducted in 2010, with members of rural women's cooperatives and in Namibia, South Africa, Swaziland, and Zimbabwe. Participants often mentioned UN MDGs and efforts from European development agencies and major foundations but seldom referred to U.S. foreign-policy bureaucracies. The single exception was the PEPFAR program, which often was mentioned as caring about women in all matters related to HIV/AIDS.

In March 2011, I interviewed a USAID officer, stationed in Washington, D.C., who worked for a regional bureau. She had recently been asked to take on the role of gender specialist, in addition to her other duties, to fulfill the requirement that every bureau have such a person. Selected because she was female and had taken one course on gender and women's politics while getting her master's degree, she reported feeling woefully ill prepared for her duties. Further, she said that although the agency had a person to coordinate its gender efforts, her success was impeded by several factors. She already had too much to do; too few knowledgeable gender specialists were on staff; and the top gender positions lacked status and, importantly, had no budget. The only way a gender project could be developed was to secure resources from a unit whose budget was flexible enough to fund a new initiative, which usually meant finding a gender-policy champion within a standing unit. If that succeeded, then the gender project had to meet all of the granting unit's metrics for accountability. Much the same was true for adding gender to a project. Problematically, it would be an add-on rather than the "real" project and would not carry its own funding or measures for success. In short, my contact reported that gender had little claim to USAID's organizational capacity, with few personnel, no budget, and poor coordination. Consultation with other personnel confirmed that these constraints were prevalent throughout all foreign-policy and development agencies.

Just over a year later, in July and August 2012, I again visited producer groups in Namibia, Botswana, and Swaziland to undertake follow-up interviews. I conducted focus groups in Botswana. UN MDGs were again mentioned the most often, again with the exception of PEPFAR. Importantly, respondents seemed to have noticed that more of PEPFAR's efforts were directed specifically to women. Namibia had received MCC funding, and the projects paid heed to women and gender, although integration was uneven. Efforts were strong in the indigenous natural-products sector but weak in traditional agriculture, for example. Swaziland seemed focused on PEPFAR and MDGs, with a big push for HIV/AIDS programming that was leveraged to diminish women's poverty. USAID was pulling back, generally because Swaziland, Namibia, and Botswana had achieved middle-income-country status, with a per capita GDP greater than $875 annually (Chilonda, Machethe, and Minde 2007).

In March 2013, I attended a conference in West Africa sponsored by the USAID-funded Global Shea Alliance, which supports women in the production of shea butter. This meeting took place a year after USAID announced its policy of full gender integration. The female head of the project, who worked for a major development contract company, stated that she was happy to empower women through the project, although she had no particular training for this task. While the need to expand to gender equity and women's empowerment was broadly understood to be policy, in the field, she said, "it still hinge[d] upon individual champions inside the agencies." That is, one bureaucrat still had to function as a policy entrepreneur for gender equity and women's empowerment. Policy had changed since 2011 but continued to show the effects of idiosyncratic implementation.

In our 2013 interview, a highly placed USAID official confirmed these challenges to successful implementation:

> Some things go together. Like we can put environmental sustainability with economic development together easily. But you can't just squeeze gender and women in because you want to. We'd be better off if they had us in fewer meetings about women and gender, and spending less time at training. They should just let us do our jobs and women will benefit.

This head of mission was not happy about efforts to integrate gender and women into US development policy. He understood gender to be an add-on to more important agency goals and resisted implementing the one-year-old policy. At this point at least, he perceived gender and women's policy as out of step with the portfolio of his USAID mission.

Finally, I spent more than four months in Botswana during 2014. I spoke with a range of development professionals working in the U.S. embassy, USAID, NGOs, and contract companies whose efforts were focused in Botswana, Namibia, and South Africa. One women's group was receiving USAID support because they were women organized around sustainable livelihoods and HIV/AIDS support. The women were fully aware of the reasons for the support and knew that it came from the U.S. government. As one head of a regional USAID environmental project explained in our 2014 interview:

> Including women is natural if you do a proper community participation assessment. Really, *it's just natural to include women.* Yes, we've all had the training but really it makes sense to include women with natural products. They've been playing these roles culturally for a very long time. (Emphasis added)

It is a striking change from the past that including women was deemed to be "natural" for community projects. Significantly, this was a sentiment echoed by other personnel.

A U.S. embassy officer who worked with the commerce section in Namibia, for example, provided a similar response in our 2014 interview. He emphasized the strength of AWEP and the number of programs and awards AWEP sponsored to recognize outstanding businesswomen. He could name and describe many of the women's accomplishments in detail. He also suggested that women were more likely to participate in new programs. "Face it," he said. "We're trying to move into some new and innovative areas. If you're trying something innovative, women will be much more attracted than men. So, *it's just natural to include women*" (emphasis added). He continued, "Yes, we've had the training, and SO [Secretary's Office] reminds us all the time that we're supposed to be giving priority to gender and women's empowerment. But really, it's not hard."

Although Secretary Kerry changed program names and reoriented several economic tools of diplomacy, the emphasis on gender and female empowerment has continued and has mattered greatly. Implementation of any policy requires time to evolve and continued top-level support. Field officers commented on the fact that the SO continued to remind them of their responsibilities, ensuring that policy evaporation would not occur for gender and women's policy. Efforts in the field would be supported.

The interviews and observations suggest these agencies have made considerable progress toward full integration of gender equality and women's empowerment. While the numbers interviewed are too few to draw firm conclusions and the long-term impact on the lives of individual women is not yet known, the shift in awareness and openness regarding gender-equality and female-empowerment programs is striking. Implementation of this public policy has been comparatively swift, with significant changes occurring within one presidential term.

Conclusion

This study explores the dynamics of implementation, examining hurdles to and successes in implementation with an eye toward understanding larger patterns of implementation. Importantly, it sought to discover whether successful gender-equity and women's-empowerment policy would change the bureaucracies themselves along with incumbent officials' orientation toward gender equity and women's empowerment. It looked for evidence that the implementation of gender policy might be sustained through changes in leadership.

Several lessons are evident. First, the pattern for implementing gender policy moved through a process relevant to other policies. Predictably, after setting a new policy direction—the integration of gender equity and women's empowerment—initial stages evidenced many forms of resistance, with field officers ignoring early guidance, expressing resentment, and considering gender equity and women's empowerment as add-ons to other more important agency initiatives. Awareness of what to do and how to proceed in the field was limited. From 2010 through 2012, internal-policy entrepreneurs were pivotal, advocating for programs and fixing problems that arose. With explicit and formal mandates beginning in 2011 and 2012, which were coupled with expert staff, incentives, training, and ubiquitous field support, gender was incorporated into all project spending from the ambassador level downward.

Second, field agents came to accept gender inclusion, acknowledging it as relevant and useful to the core diplomacy and development policy. Ultimately, some referred to gender policy as "natural" to achieving mission goals. This reframing of gender policy from a moral preference to a core policy commitment proved to be powerful. The critical continuity Secretary Kerry offered avoided policy evaporation. The policy focus continued, strongly and broadly integrated.

Third, incentives for innovative approaches encouraged bottom-up proposals, bolstered by a learning-organization stance that treated failures as well as successes as lessons that were incorporated into the next proposal cycle and their accompanying guidance on best practices.

Thus, all three approaches to implementation politics discussed by Soss and Moynihan (2014) were evident. First, efforts to fully integrate gender policy were imposed on administrators top down from Foggy Bottom to remote field missions, and initially many resisted. Second, in conjunction with women's NGOs whose connections to Secretary Clinton go back at least to 1995 and her participation in the United Nations Fourth World Conference on Women, Clinton inserted gender experts into the implementation process. Third, both gender mainstreaming and gender- and women-specific programming were strategically combined and implemented through networks and focused offices. Finally, the training and reminders from the SO also shifted at least some field agents' understandings regarding the utility and naturalness of focusing on gender and women to achieve diplomatic, peace, and development aims.

Some scattered reflections warrant mention. Whether having more women in high foreign-policy posts matters for outcomes of gender policy cannot be conclusively discerned from this study, but much research suggests that it does (e.g., Brescoll 2011; Carroll 2001; Chatman and O'Reilly 2004; Croson and Gneezy 2009). Future research can dig into the details of implementation with finer precision. This preliminary analysis, however, already suggests that Secretaries Clinton and Kerry and their respective teams understood that implementing these policies would change their organizations. In fact, that change appears to have been an essential precondition for other gender-policy success.

NOTES

The research presented in this chapter was generously supported by several programs at Beloit College, including the Sanger Summer Scholars Program, the Senior Keefer Fund, and the Professional Development Fund.

1. Despite important distinctions in theory and practice among the terms, several names for these efforts are used interchangeably here: "gender policy," "gender equity" (or "gender equality"), and "women's empowerment." Later in Clinton's tenure, reference was made to "female empowerment," instead of "women's empowerment," to incorporate an attentiveness to empowering girls.

2. For a detailed discussion of the fieldwork conducted for this study in several African nations and in Washington, D.C., see the final section of this chapter. To ensure that the reader is fully informed about the sources of all information, however, interview quotations are contextualized as they appear throughout this chapter.

3. Deputy chief of mission is the highest rank many career Foreign Service officers attain; as professionals, they actually manage the embassy, while their ambassadors take the lead in performing diplomatic duties. The undersecretary is the fourth-highest post within the department; this post is nominated by the president and is subject to Senate confirmation. The G8 "refers to the group of eight highly industrialized nations—France, Germany, Italy, the United Kingdom, Japan, the United States, Canada, and Russia—that hold an annual meeting to foster consensus on global issues like economic growth and crisis management, global security, energy, and terrorism" (Laub 2014).

REFERENCES

Allen, Jonathan, and Amie Parnes. 2014. *HRC: State Secrets and the Rebirth of Hillary Clinton.* New York: Crown.

Brescoll, Victoria L. 2011. "Who Takes the Floor and Why: Gender, Power, and Volubility in Organizations." *Administrative Science Quarterly* 56 (4): 622–641.

Carroll, Susan J., ed. 2001. *The Impact of Women in Public Office.* Bloomington: Indiana University Press.

Chatman, Jennifer A., and Charles A. O'Reilly. 2004. "Asymmetric Reactions to Work Group Sex Diversity among Men and Women." *Academy of Management Journal* 47 (2): 193–208.

Chilonda, Pius, Charles Machethe, and Isaac Minde. 2007. "Poverty, Food Security and Agricultural Trends in Southern Africa." Regional Strategic Analysis and Knowledge Support System Working Paper No. 1. Available at http://pdf.usaid.gov/pdf_docs/pnads604.pdf.

Council of Europe. 1998. "Gender Mainstreaming: Conceptual Framework, Methodology and Presentation of Good Practices." Available at http://www.unhcr.org/3c160b06a.pdf.

Croson, Rachel, and Uri Gneezy. 2009. "Gender Differences in Preferences." *Journal of Economic Literature* 47 (2): 448–474.

Derbyshire, Helen. 2012. "Gender Mainstreaming: Recognising and Building on Progress: Views from the UK Gender and Development Network." *Gender & Development* 20 (3): 405–422.

Duerst-Lahti, Georgia. 1989. "The Government's Role in Building the Women's Movement." *Political Science Quarterly* 104 (2): 249–268.

Duerst-Lahti, Georgia, and Rita Mae Kelly. 1995. *Gender Power, Leadership, and Governance.* Ann Arbor: University of Michigan Press.

Edelman, Murray. 1964. *The Symbolic Uses of Politics.* Urbana: University of Illinois Press.

Halperin, Morton H., and Priscilla A. Clapp, with Arnold Kanter. 2006. *Bureaucratic Politics and Foreign Policy.* 2nd ed. Washington, DC: Brookings Institution Press.

Hawkesworth, Mary. 2012. *Political Worlds of Women; Activism, Advocacy, and Governance in the Twenty-First Century.* Boulder, CO: Westview Press.

Johnson, Cathy Marie, Georgia Duerst-Lahti, and Noelle H. Norton. 2006. *Creating Gender: The Sexual Politics of Welfare Policy.* Boulder, CO: Lynne Rienner.

Laub, Zachary. 2014. "The Group of Eight (G8) Industrialized Nations." Council on Foreign Relations, March 3. Available at http://www.cfr.org/international-organizations-and-alliances/group-eight-g8-industrialized-nations/p10647.

Majone, Giandomencio, and Aaron Wildavsky. 1978. "Implementation as Evolution." In *Policy Studies Review Annual, 1978,* edited by Howard E. Freeman, 103–117. Beverly Hills, CA: Sage.

Martin, Janet M. 2003. *The Presidency and Women: Promise, Performance, and Illusion.* College Station: Texas A&M University Press.

Mazmanian, Daniel A., and Paul A. Sabatier. 1989. *Implementation and Public Policy.* Lanham, MD: University Press of America.

McKenzie, Beatrice Loftus. 2011. "The Diplomatic Career of Constance Harvey: Gender and Consular Work, 1929–1964." Paper presented at the Society for Historians of American Foreign Relations Conference, Washington, DC, June 24.

———. 2015. "The Problem of Women in the Department: Sex and Gender Discrimination in the 1960s United States Foreign Diplomatic Service." *European Journal of American Studies* 10 (1). Available at https://ejas.revues.org/10589.

Meier, Kenneth J., and Laurence J. O'Toole. 2006. *Bureaucracy in a Democratic State: A Governance Perspective.* Baltimore: Johns Hopkins University Press.

Millennium Challenge Corporation. 2011. "Gender Policy." Available at http://www.mcc.gov/documents/guidance/mcc-policy-gender.pdf.

Nomination of Hillary R. Clinton to Be Secretary of State: Hearing Before the Committee on Foreign Relations, United States Senate. 2009. 111th Cong. 23 (statement of Hillary Rodham Clinton, U.S. Senator from New York). Available at https://www.gpo.gov/fdsys/pkg/CHRG-111shrg54615/pdf/CHRG-111shrg54615.pdf.

Obama, Barack. 2013. "Presidential Memorandum: Coordination of Policies and Programs to Promote Gender Equality and Empower Women and Girls Globally." January 30. Available at https://www.whitehouse.gov/the-press-office/2013/01/30/presidential-memorandum-coordination-policies-and-programs-promote-gende.

President's Emergency Plan for AIDS Relief. 2013. "Updated Gender Strategy, FY 2014." Available at http://www.pepfar.gov/documents/organization/219117.pdf.

Pressman, Jeffrey L., and Aaron Wildavsky. 1973. *Implementation: How Great Expectations in Washington Are Dashed in Oakland; or, Why It's Amazing That Federal Programs Work at All, This Being the Saga of the Economic Development Administration as Told by Two Sympathetic Observers Who Seek to Build Morals on a Foundation of Ruined Hopes.* Berkeley: University of California Press.

Roggeband, Conny. 2013. "Gender Mainstreaming in Dutch Development Cooperation: The Dialectics of Progress." *Journal of International Development* 26 (3): 332–344.

Ryan, Neal. 1995. "Unraveling Conceptual Developments in Implementation Analysis." *Australian Journal of Public Administration* 54 (1): 65–81.

Schneider, Anne, and Helen Ingram. 1993. "Social Construction of Target Populations: Implications for Politics and Policy." *American Political Science Review* 87 (2): 334–347.

Society of International Development, Gender in Development Workgroup. 2014. "Getting the Most out of USAID's Gender 101 Training Tool." Available at http://www.sidw .org/mc/community/eventdetails.do?eventId=438306&orgId=wdcsid&recurringId=0.

Soss, Joe, and Donald P. Moynihan. 2014. "Policy Feedback and the Politics of Public Administration." *Public Administration Review* 74 (3): 320–332.

UN Women. n.d. "Progress towards Meeting the MDGs [Millennium Development Goals] for Women and Girls." Available at http://www.unwomen.org/en/news/in-focus/mdg -momentum (accessed December 5, 2015).

U.S. Agency for International Development. n.d. *Gender 101: Gender Equality at USAID*. Available at http://usaidlearninglab.org/sites/default/files/media/GLS_USAID _Gender101_SCORM_20130918/index.html#9A69C53F-52C7-1A80-1BE5-E45B C1907FCD (accessed December 5, 2015).

———. 2012. "Gender Equality and Female Empowerment Policy." Available at https:// www.usaid.gov/sites/default/files/documents/1865/GenderEqualityPolicy_0.pdf.

U.S. Department of State. 2009. "State Department 100-Day Report." Available at http:// www.state.gov/r/pa/ei/rls/dos/122390.htm.

———. 2012a. "Advancing the Rights of Women and Girls: A Cornerstone of U.S. Foreign Policy." Available at http://www.state.gov/documents/organization/185687.pdf.

———. 2012b. "U.S. Department of State Policy Guidance: Promoting Gender Equality to Achieve Our National Security and Foreign Policy Objectives." Available at http:// www.state.gov/documents/organization/189379.pdf.

———. 2013. "Advancing the Status of Women and Girls around the World." Available at http://www.state.gov/r/pa/prs/ps/2013/03/205866.htm.

———. 2014. "U.S. Department of State Policy Guidance: Promoting Gender Equality and Advancing the Status of Women and Girls." Available at http://www.state.gov/s/gwi/ rls/other/2014/228735.htm.

U.S. Department of State and U.S. Agency for International Development. 2010. "Leading through Civilian Power: The First Quadrennial Diplomacy and Development Report." Available at http://www.state.gov/documents/organization/153108.pdf.

Verloo, Meike. 2001. "Another Velvet Revolution? Gender Mainstreaming and the Politics of Implementation." Institute fur die Wissenschaften vom Menschen Working Paper No. 5/2001. Available at http://www.iiav.nl/epublications/2001/anothervelvet revolution.pdf.

White House. n.d. "Obama Administration Record for Women and Girls." Available at http://www.whitehouse.gov/sites/default/files/docs/womens_record.pdf (accessed December 5, 2015).

———. 2013. "Fact Sheet: The Obama Administration's Comprehensive Efforts to Promote Gender Equality and Empower Women and Girls Worldwide." Available at http:// www.whitehouse.gov/the-press-office/2013/04/19/fact-sheet-obama-administration-s -comprehensive-efforts-promote-gender-e.

12

Presidential Power, Partisan Continuity, and Pro-Women Change in Chile, 2000–2010

CATHERINE REYES-HOUSHOLDER

This chapter compares how successive Chilean presidents have exercised executive power to effect policy changes for women. Michelle Bachelet, the first female president of Chile, is often described as instituting policies that benefited the women of her country—yet there has been no systematic study of the extent to which, in comparison with her immediate predecessor, Ricardo Lagos, she has actually represented change or continuity. Bachelet and Lagos hail from the same party, have maintained similar core constituencies, and have enjoyed similar popularity levels. In this chapter, "pro-women change" is defined as policy congruent with that of the UN Convention on the Elimination of Discrimination Against Women (to which Chile is a signatory); the policy agenda of the Chilean government's agency for women; or the Gender and Equality Observatory, Chile's main umbrella organization for women's groups. Working with all legislation proposed from 2000 to 2010, encompassing Lagos's term and Bachelet's first term, this chapter examines legislative-executive relations in more than 250 bills. Comparing and contrasting the two presidents' exercise of power, it demonstrates that Bachelet, far more than Lagos, used her executive power to advance a greater number of and a more diverse array of pro-women policies.

A growing number of case studies document how some female presidents (*presidentas*) in Latin America have advanced gender equality (Franceschet 2010; Jalalzai and dos Santos 2015; Staab and Waylen 2016; Stevenson 2012). Yet no study has systematically compared female and male presidents. This lack of variation in the independent variable (sex of president) makes it difficult to assess the impact of *presidentas* on reforms benefiting women.

This chapter advances scholarship on *presidentas* by closely examining the use of power by two similarly situated presidents who differ by sex. Chile's first female president, Michelle Bachelet, and her immediate male predecessor, Ricardo Lagos, both hailed from the Socialist Party and professed a center-left ideology. Governing the same country during the same decade, they faced similar political, economic, and cultural opportunities and constraints.[1]

In addition to providing a comparative study of a female and male president's use of power while controlling for party, the chapter contributes to a long-standing debate on how to measure women's interests. I argue for a three-tier operationalization of pro-women change (PWC) in Chile. Employing this operationalization offers a theoretical advantage of avoiding essentialism,[2] yields the largest data set on PWC bills in Chile to date, and reveals uses of presidential power to promote PWC that extant literature has generally overlooked.

My analysis of more than 250 bills benefiting women reveals that Bachelet used her legislative powers more frequently than Lagos to advance PWC. These presidents also differed in the kinds of PWC legislation that they promoted. Bachelet's PWC legislation often delivered material benefits to diverse groups of women—particularly low-income mothers. In contrast, Lagos focused primarily on compliance with international treaties.

I first review Lagos's and Bachelet's elections and suggest that their winning constituencies differed in sex-specific ways. I then operationalize PWC in Chile, explain the empirical method used in my analysis, and discuss my findings. Finally, I discuss some of Lagos's and Bachelet's PWC legislative highlights and outline avenues for future research.

Lagos and Bachelet: Women Voters and the Elections of 1999–2000 and 2005–2006

After Chile's return to democracy following a military dictatorship from 1973 to 1989, Chile's center-left Concertación coalition won the presidency four consecutive times (1989, 1993, 2000, and 2006). Ricardo Lagos, a socialist minister under the first two Concertación presidents, won in 2000. Michelle Bachelet, also a socialist with ministerial experience under Lagos, triumphed in 2006.

Ricardo Lagos and the Elections of 1999–2000

Born in the capital of Santiago, Ricardo Lagos earned his Ph.D. in economics in 1966 from Duke University and then returned to Chile to work as an economics professor. Lagos emerged as a national leader of the opposition to the military dictatorship (1973–1989). After the democratic transition, he served as education minister (1990–1992) and then as public works minister (1994–1998). Lagos resigned from the cabinet to run for president, and he won the Concertación coalition's nomination via a primary contest in 1999.

In the ensuing general election, Lagos confronted Joaquín Lavín, a charismatic leader of the far right's Independent Democratic Union Party and successful mayor of the wealthy Las Condes commune. An ongoing economic crisis meant that many of the campaign debates focused on economic issues. Lagos's platform began by evoking the Concertación's success in creating economic growth in the 1990s, its historic fight for democracy, and its pursuit of social justice (Centro de Estudios Miguel Enriquez and Archivo Chile 1999b). Lavín's main campaign promises were to create one million new jobs and help small and medium businesses thrive and fight crime (Centro de Estudios Miguel Enriquez and Archivo Chile 1999a).

In the first round, Lagos failed to capture the majority needed to win, earning just 47.96 percent to Lavín's 47.51 percent of the vote. Lagos won 49 percent of the male vote and 44 percent of the female vote (Servicio Electoral de Chile 2013), continuing a trend set by his predecessors; both Concertación presidents before him performed comparatively worse among women.[3] (Lavín won 43 percent of the male vote and 49 percent of the female vote.) The second-round strategy thus focused on securing women's support. To achieve this, Lagos named former Concertación minister Soledad Alvear his new campaign spokesperson.[4] The choice was based on the assumption that women voters in Chile were more likely to support a campaign with a female face (Arriagada and Navia 2006).

In the second round in January 2000, Lagos defeated Lavin 51.3 percent to 48.7 percent. Naming a prominent female ex-minister as a spokesperson did not seem to help Lagos earn female support, since Lagos again underperformed among women, earning 53 percent of the male vote and just 48 percent of the female vote. Lavín, meanwhile, won 45 percent of the male vote and 50 percent of the female vote (Servicio Electoral de Chile 2013; Zúñiga Urbina and Gutiérrez Moya 2000).

Like that of his Concertación predecessors, Lagos's winning constituency consisted of more men than women. His advantage among men seemed to continue during his presidency. For example, in a Centro de Estudios Públicos (CEP) June/July 2004 poll, 61 percent of men but only 55 percent of women approved of Lagos's performance, and 53 percent of men but just 46 percent of women approved of his economic performance.[5] Women voters would not become a key constituency for any Concertación presidential candidate until Chile elected its first female president, Michelle Bachelet.

Michelle Bachelet and the Elections of 2005–2006

Michelle Bachelet is the daughter of a general who died under torture during the dictatorship. She and her mother lived as exiles in Australia and then East Germany during the military regime. She returned to Chile in 1979, completed her studies in medicine, and worked as a pediatrician. She also completed course work in military affairs in Chile in the 1990s and then studied for one year at the Inter-American Defense College in Washington, D.C. Like Lagos, Bachelet served in prominent ministerial positions before becoming president. She emerged as a national politician in 2000 when Lagos named her health minister. Two years later, Bachelet became Latin America's first female defense minister.

Bachelet emerged as a candidate at a time when the Concertación had wielded presidential power for over ten consecutive years. The center-left coalition sought ways to offer the Chilean public change, and some leaders hinted that nominating a woman could help renew the coalition. In this context, Foreign Affairs Minister Soledad Alvear and Defense Minister Bachelet were relatively well positioned to seek the presidency. Bachelet soon outpaced Alvear in the polls, and Alvear dropped out of the primary race in May 2005 (Morales Quiroga 2008; Ríos Tobar 2008). Meanwhile, Lavín, again representing Chile's far-right party, was sinking according to public opinion surveys. This opened up space for billionaire businessman and former senator Sebastián Piñera, soon nominated for president by the center-right National Renovation Party.

In contrast to the previous presidential contest, gender issues became salient during the 2005 campaigns because of the novel possibility of electing Chile's first *presidenta* and to Bachelet's campaign, which became decidedly pro-women once she pledged to name Chile's first gender-parity cabinet. The public commitment met with some resistance from the political establishment but also received strong support from Chilean women activists. Bachelet promised child subsidies for mothers, an improved social safety net for children, massive social-security reforms through new provisions to reduce gender inequalities, more effective divorce laws, more reproductive rights, greater participation of women in politics, and a strengthening of gender-violence laws (Centro de Estudios Miguel Enriquez and Archivo Chile 2005).

In addition to campaigning on the most women-friendly presidential platform in recent Chilean memory, historical accounts suggest that Bachelet discursively employed her identity as a single mother to successfully mobilize a female constituency on the basis of gender identity (Ríos Tobar 2008; Thomas and Adams 2010). For example, in 2004, a journalist asked Bachelet, "How do you handle the guilt involved in spending so little time with your 11-year-old daughter?" Bachelet probably would not have received questions about her maternal duties if she had been a man, and questions about children posed to a female presidential candidate could be interpreted as sexist. Instead of refusing to answer, Bachelet spoke freely about her feelings and experiences as a single mother.

> With my youngest girl it hurts when she gets angry with me for how little we see each other, and when I get the impression that she doesn't need me, that she's learned to live without me. That's something I hate. The help that my mother's provided has been fundamental. When one works and is separated, the presence of another adult is crucial. . . . I will try to protect my loved ones, so that they aren't hurt because their mother is a public figure. . . . I'm not stupid and I know that my showing in the polls has made me a target. But I would hope that there is fair play in politics. ("The Best Alternative" 2004)

Bachelet appeared to turn a potential vulnerability—her status as a single mother—into a political advantage—an ability to connect with Chilean mothers. Polling evidence helped confirm the conventional wisdom that Bachelet attracted women voters. For example, in a CEP June–July 2005 poll, 52 percent of women and 46 percent of men said that Bachelet was the most trustworthy (*confiable*) candidate, while 23 percent of women and 22 percent of men said the same about Lavín, and 13 percent of women and 20 percent of men said the same about Piñera (Centro de Estudios Públicos 2005).[6] Political pundits at the time in Chile repeatedly interpreted these polling results—and similar results from other national surveys—as evidence that Bachelet's status as a woman appeared to help her identify with, establish trust, and gain support from women, particularly low-income mothers (Morales Quiroga 2008; Ríos Tobar 2008; Valdés 2010b).

In December 2005, Bachelet captured 45.96 percent of the vote; Lavín, 23.23 percent; and Piñera, 25.41 percent. She became the first Concertación presidential candidate to perform better among women than men, winning 45 percent of the female and 43 percent of the male vote. In the second round, Bachelet defeated Piñera soundly, 53.5 percent to 46.5 percent. Many political analysts noted that, thanks to women, Bachelet won more decisively in the second round than Lagos had in 2000 (Ríos Tobar 2008): Lagos earned 45.3 percent of the women's vote in 2000, and Bachelet captured 53.5 percent.

Bachelet's horizontal leadership style, which emphasized coalition building and cooperation rather than command, and her distinctly feminine (if not maternal) charisma contrasted with Lagos's professorial, paternal public image (Thomas and Adams 2010). Bachelet's team *and* the opposition acknowledged that Bachelet's gendered public image helped her build a core constituency of female voters. Bachelet's campaign strategist, Francisco Javier Díaz, described the importance of Bachelet's constituency of women: "We saw that we could continue growing among women, something that we had believed would be impossible" (quoted in Gerber 2005, 46). Conservative deputy and member of the opposition campaign Lily Pérez acknowledged Bachelet's strong female base and remarked that "Bachelet has the advantage of conquering the women's vote because it is very easy for many women to identify with her because of the gender issue" (Estrada 2006). "Gender issue" is an ambiguous phrase, and here it could refer to either Bachelet's pro-women platform, identity as a woman, status as a single mother, or distinct leadership style. It was likely that all of these gender-related factors were in play.

In sum, Lagos and Bachelet's winning constituencies appeared to vary in sex-specific ways. Although Lagos tried to mobilize women in the 2000 second-round election by appointing Soledad Alvear as his campaign spokesperson, he continued a pattern of Concertación presidential candidates performing better among men than women. Bachelet's identity as a single mother and her pro-women campaign promises seemed to help her secure strong support among women. There is evidence that her core constituency of women remained loyal during her presidency. For example, polls showed that Bachelet earned her highest approval ratings among low-income women throughout her term (Fernández and Rubilar Lear 2011). In addition, a CEP October 2009 poll showed that 81 percent of women and 75 percent of men approved of Bachelet's performance, while 9 percent of women and 14 percent of men disapproved (Centro de Estudios Públicos 2009).[7]

Could sex-specific differences in constituencies affect Lagos's and Bachelet's decision making on PWC? Possibly. But before presenting the evidence for this, I discuss PWC in the Chilean context.

Pro-Women Change in Chile

A rich scholarship on women and politics in Chile has examined abortion, marriage, the family, and domestic-violence reforms (Haas 2010; Htun 2003). Other research focuses on Bachelet's gender-equality agenda (Staab and Waylen 2016). This literature has expanded our knowledge of specific policies. For this study, however, conceptualizing PWC based on prior research would not capture the potential diversity of women's interests. Moreover, operationalizing PWC in the ways extant scholarship has done could limit the concept's applicability to other contexts because these particular issues may not be relevant in other countries or in other historical moments.

This chapter approaches PWC in a way that addresses the limitations in existing studies while avoiding the long-standing problem of essentializing women's identities—assuming that all women have common, exogenously given interests (Schwindt-Bayer and Taylor-Robinson 2011). Recognizing that women's interests are socially constructed (Beckwith 2011), I maintain that certain actors can be identified as exercising authority to determine which policies advance women's interests. I define PWC in Chile according to three sets of authorities located at the international, national, and local levels. These actors interact, influence each other, and express socially constructed and overlapping—but not identical—ideas about PWC.[8]

At the international level, the UN Convention on the Elimination of All Forms of Discrimination Against Women (CEDAW) asserts that discrimination against women is recurrent and detrimental to society (Baldez 2011). The CEDAW text, designed to be adaptable to the policy agendas of diverse world leaders, addresses a broad range of issues. By signing CEDAW in 1979 and ratifying it in 1989, Chile promised to advance women's interests and gender equality.[9] Panels of experts from around the world regularly analyze signatory countries' progress on gender equality and offer recommendations on how to better comply with CEDAW.

At the national level, Chile's women's agency Servicio Nacional de la Mujer (SERNAM) is the authority that defines PWC within the Chilean context. Like national women's bureaus in other countries, SERNAM studies CEDAW's reports and strives to comply with the treaty (Towns 2010; see also Chapter 9). SERNAM conducts some of its own studies on women's status in Chile and tailors CEDAW's general guidelines into concrete policies. The agency also aims to mainstream gender policy throughout the executive branch.[10] Notwithstanding its small budget (about 1 percent of Chile's national budget), its efforts are generally believed to be effective (Thomas 2016).

Finally, at the local level, groups of organized women within Chile have been debating and (re)defining PWC for decades (Baldez 2002; Franceschet 2005). Domestic women's groups lobbied for the creation of SERNAM, and many local activists went to work for the agency. Nevertheless, the influence of nongovernmental organizations (NGOs) in SERNAM has fluctuated over time, suggesting that it does not always share their ideas of women's interests (Haas 2010). For example, SERNAM's support for women's health issues has varied over the years, while Chilean women's groups have consistently pushed for change in this area. Any conceptualization of PWC in Chile needs to account for possible discrepancies between SERNAM and women's organizations.

This three-tier operationalization of PWC offers several advantages. First, avoiding a preselection of issues permits the pro-women change concept to encompass a broader range of policy areas than found in existing scholarship. Second, recognizing that women's interests are socially constructed by a variety of actors avoids essentialism. Third, this method of operationalization could be applied to study contexts outside Chile—in any CEDAW signatory country that features some sort of women's agency and organized women's groups.[11] This operationalization thus has the potential to advance the comparative study of pro-women change.

Data and Empirical Method

Measuring and evaluating the presidential promotion of PWC requires a brief discussion of presidents' legislative powers. In Chile, both the president and Congress draft legislation (Siavelis 2000). Messages are bills initiated by the executive, and motions are bills initiated by Congress. The constitutional power to assign "urgencies," which in essence constitute deadlines for legislative action, confers agenda-setting power on presidents. A "simple" urgency is meant to compel Congress to address the bill within thirty days; a "high" urgency gives Congress fifteen days; and an "immediate-discussion" urgency, six days.

Presidents can maintain or intensify pressure on Congress by issuing a simple, high, or immediate-discussion urgency to any message or motion in Congress at virtually any moment during the legislative process. A president can assign multiple urgencies to the same bill over a period of time. While Congress usually respects presidential urgencies, the Constitution does not stipulate a penalty when Congress ignores the urgency. As a result, the president sometimes issues an urgency, and if Congress does nothing, the president may issue another urgency to insist on the bill's priority. Exercising urgency power to the maximum would mean assigning the most powerful kind of urgency—immediate-discussion urgencies—one right after the other.

A quick example illustrates how presidential urgencies may be used. Bachelet's reproductive-rights message entered Congress on June 30, 2009. On that same day, she assigned a high urgency on the message, meaning that Congress had fifteen days to react. On July 7, she withdrew this high urgency and replaced it with another high urgency—in effect, extending the congressional deadline. On July 13, the lower chamber's health committee issued its first report. The chamber discussed and approved the bill. The bill moved to the Senate's health committee, and on July 28 Bachelet placed a simple urgency, giving Congress thirty days to act. On August 18, she issued a high urgency, and when that urgency expired on September 1, she assigned another high urgency. The Senate health committee produced its report on September 2. Bachelet assigned high urgencies on September 16, on September 29, and again on October 13. The Senate finally agreed to address the bill in the legislative session on October 27. On that day, Bachelet attached an immediate-discussion urgency to the bill, and the Senate health committee reacted by promptly presenting its first committee report to the entire Senate, with a vote immediately following. This pattern of Bachelet issuing urgencies and Congress reacting continued until Bachelet was able to push her reproductive-rights bill through the legislature in 2010 (Boletin 6582-11). Urgencies therefore constitute a formidable tool for Chilean presidents who strive to push a particular bill through Congress as quickly as possible.

Bill initiation and urgency assignments are the most relevant measures of Chilean presidents' use of legislative power to advance PWC.[12] The empirical goal, therefore, was to collect all bills initiated by either branch of government—regardless of whether they were successful—and the corresponding urgencies.[13]

Pro-Women Change Keyword Searches

The PWC operationalization guided the selection of search words in Chile's online legislative database found on the Senate's website, www.senado.cl. I drew keywords and phrases from the CEDAW text, official SERNAM documents, and publications of Chilean women's organizations. Table 12A.1 in the chapter appendix displays the keywords used, with their English translations, and the number of results from each search. Individual searches with these keywords generated a total of 1,088 results. The number of bills dropped to 602 after I deleted all duplicates and narrowed the search to bills proposed in Lagos's term (2000–2006) or in Bachelet's first term (2006–2010).

These 602 bills contained at least one keyword or phrase and covered the targeted time period. To evaluate whether these bills actually promoted PWC, I read the bill summaries and referred to texts from each of the three authorities. I employed the text of the CEDAW treaty; SERNAM's *Memorias*, which are found in the SERNAM library in Santiago and contain accounts of SERNAM's goals and activities since 1991; and documents from the Gender and Equality Observatory, Chile's main umbrella organization for dozens of women's groups (Valdés 2010a). This last set of materials served as a strong proxy for Chilean women's groups' conceptions of pro-women change.

To qualify as "pro-women," a bill had to correspond to the goals and objectives of at least two of the three authorities—CEDAW, SERNAM, and/ or Chilean women's organizations. I excluded any bill that was unrelated or that hindered rather than advanced PWC. For example, if I did not find evidence that a particular bill related to any PWC ideas according to the Gender and Equality Observatory in Chile, but I did find evidence that it corresponded to both CEDAW articles and SERNAM's stated goals, then the bill was included in the data set as PWC. If I found evidence that a bill reflected only CEDAW articles but did not reflect SERNAM's goals or any PWC ideas stated by the Gender and Equality Observatory, then it was not included in the data set as a PWC bill.

Coding the Legislation: Presidential Urgencies

Of the 602 bills, only 252 actually qualified as promoting PWC. I coded these as messages or motions, by types and quantities of presidential urgencies and whether the bill became law. Prior to this data set, the most comprehensive data collection effort of this kind was Liesl Haas's (2010) list of sixty-three gender-equality bills in Chile from 1990 to 2008. My PWC data set includes almost ten times as many bills, in part because it includes large pieces of legislation that had relatively minor PWC provisions. It also includes bills from ministries usually not associated with PWC and overlooked by previous research. For example, in 2004, Lagos sent a bill related to women in the police force (Carabineros) to Congress (Boletin 3694-02).[14] The bill combined women's and men's promotion lists, thereby lessening sex-based inequalities and allowing women to assume the highest ranks of the national police. As defense minister, Bachelet championed the bill before Congress, and it became law during the Lagos administration.[15] The data set, then, facilitates an appropriately inclusive examination of pro-women legislation during the years of the Lagos and Bachelet presidencies. The following section examines the descriptive statistics generated from this data set.

Lagos versus Bachelet: Using Legislative Power to Promote Pro-Women Change

Table 12.1 displays descriptive statistics for each president's messages to Congress and urgencies. It distinguishes between (1) all messages initiated by the president during his or her term and (2) PWC messages, which are a subset of all messages. An examination of *all messages* reveals that Lagos and Bachelet deployed their legislative powers in similar ways, while the examination of *PWC messages* shows that these presidents behaved differently in promoting pro-women reforms.

Table 12.1 shows that Lagos initiated more messages (544) than Bachelet (392), in part because Lagos governed for more years. (A constitutional

TABLE 12.1: PRO-WOMEN CHANGE MESSAGES AND URGENCIES PROPOSED BY
PRESIDENTS LAGOS AND BACHELET, 2000–2010

	All messages		PWC messages	
	Lagos	Bachelet	Lagos	Bachelet
Total number	544	392	11	17
Average number of messages per year	90.7	98.0	1.8	4.3
Percentage of messages that became law during term	78.1	73.2	18.2	76.5
Percentage of messages with at least one urgency	48.0	52.6	54.5	82.4

reform in 2005 reduced the Chilean presidential term from six to four years. In the data set, Lagos accounts for data from March 11, 2000, to March 11, 2006, and Bachelet for data from March 11, 2006, to March 11, 2010.) On average, Lagos initiated 90.7 messages per year, while Bachelet initiated 98 messages, indicating both presidents were similarly active legislators. Lagos enjoyed a slightly better success rate of messages becoming law than Bachelet, 78.1 percent and 73.2 percent, respectively. A two-sample t-test reveals that this difference is borderline statistically significant ($p = 0.07$).

Turning to the subset of PWC messages, the findings reveal that Lagos and Bachelet contrasted dramatically in their exercise of PWC message and urgency powers. Lagos sent Congress 11 PWC messages, averaging 1.8 per year. Just 2 percent of Lagos's messages promoted PWC. In contrast, Bachelet sent Congress 17 PWC messages, averaging 4.3 per year, and 4.3 percent of Bachelet's messages advanced PWC. The difference in Lagos's and Bachelet's share of messages that promoted PWC is statistically significant ($p = 0.05$).

Lagos not only initiated fewer PWC messages than Bachelet but was also far less successful in passing the PWC messages that he did send Congress. Just two of Lagos's PWC messages passed during his presidential term, a success rate of 18.2 percent, much lower than his overall success rate of 78.1 percent in securing passage of his messages. In contrast, 13 of Bachelet's PWC messages became law during her administration, a 76.5 percent success rate. Lagos's and Bachelet's success rates on PWC messages are statistically different ($p = 0.002$). To summarize, when we observe all messages, Lagos enjoyed a slightly higher rate of success than Bachelet. However, Bachelet was far more prolific and successful than Lagos in securing passage of PWC messages.

Why was Bachelet more successful in passing her PWC messages? One reason could be her greater propensity to assign urgencies to PWC legislation. This is a Chilean president's key agenda-setting instrument. Table 12.1 shows that the presidents differed greatly in their rates of assigning at least one urgency to PWC messages. Lagos issued at least one urgency for 54.5 percent of his PWC messages, while Bachelet issued at least one urgency to 82.4 percent of her PWC messages.[16]

Table 12.2 extends the analysis by displaying the number of simple, high, and immediate-discussion urgencies that each president assigned to PWC messages and PWC motions initiated during each president's term. Lagos assigned a total of 16 simple urgencies on his PWC messages, while Bachelet assigned 41 (about 2.5 times as many). Lagos also assigned 6 high urgencies to his PWC messages, while Bachelet assigned 65 (about 10 times as many). Finally, Lagos issued no immediate-discussion urgencies to his PWC messages, while Bachelet issued 11 to hers. These descriptive statistics underscore the extent to which Bachelet prioritized PWC messages more highly than Lagos. Bachelet made greater use of each type of urgency in advancing PWC legislation than did Lagos.

What about the use of presidential urgencies on PWC motions? Congress initiated 58 PWC motions during Lagos's term. Of these, Lagos assigned an urgency only once—an immediate-discussion urgency. He placed no simple and no high urgencies on any PWC motions initiated during his term. During Bachelet's first term, Congress initiated 165 PWC motions; and the *presidenta* issued 65 simple, 47 high, and 3 immediate-discussion urgencies on 11 different PWC motions. Lagos's 1.7 percent rate of issuing at least one urgency on a PWC motion is borderline statistically different from Bachelet's 6.7 percent rate ($p = 0.06$).

In summary, compared to Lagos, Bachelet submitted more PWC messages, on average, each year; more often attached at least one urgency to PWC messages and PWC motions; and more often succeeded in passing her PWC messages.

The next section's case studies of PWC messages reveal that both presidents promoted policies that benefited women in ways congruent with their presidential campaign platforms. In his 1999 presidential platform, Lagos

TABLE 12.2: URGENCIES ASSIGNED TO PRO-WOMEN CHANGE MESSAGES BY PRESIDENTS LAGOS AND BACHELET, 2000–2010

	PWC messages		PWC motions	
	Lagos	Bachelet	Lagos	Bachelet
Total number	11	17	58	165
Total number of simple urgencies	16	41	0	65
Total number of high urgencies	6	65	0	47
Total number of immediate discussion urgencies	0	11	1	3

Note: Messages are bills initiated by the president; motions are bills initiated by the Congress.

promised to ratify international human-rights agreements and to better comply with Chile's preexisting agreements that protected women's and children's rights. Four of Lagos's eleven PWC messages related to international agreements. Other PWC messages related to the Defense Ministry (two messages) and anti-discrimination, citizen participation, maternity rights, nationality, and preschools (one each) and fulfilled Lagos's rights-centered campaign promises.

Bachelet's PWC messages also reflected her campaign platform, which committed the *presidenta* to delivering material benefits to different subgroups of women, including low-income mothers (four messages), female politicians (three), divorced women (two), and women seeking to prevent pregnancy, women who rely on pensions, and female victims of violence (one each).[17] The fact that Lagos and Bachelet used their legislative powers in ways that fulfilled their campaign promises does suggest that both presidents were motivated to satisfy their constituency's needs. In this chapter, because of space constraints, I discuss the PWC messages that appear most frequently in the total population of each president's PWC messages—that is, Lagos's messages relating to international agreements and Bachelet's messages relating to low-income mothers.

Lagos's Legislative Highlights: Advancing International Agreements

The first PWC message that Lagos sent Congress was emblematic of the international women's movement. Signed by SERNAM's minister, this message sought approval of CEDAW's Optional Protocol, which would have allowed an individual or group to formally complain to the UN about a CEDAW violation. Opposing the bill, members of the conservative coalition in Congress interpreted the protocol as a potential threat to Chilean sovereignty. No congressional or presidential action has advanced the bill since 2004 (Boletin 2667-10). Lagos's decision not to use urgency powers suggests that, in essence, the president was unwilling to spend political capital. He gave up trying to win congressional approval for his bill.

Lagos also sent Congress a message to approve the Protocol to Prevent, Suppress and Punish Trafficking in Persons, Especially Women and Children (Boletin 3445-10). This protocol supplements the UN Convention against Transnational Organized Crime. Lagos apparently did not need to issue any urgencies to speed the bill through Congress; congressional debate transcripts suggest that deputies and senators tended to agree on the importance of taking a stand against transnational trafficking and did not interpret the legislation as an infringement on Chilean sovereignty. This less controversial bill became law in 2005.

In July 2004, Lagos introduced SERNAM-sponsored legislation on the protection of childhood (Boletin 3596-18) to better comply with the Convention on the Rights of the Child, signed by Chile in 1990. The bill sat in the lower chamber's Family Committee for over six months. Lagos withdrew it; then, a few days later, he sent Congress a bill with the same title and similar content. Again, he attached no urgencies (Boletin 3792-07). Finally, about six weeks before leaving office, Lagos directed a message to approve the Protocol of San Salvador, the Additional Protocol to the American Convention on Human Rights in the Area of Economic, Social and Cultural Rights (Boletin 4087-10; Department of International Law 1988). This text includes several provisions specific to women's rights and autonomy. The bill received little attention from Congress, and Lagos did not exercise any urgency prerogatives. Therefore, these pieces of legislation were not a major priority for Lagos. In several instances, he initiated these bills toward the end of his administration and opted out of assigning urgencies. Not surprisingly, not all of these bills were approved.

Lagos kept his campaign promises by initiating these PWC bills. However, he also decided against spending political capital on this legislation and did not assign urgencies to bills that displeased Congress. This was in marked contrast to Bachelet's use of presidential power to advance PWC legislation.

Bachelet's Legislative Highlights: Responding to Low-Income Mothers

Several of Bachelet's PWC messages targeted low-income mothers, who were among the *presidenta*'s constituents. Her first PWC message stipulated that mothers rather than male partners would receive the family *asignaciones* (Boletin 4204-13; Biblioteca del Congreso Nacional de Chile 2007a, 15). These government payments benefited workers who contributed to social security and could provide for their family. According to a congressional report, the bill recognized an important reality: most mothers were the primary caregivers for their children, and therefore mothers should receive the *asignaciones* directly. Bachelet applied high urgencies three times to push Congress to act, and the message became law in 2007.

Bachelet's *asignaciones* bill was the beginning of a series of measures to deliver material assistance to low-income mothers. In January 2007 and December 2008, Bachelet sent Congress two messages that helped launch and institutionalize "Chile Grows with You" (Boletin 4812-13). The program sought to protect children from birth through kindergarten by improving maternity care, universal preschools, and health services. Serving the poorest 40 percent of households, it was estimated that Chile Grows with You would cost 4.8 billion Chilean pesos in 2007 (Biblioteca del Congreso Nacional de Chile 2007b, 4–10).

The first Chile Grows with You bill was a direct outcome of the Presidential Advisory Council for Childhood Policy Reforms (Consejo Asesor Presidencial para la Reforma de las Políticas de Infancia), which Bachelet commissioned in her first year in office. The bill established "automatic access to family subsidies to all pregnant women and children under 18 years old who comply with certain characteristics" (Boletin 4812-13). Bachelet issued two simple urgencies and four high urgencies to shepherd the legislation through Congress, and the message became law during her term in office. The second Chile Grows with You message established the Intersectoral System of Social Protection, intended to safeguard the program's future (Boletin 6260-06). Bachelet assigned three simple urgencies and thirteen high urgencies, and the bill became law in 2009.

Bachelet targeted low-income mothers with material aid via other legislation. She sent a message and exercised urgency powers to augment the minimum wage and family/maternal subsidies (Boletin 6568-05). She also included a special provision in a youth-employment bill so that any young woman who became pregnant had the right to a subsidy for pre- and post-maternity leave (Boletin 6393-05). Bachelet assigned two high urgencies to this bill, which became law in 2009.

These case studies suggest that both Bachelet and Lagos strategically deployed their legislative powers to fulfill their campaign promises. Many of Bachelet's most important pieces of PWC legislation targeted an important electoral base: low-income mothers. Bachelet initiated legislation that delivered substantial material benefits to this group and prioritized the legislation, initiating it early in her term and frequently assigning powerful urgencies to help push the messages through Congress. These findings document the use of formal prerogatives to promote PWC but cannot tell us how Lagos and Bachelet used informal powers (for example, powers of oral persuasion). Nevertheless, this chapter's evidence, drawn from government archives, clearly indicates that Lagos and Bachelet, although they were from the same party, exercised their formal powers very differently in response to diverse groups of Chilean women.

Conclusion

This sex-difference study has important implications for gender, which could be explored and tested in future research. Lagos and Bachelet exercised their powers in similar ways with regard to initiating messages and assigning urgencies overall. Lagos and Bachelet were also similar in promoting pro-women change that fulfilled their campaign promises.

Nevertheless, these presidents contrasted in statistically significant ways concerning the rates at which they deployed their initiation and urgency prerogatives to promote PWC bills. Bachelet exploited her powers to a far greater extent to deliver material assistance to specific groups of women. The *presidenta*'s PWC bills enjoyed higher success rates than did Lagos's, in part because of her frequent use of urgencies, a powerful agenda-setting tool.

What explains these sex differences in the use of power to promote policies benefiting women? Scholars have attributed Bachelet's pro-women agenda to her "feminist" consciousness (Staab and Waylen 2016), but they have not connected her PWC decision making to constituency incentives. Yet theories of democratic representation would predict that a president would respond to constituency demands. Moreover, many political scientists recently have provided compelling observational and experimental evidence that Latin American presidents are rewarded in the polls when they target their constituencies with social policy (De la O 2013; González and Mamone 2015; Melo and Pereira 2013; Zucco 2013). There is reason to extend this theorizing to the presidencies of Ricardo Lagos and Michelle Bachelet: their winning electoral constituencies clearly differed along gendered lines, suggesting that their decision making would also differ, reflecting their contrasting incentives to deliver benefits to their voters. Supported to a greater extent by women, Bachelet had the greater incentive to deliver pro-women change and therefore invested more effort in proposing and advancing legislation that provided women throughout the society with material benefits.

This chapter provides a foundation for investigating sex differences in presidential decision making about pro-women change, in both its operationalization of pro-women change and its examination of presidential powers. It also begins to suggest important connections among presidents' campaign promises, electoral coalitions, and constituent-driven incentives to advance legislation. In addition, the receptivity of the legislature in approving such legislation is an additional area of research, as one of my legislative cases suggests.

To test and develop these findings and the associated hypotheses, comparisons of male and female presidents need to be conducted in many more countries. Future research could compare, for example, the Brazilian male and female presidents from the center-left Workers' Party: Luiz Inácio Lula da Silva, elected in 2002 and reelected in 2006, and Dilma Rousseff, elected Brazil's first *presidenta* in 2010 and reelected in 2014. Did these Brazilian presidents differ in their PWC decision making in ways analogous to those of their Chilean counterparts? The emergence of Latin American *presidentas* has opened opportunities to explore the sex differences among presidents as they set their policy priorities, negotiate with their legislatures, and respond to their perceived constituents.

Appendix

TABLE 12A.1: PRO-WOMEN CHANGE KEYWORD SEARCHES

Keyword	Translation	Results
mujer	woman	431
maternidad	maternity	127
divorcio	divorce	93
aborto	abortion	72
femenino	feminine	56
femenina	feminine	48
violencia intrafamiliar	domestic violence	35
SERNAM	National Women's Service	27
matrimonio civil	civil marriage	25
postnatal	postmaternity	24
tribunales de familia	family courts	22
subsidio familiar	family subsidy	21
femicidio	femicide	16
educacion parvularia	preschool education	13
jardines infantiles	kindergartens	13
CEDAW	Convention on the Elimination of All Forms of Discrimination Against Women	9
acoso sexual	sexual harassment	9
sala cuna	day care	9
teletrabajo	teleworking	9
posnatal	postmaternity	7
amamantamiento	breast-feeding	6
salas cunas	day cares	5
interrupcion del embarazo	interrupting pregnancy	4
prenatal	prenatal	3
tribunal de familia	family court	1
trabajadoras temporeras	female temporary workers	1
jardin infantil	kindergarten	1
bono por hijo	child subsidy	1
violencia contra la mujer	violence against women	0
contracepcion de emergencia	emergency contraception	0
cuidado infantil	child care	0
participacion laboral	work participation	0
jefas de hogar	female heads of household	0
brecha salarial	wage gap	0

NOTES

Research for this chapter was made possible, in part, through support provided by the Fulbright-Hays Doctoral Dissertation Research Abroad Program.

1. Bachelet was reelected in 2013. Because her second term is still under way as this book goes to print, I focus exclusively on her first term.

2. Essentialism here refers to the assumption that all females share exogenously given common interests.

3. The Concertación's president Patricio Aylwin won 50 percent of the female and 58 percent of the male vote in 1989, and President Eduardo Frei had captured 54 percent of the female and 55 percent of the male vote.

4. Alvear had been a justice minister (1994–1998) and minister of SERNAM, the Chilean women's agency (1991–1994). After Lagos won presidential office, he named Alvear as his minister of foreign affairs (2000–2004).

5. The margin of error is plus or minus 2.7 percent.

6. The margin of error is plus or minus 2.7 percent.

7. The margin of error is plus or minus 3.0 percent.

8. I employ the term "pro-women" rather than "feminist" because most Latin American women and many activists whose ostensible goal is to promote women's interests do not identify as feminists (Stephen 2010).

9. The UN General Assembly adopted CEDAW in 1979 with 130 votes in favor, 0 against, and 10 abstentions (Baldez 2011). As of 2016, some 189 countries have ratified this treaty (United Nations Office of the High Commissioner on Human Rights, n.d.).

10. "Mainstreaming" refers to promoting gender-sensitive public policies in all government ministries. See also Chapter 11 for a discussion of this approach to facilitating gender equality.

11. Two-thirds of all UN member states have some kind of women's agency (Towns 2010).

12. I focus exclusively on bill initiation and urgency assignments because presidents use these powers far more frequently than other legislative prerogatives such as veto and referendum. Neither Lagos nor Bachelet ever vetoed legislation that hindered or favored PWC, and no president has called a referendum on a PWC issue.

13. Presidents can assign urgencies to any bill in Congress, including bills initiated before the president's inauguration. To provide balance between the analysis of Lagos's and Bachelet's urgency assignments, this study focuses on urgencies placed on bills initiated only during each president's term.

14. Until 2011, Chile's police force was housed in the Defense Ministry, a legacy of Chile's military dictatorship.

15. This was Bachelet's last bill as defense minister before she left the post to run for president.

16. This difference, however, is not statistically significant ($p = 0.12$), potentially because of the small number of total PWC messages (eleven for Lagos and seventeen for Bachelet).

17. Case studies of gender-equality policies during the Bachelet administration have examined, for instance, reproductive rights (Sepúlveda-Zelaya 2016) and social security reform (Staab 2016).

REFERENCES

Arriagada, Arturo, and Patricio Navia. 2006. "Jefes de campaña en elecciones presidenciales en Chile, 1970–2005" [Heads of campaigns in presidential elections in Chile,

1970–2005]. Instituto de Investigación en Ciencias Sociales Working Paper No. 12. Available at http://www.icso.cl/images/Paperss/septimo.pdf.

Baldez, Lisa. 2002. *Why Women Protest: Women's Movements in Chile*. New York: Cambridge University Press.

———. 2011. "The UN Convention to Eliminate All Forms of Discrimination Against Women (CEDAW): A New Way to Measure Women's Interests." *Politics & Gender* 7 (3): 419–423.

Beckwith, Karen. 2011. "Interests, Issues, and Preferences: Women's Interests and Epiphenomena of Activism." *Politics & Gender* 7 (3): 424–429.

"The Best Alternative." 2004. *Santiago Times*, April 12. Available at http://santiagotimes.cl/the-best-alternative/.

Biblioteca del Congreso Nacional de Chile. 2007a. "Historia de la Ley No. 20.172: Regula el derecho de la madre a percibir directamente las asignaciones e incorpora nuevo causante de dicho beneficio" [The history of Law No. 20.172: Regulating the right of mothers to receive directly family allowances and incorporating a child as a new cause of those allowances]. Available at http://www.leychile.cl/Consulta/portada_hl?tipo _norma=XX1&nro_ley=20172.

———. 2007b. "Historia de la Ley No. 20.203: Modifica normas relativas al subsidio familiar y a la adopción" [The history of Law No. 20.203: Amending rules on family subsidy and adoption]. Available at http://www.leychile.cl/Consulta/portada_hl?tipo _norma=XX1&nro_ley=20203.

Centro de Estudios Miguel Enriquez and Archivo Chile. 1999a. "Programa de gobierno candidatura presidencial de Joaquín Lavín, 1999: Crear un millón de nuevos empleos" [The governing program of presidential candidate Joaquín Lavin, 1999: Creating a million new jobs]. Available at http://www.archivochile.com/Partidos_burguesia/ udi/de/PBdeudi0006.pdf.

———. 1999b. "Programa de gobierno de Ricardo Lagos: Para crecer con igualdad" [The governing program of presidential candidate Ricardo Lagos: Growing with equality]. Available at http://www.archivochile.com/Gobiernos/gob_rlagos/de/GOBdelagos 0002.pdf.

———. 2005. "Estoy contigo: Programa de gobierno, Michelle Bachelet" [I am with you: The governing program of Michelle Bachelet]. Available at http://www.archivochile .com/Chile_actual/Elecciones_2005/Bachelet/01%20Programa_de_Gobierno.pdf.

Centro de Estudios Públicos. 2004. "Estudio nacional de opinión pública n 47, Junio–Julio 2004" [National public opinion study no. 47, June–July 2004]. Available at http://www .cepchile.cl/bannerscep/bdatos_encuestas_cep/base_datos.php.

———. 2005. "Estudio nacional de opinión pública n 49, Junio–Julio 2005" [National public opinion study no. 49, June–July 2005]. Available at http://www.cepchile.cl/banner scep/bdatos_encuestas_cep/base_datos.php.

———. 2009. "Estudio nacional de opinión pública n 61, Octubre" [National public opinion study no. 61, October]. Available at http://www.cepchile.cl/bannerscep/bdatos _encuestas_cep/base_datos.php.

De la O, Ana L. 2013. "Do Conditional Cash Transfers Affect Electoral Behavior? Evidence from a Randomized Experiment in Mexico." *American Journal of Political Science* 57 (1): 1–14.

Department of International Law. 1988. "Additional Protocol to the American Convention on Human Rights in the Area of Economic, Social and Cultural Rights 'Protocol of San Salvador.'" Available at http://www.oas.org/juridico/english/treaties/a-52 .html.

Estrada, Daniela. 2006. "Women—Chile: Steps in the Right Direction." *Inter Press Service News Agency,* February 9. Available at http://www.ipsnews.net/2006/02/women-chile -steps-in-the-right-direction/.

Fernández, Maria de los Angeles, and Fernando Rubilar Leal. 2011. "En el nombre de género: El caso de Michelle Bachelet" [In the name of gender: The case of Michelle Bachelet]. *Desigualdade y Diversidade* [Inequality and Diversity] 9:135–156.

Franceschet, Susan. 2005. *Women and Politics in Chile.* Boulder, CO: Lynne Rienner.

————. 2010. "Continuity or Change? Gender Policy in the Bachelet Administration." In *The Bachelet Government: Conflict and Consensus in Post-Pinochet Chile,* edited by Silvia Borzutzky and Gregory Weeks, 158–180. Gainesville: University of Florida Press.

Gerber, Elisabet. 2005. "Comunicación y política: Análisis de la campaña presidencial de Michelle Bachelet" [Communication and policy: Analyzing the presidential campaign of Michelle Bachelet]. Centro de Competencia en Comunicación para América Latina, July. Available at http://docplayer.es/2215220-Comunicacion-y-politica-analisis-de -la-campana-presidencial-de-michelle-bachelet-elisabet-gerber.html.

González, Lucas, and Miguel Ignacio Mamone. 2015. "Who Distributes? Presidents, Congress, Governors, and the Politics of Distribution in Argentina and Brazil." *Revista Ibero-Americana de Estudios Legislativos* [Review of Iberian-American Legislative Studies] 4 (May): 17–32.

Haas, Liesl. 2010. *Feminist Policymaking in Chile.* University Park: Pennsylvania State University Press.

Htun, Mala. 2003. *Sex and the State: Abortion, Divorce, and the Family under Latin American Dictatorships and Democracies.* New York: Cambridge University Press.

Jalalzai, Farida, and Pedro G. dos Santos. 2015. "The Dilma Effect? Women's Representation under Dilma Rousseff's Presidency." *Politics & Gender* 11 (1): 117–145.

Melo, Marcus André, and Carlos Pereira. 2013. *Making Brazil Work: Checking the President in a Multiparty System.* New York: Palgrave Macmillan.

Morales Quiroga, Mauricio. 2008. "La primera mujer presidenta de Chile: ¿Qué explicó el triunfo de Michelle Bachelet en las elecciones de 2005–2006?" [The first woman president of Chile: What explains the triumph of Michelle Bachelet in the elections of 2005–2006?]. *Latin American Research Review* 43 (1): 7–32.

Ríos Tobar, Marcela. 2008. "Seizing a Window of Opportunity: The Election of President Bachelet in Chile." *Politics & Gender* 4 (3): 509–519.

Schwindt-Bayer, Leslie A., and Michelle M. Taylor-Robinson. 2011. "Introduction." *Politics & Gender* 7 (3): 417–418.

Sepúlveda-Zelaya, Carmen. 2016. "Formal and Informal Institutional Challenges to Women's Reproductive Rights: Emergency Contraception and the Constitutional Tribunal in Chile." In *Gender, Institutions and Change in Bachelet's Chile,* edited by Silke Staab and Georgina Waylen, 171–186. New York: Palgrave Macmillan.

Servicio Electoral de Chile. 2013. "Elecciones presidenciales 1989 al 2013 por circunscripción electoral" [Presidential elections, 1989 to 2013, by electoral district]. Available at http://www.servel.cl/elecciones-presidenciales-1989-al-2013-por-circunscripcion -electoral/.

Siavelis, Peter M. 2000. *The President and Congress in Postauthoritarian Chile: Institutional Constraints to Democratic Consolidation.* University Park: Pennsylvania State University Press.

Staab, Silke. 2016. "Opportunities and Constraints for Gender-Egalitarian Policy Change: Michelle Bachelet's Social Protection Agenda (2006–2010)." In *Gender, Institutions and Change in Bachelet's Chile*, edited by Silke Staab and Georgina Waylen, 121–146. New York: Palgrave Macmillan.

Staab, Silke, and Georgina Waylen. 2016. *Gender, Institutions and Change in Bachelet's Chile*. New York: Palgrave Macmillan.

Stephen, Lynn. 2010. *Women and Social Movements in Latin America: Power from Below*. Austin: University of Texas Press.

Stevenson, Linda S. 2012. "The Bachelet Effect on Gender-Equity Policies." *Latin American Perspectives* 39 (4): 129–144.

Thomas, Gwynn. 2016. "Promoting Gender Equality: Michelle Bachelet and Formal and Informal Institutional Change within the Chilean Presidency." In *Gender, Institutions and Change in Bachelet's Chile*, edited by Silke Staab and Georgina Waylen, 95–120. New York: Palgrave Macmillan.

Thomas, Gwynn, and Melinda Adams. 2010. "Breaking the Final Glass Ceiling: The Influence of Gender in the Elections of Ellen Johnson-Sirleaf and Michelle Bachelet." *Journal of Women, Politics & Policy* 31 (2): 105–131.

Towns, Ann E. 2010. *Women and States: Norms and Hierarchies in International Society*. New York: Cambridge University Press.

United Nations Office of the High Commissioner on Human Rights. n.d. "Ratification Status for CEDAW." Available at http://tbinternet.ohchr.org/_layouts/TreatyBody External/Treaty.aspx?Treaty=CEDAW&Lang=en (accessed May 9, 2016).

Valdés, Teresa, ed. 2010a. *¿Construyendo igualdad? 20 años de políticas públicas de género* [Building equality? Twenty years of public policies relating to gender]. Santiago de Chile: Centro de Estudios para el Desarrollo de la Mujer.

———. 2010b. "El Chile de Michelle Bachelet ¿Género en el poder?" [Michelle Bachelet's Chile: Gender in power?]. In "Living in Actually Existing Democracies," edited by Nancy Postero, special issue, *Latin American Research Review* 45:248–273.

Zucco, Cesar. 2013. "When Payouts Pay Off: Conditional Cash Transfers and Voting Behavior in Brazil, 2002–2010." *American Journal of Political Science* 57 (4): 810–822.

Zúñiga Urbina, Francisco, and Carlos Gutiérrez Moya. 2000. "Crónica de la elección presidencial en Chile (December-1999 and January-2000)" [Chronicling the presidential election in Chile (December 1999 and January 2000)]. *Revista de Derecho Político* [Journal of Constitutional Law] 47:289–307.

13

"First Women" and "Women's Posts"

Examining the Backgrounds and Credentials
of Ministers in Five Presidential Democracies

MARIA C. ESCOBAR-LEMMON
AND MICHELLE M. TAYLOR-ROBINSON

This comparative study of presidential cabinets assesses the resources that contribute to ministerial power and influence. Women are being appointed to presidential cabinets in increasing numbers and to a greater diversity of posts. How do the skills, experiences, and connections of these women compare to those of the men holding the same ministerial portfolios? This chapter examines the backgrounds, connections, and political capital resources of ministers from sixteen presidential administrations in Argentina, Chile, Colombia, Costa Rica, and the United States. The analysis focuses on two special types of cases: (1) first-women posts, the first appointment of a woman to a given portfolio in a country, and (2) majority-women posts, in which a majority of ministers have been women. The authors find that first women appear to conform to the male norm for credentials in their post in their country and are typically as qualified for the post as their male colleagues. In majority-women posts, the resources and skills the women ministers bring to the administration indicate that those posts have not been downgraded in prestige. There is an exception to this finding, however. Women in majority-women posts typically do not appear to be providing political-capital resources to the administration. As a result, presidents may appear more inclusive of women than those presidents actually are.

Since 1933, when Franklin D. Roosevelt made history by appointing the first woman to the U.S. cabinet, women have made significant strides, becoming almost familiar faces in presidential cabinets. Yet there is still room for progress, because only in recent decades have we seen the first (or only) women appointed to positions in stereotypically masculine policy domains such as finance and defense. Are the women holding these posts different from the men who have held them, or are they like the men in all regards except their sex?

Full cabinet-rank posts are very limited in number, so they are a scarce and valuable resource, and the people who hold them are a critical part of a successful administration, raising the stakes for nominators. Social-control theory predicts the group who has traditionally held power—white men—will give posts to representatives of new groups only if they view the political cost of not doing so to be dangerously high. However, to avoid policy change that would harm their privileged position, they will select as representatives of the new group people who are minimally different (see Carroll 1984; Duke 1976; Gamson 1968; Leyenaar 2014; Lovenduski 1986; Lukes 1974; Mills 1959; Skard and Haavio-Mannila 1985; Zimmer 1988). For women appointed to presidential cabinets, this leads to the prediction they will closely resemble their male colleagues in their professional, political, and group-linkages background.

There are, however, two instances in which this prediction might not hold: when the first woman is appointed to head a department and when appointment of women to a portfolio has become what might be viewed as the norm in a country. In these cases, presidents may benefit from appointing women with different credentials. In the first scenario the woman might be different from the male norm because her appointment may be intended to draw attention to diversity appointments. In the second scenario, a "female norm" for credentials could be established for a post that may have come to be viewed as a "woman's seat" (Borrelli 2010, 737).

The question of whether female ministers are different from male appointees is interesting because cabinets—like presidencies—have always been male-dominated institutions and would be expected to be steeped in masculine norms about proper credentials. In addition, regardless of whether it is novel to appoint a woman to a particular post or if appointing women to a particular post has become the norm, the small number of full cabinet-rank posts forces presidents to carefully consider the political-capital resources (PCRs) each appointee can bring to the administration (Wyszomirski 1989).[1] Consequently, we examine whether first women and appointees to a women's post bring the same types and quantity of PCRs to the administration as is the norm for men. This is important for evaluating whether the women will have the capacity to be equal players with the men at this highest level of executive branch politics.

Women breaking new ground are likely to receive extra media attention, with their sex, rather than their credentials, dominating the coverage (Borrelli 2010; Kanter 1977; Wilson 2007).[2] In this chapter we look at cases in which a woman is appointed to a particular post for the first time, even though appointment of some women to the cabinet has become the norm.[3] Many of these first women are appointed to posts outside stereotypically feminine policy domains, so they enter new territory not just with respect to their specific portfolio but also regarding the broader category of masculine policy-domain posts where women may draw extra criticism as potentially inappropriate appointees. According to role congruity theory, "When a stereotyped group member and an incongruent social role become joined in the mind of the perceiver, this inconsistency lowers the evaluation of the group member as an actual or potential occupant of the role" (Eagly and Karau 2002, 574; see also Ritter and Yoder 2004). The woman appointee is likely to be stereotyped as lacking traits associated with men (e.g., assertiveness, decisiveness, aggressiveness), though such stereotypes appear to be changing as more women enter positions of power (Diekman, Goodfriend, and Goodwin 2004).

We hypothesize that first women will be expected to conform to male norms in the credentials they bring to their post. MaryAnne Borrelli (2002) found that women are disproportionately appointed to buffer the president from a constituency that is unlikely to receive representation of its interests during the administration. When this occurs, a woman might have credentials different from those of her male predecessors in the post, so some may conclude that she lacks the necessary credentials for her post. That does not mean she lacks credentials in general but that she is appointed to a post that does not match her credentials, and consequently she is marginalized in her post and likely to be dependent on the president because she lacks an independent power base (Borrelli 2010, 735). Alternatively, if first women have their own power base and skills that match the post to which they are appointed, that should enable them, as much so as the men who have their own power base, to be full players in cabinet politics.[4]

In contrast, for a portfolio in which it has become common in a country to appoint a woman, appointing another woman should not attract attention because of her sex, though her credentials might be compared to those of women who have previously held the post. Additionally, for posts to which women are frequently appointed, a man might be expected to have credentials that conform to a female norm.[5] Norms about appropriate qualifications may change as the gender balance in a particular post changes. For a post that, in a particular country, has become dominated by women, we want to observe whether the men that are appointed to that post "look like the women" in terms of their credentials and whether the credentials of the women enable them to bring as many PCRs to the administration as is the norm for their country.

To preview our findings, first women appear to conform to the male norm for credentials in their post in their country, and they bring as many PCRs to the administration as the men appointed to the same post. It is more difficult to draw strong conclusions about norms for credentials in portfolios where appointment of women has become common because of the small number of individual observations we have per country-post. However, in majority-women posts, ministers commonly are sources of multiple PCRs for the administration, which indicates that those posts have not been downgraded in prestige since they have become common posts for women (Reskin 1988; Yoder 1991). But in all-women posts, those ministers typically are not sources of multiple PCRs for the administration, which may mean the posts carry little prestige.

Case Selection, Data, and Variables

We examine backgrounds, experience, connections, and PCRs of cabinet ministers in five presidential democracies: Argentina, Chile, Colombia, Costa Rica, and the United States.[6] Focusing on cabinets allows us to broaden our understanding of the executive beyond the president by examining those men and women with whom presidents surround themselves. To learn whether first women and ministers in women's posts have the same or different credentials from the (male) norm, we need data about the backgrounds of *all* members of the cabinet for a presidential administration. Our data set comprises all appointees to posts of full cabinet rank in administrations in Argentina (1999–2011), Chile (2000–2010), Colombia (1998–2010), Costa Rica (1998–2010), and the United States (1993–2009), giving us a full data set of 447 ministers, of whom 110 are women (see Figure 13.1).[7] Our unit of analysis is person-post, not the individual. Thus, a minister who served in the same post in two administrations contributes two observations, as does the individual who served in two different posts in the same administration.[8]

Including five countries in our study broadens knowledge about the credentials of women in presidential cabinets beyond the case of the United States. Broader knowledge is important because many democratic countries have presidential-style systems. To facilitate comparison with the United States, and because collection of background data about *all* members of a cabinet is labor intensive, we selected a few countries with established presidential systems, stable democratic institutions, high levels of economic development and inclusion of women in education and the workforce, and

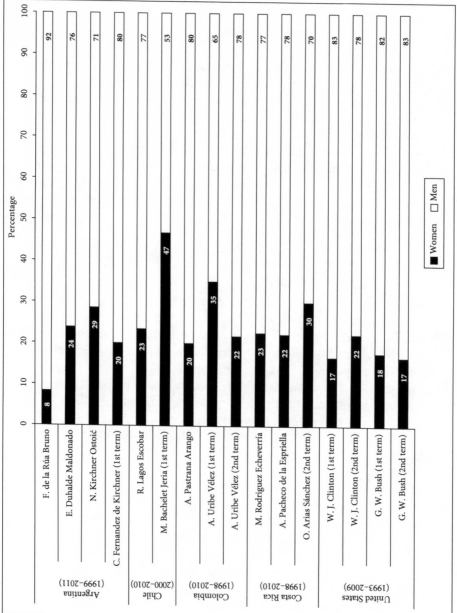

Figure 13.1 Percentage of women and men in cabinet by country and presidential administration

most important, relatively high levels of representation of women in recent cabinets.[9] Though analysis of only five countries limits the generalizability of assessments about how women's credentials compare to men's, these countries provide variance on several dimensions that may affect norms about expected backgrounds for cabinet ministers. They encompass highly federal (Argentina, United States), decentralized (Colombia), and strongly unitary forms of government (Chile, Costa Rica). Party systems range from an established two-party system (United States, Costa Rica, though more recently Costa Rica's two-party system has become more fragmented), to a historically two-party system where one party has recently been dominant (Argentina), to a historically two-party system that has become multiparty (Colombia), to a historically multiparty system that now operates with two well-established coalitions (Chile). These countries vary in the formal institutional powers of the president, from a president with very few and limited constitutional legislative powers (United States, Costa Rica), to the country argued to have the presidency with the most extensive formal powers (Chile), to intermediate formal legislative powers for the president (Argentina, Colombia) (Mainwaring and Shugart 1997). These countries also offer an interesting comparison because during the period under study, Argentina and Costa Rica had effective gender quotas for the legislature, Colombia had a gender quota for administrative posts, and Chile and the United States had no national gender quota law, although Chile adopted one in 2015.[10] Additionally, Argentina, Chile, and Costa Rica have elected female presidents, though Costa Rica's Laura Chinchilla was president from 2010 to 2014, after the end of our data-collection period.

To compare male and female cabinet ministers, we collected data on fifteen dimensions to measure their background, political experience and connections, and group linkages. Our information comes from publicly available sources, primarily Internet searches for newspaper coverage of the minister, but also résumés posted by employers after the minister left the cabinet, award announcements, university web pages with information about faculty, and campaign information when ministers ran for office. It is possible that a minister had additional undisclosed credentials or links that contributed to a selector's evaluation of her or his qualifications for the post. However, we view cabinet appointments as a public signal by the administration about its policy aims and constituencies. Thus, if information was not publicly available, it was at best a very weak signal. Both authors coded all variables. Variables are binary, indicating that a minister had or did not have a credential or connection at the time of appointment. Variables are not mutually exclusive, and as noted later, some are nested within each other. In this chapter, we study three PCRs: policy expertise (extensive work and educational background); political skills (experience in government and politics), and support resources (connections to interest groups, associations, and organizations).

We evaluate work and educational background in three ways: (1) *public-sector career*, indicating the minister previously had worked primarily for the government in some capacity; (2) *related degree*, indicating an academic field of study related to the ministry's policy purview; and (3) *extensive experience*—our proxy for the PCR of policy expertise—indicating that the minister had *many* years of work experience related to her or his portfolio's policy jurisdiction, frequently including academic training in the area. A related academic degree alone, a few years of work, or work decades ago would not meet the standard for extensive experience.

Political background is evaluated in six ways: (1) *Organizational partisans* have held formal leadership posts in their party at the local or national level or inside the legislature (e.g., party whip) or have been involved in campaigns (Cohen 1988).[11] (2) *Campaign experience* indicates that the minister worked in a top post in a political campaign (including as an adviser), though not necessarily for the president who appointed her or him to the cabinet.[12] (3) *Prior minister* indicates previous service as a minister or vice minister. (4) *Elected post* means that the minister had previously been elected to any office at the national or subnational level. (5) *Appointed post* indicates that the minister had held a high-level appointed post prior to appointment to the cabinet (e.g., ambassador, head of an agency or the central bank, vice minister, or minister). (6) *Government insider*—our proxy for the PCR of political skills—is a somewhat relaxed coding of Borrelli's (2002) insider trait, meaning that the minister had previously served in the cabinet as a minister or vice minister or had built a career in the congress.[13] We also code political connections: (1) *Connected to the president* indicates the person had close ties with the president that could be formal (i.e., campaign manager) or personal. (2) Personal linkages make the person a *president's friend*. (3) *Political family* indicates the minister is part of a major family in the country's politics (e.g., Colombia's Barco family; the U.S. Kennedy or Bush families), which does not have to be the president's family.[14]

We evaluate group linkages in three ways: (1) *Links to business* means the minister has known links to business, through membership or holding a leadership post in a business organization or sitting on company boards of directors. (2) *International links* indicates that the minister has known links to external organizations, for example, the United Nations, transnational environmental organizations, or international legal organizations. (3) *Links to clients*—our proxy for the PCR of support resources—means that the minister has known connections to at least one constituency of her or his portfolio.

First-Women Portfolios

Here we consider fourteen women who are the first to hold a portfolio in their country during the period covered by our data set (see Table 13.1). In eight cases, a second woman has also been appointed to lead the ministry, including three first women reappointed in another presidential term (Nilda Garré, defense in Argentina; Gale Norton, interior in the United

TABLE 13.1: FIRST WOMEN APPOINTED TO A POST IN A COUNTRY

Country	Administration	Portfolio	Minister (dates in post)	When appointed
Argentina (1999–2011)	N. Kirchner Ostoić	Defense	Nilda Cecilia Garré (2005–2007, 2007–2010)	Replacement
	F. de la Rúa Bruno	Labour, Employment, and Social Security	Patricia Bullrich (2000–2001)	Replacement
Chile (2000–2010)	M. Bachelet Jeria (first term)	Agriculture	Marigen Hornkohl Venegas (2008–2010)	Replacement
	R. Lagos Escobar	National Defense	Michelle Bachelet (2002–2004)	Replacement
	R. Lagos Escobar	Foreign Affairs	Soledad Alvear Valenzuela (2000–2004)	Initial
	M. Bachelet Jeria (first term)	General Secretariat of Government	Carolina Tohá Morales (2009)	Replacement
Colombia (1998–2010)	A. Pastrana Arango	Culture	Consuelo Araújo Noguera (2000–2001)	Replacement
	A. Uribe Vélez (first term)	Defense	Marta Lucía Ramírez (2002–2003)	Initial
Costa Rica (1998–2010)	O. Arias Sánchez (second term)	Finance	Jenny Phillips Aguilar (2009–2010)	Replacement
	O. Arias Sánchez (second term)	Transportation and Public Works	Karla Gonzalez Carvajal (2006–2009)	Initial
United States (1993–2009)	G. W. Bush (first term)	Agriculture	Ann Veneman (2001–2005)	Initial
	G. W. Bush (first term)	Interior	Gale Norton (2001–2005, 2005–2006)	Initial
	W. J. Clinton (first term)	Justice	Janet Reno (1993–1997, 1997–2001)	Initial
	W. J. Clinton (second term)	State	Madeleine Albright (1997–2001)	Initial

Note: These are instances when the first woman was appointed to a post during the period covered by our data. In other posts, the first woman was appointed before we started observing or after we stopped data collection, or there has never been a female minister.

States; Janet Reno, justice in the United States) and five posts in which a different woman (or women) was later appointed. We see that in the United States, all first women were appointed as part of the initial cabinet, appointments that would receive high media coverage, enhancing the president's political standing. In our Latin American cases, most first women were appointed during reshuffles, so the breadth of assignments given to women was expanding even when media coverage was less likely to give the president credit for enhancing cabinet diversity. These first women (who were *not* the first woman to be appointed to the cabinet) appear in a broad array of portfolios. None held social welfare posts, and only one—Colombia's minister of culture—is in a stereotypically feminine policy domain, which is where women have most often been appointed to cabinets (Annesley and Gains 2010; Blondel 1988; Davis 1997; Escobar-Lemmon and Taylor-Robinson 2005, 2009; Franceschet and Thomas 2013; Krook and O'Brien 2012; Luna, Roza, and Vega 2008; Paxton and Hughes 2007, 97; Reynolds 1999, 564; Skard and Haavio-Mannila 1985, 79; Studlar and Moncrief 1999, 379).[15]

Do first women resemble the men in our data set who were appointed to the same post in their country before and after them? Table 13.2 summarizes the number of similar traits and compares PCRs of each first woman and male ministers in our data set from her country who held the same post. First, for the fifteen traits we count the number of traits for which this woman is coded the same as the majority of the men. If a majority of the men lack the trait (or have the trait), and the first woman also lacks the trait (or has the trait), we count her as having the same credentials as the men. Second, we determine if these first women appear to bring as many PCRs, and the same types of PCRs, to the administration as do their male colleagues in the same post.

Our findings indicate support for the expectations of social-control theory. Most first women have backgrounds and links that match the pattern of their male colleagues on a majority—often the vast majority—of traits, though there are a few exceptions. Seven first women are coded the same as the men on most of the fifteen traits (defense in Argentina and Colombia, foreign relations in Chile, finance and public works and transport in Costa Rica, justice and interior in the United States). Four others are coded the same as the men for a majority (eight or more) of traits (labor in Argentina, defense and general secretary for government in Chile, agriculture in the United States).

The remaining three first women are quite different from the men, although this is partly due to the difficulty in identifying a clear male norm in these cases. Chile's minister of agriculture, Marigen Hornkohl Venegas, has the same credentials as the men only in being connected to the president, friend of the president, coming from a political family, and having links to

TABLE 13.2: SHARED TRAITS OF FIRST WOMEN APPOINTED TO A POST AND MALE MINISTERS IN THE SAME POST

| | | | | Majority of ministers have this PCR[3] | | | | | |
| | | | | Policy expertise | | Political skills | | Support resources | |
Country	Portfolio	Number of person-posts, by sex[2]	Number of traits first woman shares with majority of men[2]	Men	First woman	Men	First woman	Men	First woman
Argentina	Defense	2 women, 5 men	12	no	no	yes	yes	no	yes
	Labour, Employment and Social Security	2 women, 5 men	9	yes	no	yes	yes	yes	no
Chile	Agriculture	1 woman, 2 men	4	split	no	no	yes	split	no
	National Defense	2 women, 4 men	8	no	yes	yes	yes	no	no
	Foreign Affairs	1 woman, 3 men	12	no	no	yes	yes	yes	yes
	General Secretariat of Government	2 women, 6 men	8	no	yes	yes	yes	no	no
Colombia	Culture	5 women, 2 men	5	split	yes	split	no	split	yes
	Defense	1 woman, 7 men	11	no	no	yes	yes	no	no
Costa Rica	Finance	1 woman, 7 men	13	yes	yes	yes	yes	no	no
	Transportation and Public Works	1 woman, 7 men	12	no	yes	yes	yes	no	no
United States	Agriculture	1 woman, 5 men	9	yes	yes	yes	yes	no	no
	Interior	2 women, 3 men	12	yes	yes	no	no	yes	no
	Justice	2 women, 3 men	14	yes	yes	no	no	yes	yes
	State	2 women, 2 men	7	yes	yes	yes	yes	split	yes

[1] A minister who serves in the same post in two (or three) administrations contributes two (or three) person-posts to the analysis. A minister who switches from one post to another during the course of an administration also contributes two person-posts to the analysis. Three women (Nilda Cecilia Garré [minister of defense in Argentina], Janet Reno [U.S. attorney general] and Gale Norton [U.S. secretary of the interior]) and six men each contribute two person-posts.

[2] We assess credentials on fifteen traits: public-sector career, related degree, extensive experience (PCR of policy expertise), organization partisans, campaign experience, prior minister, elected post, appointed post, government insider (PCR of political skills), connected to the president, president's friend, political family, links to business, international links, and links to clients (PCR of support resources). Note that we count whether the women are the same as a majority of men (having or lacking the trait) and not whether women have the trait.

[3] "Majority" refers to a simple majority of person-posts. "Split" refers to instances where there are an even number of person-posts and they are divided 50-50.

business. On five traits she is the opposite of the male norm. However, she had more political experience than both her male colleagues in the post (as a government insider, prior minister, and prior high-level appointed post), and she is an organizational partisan and has campaign experience, as does one of the men. The two men differed from each other on the remaining six traits, making it difficult to determine a men's norm in this post. For Colombia's Ministry of Culture, only two men held the position prior to the five women included in our data set, and they were split in the coding for seven traits, again making it challenging to identify a male norm. The first woman culture minister, Consuelo Araújo Noguera, is different from both men in that she came from a political family, had not previously held a high-ranking appointed post, and had a private-sector career, while the men had revolving-door careers, but as discussed later, she arguably brought more PCRs to the administration than the men did. The first woman U.S. secretary of state, Madeleine Korbel Albright, is coded as having the same background as the men on seven traits, and similar to the case of agriculture in Chile, the two men are split on the remaining eight traits, making it difficult to determine a male norm.

Our second method for comparing first women to their male predecessors/successors in our data set looks at PCRs. Again, first women generally resemble the men (see Table 13.2). Across countries, having the PCR of policy expertise was the male norm in six posts (and men were split in two additional posts), but in nine posts the first woman appointed brought the PCR of policy expertise. In examining these fourteen portfolios on the PCR of political skills, we observe that in ten posts a majority of the men have this trait (and in one additional post the men are split), but in eleven posts the first woman appointed brought this PCR. Finally, for the PCR of support resources we find that in four posts the male norm is to have this PCR (and the male norm is split in three additional posts); however, in five posts the first women brought the PCR of support resources. It is worth pointing out that there is not perfect overlap between instances in which the male norm is to possess a PCR and the first woman appointed to that post also has it. In some instances, women bring a PCR to a post where it is not traditionally expected, but in other instances, they diverge from the male norm and do not bring that PCR to the administration.

We also find that most first women bring at least two kinds of PCRs to the administration. Madeleine Albright brought all three types of PCRs, and none of the first women appear to bring no PCRs to the administration. In three posts the norm for men is to provide all three types of PCRs, and there are no posts where the men typically provide no PCRs. On the whole, the evidence indicates that the first women are a source of PCRs for the administration at least as much as the men are.

These first women are as qualified as the men, which could indicate that women must conform to male norms in order to receive new types of posts. A more positive interpretation is that first women appear to be just as likely as the men to have an independent power base (i.e., not to be dependent on the president) and to have been appointed to posts that will allow them to use the policy expertise and group links they developed in their careers. It does not appear that they are marginalized or "gender outsiders" in their posts (Borrelli 2002, 61; Martin 1989, 166). Instead, the résumés of first women indicate that gender integration appears to be occurring in these cabinets.[16] These women were appointed to posts that stretch stereotypical gendered boundaries for occupations (Alexander and Andersen 1993; Borrelli 2002; Dolan 2010; Huddy and Terkildsen 1993a, 1993b; Koch 2000; Lawless 2004), and they are as likely as their male colleagues in the post to bring multiple PCRs to the administration. These women should have the resources to be full players in the cabinet, similar to male cabinet members who have their own power base.

Majority-Women and All-Women Portfolios

Appointing a woman minister is new in some portfolios, particularly in stereotypically male policy domains (e.g., defense, finance, public works). Yet during the period we observe, there are ten instances in which more than half of the ministers appointed to a portfolio in a given country are women, and in three of those everyone appointed is a woman (women's-issues ministries in Chile and Costa Rica, communications in Colombia; see Table 13.3). Here we are interested in identifying whether the men in these posts conform to

TABLE 13.3: PORTFOLIOS IN WHICH WOMEN ARE A MAJORITY OF APPOINTEES

Country	Portfolio	Number of women and men in post (in our data set)
Argentina (1999–2011)	Health	3 women, 2 men
	Social Development	6 women, 2 men
Chile (2000–2010)	Education	4 women, 2 men
	Housing and Urban Planning	5 women, 1 man
	National Women's Service	4 women, 0 men
Colombia (1998–2010)	Culture	5 women, 2 men
	Information Technologies and Communications	5 women, 0 men
Costa Rica (1998–2010)	Health	2 women, 1 man
	Women's Issues	5 women, 0 men
United States (1993–2009)	Labor	3 women, 1 man

a female-determined norm and whether these majority-women posts have become devalued by the administration because the women are less likely to bring PCRs.

For these country-posts—which might be called "women's seats"—we assess minister credentials in two ways. First, we examine credentials (using the same traits as in the previous section) to determine if the men appointed to these posts look like their female predecessors/successors in our data set.[17] Second, we investigate whether it is the norm for the ministers appointed to these posts to bring multiple PCRs to the administration. Literature argues that as women enter an occupation in greater numbers, the occupation's prestige often diminishes (Kenney 1996; Reskin 1988). According to Janice D. Yoder, a "discriminatory reaction to the intrusion of women into prestigious male-dominated occupations may be the channeling of women into less prestigious subspecialties or female-dominated 'ghettos' within the occupation" (1991, 189).[18] If this has occurred with female-dominated cabinet posts, we would expect these ministers to be less likely than the norm to bring multiple PCRs to the administration. However, literature from psychology predicts that expectations of appropriate gender roles may change as more women hold leadership posts (Sczesny et al. 2004). If adaptation of views about gender is occurring, then we would expect women in women's seats to have credentials that enable them to bring PCRs to the administration. If posts to which multiple women have been appointed are also posts in which ministers commonly have independent power bases and are sources of multiple types of PCRs, then this would be evidence of incorporation of women (Borrelli 2002).

First, we explore whether a female norm for credentials may have developed in these posts where appointing women has become common (see Table 13.4). This judgment is complicated in instances where there is not a clearly defined female norm for the trait. However, we can cautiously conclude that in two ministries—planning in Chile and health in Costa Rica—the one man in our data set appointed to these posts looks like the women for at least two-thirds of the traits examined. In one other ministry—health in Argentina—the men look like the women on a majority of traits. (Again, "looking like" means having the trait when the women do and lacking it when the women do not.) If we exclude political-connection traits from the analysis (connected to president, president's friend, political family), men and women overlap on a majority of traits for the social development portfolio in Argentina and labor in the United States. In the remaining two cases, however, there are few traits where the women and men are clearly alike, and there is great inconsistency within a given sex's credentials. For the education portfolio in Chile there does not appear to be a clear norm for credentials. The two men are coded the same for twelve of fifteen traits, and for four

TABLE 13.4: SHARED TRAITS OF MALE AND FEMALE MINISTERS IN MAJORITY-WOMEN AND ALL-WOMEN POSTS

Country	Portfolio	Number of person-posts, by sex[1]	Number of traits men share with majority of women[2]	Policy expertise Men	Policy expertise Women	Political skills Men	Political skills Women	Support resources Men	Support resources Women	Average number of PCRs in country (all posts)	Average number of PCRs among women in post
Argentina	Health	3 women, 2 men	9	yes	yes	no	no	yes	yes	1.67	1.67
	Social Development	6 women, 2 men	7	split	yes	no	no	split	no	1.67	1.17
Chile	Education	4 women, 2 men	5	no	yes	split	split	no	yes	1.4	2.25
	Housing and Urban Planning	5 women, 1 man	10	yes	yes	yes	no	no	no	1.4	1
	National Women's Service	4 women	N/A (all women)	—	yes	—	yes	—	no	1.4	2
Colombia	Culture	5 women, 2 men	6	split	yes	split	no	split	yes	1.35	1.4
	Information Technologies and Communications	5 women	N/A (all women)	—	no	—	no	—	no	1.35	0.2
Costa Rica	Health	2 women, 1 man	13	yes	yes	no	no	yes	yes	1.71	2
	Women's Issues	5 women	N/A (all women)	—	no	—	no	—	yes	1.71	1.4
United States	Labor	3 women, 1 man	7	no	yes	no	yes	no	yes	1.83	2.67

[1] A minister who serves in the same post in two (or three) administrations contributes two (or three) person-posts to the analysis. A minister who switches from one post to another during the course of an administration also contributes two person-posts to the analysis. None of the men, but three of the women (Minister of Health Gines Gonzales Garcia [Argentina], Minister of Social Development Alicia Kirchner Ostoić [Argentina], and Secretary of Labor Elaine Chao [United States]) contribute two person-posts to the analysis.

[2] We assess credentials on fifteen traits: public-sector career, related degree, extensive experience (PCR of policy expertise), organization partisans, campaign experience, prior minister, elected post, appointed post, government insider (PCR of political skills), connected to the president, president's friend, political family, links to business, international links, and links to clients (PCR of support resources). Note that we count whether the man (or both men when there are two) are the same as a majority of women, which in some instances means having and in others lacking the trait.

[3] "Majority" refers to a simple majority of person-posts. "Split" refers to cases where there are an even number of person-posts and they are divided 50-50.

of these traits they both differ from the norm for women, and on an additional three traits there is no female norm because the women are split. For the culture portfolio in Colombia, one of the men (Juan Luis Mejía Arango) has credentials that for the most part resemble the credentials of the women, though the other man (Alberto Casas Santamaría) does not. However, since both men preceded the women, it would be hard to argue that Minister Mejía was conforming to a female norm.

Overall, for most of these majority-women posts, male and female appointees generally have similar backgrounds and credentials. However, because of the relatively short time period for which we have data and the resultant small number of ministers in each post, it is not possible to conclude that those traits are a female norm or continuance of the male norm. We can make more definitive, though cautious, determinations about whether the men appointed to these posts match the female norm during this period for the post with regard to PCRs.

Looking at PCRs individually, the record for the female norm is at least as strong as the record for the men for majority-women posts. Half or more of the men have the PCR of policy expertise in five cases (country-portfolio), but in all seven cases a majority of women have policy expertise. Half or more of the men are a source of the PCR of political skills in three cases, and half or more of the women in two of seven cases. In four cases half or more of the men are a potential source of the PCR of support resources, while women are a potential source of this PCR in five of seven. The fact that in terms of PCRs the men and the women look similar, with the women bringing at least as many PCRs to the administration, provides evidence that these posts have not become devalued or populated by individuals with limited political experience and that if there is a female norm, it is not one that lowers standards. Of course, we lack a long-term stream of data on previous ministers to determine whether the women and, consequently, these men are conforming to a previously defined male standard in terms of PCRs or if the women in these posts have increased the number of PCRs ministers in these portfolios are expected to bring to the administration.

However, all-women posts (communications in Colombia, women's issues in Chile and Costa Rica) present a stark contrast. In only one of the three cases do we find the PCRs of policy expertise or political skills to be the norm (both in Chile's women's-issues ministry), and support resources (client links) are the norm only in Costa Rica's women's-issues ministry. For the communications portfolio in Colombia none of the three PCRs coded here are the norm, but it is possible that these women are tasked with bringing a new PCR of representativeness to the administration instead.

We also examine how the women appointed to majority-women posts compare to the PCR norm observed for all ministers in their country (all ministers from the country in our data set). We report the country average and the average among all women in that post in the last two columns in Table 13.4. In five of seven cases, the PCR norm for women appointed to a majority-women post equals or exceeds the national average. In education in Chile and labor in the United States, the women are impressively qualified, bringing between two and three of the PCRs we code. In the other two cases (social development in Argentina, planning in Chile), the women bring, on average, one PCR to the administration, which while not insignificant, is less than the country averages.

For the all-women posts, the findings again are more negative. In two of three cases, the norm for PCRs falls short of the national average. In the communications portfolio in Colombia, the women do not typically bring any PCRs to the administration. One of the five ministers is a source of the political skills resource, and none are a source of policy expertise or support resources. In the women's-issues ministry in Costa Rica, three of the five ministers have links to ministry clients, so they are a source of support resources, but only two ministers are a source of policy expertise or political skills, leaving them below the country average of 1.71. In Chile's women's-issues ministry, a majority of ministers bring the PCRs of policy expertise and political skills, and one of the four ministers has the PCR of support resources.[19] This record makes it appear that in Colombia and Costa Rica all-women posts are devalued in the cabinet at least with respect to bringing PCRs to the administration. These are likely to be posts where women are going to be showcased for their sex rather than valued for their experience. In women's-issues ministries, it may not be only the minister who is being showcased but also the administration's attentiveness to women as a group.[20]

Overall, it appears the women appointed to majority-women posts in our data set have similar credentials to those of their male colleagues in the same post and are similarly robust sources of PCRs for the administration. When the number of ministers is so small and ministers of the same sex often differ for a trait, it is difficult to say whether a new female norm for credentials is developing in a post, breaking the unspoken male norm for cabinet ministers. The men appointed to these posts typically resemble the women in credentials, but it may be that the women—while a majority of appointees in recent years—may be conforming to a long-established male norm for credentials. Both men and women appointed to majority-women posts are frequently sources of multiple PCRs, suggesting that women are not consistently required to display higher levels of qualifications in order to enter the cabinet but also that these posts are not devalued. Statistically, there is no difference in the average number of PCRs men and women appointed to majority-women and all-women posts bring when compared with the national average, with one important exception. Women appointed to head communications in Colombia (an all-women post) bring notably fewer PCRs to the cabinet ($p = 0.01$).

Conclusion

Our analysis indicates that both the first woman appointed to a post in a country and women appointed to majority-women posts (but perhaps not to all-women posts) conform to the male norm, supporting the expectations of social-control theory. This may mean that they are able to play a male-dominated game by established rules but that these women are unlikely to bring as fresh a perspective to the representation of interests as could be brought by other women whose backgrounds differed more from those of the men—for example, by women with strong connections to female organizations or to organizations representing other historically underrepresented groups.[21] Susan Carroll reached a similar conclusion in her earlier study of the appointment of women to cabinets by U.S. governors: "Women selected for political appointments are likely to be those who will play the game by existing rules and not challenge the power of governing elites. . . . Since existing elites seem to apply standards for elite membership more strictly when selecting women to hold positions of power, women who might pose a significant threat to the status quo are likely to be excluded" (1984, 104).

But conforming to the male norm in work background, political experience, and group links means that these women are as strong as their male colleagues in their ability to bring PCRs to the administration. It also suggests that these women should have the ability to be equally effective in wielding those PCRs to advance women's interests. However, we leave to future research the question of whether (and how) they actually choose to do so. We acknowledge that in drawing this conclusion, we are adopting the male norm about PCRs. There may be new, women's sources of PCRs. But the use of the male norm in this analysis seems reasonable since the literature was developed from the study of male-dominated cabinets and cabinets remain male dominated. The overall picture that can be drawn from this analysis is an indication that gender integration (Borrelli 2010) is occurring in the recruitment and appointment of women to these cabinets.

It appears that, in general, women who are the first to hold a portfolio in their country and women appointed to majority-women posts both come to the cabinet with the credentials needed to get things done. The major exception to this conclusion are the all-women posts, at least in Colombia and Costa Rica, where the below-average PCRs of ministers could be a signal of the marginalization of those posts and of the women appointed to run them. Claire Annesley and Francesca Gains argue that we need to study women in their institutional context (2010, 912). Their particular interest is to understand when women in government will be successful at gendering policy; they contend that it is not sufficient for the woman minister to be a feminist; she also needs political and organizational resources to enable her to "shape policy outcomes" (917). "Feminists intent on pursuing gendered policy change need to hold positions that grant access to power and resources," head a department with a large budget, have "the ear of vested interests," and have "personal links and relationships that exist between individuals" or informal networks (918). Probably men need these types of resources to be successful as well. The vast majority of the women appointed to the posts that are the focus of our study appear to have multiple PCRs they can marshal toward achieving policy goals and administering their departments. This appears to be the case in all five of the countries we examined, and it indicates that women in these presidential cabinets are being appointed for their credentials—to do a job—not to showcase them for their sex (Borrelli 2002, 54).

NOTES

1. There is variation across countries and over time in what constitutes the cabinet because of appointment of ministers without portfolio, separations or fusion of departments, and designation of other appointees as "cabinet rank." As Janet M. Martin (1997) notes, this can be a way to include women without really including them in the cabinet. To achieve consistency in the unit of study across countries, when we use the term "full cabinet-rank posts" or "portfolios," we mean ministers who are heads of departments, so we exclude positions in the United States such as chief of staff, United Nations ambassador, or Environmental Protection Agency administrator, which presidents have sometimes designated as cabinet rank.

2. Rosabeth Kanter (1977) explains that in skewed groups (i.e., where women are 15 percent or less of the group) women's appearance and personal life are the subject of intense attention, but their credentials for the job are not. Borrelli notes the difference when Hillary Clinton was nominated to be secretary of state by President Obama (2010, 745). Clinton was the third woman to be nominated for that portfolio, and the media coverage did not focus on her sex but on her credentials and politics.

3. The first woman was appointed to the U.S. cabinet in 1933: Frances Perkins as secretary of labor. In Argentina, Susana Ruiz Cerutti was the first woman appointed in 1989, though this was a short-term placeholder as minister of foreign relations. The next woman was appointed in 1996, Susana Decibe as minister of education (Barnes and Jones 2011, 111; Waylen 2000, 778). In Chile, the first woman was appointed in 1952, Adriana Olguín de Baltra as minister of justice at the end of President González Videla's 1946–1952 term, and his successor appointed a woman as minister of education (Barnes and Jones 2011, 112). In Colombia in 1956, Josefina Valencia de Hubach was appointed minister of education, and in Costa Rica in 1958 Estela Quesada Hernandez was appointed as minister of education (Luna, Roza, and Vega 2008).

4. We sidestep the question of whether these credentials are really necessary to do the job. For instance, it is debatable whether one needs a Ph.D. in economics to be a successful minister of finance. If the norm is to have a Ph.D. and the first woman does not,

she may be perceived as less qualified and consequently be less effective, regardless of her actual ability.

5. We thank Karen Beckwith and Christina Bergqvist for bringing this point to our attention.

6. For extended discussion of the countries, data, variables, and how background affects treatment and success of women in presidential cabinets, see Escobar-Lemmon and Taylor-Robinson 2016.

7. Years covered vary across countries based on when presidential administrations began and ended. A list of the portfolios included in the analysis and discussion of the nature of cabinet appointments in each case can be found in Escobar-Lemmon and Taylor-Robinson 2016, chaps. 2 and 3.

8. The person-post structure of our data set diverges from the way cabinet appointments are analyzed in the United States. We organized the data set this way because in Latin America changing posts and movement in and out of the cabinet are more frequent than in the United States. We needed a coding scheme that explicitly recognized that a person's prior work experience might be highly relevant for one post but not another. Additionally, we treat those reappointed to the same post (by the same president or another) as being a separate observation, because even though the president or post might be the same, the individual enters the second term with experience not brought to the first term (e.g., established relationship with budget makers and known management style), and the political context in which they operate is undoubtedly different (e.g., the perception of president as a "lame duck"). To allow updating of the independent variables (background traits) to include experience gained in the first term, we treat the two terms as separate appointments even though we acknowledge that in the United States, a secretary who continues in a post does not require reconfirmation by the Senate, although the second inauguration for a president does symbolically mark a new beginning. Latin American presidents appoint cabinet ministers without needing confirmation of appointments by another body, though in some countries the legislature can dismiss a minister, which rarely happens. Additionally, cabinet departments in Latin America have been more fluid because ministries are combined, divided, or recombined during the span covered by our data set.

9. Colombia and Costa Rica are the oldest continuous democracies in Latin America with regimes installed in 1957 and 1949, respectively, although violence in Colombia has placed democracy under stress in recent decades. Argentina and Chile reinstalled democracy in 1983 and 1991, respectively, although prior to 1973 Chile had the longest continual experience with democracy in the region.

10. In Colombia, Law 581 of 2000 established a 30 percent quota for appointed administrative posts, but it did not apply to posts appointed completely on merit, such as cabinet posts. See "Colombia" 2013.

11. Committee chairs in the legislature are not counted as organizational partisans.

12. We acknowledge the important role of donors in U.S. campaigns but do not capture monetary support with this variable. Because of differences in campaign finance in our Latin American cases, it would not be possible to include background as a donor in our analysis.

13. Borrelli's coding required that the person had served in the cabinet, been an assistant secretary, or had a primary career in national government immediately prior to appointment to the cabinet post. Given the different career patterns in our Latin American countries, a government insider may have had a short break between the prior service and the cabinet appointment.

14. Political families are ones in which politics is the family business, especially with traditions of dominating subnational politics, and in which prominent party factions are associated with a particular family, so we conceive of family primarily as blood ties and long-standing networks, not simply marriage between two elected leaders.

15. Most of the ministers in our data set who held the culture post in Colombia are women (five women, two men), so we also include this case in the analysis of majority-women posts. Here we compare the first woman to the two men, both of whom held the post before she did.

16. First women who are recent appointments do not appear to be marginalized. With our data we cannot assess if that was true for the earliest women appointed to the cabinet in these countries.

17. This part of the analysis includes only the seven cases in which at least one of the ministers is a man.

18. Some of these posts, in particular communications in Colombia and labor in the United States, may represent instances of regendering; however, an analysis of whether this is the case and the process by which it occurred are beyond the scope of this chapter.

19. The lack of links to women's groups by ministers of women's issues in Chile is surprising given the organized women's sectors in parties. This has been the subject of much research; see Baldez 2002, Franceschet 2005, Haas 2010, and Weeks and Borzutzky 2012.

20. Raising the visibility of an issue or group by elevating an agency to cabinet rank, creating a minister without portfolio to respond to the issue, dividing a ministry to make each part full cabinet rank, or creating a policy czar are all ways a president can call attention to particular issues. During the period under study, this may be the case with the women's-issues portfolio, but it is not unique to that policy area or to these countries, because similar changes in attentiveness to various clientele groups take place in others.

21. Women are, of course, not the only group who has traditionally been excluded from access to power. Future research should explore if and how members of other minority groups provide representation of their interests and how the intersection of gender and other identities determines representation of interests.

REFERENCES

Alexander, Deborah, and Kristi Andersen. 1993. "Gender as a Factor in the Attribution of Leadership Traits." *Political Research Quarterly* 46 (3): 527–545.

Annesley, Claire, and Francesca Gains. 2010. "The Core Executive: Gender, Power and Change." *Political Studies* 58 (5): 909–929.

Baldez, Lisa. 2002. *Why Women Protest: Women's Movements in Chile.* Cambridge: Cambridge University Press.

Barnes, Tiffany D., and Mark P. Jones. 2011. "Latin America." In *Women in Executive Power: A Global Overview*, edited by Gretchen Bauer and Manon Tremblay, 105–121. New York: Routledge.

Blondel, Jean. 1988. "Introduction: Western European Cabinets in Comparative Perspective." In *Cabinets in Western Europe*, edited by Jean Blondel and Ferdinand Müller-Rommel, 1–16. New York: Palgrave Macmillan.

Borrelli, MaryAnne. 2002. *The President's Cabinet: Gender, Power, and Representation.* Boulder, CO: Lynne Rienner.

———. 2010. "Gender Desegregation and Gender Integration in the President's Cabinet, 1933–2010." *Presidential Studies Quarterly* 40 (4): 734–749.

Carroll, Susan J. 1984. "The Recruitment of Women for Cabinet-Level Posts in State Government: A Social Control Perspective." *Social Science Journal* 21 (1): 91–107.

Cohen, Jeffrey E. 1988. *The Politics of the U.S. Cabinet: Representation in the Executive Branch, 1789–1984.* Pittsburgh: University of Pittsburgh Press.

"Colombia." 2013. *QuotaProject: Global Database of Quotas for Women*, December 4. Available at http://www.quotaproject.org/uid/countryview.cfm?country=48.

Davis, Rebecca Howard. 1997. *Women and Power in Parliamentary Democracies: Cabinet Appointments in Western Europe, 1968–1992.* Lincoln: University of Nebraska Press.

Diekman, Amanda B., Wind Goodfriend, and Stephanie Goodwin. 2004. "Dynamic Stereotypes of Power: Perceived Change and Stability in Gender Hierarchies." *Sex Roles* 50 (3–4): 201–215.

Dolan, Kathleen. 2010. "The Impact of Gender Stereotyped Evaluations on Support for Women Candidates." *Political Behavior* 32 (1): 69–88.

Duke, James T. 1976. *Conflict and Power in Social Life.* Provo, UT: Brigham Young University Press.

Eagly, Alice H., and Steven J. Karau. 2002. "Role Congruity Theory of Prejudice toward Female Leaders." *Psychological Review* 109 (3): 573–598.

Escobar-Lemmon, Maria C., and Michelle M. Taylor-Robinson. 2005. "Women Ministers in Latin American Government: When, Where, and Why?" *American Journal of Political Science* 49 (4): 829–844.

———. 2009. "Getting to the Top: Career Paths of Women in Latin American Cabinets." *Political Research Quarterly* 62 (4): 685–699.

———. 2016. *Women in Presidential Cabinets: Power Players or Abundant Tokens?* New York: Oxford University Press.

Franceschet, Susan. 2005. *Women and Politics in Chile.* Boulder, CO: Lynne Rienner.

Franceschet, Susan, and Gwynn Thomas. 2013. "Changing Representational Norms in the Executive Branch: Parity Cabinets in Chile and Spain." Paper presented at the Third European Conference on Politics and Gender, Barcelona, Spain, March 21–23.

Gamson, William A. 1968. *Power and Discontent.* Homewood, IL: Richard D. Irwin Press.

Haas, Liesl. 2010. *Feminist Policymaking in Chile.* University Park: Pennsylvania State University Press.

Huddy, Leonie, and Nayda Terkildsen. 1993a. "The Consequences of Gender Stereotypes for Women Candidates at Different Levels and Types of Office." *Political Research Quarterly* 46 (3): 503–525.

———. 1993b. "Gender Stereotypes and the Perception of Male and Female Candidates." *American Journal of Political Science* 37 (1): 119–147.

Kanter, Rosabeth M. 1977. "Some Effects of Proportions on Group Life: Skewed Sex Ratios and Responses to Token Women." *American Journal of Sociology* 82 (5): 965–990.

Kenney, Sally J. 1996. "New Research on Gendered Political Institutions." *Political Research Quarterly* 49 (2): 445–466.

Koch, Jeffrey W. 2000. "Do Citizens Apply Gender Stereotypes to Infer Candidates' Ideological Orientation?" *Journal of Politics* 62 (2): 414–429.

Krook, Mona Lena, and Diana Z. O'Brien. 2012. "All the President's Men? The Appointment of Female Cabinet Ministers Worldwide." *Journal of Politics* 74 (3): 840–855.

Lawless, Jennifer L. 2004. "Women, War, and Winning Elections: Gender Stereotyping in the Post–September 11th Era." *Political Research Quarterly* 57 (3): 479–490.

Leyenaar, Monique. 2014. "A Matter of Time? A Historical and Empirical Analysis of Women Cabinet Ministers in the Netherlands." Paper presented at the European Consortium for Political Research Joint Sessions Workshop, Salamanca, Spain, April 10–15.

Lovenduski, Joni. 1986. *Women in European Politics: Contemporary Feminism and Public Policy.* Amherst: University of Massachusetts Press.

Lukes, Steven. 1974. *Power: A Radical View.* New York: Macmillan.

Luna, Elba, Vivian Roza, and Gabriela Vega. 2008. "El camino hacia el poder: Ministras latinoamericanas, 1950–2007" [The road to power: Latin American women ministers, 1950–2007]. Interamerican Development Bank. Available at http://www.iadb .org/document.cfm?id=1415084.

Mainwaring, Scott, and Matthew Soberg Shugart, eds. 1997. *Presidentialism and Democracy in Latin America.* New York: Cambridge University Press.

Martin, Janet M. 1989. "The Recruitment of Women to Cabinet and Subcabinet Posts." *Western Political Quarterly* 42 (1): 161–172.

———. 1997. "Women Who Govern: The President's Appointments." In *The Other Elites: Women, Politics, and Power in the Executive Branch,* edited by MaryAnne Borrelli and Janet M. Martin, 51–72. Boulder, CO: Lynne Rienner.

Mills, C. Wright. 1959. *The Power Elite.* New York: Oxford University Press.

Paxton, Pamela, and Melanie M. Hughes. 2007. *Women, Politics, and Power: A Global Perspective.* Los Angeles: Pine Forge Press.

Reskin, Barbara F. 1988. "Bringing the Men Back In: Sex Differentiation and the Devaluation of Women's Work." *Gender & Society* 2 (1): 58–81.

Reynolds, Andrew. 1999. "Women in Legislatures and Executives of the World: Knocking at the Highest Glass Ceiling." *World Politics* 51 (4): 547–572.

Ritter, Barbara A., and Janice D. Yoder. 2004. "Gender Differences in Leader Emergence Persist Even for Dominant Women: An Updated Confirmation of Role Congruity Theory." *Psychology of Women Quarterly* 28 (3): 187–193.

Sczesny, Sabine, Janine Bosak, Daniel Neff, and Birgit Schyns. 2004. "Gender Stereotypes and the Attribution of Leadership Traits: A Cross-Cultural Comparison." *Sex Roles* 51 (11–12): 631–645.

Skard, Torild, and Elina Haavio-Mannila. 1985. "Women in Parliament." In *Unfinished Democracy: Women in Nordic Politics,* edited by Elina Haavio-Mannila, Drude Dahlerup, Maud Eduards, Esther Gudmundsdóttir, Beatrice Halsaa, Helga Maria Hernes, Eva Hänninen-Salmelin, Bergthora Sigmundsdóttir, Sirkka Sinkkonen, and Torild Skard, translated by Christine Badcock, 51–80. New York: Pergamon Press.

Studlar, Donley T., and Gary F. Moncrief. 1999. "Women's Work? The Distribution and Prestige of Portfolios in the Canadian Provinces." *Governance: An International Journal of Policy and Administration* 12 (4): 379–395.

Waylen, Georgina. 2000. "Gender and Democratic Politics: A Comparative Analysis of Consolidation in Argentina and Chile." *Journal of Latin American Studies* 32 (3): 765–793.

Weeks, Gregory, and Silvia Borzutzky. 2012. "Michelle Bachelet's Government: The Paradoxes of a Chilean President." *Journal of Politics in Latin America* 4 (3): 97–121.

Wilson, Marie C. 2007. "It's Woman Time." In *Women and Leadership: The State of Play and Strategies for Change,* edited by Barbara Kellerman and Deborah L. Rhode, 271–282. San Francisco: Jossey-Bass.

Wyszomirski, Margaret Jane. 1989. "Presidential Personnel and Political Capital: From Roosevelt to Reagan." In *Pathways to Power: Selecting Rulers in Pluralist Democracies,* edited by Mattei Dogan, 45–73. Boulder, CO: Westview Press.

Yoder, Janice D. 1991. "Rethinking Tokenism: Looking beyond Numbers." *Gender & Society* 5 (2): 178–192.

Zimmer, Lynn. 1988. "Tokenism and Women in the Workplace: The Limits of Gender-Neutral Theory." *Social Problems* 35 (1): 64–77.

Contributors

Amy C. Alexander is an assistant professor at the Quality of Government Institute and Department of Political Science at the University of Gothenburg, Sweden. A scholar of comparative politics, she has published in both political science and sociological peer-reviewed journals, including *Comparative Politics, International Review of Sociology, International Political Science Review*, and *Politics & Gender*.

MaryAnne Borrelli is a professor of government at Connecticut College. Her research investigates gender in the U.S. presidency. She has authored *The Politics of the President's Wife* (2011) and *The President's Cabinet: Gender, Power, and Representation* (2002); coedited *The Other Elites: Women, Politics, and Power in the Executive Branch* (1997); and coauthored *Understanding American Government* (2013). The author of several book chapters, her peer-reviewed journal articles have appeared in *Presidential Studies Quarterly* and *Women & Politics*.

Sheetal Chhabria is the Jacob and Hilda Blaustein Assistant Professor of History at Connecticut College. Her research investigates social policy in South Asia and transnational poverty, drawing on the intellectual resources of postcolonial studies. Her book manuscript is titled "Making the Modern Slum: Housing in Colonial Bombay."

Georgia Duerst-Lahti is a professor of political science at Beloit College. Her extensive academic and professional writings span U.S. politics, public administration, foreign policy, and fair trade. She is the coauthor of *Creating Gender: The Sexual Politics of Welfare Policy* (2007) and the coeditor of *Gender Power, Leadership, and Government* (1995). In addition to numerous book chapters, she has published articles in *Administration and Society, PS: Political Science & Politics, Public Administration Review, Political Science Quarterly*, and *Sex Roles*.

Maria C. Escobar-Lemmon is an associate professor of political science at Texas A&M University. A Latin Americanist and methodologist, she is the recipient of a grant from the National Science Foundation. She is the coauthor of *Women in Presidential Cabinets: Power Players or Abundant Tokens?* (2016) and the coeditor of *Representation: The Case of Women* (2014); her peer-reviewed articles have been published by such journals as the *American Journal of Political Science*, the *Journal of Politics*, *Policy Studies Journal*, and *Political Research Quarterly*.

Cory Charles Gooding is an assistant professor of political science at the University of San Diego. A scholar of race, ethnicity, and U.S. politics, his book manuscript is titled "Public Identities: Afro-Caribbean Political Incorporation in the Obama Era."

Lilly J. Goren is a professor of political science and global studies at Carroll University. Her publications extend from political theory to popular culture; she examines portrayals and interpretations of U.S. politics. She is a coeditor of *Mad Men and Politics: Nostalgia and the Remaking of Modern America* (2015) and the award-winning *Women and the White House: Gender, Popular Culture, and Presidential Politics* (2012) and the editor of *"You've Come a Long Way, Baby": Women, Politics, and Popular Culture* (2009). She is also the author of *Not in My District: The Politics of Military Base Closures* (2003) and a coauthor of *The Comparative Politics of Military Base Closures: A United States–Canadian Case Study of De-distributive Decisions and Domestic Military Bases* (2000). In addition to a number of book chapters, she has published in the *Political Research Quarterly* and *White House Studies*.

Karen M. Hult is a professor of political science and a core faculty member and chair of the Center for Public Administration and Policy at Virginia Tech. Her research centers on organizational and institutional theory and the presidency and the executive branch. She is the coauthor of the books *Empowering the White House: Governance under Nixon, Ford, and Carter* (2004); *Governing the White House: From Hoover through LBJ* (1995); *Governing Public Organizations: Politics, Structures, and Institutional Design* (1990); and *Agency Merger and Bureaucratic Redesign* (1987). She has also written many journal articles and book chapters. Her current book project (with David Cohen and Charles Walcott) examines the White House chief of staff. Professor Hult received the Excellence in Mentoring Award from the APSA Policy Section in 2015 and the Career Service Award from the APSA Presidents and Executive Politics Section in 2012.

Farida Jalalzai holds the Hannah Atkins Endowed Chair and is an associate professor of political science at Oklahoma State University. Her research focuses on comparative politics, gender, and executive politics. She is the author of *Beyond Family Ties: Women Presidents of Latin America* (2015) and *Shattered, Cracked or Firmly Intact? Women and the Executive Glass Ceiling Worldwide* (2013). In addition to her many book chapters, she has published in a diverse array of journals, including *International Journal of Diversity in Organisations, Communities and Nations*, the *International Political Science Review*, *Politics & Gender*, and *Politics and Religion*.

Janet M. Martin is a professor of government and legal studies at Bowdoin College. Her research centers on women and the U.S. presidency, and she is the author of the award-winning book *The Presidency and Women: Promise, Performance, and Illusion* (2003).

She is also the author of *Lessons from the Hill: The Legislative Journey of an Education Program* (1994) and the coeditor of *The Other Elites: Women, Politics, and Power in the Executive Branch* (1997). Her journal articles, essays, and book chapters are wide ranging and comment on women as global and national leaders and on women in the executive branch and presidency. Her current book project focuses on the U.S. presidency, human rights, and women's rights; she is also developing the documentary film *After Revolution: An American Story*.

Daniela F. Melo is an adjunct assistant professor at Connecticut College. A Europeanist, her research examines social movements, political participation, and public policy in comparative perspective. The recipient of a Fulbright Research Grant, she has published articles in *Comparative European Politics*, the *Journal of Women, Politics & Policy*, and *Social Movement Studies*. Her book project addresses the impacts of democratization and Europeanization on the development of the Portuguese women's movement.

Catherine Reyes-Housholder is a Ph.D. candidate in the Department of Government at Cornell University. Her dissertation is titled "*Presidentas*, Power and Pro-Women Change in Latin America," and she has published in *Latin American Politics and Society*.

Ariella R. Rotramel is the Vendana Shiva Assistant Professor of Gender and Women Studies at Connecticut College. Her research encompasses gender and leadership, queer and sexuality studies, and social movements. In addition to many professional presentations and workshops, her publications include a peer-reviewed article in *AAPI Nexus: Asian Americans and Pacific Islanders Policy, Practice, and Community Journal*. Her forthcoming book is titled *Pushing Back: Women-Led Grassroots Activism in New York City's Transnational Communities of Color*.

Leslie A. Schwindt-Bayer is an associate professor of political science at Rice University. Her research examines gender in executive and in legislative politics, focusing on Latin American politics. She is the coauthor of *The Gendered Effects of Electoral Institutions: Political Engagement and Participation* (2012) and the author of *Political Power and Women's Representation in Latin America* (2010). In addition to her many book chapters, she has published in such diverse peer-reviewed journals as *American Journal of Political Science*, *British Journal of Political Science*, the *Journal of Politics*, *Legislative Studies Quarterly*, *Perspectives on Politics*, *Politics & Gender*, and *Revista Uruguaya de Ciencia Política*.

Michelle M. Taylor-Robinson is a professor of political science at Texas A&M University. A comparativist, her research focuses on Latin American politics, including gender and the executive, electoral politics, legislative politics, and representation. She is the author of *Do the Poor Count? Democratic Institutions and Accountability in a Context of Poverty* (2010), a coauthor of *Women in Presidential Cabinets: Power Players or Abundant Tokens?* (2016) and *Negotiating Democracy: Transitions from Authoritarian Rule* (1996), and a coeditor of *Representation: The Case of Women* (2014). The author of many book chapters, she has also published in the *American Journal of Political Science*, the *Journal of Politics*, the *Journal of Theoretical Politics*, *Party Politics*, *Political Research Quarterly*, *Revista Latinoamericana de Opinión Pública*, and *Revista Uruguaya de Ciencia Política*.

Index

Page numbers in italics indicate material in figures or tables.